The World's Greatest
Unsolved Mysteries

By the same author:

Strange but True series
The Mammoth Book of Nostradamus and Other Prophets
The Encyclopedia of Unsolved Mysteries (with Colin Wilson)
Murder Most Foul (with Rowan Wilson)
Unsolved Mysteries: Past and Present (with Colin Wilson)

The World's Greatest Unsolved Mysteries

Edited by
Damon Wilson

BARNES & NOBLE

NEW YORK

Copyright © 1994, 2004, 2006 by Constable & Robinson Ltd

This edition published by Barnes & Noble, Inc.

2006 Barnes & Noble Books

ISBN-13: 978-0-7607-6990-4
ISBN-10: 0-7607-6990-7

Printed and bound in the EU

06 07 08 09 10 M 9 8 7 6 5 4 3

CONTENTS

Chroniclers of the UnXplained

We often use the phrase 'mind over matter' to explain psychic phenomena, but is it possible that mind and matter are not divided? How else can we explain the experience of two people who stepped 200 years back in time? Today nuclear science speaks of a particle in the brain that may communicate with other minds or with matter – and may not be hindered by space or time. Are scientists coming closer to the occult, as represented by science debunker Charles Hay Fort? Do the numerous odd occurrences he recorded indicate that there is less disparity between mind and matter than we now believe?

On the afternoon of 10 August 1901 two Englishwomen on a visit to the palace of Versailles had an extraordinary experience – they stepped back in time. The incredible happened as they walked along a shaded lane on their way to the *Petit Trianon*, the small secluded eighteenth-century mansion that had once been the private retreat of Queen Marie-Antoinette. The features of the garden, the buildings, even the people they met, obviously belonged to a time much earlier than 1901.

For Charlotte Moberly and Eleanor Jourdain, this was their first visit to Versailles, and they were puzzled by what was happening to them. They had missed the direct way to the *Petit Trianon*, and turned down a sunken lane that led past buildings of a domestic sort. Gradually they were overcome by an unaccountable depression, 'as if something were wrong', Eleanor Jourdain recalled. They could think of no reason to account for the feeling of gloom and isolation that filled them, which they were unable to shake off. Miss Jourdain later said, 'I began to feel as if I were walking in my sleep; the heavy dreaminess was oppressive.'

The two women passed a stone cottage where Miss Jourdain noticed a woman handing a jug to a young girl. The old-fashioned dress of this girl struck her as odd. Then they asked the way of two distinguished looking men carrying staffs and wearing long, greenish-grey coats and three-cornered hats. The men were standing near some gardening tools that included a wheelbarrow and a plough, and though the two women assumed they were gardeners, their dignified bearing suggested they were persons of authority. They directed the women on toward a wood where the two saw a circular kiosk, something like a small bandstand. On the steps sat a man wearing a heavy black cloak around his shoulders and a slouch hat. 'At that moment', Miss Jourdain later wrote, 'the eerie feeling that had begun in the garden culminated in a definite impression of something uncanny and fear-inspiring.' As Miss Moberly put it, 'Everything suddenly looked unnatural, therefore unpleasant; even the trees behind the building seemed to have become flat and lifeless, like a wood worked on tapestry.'

When the man turned his head they could see that his face was dark and disfigured by smallpox. His expression struck them both as 'very evil and yet unseeing', and though he did not seem to be looking at them, neither of them wanted to step any closer to him. While they were hesitating, they heard the sound of running foot-steps along a nearby path. The rocks separating the paths concealed the runner from their view, until suddenly he was behind them and quite close. This man also wore a thick cloak and large hat, though only afterward did the two wonder at such odd clothes for a hot August afternoon. He was handsome, 'distinctly a gentleman', and he called out to them in an excited manner and in oddly-pronounced French that they were not to go toward the kiosk but to the *Petit Trianon*. Curiously, he referred to it as 'la maison', the word used by Marie-Antoinette to describe her palace.

The two tourists crossed a small rustic bridge above a tiny ravine and came out into an English landscape garden, that at last gave them a sight of the *Petit Trianon*. The windows were shut-tered, but on the terrace sat a middle-aged woman wearing a light summer dress and a large white hat over her fair hair. She was sketching the trees. They could see no way of entering the building on this side, so they walked around the west corner onto a terrace looking down on the formal beds of the French garden. All but one of the windows were shuttered, but from a door in what seemed to be a separate house beyond the *Petit Trianon* itself, a man with the jaunty air of a footman emerged, banging the door behind him. He told them that the way to 'la maison' lay through the courtyard on the other side of the kitchen and he offered to show them the way. 'He looked inquisitively amused as he walked by us down the French garden', said Miss Moberly. When he left them, they at last made their way into the *Petit Trianon* and followed a merry French wedding party around the rooms. Both felt lively and normal again.

Later they discovered that only Miss Moberly had seen the lady sketching and only Miss Jourdain had seen the cottage woman and the child. Neither of them could understand how the other had failed to see people so close. This discrepancy set them thinking that they must have glimpsed some sort of apparition, so they wrote down separate accounts of that afternoon in Versailles. Both were keen observers with skill in expressing themselves. Miss Moberly, elder of the two, had been for fifteen years principal of St. Hugh's Hall (later College) at Oxford University; Miss Jourdain, later to be her successor at St. Hugh's, was in 1901, headmistress of a successful private school outside London.

The following year Miss Jourdain made a second visit to Versailles, and because of what she saw there – or rather, because of what she didn't see – she and Miss Moberly subsequently went again together. To their astonishment, derelict gates, unopened for many years, blocked the paths they had followed in 1901. No stone cottage existed, no kiosk; neither the little bridge nor the ravine it crossed could be found. In place of the rough and shaded meadow of the English garden, they saw a broad gravel sweep leading up to the terrace, and where the woman had sat sketching, they found large rhododendron bushes of many years growth. Besides these changes in the surroundings, they found numerous groups of visitors on all sides where previously they had been unpleasantly aware of being alone in that part of the garden. Miss

Moberly recounted that, 'Garden seats placed everywhere and stalls for fruit and lemonade took away from any idea of desolation.'

The discovery that there had been an alteration of the very scenery of the place gave an altogether more remarkable quality to their experience. They had not merely seen ghosts from the past, but in some unknown way they had entered a past where those 'ghosts' were still living people and the scenery that of their own earlier time.

The two women continued their research on Versailles in whatever hours they could spare from their academic work, and also paid further visits to the palace. They discovered that the door through which the footman had come to show them the way had been locked for many years, and the passages and stairways behind the door were all broken and unusable. When they asked an official about the green coats worn by the gardeners, they were told that green had been one of the colours of the long-vanished royal livery. No plough of the kind Miss Jourdain had seen was any longer in use at the *Petit Trianon*, but throughout the reign of King Louis XVI and Queen Marie-Antoinette, an old plough had been preserved there. The same sentimental view of the simple life that had prompted Marie-Antoinette to dress as a milkmaid had made her husband pose as a ploughman. The discovery of long-forgotten maps and paintings of the gardens confirmed the existence in the eighteenth century of many features seen by Miss Moberly and Miss Jourdain on 10 August 1901 – but long since swept away in the aftermath of the French Revolution.

Coincidences of this kind, requiring a special knowledge neither of the two Englishwomen possessed on their first visit, seemed to confirm that they had gone back in time, and that in some incomprehensible manner the past had remained available for them to experience it. In 1911 they published a record of their experience and subsequent research, calling the book *An Adventure*. The attempt to understand their 'adventure' has been continuing ever since.

Suggestions that the two tourists had interrupted a group of people rehearsing a play or making a film had been investigated at the start and proved unfounded. In *The Trianon Adventure*, the principal author, Arnold O. Gibbons, has suggested the existence of some power, at present unknown, that enables an image of reality as it once existed to become available again to a living brain. The image is so vividly accurate – even to the precise details of a costume, the features of a face, and the surrounds – that those who receive the image are convinced of its reality. While the trancelike experience lasts, it entirely supplants the ordinary environment of the everyday lives of those involved.

The eighteenth-century person who may have been behind this image is identified by Gibbons and other contributors to the book as Antoine Richard, head gardener at the *Petit Trianon* from 1765 –1795. Richard had helped save the royal garden from destruction by the revolutionary government, having carried the fight on all alone. At one point he even paid workers himself. He certainly seems a likely candidate for the role of agent, capable of triggering off a sense of reality when conditions are right. An analysis of where the Moberly–Jourdain experience occurred has shown that most of the incidents happened in the neighbourhood of the gardener's house. None took place inside the *Petit Trianon* where the memories of Marie-Antoinette, whom Miss Moberly tentatively identified as the agent, might be expected to linger. Possibly Antoine Richard was one of the authoritative-looking gardeners encountered by the two women at the start of their adventure, accompanied by his father Claude, his predecessor as head gardener.

When asked why they should have been singled out for this paranormal experience, Miss Moberly replied that she had come to think such experiences might not be so unusual. 'We can imagine,' she wrote, 'that people, even if they suspected anything unusual, may have thought it best not to follow it up.'

Until about 350 years ago, paranormal experiences were accepted and appreciated in Western, as in other, cultures. They fitted readily with the way people pictured the universe as having everything interrelated by seen or hidden affinities called 'correspondences', of colour, shape, position, or mood. Supernatural beings were believed to move among the natural world and act upon it. If the consequences of mysterious happenings seemed good, they were explained as the intervention of angels; if evil, they were attributed to witchcraft.

These beliefs served to encourage credulity and among the

mysterious happenings recorded in the chronicles of earlier times, are to be found reports of such impossibilities as women giving birth to puppies and cows producing lambs. The system of belief also encouraged rigidity of mind in particular areas of knowledge. For example, Flemish-born Andreas Vesalius met violent opposition when he began revising the anatomical theories of Galen, the Roman physician whose books had been the foundation of medicine for 1300 years (though much of Galen's work on anatomy was wrong). Rigidity of thought could affect even so clear-headed an observer as Leonardo da Vinci. Having dissected a woman's body to examine the position of the foetus in the womb, he still drew it according to his preconception.

The Renaissance and Elizabethan view of the world held tight to the ancient belief that 'there is one common flow, one common breathing, all things are in sympathy'. The Italian humanist, Pico della Mirandola neatly expresses this feeling of interdependence, 'Firstly, there is the unity in things whereby each thing is at one with itself, consists of itself, and coheres with itself. Secondly, there is the unity whereby one creature is united with the others and all parts of the world constitute one world.'

This system of mutually-supporting parts and the interplay of the natural and the supernatural, had to give way as the scientific revolution began. By 1700 a mechanistic view of the world was firmly established. The bodies of living things were regarded as material objects, moving and interacting like the parts of a machine. The divorce of one area of knowledge from another began, and different sciences went their different ways. The study of the physical and chemical properties of matter, the behaviour of living things and human experiences and thoughts, were cut off from one another and remained so for 250 years. Only recently has the attempt begun to draw the separate threads of knowledge together again and to try to fashion an understanding of the unity that underlies our existence. Paranormal events are now studied by physicists, biochemists, mathematicians and other scientists. Many scientists admit that no picture of our existence can be considered complete if it deliberately ignores what we now call the paranormal and the mysterious – but which at some future date may well be seen as normal and everyday.

An implacable opponent of all scientists who held strong

mechanistic views was Charles Hay Fort, intellectual rebel and recluse who died in New York in 1932 at the age of 57. He made it his life work to painstakingly collect and catalogue thousands of inexplicable events that scientists had either ignored or dismissed as of no importance.

Fort's father was a wealthy businessman who ruled his family with autocratic severity, often beating young Fort with a dogwhip. An intelligent and strong-willed child, Charles grew up with a passionate hatred of authority and stupidity. In his teens he decided to be a writer but his one published novel was a failure, perhaps because of his writing style which is a series of brief statements, often without verbs; he also darts from one idea to another without any particular order. To say that his style lacks flow and readability is an understatement.

From an early age Fort had been obsessed by the mysterious and the unexplained. He devoured books on the lost continent of Atlantis, the hollow earth theory and the mystery of the pyramids. One of his earliest books, which he simply named *X*, argued that our civilization was controlled by Mars. Subsequently, he wrote a book titled *Y* and planned another titled *Z*. He wrote *X* and *Y* with tongue-in-cheek, but later he attempted a reasoned statement of his beliefs in *The Book of the Damned*, published in 1919. By 'damned' he meant phenomena that had been discredited and excluded by orthodox science. Here is a typical Fort entry,

'Extract from the log of the bark *Lady of the Lake*, by Capt. F. W. Banner:

"That upon the 22nd of March 1870 at Lat. 5*47'N., Long. 27*52'W., the sailors of the *Lady of the Lake* saw a remarkable object, or cloud, in the sky. They reported to the captain.

"According to Capt. Banner, it was a cloud of circular form, with an included semicircle divided into four parts, the central dividing shaft beginning at the centre of the circle and extending far outward, and then curving backward.

"Geometricity and complexity and stability of form: and the small likelihood of a cloud maintaining such diversity of features, to say nothing of appearance of organic form . . .

"Light grey in colour, or it was cloud-colour.

"That whatever it may have been, it travelled against the wind.

"For half an hour this form was visible. When it did finally disappear that was not because it disintegrated like a cloud, but because it was lost to sight in the evening darkness".'

This might make the reader think at once of a flying saucer, especially since Captain Banner's description sounds like many other UFO sightings. But Fort recorded this account in 1919, 30 years before the start of the UFO craze, and he was quoting from the *Journal of the Meteorological Society,* an eminently respectable publication. He makes no attempt to draw conclusions from the report. It is simply one of hundreds of similar mysterious occurrences that he quotes at length and in detail.

Fort's contemporaries regarded him as mildly insane, and it is easy to understand why. He spent 30 years of his life in the New York Public Library, searching through piles of old newspapers and magazines for items like the one quoted. He was particularly fond of tales of odd things falling from the sky – frogs, fish, blood, stones, or two-feet-square snowflakes. He collected reports of sudden floods, vanishing ships, strange lights in the sky, luminous birds, people who disappeared into thin air, children who came from nowhere. In his third book *Lo!,* he wrote, 'I labour, like workers in a beehive, to support a lot of vagabond notions. But how am I to know? How am I to know but that sometimes a queen-idea may soar to the sky, and from a nuptial flight of data, come back fertile from one of these drones?'

Fort's intuition told him there was something wrong with the neat and orderly universe as pictured by science, and that it was a thousand times stranger than even the most brilliant scientists of his day could imagine. It was this intuition that rang a bell when he read the flying saucer story and dozens more like it. Toward the end of his life he put forward some highly personal theories to account for the phenomena he had recorded, but generally he was not concerned with explanation. He felt there could be any number of possible explanations, all equally at variance with scientific thinking, all equally exciting and fruitful.

'Newtonism is no longer satisfactory', he wrote. 'There is too much that it cannot explain.

'Einsteinism has arisen.

'If Einsteinism is not satisfactory, there is room for other notions.'

Fort had no patience with scientific experts because of cases like the Valparaiso earthquake. Among the many records he collected of 'fires in heaven' that had been seen before or accompanying earthquakes, is a reference to the one in Valparaiso on 16 August 1906. 'Chile lit up', he wrote. 'Under a flaming sky, the people of Valparaiso were running from the smashing city. . . .' He goes on to remark that 136 reports of illuminations in the sky were examined by Count De Ballore, a noted seismologist, who dismissed them all as indefinite or impossible.

'The lights that were seen in the sky', said De Ballore, 'were very likely only searchlights from warships. Or the people may have seen lights from streetcars.' Fort comments, 'It does not matter how preposterous some of my own notions are going to seem. They cannot be more out of accordance with events upon this earth than is such an attribution of the blazing sky of a nation to searchlights or to lamps in streetcars.'

Astronomers fared no better at his hands than seismologists. In a flash of barbed wit, he compares the slit in the dome of an observatory with the fixed grin of a clown. To show he had good historical reasons for his criticism, he gives an account of how astronomers long disbelieved in meteorites.

'About one hundred years ago, if anyone was so credulous as to think that stones had ever fallen from the sky, he was reasoned with:

"In the first place there are no stones in the sky:

"Therefore no stones can fall from the sky." '

He goes on to tell about a report in 1772 that a blazing stone had fallen from the sky at Luce, France. One of the members of the committee appointed by the French Academy to investigate the report was the distinguished scientist Antoine Lavoisier, who wrote the first modern chemistry textbook, among other achievements. But where meteorites were concerned, Lavoisier took the conventional line of his time. The object that fell at Luce, like any meteorite, showed signs of fusion as a result of its passage through the earth's atmosphere. Lavoisier explained this by saying that a stone on the ground had been struck by lightning, which heated and melted it. As Fort sarcastically put it, Lavoisier 'absolutely proved' that there were no meteorites with this explanation.

After Lavoisier's time, an increased flow of data and fresh

theories about the earth's place in the universe led to a new under-standing of meteorites. Perhaps it is not a full understanding, but at least the luminous objects are no longer incorrectly thought to be stones struck by lightning, or boulders flung out by volcanoes. Fort hoped that by accumulating data concerning other strange phenomena, a body of information could be built up to help future thinkers reconsider other accepted theories about life on earth. He kept a meticulous record of his sources of information in newspa-pers and journals.

As could be expected, most of Fort's contemporaries ignored him, but he also ignored them. Even when he was recognized he did not respond. On the launching of a Fortean Society in his honour by the writer Tiffany Thayer, Fort firmly declined to become a member. He may have feared that his disciples would try to pin him down to a definite set of ideas and beliefs and he had no intention of being pinned down.

Day after day and year after year, he continued his obsessive search through the world's publications, making endless notes on slips of paper that he kept in shoe boxes. After *The Book of the Damned* came *New Lands*, then *Lo!*, and finally *Wild Talents*. He became more and more of a hermit. Almost his only recreation was going to the movies and he said he did that only to keep his wife company. For himself, most films 'bored him to death'.

While finishing *Wild Talents* Fort's health began to break down – understandably in view of his dreary existence. He finally became so weak that his wife had to send for an ambulance to take him to the hospital. When his publisher brought a copy of *Wild Talents* to him he was too weak to hold it. He died later the same day.

Fort was ignored in death as in life. Although the Fortean Society continued, it was composed of a small group of eccentrics who admired his fierce individualism. So far as the general public was concerned, his lack of style and unsystematic organization of material kept his books unread and almost forgotten for a quarter of a century after his death.

He was resurrected in France in the mid-1950s by two ardent admirers, Jacques Bergier and Louis Pauwels. Bergier had been trained as a chemist, but was fascinated by alchemy and the occult. Pauwels was a successful journalist and student of the paranormal. After pooling their talents they produced the book Fort had tried to write all his life. They called it *The Morning of the Magicians*. First published in 1960, it became an immediate success and has been a best-seller in many languages. Pauwels and Bergier, like Fort, are critical of the mechanistic views of nineteenth-century science. They devote a chapter to Fort's life, quoting extensively from his works and drawing attention to his call for a revision of the very structure of our knowledge. 'He sees science', they explained, 'as a highly sophisticated motor car speeding along on a highway. But on either side of this marvellous track, with its shining asphalt and neon lighting, there are great tracts of wild country, full of prodigies and mystery. Stop! Explore in every direction! Leave the high road and wander!' With the international success of their book, interest in Fort revived along with interest in all studies of the paranormal and the non-mechanistic. All Fort's books were re-issued and translations appeared all over the world. Recognition had finally arrived.

Ironically, assistance to this contemporary surge of interest in the paranormal has come from science, in particular from that branch of science devoted to probing the atom. Very mysterious 'states of being' occur within the atom, and to understand them nuclear physicists have become increasingly daring in their hypotheses. Matter has become progressively dematerialized. A single electron has been made to pass through two holes in a screen at the same time – a feat, it has been said, that not even a ghost can manage! The Nobel Prize-winning British physicist, Paul Direc has suggested that interstellar space is not empty, but filled by a bottomless sea of electrons with negative mass. Does this not begin to sound like Fort's 'Super-Sargasso Sea'? Fort theorized that many strange objects falling from the sky came from this 'Super-Sargasso Sea', which he described as a 'region somewhere above the earth's surface in which gravitation is inoperative.'

Experiments of investigators into the paranormal have become more sophisticated and scientific. The card-guessing and dicethrowing experiments pioneered by J. B. Rhine at Duke University in North Carolina, gave place to the advanced electrical equipment of his successor, Helmut Schmidt. In Schmidt's first precognition experiment in 1969, subjects were asked to predict the order in which four coloured lamps would be lit. The lamps were lit in an entirely random sequence provided by the discharge of electrons from radioactive strontium-90. In a series of nearly 74,000 trials, the subjects gave about 900 more correct guesses than would be expected by chance. This is a very high achievement by the laws of probability.

In 1970, Schmidt designed an experiment to see if subjects could influence events on the sub-atomic scale by means of thought – that is, by psychokinesis. Subjects were seated in front of a circle of nine lamps that could light up in either a clockwise or a counterclockwise direction. The direction depended on which of two numbers was produced by the Random Number Generator, and this in turn was governed by the decay of radioactive strontium-90. The subjects were asked to select a particular direction and try to cause the lamps to go on lighting up in that direction. In a run of 30,000 trials, 300 more occurred in the direction desired than could be accounted for by chance. In fact, the odds against such a score by chance, over so long a run, are 1,000 to one. The conclusion that interested physicists and parapsychologists alike was that the emission of the electrons had been affected by human thought to some degree.

Sir John Eccles, winner of a Nobel Prize in 1963 for his work on the transmission of nerve impulses in the brain, regards such experiments as evidence for the power of mind over matter. Several physicists have suggested the existence of certain particles – variously named mindons, psychons, or psitrons – that might carry information between mind and matter and between mind and mind. Even the vast distances of interstellar space and the passage of time – for example, between the eighteenth and the twentieth century – might be no hindrance to these particles.

Insights along these lines may help to explain the constantly-puzzling phenomenon of coincidence. When the mechanistic view of the world was fully accepted, very little consideration was given to coincidence. If two strangers met and discovered they shared the same birthday, it meant nothing more than the workings of blind chance. It was argued that the year contained 365 days; people met strangers all the time; sooner or later, by the laws of chance, two people whose birthdays were on the same day would meet. Any person claiming to be scientific, who devoted any further time to the matter, was branded as superstitious.

In the course of the twentieth century this attitude has altered, though it is still to be met with in many branches of science and among people who pride themselves on their rationalist approach to existence. It took a remarkable coincidence in the life of Arthur Koestler, Hungarian-born author and historian of scientific ideas, to change his attitude toward the paranormal.

During the 1930s, Koestler had the misfortune of being arrested and imprisoned by both the Fascists and the Communists. In 1937, during the Spanish Civil War, he was imprisoned for three months and threatened with execution by the Franco regime as a suspected spy.

'In such situations', he recalled, 'one tends to look for metaphysical comforts, and one day I suddenly remembered a certain episode in Thomas Mann's novel, *Buddenbrooks*. One of the characters, Consul Thomas Buddenbrook, though only in his forties, knows that he is going to die. He was never given to religious speculation, but now he falls under the spell of a "little book" in which it is explained that death is not final, merely a transition to another, impersonal kind of existence, a reunion with cosmic oneness.'

The 'little book' was an essay by the nineteenth-century German philosopher Schopenhauer, *On Death and its Relation to the Indestructibility of our Essential Selves*. Remembering the passage gave Koestler, as it had given the Consul in the novel, just the comfort he needed. The day after his release from prison he wrote to Mann, whom he had never met, thanking him for the help he had derived from the book. Mann's reply reached him a few days later in London. Mann explained that he had not read Schopenhauer's essay since writing *Buddenbrooks* 40 years before; but the previous day, sitting in his garden, he had felt a sudden impulse to read the essay once more. He went indoors to get the volume from his library. At that moment there was a ring at the door and the mailman handed him Koestler's letter.

Perhaps this coincidence is simply an impressive demonstration of the powers of telepathy. But what is to be made of the following incident, quoted by Koestler in his book, *The Roots of Coincidence*? It was recounted by the psychologist Carl Jung, who kept a logbook of coincidences. Jung writes,

'A young woman I was treating had, at a critical moment, a dream in which she was given a golden scarab. While she was telling me this dream I sat with my back to the closed window. Suddenly I heard a noise behind me, like a gentle tapping. I turned around and saw a flying insect knocking against the windowpane from outside. I opened the window and caught the creature in the air as it flew in. It was the nearest analogy to a golden scarab that one finds in our latitudes, a scaraboid beetle, the common rose-chafer (*Cetonia aurata*), which contrary to its usual habits had evidently felt an urge to get into a dark room at this particular moment.'

Koestler asks, 'What does this scarab at Jung's window mean?'

In our present state of knowledge, all answers are obliged to be speculative but Koestler suggests that the right approach to an answer lies in considering once more the views of the universe held by thinkers before the mechanistic revolution, 'There is one common flow, one common breath, all things are in sympathy.' Schopenhauer set his thinking firmly against the prevailing mechanistic views of his age. Where they insisted that physical cause must precede physical effect, he believed that there was also a metaphysical realm, a kind of universal consciousness, so that the events in a person's life existed at one and the same time in the reality of ordinary, everyday perceptions and in a greater reality. Each person is the hero of his or her own drama while simultaneously figuring in a wider drama. 'Thus everything is interrelated and mutually attuned', said Schopenhauer. In his view, a coincidence is a single event occurring in two different realities.

This profound interrelationship is accepted in nuclear physics. 'What we call an isolated particle', writes Dr F. Capra, 'is in reality the product of its interaction with its surroundings. It is therefore impossible to separate any part of the universe from the rest.'

The 300-year-old division of the universe by science into 'mind' and 'matter' shows signs of coming together as the matter of the atom is disclosed to be a form of energy. The relationship between this energy and the human mind is still far from clear, but a readiness to consider the relationship now exists.

Schopenhauer believed that existence was 'a great dream' dreamed by an entity he termed 'the Will to Life'. Others who have followed him in calling the universe a dream or a thought, have done so not from any temptation toward mysticism, but as the outcome of their scientific thought. The kind of scientist against whom Charles Hay Fort pitted himself no longer holds undisputed sway.

In spite of this new approach, however, an explanation may never be found for some of the mysterious happenings of the past. For example, in August 1887 peasants of the small village of Banjos, Spain, saw two young children walk out of a cave. Their clothes were unfamiliar and they could speak no Spanish, but even more extraordinary, their skin was green. Where they came from no one has ever discovered. There have been other sudden appearances – and sudden disappearances – equally unexplained. David Lang, a farmer of Texas, vanished from the middle of a field in full view of four witnesses. No one is ever likely to find out what happened to him.

Shall we ever solve the mystery of crewless ships like the *Mary Celeste*? Will we discover who planned and built some of the mysterious structures in the world? Our increasing knowledge of our surroundings can solve some puzzles that baffled our ancestors. Black rain, showers of blood, fish, and other creatures falling from the sky – we think we know their true nature. Further study may bring the answer to the perplexing problem of the Bermuda Triangle, that weird area of the Atlantic where planes and ships still vanish today. But will we find the explanation to the gruesome deaths of certain people by spontaneous combustion? What about objects that seem cursed? Their evil reputation may be the effect of imagination, but could there be some innate property in the objects that brings death to those associated with them? Science has become more concerned with probing such mysteries and today seems less the full opposite of the paranormal.

Fort once said that every science is a mutilated octopus. 'If its tentacles were not clipped to stumps, it would feel its way into disturbing contacts.' Over 60 years after his death, at least some of those tentacles have been allowed to grow. It seems that we may at last be entering the age of 'disturbing contacts'.

Unsolved Mysteries

Part One

'... Things in Heaven and Earth ...'

Modern man believes he lives in the 'Age of Science' just as the Europeans of the late eighteenth century believed they lived in the 'Age of Enlightenment'. Future historians may well look on both suppositions with a certain sense of irony. By later standards, the people of the Enlightenment seem ignorant, brutal and generally unenlightened. It must also be said that we – the followers of the rational, sensible creed of Science – can behave both irrationally and nonsensically when the world does not fit into our predetermined theories.

For example, early astronomers refused to accept the existence of meteorites: stones could not fall from the sky, they reasoned, because 'it was self-evident' that there were no stones in the sky. Today we know differently, yet other mysterious falls – such as frogs, fish, slime and even blood – recorded again and again around the globe, have been quietly ignored or partially explained away by meteorologists. The phenomenon of SHC (Spontaneous Human Combustion) undoubtedly takes place, but respectable scientists prefer to leave such cases for the baffled police to puzzle over. The Bermuda Triangle is treated as a joke by most people, but to the relatives of the hundreds of people that have disappeared in that region, it isn't very funny.

Unexplained 'happenings' take place all the time, but they are virtually ignored by science. The reason is not (usually) laziness or bias, but simply the fact that we, like the early astronomers, seem to be working with too little information – our science is just not big enough to comprehend such events. In this section we will look at some of the strange events that seem to make a mockery of our scientific understanding.

CHAPTER 1

CURIOUS RAIN

Of all the strange happenings on record, one of the most common is unnatural rain. Frogs, periwinkles, jelly – these and more have poured out of the skies. What causes such falls? What about the unusual coloured rains of yellow, black, red, or the strange blankets of colour-tinted dry fogs? Charles Fort tied odd rains in with his theory of an extraterrestrial source for life on earth. Strangely enough, recent analyses of meteorites have shown them to contain substances necessary to living cells. Is there something to the idea that life as we know it originated outside of Earth?

We use the phrase 'raining cats and dogs' to describe a downpour. But rains of many kinds of living creatures have actually been reported from earliest times and all over the world. On 28 May 1881, during a thunderstorm on the outskirts of Worcester, England, tons of periwinkles and small hermit crabs fell on Cromer Gardens Road and the surrounding fields. They came down out of the sky in a broad band extending for about a mile. When news of this amazing fall reached the centre of Worcester, a town 40 miles from the sea, many people hurried to Cromer Gardens Road carrying pots, pans, bags and even trunks. One garden alone yielded two sacks of periwinkles, 10 sacks of them altogether were taken back to the markets of Worcester for sale.

Showers of fish, frogs and many other animals are rare but have long been known of. Like comets and shooting stars, they were frequently interpreted as omens of calamity. Such an attitude is understandable. People need an ordered environment if they are to feel at home in the world, and fish falling from the sky is a clear sign of disorder. In the eighteenth and nineteenth centuries, many rationalists over-reacted to what they took to be the superstitions of earlier ages, and denied altogether the possibility of such marvels. So the case of the Worcester periwinkles was explained as the result of a fish dealer who abandoned his stock on the road before the storm. Two people were found who reported that they had seen the periwinkles on the ground before it rained. It is hard to understand why a fish dealer would want to get rid of his winkles when, as was pointed out, they would sell at a high price in Worcester that day. This unseen merchant, then, introduces a solution as unlikely as the idea that periwinkles and small crabs somehow managed to get into the air and later fell out of it.

About 20 years earlier, on 16 February 1861, a weird shower had been reported from Singapore. An earthquake had been followed by three days of incessant rain, in the course of which great numbers of fish were found in the puddles of streets throughout the city. Local residents reported that the fish had fallen from the sky. One writer of an account in *La Science pour Tous* stated that he himself did not see any of the fish falling – adding that the deluge of rain was so heavy that sometimes he could not see more than three yards ahead of him. But he specifically mentioned that some of the fish had been found in his courtyard, which was surrounded by high walls. The explanation generally accepted, however, was that overflowing streams had left the fish on the land after the waters receded.

Occasionally there is some truth in the explanation that objects said to have fallen from the sky were on the ground all the time. Showers of frogs and toads have been reported many times, frequently in Italy, in both ancient and modern times. Arguments regularly broke out as to whether the animals had originated on the earth or in the clouds. Some witnesses reported that they had seen the frogs fall. Other witnesses said that they had seen them only close to the walls of houses, which could mean that they had slipped down from the gutters of the roofs. A German naturalist writing in 1874 observed that frogs said to have been rained down but not seen to fall were seldom dead, lamed, or bruised because, he implied, they had been on the ground all the time. 'The appearance of the frogs after a rain is easily accounted for by the circumstance that during a long-continued drought they remain in a state of torpor in holes and coverts, and all that the rain does is the enlivening of them, giving them new spirits, and calling them forth to enjoy the element they delight to live in.'

Thomas Cooper, a popular nineteenth-century lecturer on Christianity, witnessed the phenomenon of raining frogs during his boyhood in Lincolnshire, England. 'I am as sure of what I relate as I am of my own existence', he declared. He said that the frogs were alive and jumping and that they 'fell on the pavement at our feet, and came tumbling down the spouts from the tiles of the houses into the water tubs.' It is interesting that in most of the reports of frog showers, the size of the frogs is always very small.

There seems no reason to doubt that showers of frogs occur from time to time – which is not to deny that at other times the frogs simply emerge from holes in the ground when the first rain-drops enliven them. It seems hasty to conclude either that frogs seen after a rainstorm have always fallen from the skies, or that frogs seen after a rainstorm were always on the ground before-hand. The evidence seems to show that sometimes frogs fall from above and sometimes they don't.

The scientifically-accepted explanation for a frog rain is that they have been carried in the air, sometimes for great distances, from a pool or stream where they were sucked up by sudden strong winds. Charles Hay Fort regarded this as unlikely. But Fort was also guilty of error, and not above altering the evidence when it suited his argument. In *The Book of the Damned* he wrote, 'After one of the greatest hurricanes in the history of Ireland, some fish were found as far as 15 yards from the edge of the lake.' In these words he implied that an unprecedented hurricane is required to move a fish a few yards because he wanted to cast doubt on the likelihood of the wind moving any object a matter of miles – for instance, periwinkles, 40 miles from the mouth of the nearest river to Worcester, or the enormous number of eels that fell in Coalburg, Alabama, on 29 May 1892.

The power of the wind is enormous. On 19 August 1845 a whirlwind in France uprooted 180 large trees in a few seconds in Houlme, and destroyed three mills in Monville, dropping planks from the factory buildings half an hour later on the outskirts of Dieppe, 20 miles (32 kilometres) away. Though it takes a whirlwind to transport planks, a far less violent wind can bear away small frogs, periwinkles, and eels.

So many eels fell in Coalburg that farmers came into town with carts and took them away to use as fertilizer for their fields. Eels also fell in Hendon in the northeast of England on 24 August 1918. Hundreds of them covered a small area about 60 × 30 yards. Hendon is a coastal town, but the eels were probably carried in the air for some time and from another part of the coast because, according to witnesses, 'the eels were all dead, and indeed stiff and hard, when picked up, immediately after the occurrence.'

Fish that fall in showers generally are dead. Lunged creatures are frequently alive, making it difficult to say how long they have been in the air. Live lizards fell on the streets of Montreal, Canada on 28 December 1857. Snails fell in such quantities in Redruth, England on 8 July 1886, that people were able to gather them up in hatfuls. A yellow cloud appeared over Paderborn, Germany on 9 August 1892, and a torrent of rain from it brought hundreds of mussels. More recently, on 28 September 1953 a shower of toads fell on Orlando, Florida in the middle of the afternoon.

An uncommon shower of live fish descended on Mountain Ash, Wales on 11 February 1859. The vicar of the neighbouring town of Aberdare interviewed John Lewis, an employee of the sawmill in Mountain Ash. Said Lewis, 'I was getting out a piece of timber for the purpose of setting it for the saw, when I was startled by something falling all over me – down my neck, on my head, and on my back. On putting my hand down my neck I was surprised to find they were little fish. By this time I saw the whole ground covered with them. I took off my hat, the brim of which was full of them. They were jumping all about. They covered the ground in a long strip of about 80 × 12 yards, as we measured afterward.' These fish fell in two showers, with an interval of about 10 minutes, each shower lasting about two minutes. Some people, thinking they might be sea fish, placed them in salt water whereupon they instantly died. Those that were placed in fresh water thrived well and were later identified as sticklebacks.

Showers of living objects fall over a relatively small area, but other kinds of unnatural rain can sometimes cover an entire country. Yellow rain has been reported from all parts of the world and because of the Christian link-up between brimstone and hell, the yellow has been popularly identified as sulphur and regarded as a warning from on high. Although yellow rain does not look different while it is falling, the ground is afterward found to be covered with a fine yellow dust. This dust burns easily, encouraging the belief that it is sulphur, but in the majority of cases the accepted explanation is that the yellow is pollen from trees. A forest of hazelnut trees coming into flower in April, or beeches in May or June, or pine trees from midsummer onward, can produce a vast amount of fine pollen – and a strong wind following a spell of tranquil weather can bear away enormous quantities which may subsequently fall down with rain.

Sometimes a yellow substance falls in the absence of rain. On 27 February 1877 in Peckloh, Germany, a golden-yellow fall was found to contain four different kinds of organisms. Their shapes resembled microscopic arrows, coffee beans, horns, and discs and none was identified as pollen.

Another unnatural shower often reported is black rain. The blame for this has usually been placed fairly on smoke belching from factory chimneys in an industrial area somewhere along the path of the wind. But on 14 August 1888 there was a heavy downpour of black rain on the Cape of Good Hope, a part of South Africa remote from any large concentration of industry. Could the blackness have come from a forest fire? This was the explanation given to account for the celebrated Canadian black rain 69 years before the Cape Hope incident, when it had been said that the rainclouds had been stained by the dense smoke of forest fires south of the Ohio River. In the case of the Cape of Good Hope, however, the direction of the prevailing wind makes it unlikely that fires in the forest region could have been the cause. Nor would smoke have produced a rain so black as to be described as 'a shower of ink.'

What was not realized in the past was how enormous a quantity of material the wind can carry, and how vast the distances it can carry the burden. Concentrations of dust in major storms have been estimated to reach as much as 200,000 tons per square mile of land surface. In February 1903 large areas of Western Europe were covered by a dark sand blown from the Sahara Desert. It varied widely in colour, different reports describing it as reddish, yellowish, grey and the colour of chocolate. In one place it was described as 'sticky to the touch and slightly iridescent.' A quan-

tity amounting to about 10 million tons is calculated to have
fallen on England alone. A similar fall occurred in the south of
England and Wales on 30 June 1968, when storms broke after the
hottest day for 11 years. The following morning a fine sandy dust
was found coating parked cars, greenhouses, windows and
washing. The dust was yellow, pink or bright red, and analysis
established that it had originated in the Sahara.

Red rain – popularly mistaken for showers of blood – has in the
past understandably spread more alarm than rain of any other
colour. Homer tells of showers of blood that fell upon the Greek
heroes at ancient Troy, as an omen of their approaching death in
battle. References to similar showers in Roman times mention the
terror they caused among the populace. St. Gregory of Tours, the
sixth-century historian of the Franks, recorded that in AD 582 in
the Paris region 'real blood rained from a cloud, falling on the
clothes of many people, and so staining them with gore that they
stripped them off in horror.'

A long list of unnatural rainfalls was compiled by the French
astronomer and writer Camille Flammarion, who died in 1925.
He was fascinated with anything to do with the heavens, and in
the chapter entitled 'Prodigies' in his book *The Atmosphere*, he
listed over 40 references to 'showers of blood' before 1800 and a
further 21 that had been reported in the nineteenth century. The
reports cover a wide area, from Brussels to Baghdad and from
Hungary to Lisbon. When the reaction of the populace is given it
is invariably one of panic. Supernatural signs were sometimes
reported as accompanying the showers. During a red rain that fell
on France and Germany in March 1181, a luminous cross was
observed in the skies. Frequently the showers were said to be the
warning of death; when showers of blood persisted intermittently
for three days and nights in Brescia, Italy, they were followed by
the death of Pope Adrian II on the fourth day.

One of the first to attempt to find a cause for these fearful
showers was a man called de Peiresc. When numerous red spots
had been discovered on the walls and stones on the outskirts of
Aix-en-Provence in July 1608, the local priests attributed them to
the influence of the Devil. de Peiresc examined the spots carefully
and concluded that they were not of blood – the Devil's or otherwise – but the secretions of a butterfly. He pointed out that the

species now known as the 'Large Tortoiseshell' which has a red secretion, had been seen in unusually large numbers that month. Moreover, red spots were absent from the centre of the town, where the butterflies had not made an appearance and had been found on the higher parts of the buildings, about the level to which they flew. However, the citizens of Aix preferred to believe that the Devil was the culprit.

In general, the cause of rains of blood is, like that of yellow rain, dust originating in a desert region. Signor Sementini, professor of chemistry at Naples, was ahead of his time when in 1813 he accurately identified as dust the red shower that fell on Gerace, Italy, on 14 March of that year. He also recorded a vivid impression of the event. 'The wind had been westerly for two days', he wrote, 'when at 2 pm it suddenly became calm, the atmosphere grew cloudy, and the darkness gradually became so great as to render it necessary to light candles. The citizens, alarmed by the obscurity, rushed in a crowd to the cathedral to pray. The sky assumed the colour of red-hot iron, thunder and lightning continued for a considerable length of time and the sea was heard to roar, although six miles from the city. Large drops of rain then began to fall, which were of a blood-red colour.'

The rain deposited a yellow powder and had a slight earthy taste. Sementini analyzed it and concluded that it was a terrestrial dust of some kind but could not guess where it came from. It is now difficult to establish if it had blown from the Sahara, since one account states that the wind was westerly while another gives it as easterly. Such a basic error, made at a time when accurate observations were being attempted, throws serious doubts on earlier reports made when natural phenomena were unquestioningly regarded as direct communications from God, and reported in that light.

In this category must be included showers of crosses. In France, in the year 764, crosses were said to have appeared on men's clothes during a shower of blood. In 1094, crosses are reported to have fallen from heaven, alighting on the garments of priests. In 1501, crosses rained down in Germany and Belgium during the week before Easter, and left marks on clothes, skin, and bread.

In the annals of unusual rains, 'the Miracle of Remiremont'

holds a unique position. On the afternoon of 26 May 1907 the Abbé Gueniot was snug in his library as a storm battered down outside. Suddenly his housekeeper called to him to come see the extraordinary hailstones. She told him that images of Our Lady of the Treasures were printed on them. The Abbé later described the event like this,

'In order to satisfy her, I glanced carelessly at the hailstones, which she held in her hand. But, since I did not want to see anything, and moreover could not do so without my spectacles, I turned to go back to my book. She urged, "I beg of you to put on your glasses." I did so, and saw very distinctly on the front of the hailstones, which were slightly convex in the centre, although the edges were somewhat worn, the bust of a woman, with a robe that was turned up at the bottom, like a priest's robe. I should, perhaps, describe it more exactly by saying that it was like the Virgin of the Hermits. The outline of the images was slightly hollow, as if they had been formed with a punch, but were very boldly drawn. Mlle. André asked me to notice certain details of the costume, but I refused to look at it any longer. I was ashamed of my credulity, feeling sure that the Blessed Virgin would hardly concern herself with instantaneous photographs on hailstones.'

Nonetheless, the Abbé picked up three of the hailstones to weigh them and found they weighed between six and seven ounces. One was perfectly round and had a seam all around it, as though it had been cast in a mould. Later he collected the signatures of 50 people who had seen the extraordinary hailstones. There seems little doubt that the hail that fell on Remiremont that afternoon bore strange markings. The Secretary of the French Academy wondered whether lightning might have struck a medal of the Virgin and reproduced the image on the hailstones. Other reports state that the print was found on the inside of the hailstones after they had been split. The key to the mystery probably lies there. When hailstones are formed, they are frequently tossed up and down between layers of cold and less cold air, in the process accumulating several layers of ice that show as rings on a cross-section of the individual hailstone. The circumstances of hail formation at Remiremont may have been such as to allow an irregular layering of ice that was then seen to resemble the appearance of the Virgin. It is worth mentioning that a few days before the storm, the local government had forbidden a religious procession through the town and this had created a high degree of agitated excitement among the devout – an atmosphere conducive to the occurrence of a miracle.

Showers of a liquid looking like milk have been reported at various times in Italy. In one such rain, coins and copper pots exposed to the downfall became silvered, and kept this appearance for three days. This suggests that the rain contained mercury, although it is hard to imagine the circumstances under which this would be possible.

In the Silesian province of what is now Poland, at a time of great shortage of wheat, a violent storm broke over the countryside, and afterward the ground was covered with small round seeds. The country folk at first believed their prayers had been answered and that the skies had rained millet. Unfortunately, the seeds proved to be from a local species of the herb speedwell. In 1804 however, a real wheatfall took place in parts of Andalucia in southern Spain. A hurricane removed the grain from a threshing floor in Tutua on the Moroccan coast, carried it across the Straits of Gibraltar and dropped it on the amazed and grateful Spanish peasants.

Fort gives his own eccentric possibilities for these phenomena,

'Debris from interplanetary disasters.

'Aerial battles.

'Food-supplies from cargoes of super-vessels, wrecked in interplanetary traffic.'

In the spring of 1695, dwellers in the Irish counties of Limerick and Tipperary experienced showers of a greasy substance having a 'very stinking smell'. This grease, which the local people called 'butter', fell in lumps an inch in diameter, and was soft, clammy, and dark yellow in colour. The Bishop of Cloyne called it 'stinking dew.' Fort says, 'We'll not especially wonder whether these butter-like or oily substances were food or fuel . . .' and goes on to suggest that they fell from 'a super-construction, plying back and forth from Jupiter and Mars and Venus.'

Fort's achievement in tracking down many thousands of strange happenings – and urging people to think about them – is undermined by the weird theories he put forward to account for them. It is as though he were still a little boy deliberately pasting wrong labels on cans, as he used to do in rebellion when working in his father's store. In his rebellion against autocratic science, did he sometimes deliberately apply a wrong label? In any case, his view of the universe was something like a store out of which he pulled a variety of goods.

For example, sometimes he imagined that a circle of ice surrounded the earth, that fragments break off and fall to the earth as hail, and that we see the stars through the resulting gaps. Other times he felt that the earth is ringed with a gelatinous substance, and that globs of this jelly also fall down. He talks of a 'supergeographical pond' above the earth – his 'Super-Sargasso Sea'.

Fort may not have believed all these fanciful theories, or at least not all of them at the same time, but the space probes of the 1960s and 1970s have exposed them as nonsense. Nowadays, it is difficult to read any of Fort's books without finding a foolish and disproved theory on every page, including the gelatin ring.

But can there be a fall of jelly? In Massachussetts on the night of 13 August 1819, a bright light was seen moving above Amherst and a sound was heard that was described as being as loud as an explosion. Next morning, in the front yard of a professor, was found a substance 'unlike anything before observed by anyone who saw it. It was a bowl-shaped object, about eight inches in diameter, and one inch thick. Bright, buff-coloured, and having upon it a fine nap. Upon removing this covering, a buff-coloured, pulpy substance of the consistency of soft soap was found, which gave off an offensive, suffocating smell. A few minutes of exposure to the air changed the buff colour to a livid colour resembling venous blood. It absorbed moisture quickly from the air and liquefied.'

No explanation of this strange object was put forward at the time but a few years later, a similar one was found near the same place. It was shown to Professor Edward Hitchcock, who pronounced it to be a gelatinous fungus. He said similar fungi might spring up within the next 24 hours and sure enough two others had done so before nightfall.

The moving light and the loud sound remain unexplained, but the fungus was probably of the kind called 'nostoc'. Natural appearances of 'nostoc' in unusual places presumably gave rise to the reports of more jellylike falls in several other parts of the

United States over the years. Lumps of jelly looking like coagulated egg white have been found in Rahway, New Jersey. A mass like boiled starch was reported from West Point, New York. The flakes of a substance that looked like thin slices of beef floated down from a clear sky at Olympian Springs, Kentucky. This was a thick shower, but fell only on a narrow strip of land about 100 yards long × 50 yards wide.

'Nostoc', a word first coined by the sixteenth-century German physician and alchemist Paracelsus, is usually considered like frogs, to have been on the ground all the time, when pronounced to have fallen from the sky. But there is no reason why it should not occasionally, again like frogs, be borne in the air by winds and fall to the ground when the wind drops. A primitive alga, 'nostoc' is thought to be one of the world's oldest organisms. In dry periods, the common form of 'nostoc' can shrivel into paper-thin strands, swelling up again after rain or in the presence of moisture. Practically invisible when dry, the fungus colonies can take in water and enlarge quickly to the size of a grapefruit. These sudden appearances have often given rise to the idea that they dropped from the sky.

Some varieties of 'nostoc' are eaten by South American Indians, and one of its species may have been the substance called 'manna' in the Bible. 'Manna', which provided food for the Israelites during their wanderings in the Sinai desert, cannot now be identified with any certainty. The sweet globules produced by the lichen *Lecanora esculenta* are thought to be one of the most likely sources, although this lichen is not now found in Sinai. Another possibility is the secretions of an insect that sucks the sap of the tamarisk, small drops of which fall to the ground as sticky honeydew. At the beginning of Exodus Chapter 16, Moses tells the Israelites that the Lord will rain bread from heaven, but the belief that the 'manna' would come from above is linked to the old and widespread idea that dew falls from the sky, 'In the morning the dew lay round about the host. And when the dew that lay was gone up, behold, upon the face of the wilderness, there lay a small round thing, as small as the hoar frost on the ground.'

It is now known that dew is not a precipitation like rain, but is formed on the ground as a deposit of water vapour. But the idea that dew drops from the sky is persistent. Schoolchildren in

France in the early years of this century were still being taught that it dropped. At an earlier period, pearls were thought to be congealed dew. It was said that oysters rose to the surface of the sea during the night and caught the falling dewdrops, which in time hardened into pearls.

Although Charles Fort is mistaken in most of his theories, he is not entirely wrong in suggesting that certain mysterious happenings are extraterrestrial – meteorites for example. Their seemingly supernatural origin has frequently led to them becoming objects of worship. One that fell in Arabia about the time of Muhammad is still preserved in Mecca, built into a corner of the sacred shrine known as the Kaaba – every pilgrim must kiss it in the course of his visit to the city. The Roman Emperor Heliogabalus, had a black meteorite carried in solemn procession through streets strewn with gold dust. Even when not worshipped, the fallen meteorite was long regarded as a miraculous object. The oldest authenticated meteorite in a museum is the one that fell on the Swiss town of Ensisheim in 1492. The local church records give a good contemporary account of the event,

'On the 16th November 1492 a singular miracle happened: for between 11 and 12 in the forenoon, with a loud crash of thunder and a prolonged noise heard afar off, there fell in the town of Ensisheim a stone weighing 260 pounds. It was seen by a child to strike the ground in a field near the canton called Gisgaud, where it made a hole more than five feet deep. It was taken to the church as being a miraculous object. The noise was heard so distinctly at Lucerne, Villing, and many other places that in each of them it was thought that some houses had fallen. King Maximilian, who was then at Ensisheim, had the stone carried to the castle: after breaking off two pieces, one for the Duke Sigismund of Austria and the other for himself, he forbade further damage, and ordered the stone to be suspended in the parish church.'

Not all visiting objects that arrive from beyond the earth come as stones. The strange, dry fogs that at long intervals blanket wide parts of the globe may occur when the earth passes through the vast clouds of dust that are believed to occur in the depths of space. The dry fog that in AD 526 covered the Eastern Roman Empire with a reddish haze, may have been caused in this manner. So also, the blue fog that hung over much of the northern hemisphere for most of the summer of 1783. It began at Copenhagen on 24 May and by June had extended to Germany, France and England. Eventually it spread eastward as far as Syria and westward over a large part of North America. It showed no trace of humidity and was unaffected by rain or wind. The pale blue haze was sometimes so dense that visibility was reduced to half a mile, and the sun only became visible when it stood 12 degrees above the horizon. The fog had a strong, disagreeable odour, and caused severe catarrh in humans and animals as long as it lasted. Another strange feature of the blue fog was the peculiar phosphoric gleam that accompanied it and made reading possible at night, even small print. The same gleam came with a haze in 1831, when the sun appeared tinged with green.

Many people thought such an extraordinary event must mean the approaching end of the world. Sir Arthur Conan Doyle may have had such fears in mind when he wrote *The Poison Belt*, a story in which the earth passes into a cloud of interstellar gas, bringing death and widespread fire in its inexorable progress across the globe.

Whether or not meteoric dust brings about the end of civilization, it seems certain that meteorites helped to get it going. Of the three main types of meteorite, one is almost entirely composed of pure iron, a crucial metal in the development of civilization. Iron occurring naturally on earth is invariably combined with other elements and gives no indication of its special properties. But meteoric iron found by primitive mankind was literally 'a pure gift from heaven', needing no more attention than softening by fire and hammering to a convenient shape. The Eskimos have long used meteoric iron for spears, axe heads, and knives. Fragments of such iron have been found in the burial mounds of the prehistoric Hopewell Indians of North America.

Even Fort's theory of an extraterrestrial source for life on earth has received support from the recent chemical analysis of meteorites. In 1969, British chemists J. Brooks and G. Shaw examined the meteorite that had fallen at Murray, Kentucky in 1950 and discovered that it contained 'sporopollenin', a highly complex biological substance that forms the outer coating of pollen grains. In another meteorite, the quantity of 'sporopollenin' was found to be four percent of the total weight.

When an enormous fireball swept over the countryside of Victoria, Australia on 28 September 1969, it exploded near the town of Murchison and showered the area with fragments. Examples sent to the NASA Research Centre in Ames, California revealed large quantities of 5 of the 20 amino acids found in living cells. The presence of these chemicals is considered to be essential before life can originate on a planet. Experiments have shown that they could have been generated by the action of lightning on the gases that composed our earth's primitive atmosphere – ammonia, methane, water vapour and hydrogen. But an extraterrestrial origin for life on earth cannot be ruled out.

CHAPTER 2

STRANGE DISAPPEARANCES

A man running along the road in sight of three witnesses vanishes without trace . . . a well-known journalist is lost in puzzling circumstances while on an assignment . . . three lighthouse keepers are seemingly swallowed up by the air or the sea. What could have happened to them and others who have mysteriously vanished? Sometimes there seems to be a logical and possible explanation for disappearances, but the absence of a body always creates and sustains a doubt that there is any rational reason. Is it because the explanation is, in fact, supernatural?

James Burne Worson was a hard-drinking man, a shoemaker who lived in Leamington, England. When under the influence of liquor, he would boast of his great athletic skill and would often make foolish wagers involving some trial of strength. On 3 September 1873 he made a sizeable bet that he could run all the way to Coventry and back, a distance of something more than 40 miles. He set out at once. The man with whom he made the bet (whose name is not remembered), Barham Wise, a linen draper, and Hamerson Burns, a photographer, followed him by cart.

Worson did very well for several miles, going at an easy gait without apparent fatigue, for he genuinely had great powers of endurance. The three men in the cart kept a short distance in the rear, occasionally calling out friendly encouragement or teasing him, as the spirit moved them. Suddenly, in the very middle of the road not a dozen yards from them and with their eyes right on him, Worson seemed to stumble, pitched headlong forward, uttered a loud cry – and vanished! He did not even fall to the earth, but simply vanished before touching it. No trace of him was ever discovered.

This account, somewhat compressed, is taken from an article entitled 'Mysterious Disappearances' by the American journalist and writer, Ambrose Bierce. Toward the end of his life, this master of the vitriolic pen, scourge of corruption in high places and of incompetency in all places, made a collection of such unexplained vanishing acts. Their matter-of-fact tone is strikingly different from the ghoulish excitement of his celebrated ghost stories. They have more in common with the tales he set in the Civil War, tales that drew upon his real-life experiences as a soldier fighting on the Union side.

At this late date, it is impossible to say whether Bierce was trying to create an effect by writing about make-believe events in a straightforward style. In any case, he provides factual details for even the most ghostly of these accounts, which is that of Charles Ashmore's disappearance. This sixteen-year-old boy set off from the family farmhouse one snowy winter evening, apparently to fetch water from the nearby spring, Bierce relates. When he failed to return, his father and sister went to search for him. They found that his footsteps in the snow stopped short about halfway along the path to the spring. Young Ashmore never reappeared, though his voice was heard in the immediate area of the spring for several months after. Even that sign of his presence ended by midsummer.

Bierce's interest in disappearances becomes all the more fascinating in view of the most famous of his mysterious disappearances – in this case it happened to be his own.

In November 1913, Ambrose Bierce crossed the border into Mexico where a civil war had broken out. He was granted credentials as an observer with the revolutionary army of Pancho Villa and in a letter postmarked Chihuahua City and dated 26 December, he said he expected to be sent with Villa's troops to join the seige of Ojinaga, 125 miles to the northeast. That letter proved to be his last, for nothing more was ever heard from him.

Because of the chaotic conditions in a country torn by civil war, it was sometime before the United States government could persuade the Mexicans to search for the missing writer. No hard evidence ever emerged from the investigation, but wild rumours circulated from the start. One of these maintained that Bierce had joined Villa as a staff officer, quarrelled with him and was executed. Some versions of this persistent rumour had it that Villa personally shot Bierce after discovering he wanted to travel with the other side. In another variant, Bierce was said to have gone over to the more-or-less legitimate government of General Carranza and, when Villa's troops came upon Bierce accompanying an ammunition train, had been shot on the spot. Some people believed he had managed to cross Mexico and sail for England where, they said, he became an adviser to Lord Kitchener on the conduct of the Great War, dying at Kitchener's side when the ship carrying the British general sank in the autumn of 1916.

When it seemed likely that Bierce would not return, his secretary Carrie Christiansen left their apartment in Washington and settled in Napa, California where she had first met Bierce some years before. Because there happened to be a state hospital for the insane in Napa, her arrival started a rumour that Bierce had gone mad and was confined in the Napa institution.

Interested in Bierce, by the publicity surrounding his disappearance, people began to read his books, none of which had sold well during his lifetime. They searched for clues in his caustic volume *The Devil's Dictionary*, where among hundreds of cynical definitions are to be found such shocking statements as:

'*Birth* – the first and direst of all disasters.

'*Worm's-Meat* – the finished product of which we are the raw material.'

The hints to Bierce's disappearance probably lie in the record of his life. He grew up in a poor farming community without any formal education. At the age of 19, he was one of the first to volunteer for the Civil War and his experiences in that conflict turned him from a discontented youth stirred by unformulated longing, into a bitter man determined to make his mark. A brave and efficient soldier, he was commissioned as an officer in the field, eventually becoming a brevet major. Visits to headquarters gave him ample opportunity to study the Union generals, most of whom seemed to him reckless opportunists, who were willing to sacrifice the lives of the men under their command in order to score over their rivals. What little respect Bierce possessed for men in authority was eroded.

After the war, Bierce went to San Francisco and began writing for the newspapers. His phenomenal powers of invective quickly brought him notoriety and he continued to write his bitterly humorous columns for a variety of publications, with scarcely a break until he finally retired from journalism over 40 years later.

By that time he had lived through an unsatisfactory marriage and family tragedy. His eldest son died at 20 in a ludicrous attempt to kill his rival for a girl's love. His second son died of drink and pneumonia. His daughter took to religion, something that always drew Bierce's fiercest scorn. In middle age he began to write psychological stories about sons who kill their fathers, fathers who kill their children, sons who sleep with their mothers and criminals who escape the legal consequences of their crimes, but come to a dreadful end brought on by remorse or by the ghosts of their victims. For all his aggressive manner, 'Almighty God Bierce', as he had sometimes been called, was undoubtedly a tormented man. His *Dictionary* entry for *'ghosts'* is unusually earnest. It says, 'the outward and visible sign of an inward fear.'

What did he fear? Loneliness, certainly. Many of his Civil War tales tell of soldiers cut off from their fellows by the vicissitudes of battle. Yet in the last summer of his life, Bierce deliberately destroyed several friendships of long standing by sending brutal letters. He feared old age and knew he was out of step in a greatly changed United States. For a lifelong journalist this realization must have been particularly troubling. In the summer of 1913 he said to his daughter, 'Why should I remain in a country that is on the eve of prohibition and women's suffrage? In America you can't go east or west any more, or north; the only avenue of escape is south.'

One of the last letters he wrote was from Washington to his nephew's wife. It suggests that he would not be surprised if this 'avenue of escape' turned into a one-way street.

'Good-bye – if you hear of my being stood up against a Mexican stone wall and shot to rags please know that I think that a pretty good way to depart this life. It beats old age, disease, or falling down the cellar stairs. To be a Gringo in Mexico – ah, that is euthanasia !'

Ambrose Bierce is thought to have reached Ojinaga with

Pancho Villa's rebel troops. He was then 71 and far from well. Years of hard drinking and bouts of asthma had taken their toll on his once-legendary stamina. What happened to him during the ensuing campaign will never be known, but the most likely suggestion was made by Edwin H. Smith, who interested himself in Bierce's disappearance. He wrote in 1927, 'My own guess is that he set off to fight battles and shoulder hardships as he had done when a boy, somehow believing that a tough spirit would carry him through. Wounded or stricken with disease, he probably lay down in some pesthouse of a hospital, some troop train filled with other stricken men. Or he may have crawled off to some waterhole and died, with nothing more articulate than the winds and stars for witness.'

Bierce would probably have preferred the stone wall but however his end came, such evidence that exists suggests he chose it for himself. Could he also have planned to make it a mystery?

The disappearance of Bierce, even though shrouded in mystery, permits a rational explanation. No explanation has ever been forthcoming for the disappearance of the three lighthouse keepers of the Eilean Mor lighthouse on the Flannan Islands, off the west coast of Scotland.

These desolate rocks are situated on the outermost fringe of the British Isles. The nearest land is the island of Lewis in the Outer Hebrides, 20 miles to the east; westward the Atlantic Ocean stretches uninterrupted across to North America. The islands are small – Eilean Mor, the largest, is only 500 feet across. They have the reputation of being haunted, and though Hebridean farmers might sometimes leave their sheep for fattening on the fine green turf of the tiny isles, nothing would persuade them to remain overnight themselves. Four retired seamen looked after the lighthouse, working three at a time in shifts of six weeks on the island, followed by two weeks leave on the mainland. Every two weeks the supply vessel *Hesperus* arrived with mail, oil and food. The boat brought one man back from his two weeks off and left with another, due for his two weeks away.

On 6 December 1900 it was the turn of Joseph Moore to be relieved. When the skipper of the *Hesperus* asked him if he was looking forward to his shore leave, he replied 'Aye', and added with a nod to the tiny island fading out of sight behind them, ''Tis pretty lonely there sometimes.'

The lighthouse was just one-year-old. Moore and the others – Thomas Marshall, James Ducat and Donald McArthur – had served through one long winter. None of them looked forward to their second experience of it. The living quarters of the lighthouse gave them shelter from the howling winds but there was little to do to pass the time, except read and reread newspapers and books, play draughts and stare out at the grey, restless sea. Moore had noticed how the four of them were speaking less to each other. The natural conviviality of the mariner had given place to long periods of solitary brooding.

On 21 December Joseph Moore again boarded the *Hesperus* to return for his period of duty on Eilean Mor. The weather had been unexpectedly calm during his two weeks of leave but a severe storm blew up soon after the boat left port. For three days the *Hesperus* rode the storm off the Hebridean coast and it was only on the 24th that it was able to approach the Flannan Isles. Moore was alarmed to see that the 140,000-candlepower light of the lighthouse was out but, anxious though he was to land and find out what was wrong, it was two more days before the *Hesperus* could safely approach the island's east dock.

No preparations had been made for their arrival. There were no empty packing-cases or mooring ropes on the jetty. Repeated blasts on the foghorn brought no one from the lighthouse. A boat was let down and Joseph Moore was the first ashore. The entrance gate and the main door of the lighthouse were closed. Moore went inside and shouted. There was no reply. The place was cold and empty and the clock on the shelf had stopped. Moore ran back to the jetty for help, afraid that he might find the keepers dead in the lighthouse turret. Two men climbed the stairs with him to investigate but there was no sign of life. The entire lighthouse was empty but everything was neat and in order. The wicks of the lanterns had been cleaned and trimmed and the lamps filled with oil ready to be lit after dark. The last entry on the record slate had been made on 15 December. The only unusual thing was that two of the three sets of oilskins and seaboots belonging to the men were missing.

Sailors from the *Hesperus* searched the island. They found no trace of the missing men but came upon some clues that at first suggested an answer to the mystery. The west dock had suffered extensive storm damage. On a concrete platform, 65 feet above the water, stood a crane with ropes trailing down from it. These ropes were usually stored in a tool chest, kept in a crevice 110 feet above sea level. Had some tremendous storm, with waves over 100 feet high, battered this island and carried away the chest, draping its ropes over the crane? Had it also swept the three men to their deaths? This was unlikely because such exceptionally high waves are extremely rare. Besides, experienced lighthouse keepers would hardly have been so foolish as to venture onto a jetty during a storm but if they had, all three oilskins would have been missing instead of two.

Meanwhile, Moore was examining the log with the captain of the *Hesperus* at his side. Thomas Marshall had written the log and from his brief entries sprang the image of an unnameable terror that had overwhelmed the men on their isolated rock. The log said,

'December 12: Gale, north by northwest. Sea lashed to fury. Stormbound. 9 p.m. Never seen such a storm. Waves very high. Tearing at lighthouse. Everything shipshape. Ducat irritable.'

Moore and the captain glanced at each other. On 12 December no storm had been reported at Lewis, 20 miles away. The reference to Ducat's temper was also unusual.

The next entry had been written the same day at midnight,

'Storm still raging. Wind steady. Stormbound. Cannot go out. Ship passing sounding foghorn. Could see lights of cabins. Ducat quiet. McArthur crying.'

Again Moore and the captain stared at each other. What extremity could have caused the veteran seaman, Donald McArthur to weep? They read on,

'December 13: Storm continued through night. Wind shifted west by north. Ducat quiet. McArthur praying.'

Yesterday McArthur had been crying, today he prayed.

'12 Noon. Grey daylight. Me, Ducat, and McArthur prayed.'

When Moore spoke before the board of inquiry that investigated the disappearance, he stated that he had never known any of his companions to pray. Fear of the storm was unlikely to have made them do so, since all had experienced many storms during their long years on the high seas.

One last entry remained in the log,

'December 15: 1 p.m. Storm ended. Sea calm. God is over all.'

There was no entry for 14 December. Why? It will probably never be known, just as what happened after the final log entry remains a mystery. At the inquiry it was reported that on the night of 15 December the *SS Archer* narrowly escaped running onto the rocks of Eilean Mor because no light was visible. It can be presumed that all three men were gone by then.

Could a freak storm, undetected elsewhere, have broken over the island? Could Ducat and McArthur have gone down to the west dock and been swept away? It seems more likely that the men went out in calm weather after the storm to inspect it, especially since Marshall's last entry reports the end of the storm. No one can say what happened next. One suggestion that gained wide acceptance is that one of the three went insane, killed his two companions and then himself. Although hammers, knives and axes were all untouched in their proper places, the attacker could have used a rock as a weapon. He could have pushed their bodies into the sea, plunging after them to his own death.

Did some overmastering religious mania come upon one of the men? Did he see visions as St. Flannan, a hermit on the island long ago, is said to have seen God? Could the raging storm of the log entry have been in his mind only? After all, the damage to the dock could have been caused by the storm that delayed the *Hesperus*, after the unknown events of the lighthouse had taken place. Whatever happened during those terrible days and nights, the rocks of Eilean Mor have kept their secret.

Some disappearances are so baffling that people have been tempted to put forward supernatural explanations. Even so pronounced a sceptic as Ambrose Bierce was tempted by a theory – very much ahead of its time – that there are voids or holes in the visible world that exist 'as caverns exist in the earth, or cells in a Swiss cheese'. In such a cavity Bierce suggests, 'there would be absolutely nothing. Through one of these cavities light could not pass, for there would be nothing to bear it. Sound could not come from it; nothing could be felt in it. . . . A man inclosed in such a closet could neither see nor be seen; neither hear nor be heard; neither feel nor be felt; neither live nor die.. . . . Are these the awful conditions (some will ask) under which the friends of the lost are to think of them as existing, and doomed forever to exist?'

As an attempt to explain the phenomenon of disappearances, this bears a striking resemblance to the theories advanced by physicists of the present, concerning the so-called 'black holes' in space. These conjectural objects are regarded as the final relics of massive stars that have consumed all their fuel and have collapsed in on themselves. Becoming even smaller and denser, they generate a gravitational attraction so unimaginably powerful that no matter, light or other radiation can ever escape from them – hence the term 'black hole'. Anything falling into a black hole will never get out again. Any spaceship or planet that finds itself being sucked into such a whirlpool of destruction has no hope of escape.

Of course nothing like a collapsed star can exist on earth but occasionally strange events are reported that make one wonder if there is a terrestrial version of a 'black hole'. An extraordinary incident that could lead to the conclusion of a 'black hole' on earth occurred in Bristol, England early in the morning of 9 December 1873.

Police were called to the railway station where a married couple had been found, quaking with fear. They were clad in only their nightclothes. When the police discovered that the man had been firing a pistol, the couple was arrested. At the police station the man, who proved to be Thomas B. Cumpston, was still so excited that he could hardly express himself, although there was no indication that either he or his wife had been drinking. He told the police that he and his wife had arrived the previous day from Leeds and had taken a room in the Victoria Hotel. Early in the morning, the floor had suddenly opened up and Cumpston had found himself being dragged down into the opening. His wife had managed to pull him back after a desperate struggle. Both of them were so terrified that they had jumped out of the window and had run to the station for safety. Cumpston insisted that he was telling the truth.

Mrs Cumpston's testimony added a few details. She said that both of them had been alarmed by sounds earlier in the evening but had been reassured by the hotel manager that they meant nothing. At three or four in the morning, she said, they heard the sounds again, jumped out of bed onto the floor and felt it giving way under them. When they cried out, their cries were repeated but they were not sure if by other voices or by an echo of their own voices. The floor had opened up, and only with great difficulty had she been able to stop her husband from disappearing into the hole.

When the hotel manager was contacted, she confirmed that sounds had been heard but she was unable to describe them clearly. Police examined the hotel room and found nothing out of the ordinary. Mr and Mrs Cumpston continued to believe that they had been exposed to extreme danger but they were regarded as victims of a collective hallucination.

Is there a simple and rational explanation based on the fact that the Cumpstons were elderly people in a strange town and in unfamiliar beds? Could the story go like this? The couple slept in an awkward position that interfered with the supply of blood to their legs. If they woke abruptly and stepped onto the floor without thinking, their legs would have collapsed under them, giving a strong sensation that the floor was in motion or no longer there.

What if this is not the explanation however? Might one of Bierce's 'caverns' have opened up beneath their hotel room? The Cumpstons are not alone in reporting the phenomenon of a powerful force, usually operating inside a building, that drags a person away from companions who have to exert all their strength to effect a rescue. But no consistent pattern can be found for these various disappearances.

Take this mystery, for example. Owen Parfitt, a former soldier and tailor, disappeared from the chair in which he was sitting in the doorway of his cottage. The door opened directly onto a busy road along which people, carts, and wagons were passing all the time. When his sister discovered that he was gone, she raised the alarm and within a short time parties of men searched the neighbourhood for several miles around. He was never found. That was in 1768, in the small English town of Shepton Mallet.

Not much in that story to arouse interest, perhaps, after more than 200 years – until one further fact is added. Parfitt, aged 70, had been a bedridden cripple for years, he could not move his body an inch without assistance.

His sister (older than himself but still active) and a young girl of the town, Susannah Snook, had lifted the old man from his bed that afternoon and carried him downstairs to the door. When they left him he was settled in his invalid chair, wearing his nightdress and an old greatcoat he used against the cold he felt, even in July.

His sister was away for less than a quarter of an hour, making his bed. When she returned the old man was gone from his chair, his greatcoat lying beside it. She called out, 'Owen, where are you?', but no answer came. And no answer ever came.

One witness reported that a noise had been heard at the time of the disappearance. It was the single meagre clue to a puzzle that has never been solved. Brooks were dragged and woods and fields searched as far as the cathedral city of Wells, six miles away. That Parfitt had been seriously crippled for a long time is beyond doubt. Many people in the town had come to him for tailoring work, until his growing paralysis forced him to give up the work. Susannah Snook said that 'he could not move at all without aid of someone else.' As for his character, a neighbour said of him, 'He was not a very good or a very bad man.' In his youth he had lived a wild life, soldiering in the New World and Africa. But if a longing to roam once more came over him in old age that warm July day, how could he have moved from his chair? If he had managed to move, why didn't the haymakers working on both sides of the road see him along the way? How could he have been missed by the search parties that were out looking for him within minutes ?

Perhaps, it was said, a passing cart took him away. If so, he probably did not go willingly considering he only wore his night clothes without the greatcoat he had around his shoulders. A man who had known him well said later, 'Many folk round here at the time believed that Owen Parfitt had been spirited off by supernatural means.'

Forty years later a skeleton was found buried in a garden a field away from where Owen Parfitt's cottage had stood. The skeleton, which lay face downward as though it had been thrown down hastily, was covered with two feet of soil. It was thought that the mystery of old Owen's disappearance had been solved, until an anatomist established that the bones were those of a young woman.

Shepton Mallet is an old sheep trading settlement dating back to Saxon times. Many remarkable incidents must have taken place there, but few could have been stranger than the vanishing of an old invalid that warm summer day in 1768.

Another celebrated case in which a man vanished while people were close by is that of Benjamin Bathurst, British envoy to Vienna during the Napoleonic Wars. In November 1809, this handsome and youthful diplomat, a cousin of Britain's foreign minister, was returning to England with important dispatches. Napoleon had recently defeated Austria at the Battle of Wagram and had imposed a peace treaty on the conquered country. French spies were active throughout Europe and Bathurst had to follow a circuitous route. He went by way of Berlin, where he obtained false passports for himself and his Swiss servant and then made for the still independent city of Hamburg, along roads bristling with French troops. On Saturday 26 November when the coach had covered about half the distance, Bathurst stopped in the small Westphalian town of Perleberg for a change of horses. The four occupants of the coach – Bathurst, his servant, and two other travellers – dined in the post house, and at 9 o'clock went out to the coach to continue their journey. While their belongings were being packed, Bathhurst stepped behind the coach for some unknown purpose – and vanished. The others waited for him, looked for him, called for him, all in vain.

Finally Bathurst's servant went to Captain Klitzing, the Prussian Governor of the town and acquainted him with what had occurred. Klitzing already knew of the presence of the travellers because one of them, possibly Bathurst himself, had asked for protection during the stay in Perleberg. Two soldiers had been sent to the post house for that purpose, and had remained there until 7 o'clock, when one of the travellers – which one is not known – sent them away. On learning of the disappearance, Klitzing arranged for the others to be accommodated in the Gold Crown Hotel, assigned a detachment of guards and ordered all the belongings of the missing man to be brought to him.

At that stage the disappearance was being treated as a straightforward case of abduction, possibly murder, for the sake of the money the vanished man was presumed to be carrying. A fur cloak of sable, trimmed with violet velvet, was found to be missing from his belongings. This was eventually discovered in a woodshed of the post house, covered up with firewood. The wastrel son of the family who ran the post station was later arrested for theft and briefly imprisoned, but the reappearance of the cloak threw no light on the disappearance of the man.

The town's four magistrates were roused from their sleep and they searched the taverns and coffee houses of the area until far into the night. The next Sunday, a fisherman was instructed to explore the Stepnitz River that passes through and around the town. He discovered nothing. Also on Sunday the Governor left town, for an unannounced destination – perhaps Berlin, perhaps one of the French garrisons that had been placed at strategic positions throughout Prussia. On his return the following day, he seems to have become aware that Bathurst was a diplomat trying to elude the French and that the missing man's valuables consisted of his dispatches. What these contained was never to be known.

Klitzing's loyalties seem to have been for his own nation rather than for the French but whatever the precise nature of his sentiments, he was forced to act carefully. Gamekeepers and huntsmen were sent out to search the entire countryside with hounds. The river was dammed so that the bed could be examined. Was he just going through the formalities? Did he know that none of this activity would be productive?

One of Bathurst's other two fellow travellers turned out to be a British courier. He was allowed to return to Berlin accompanied by his servant. Bathurst's own servant remained in Perleberg, however, and so was on hand when a female labourer gathering brushwood in a remote beech forest, discovered a pair of Bathurst's trousers on a lonely path. They had been turned inside out and placed on the ground, as though someone had intended them to be found, she declared. The trousers had been perforated by two pistol balls fired at them after they had been removed from their wearer. In one of the pockets was found a scrap of dirty paper on which Bathurst had scribbled a letter to his wife. In this he expressed his fear that he would not see her again and blamed his perilous situation on a certain Comte d'Entraigues. There was no way of telling whether he had written this letter while at the post house or after he had vanished.

When the British government learned of their envoy's disappearance, they offered a reward of £1,000. Bathurst's influential family offered a similar sum. In spite of this, no news was forthcoming. In the spring of 1810, Bathurst's young wife travelled to Perleberg and then throughout Germany and France, having obtained a passport from Napoleon himself, in search of information concerning her missing husband. She heard from one source that he had escaped to the north coast of Germany and drowned in the Baltic, from another that he had been drowned while trying to cross the Elbe, from a third that he had been killed by a disgruntled servant. More significantly, she learned that the governor of Magdeburg prison had been overheard to say, "They are looking for the English ambassador, but I have him up there', pointing to the fortress in which prisoners were kept. When Mrs Bathurst faced the governor with his words, he did not deny uttering them but explained that he had been mistaken in the identity of his prisoner. Her comment on this reply was, 'I thought that governors of state prisons do not make mistakes.' In spite of all her efforts, however, she was unable to learn more of Magdeburg's mysterious prisoner.

Back in England, Mrs Bathurst had a visit from Comte d'Entraigues, the man mentioned as a danger in her husband's last note to her. Mrs Bathurst treated his approach with great caution – wisely, as it proved, because d'Entraigues was a double agent. He told Mrs Bathurst that her husband had indeed been taken to Magdeburg. Since she did not know whether to believe him or not, she asked for proof and he agreed to obtain it. Whether he actually tried to is unknown because a few days later he met the not unusual fate of double agents – death by assassination. He and his wife, who was privy to all his secrets, were stepping out of their house in Twickenham, when a newly hired French servant plunged a dagger into her bosom and she fell dead on the spot. The count ran back to his bedroom for his pistols, followed closely by the man. Two gun shots were heard. When the other servants ran into the room, both the count and his assailant were dead. After these sensational deaths no further clues to Bathurst's whereabouts were uncovered. His wife accepted the fact that he had been killed but his mother never gave up hope of his return.

It is presumed that Bathurst's disappearance was arranged by the French, but how remains a mystery. If French spies or soldiers overpowered him as he walked behind the coach, it is remarkable that his fellow travellers – only too conscious of the perils of their situation – heard or saw nothing. A German chronicler of the events writes, 'The disappearance of the English ambassador seems like magic. It is just as if the ground had opened itself under his feet and swallowed him up, closing itself upon him without leaving the least trace behind.'

It is not only during wars that nations have disposed of troublesome individuals by causing them to disappear. Such is thought to have been the fate of Rudolf Diesel, inventor of the type of engine that bears his name.

On the night of 29 September 1913, 10 months before the outbreak of World War I, Diesel and two friends embarked at Antwerp, Belgium on the steamer *Dresden* for the overnight trip to Harwich, England. He was due in London to meet naval officers and industrialists interested in his latest invention. A man of 56, of German nationality though born in Paris, he had found it difficult to get enough backing to develop the engine he claimed was the most efficient in the world. The German firm of Krupps had originally underwritten him but Diesel had run foul of certain American firms and by 1913 his personal and business finances were in bad shape. The forthcoming discussions in London were therefore very important to him and he hoped they would lead to a change in his financial situation. As the *Dresden* steamed across the North Sea, he dined with his companions Georg Carels, a fellow director and an engineer named Luckmann. After dinner they took a stroll around the deck and at 10 o'clock retired to their cabins.

The next morning, Diesel did not appear. A search in his cabin revealed that his bed had not been slept in, although his belongings were arranged as though he had intended to go to bed. For example, his watch had been placed in a high position so that he could see it from where he lay. Since Diesel suffered from insomnia and in recent weeks had seldom slept for more than two hours a night, it was assumed that he had gone for a walk on deck and fallen overboard. Even though the deck was surrounded by a rail four feet high, no other explanation seemed possible. Accidental death was presumed, when his two companions said he had been in excellent spirits at dinner and showed no sign of mental breakdown or thoughts of suicide.

Ten days later, a fishing crew off the coast of the Netherlands observed a body floating in the water. For some reason the fishermen were unable to bring the body ashore but they retrieved certain articles from it, including a diary and an eyeglass which Diesel's son recognized as belonging to his father. The family offered a reward for the recovery of the body but it was never seen again. Was the body that of Diesel? The failure to bring it ashore and the removal of identifiable objects from it, look most suspicious. In addition, the body had been described as being in an advanced state of decomposition, which is surprising after so short a time in the water.

In 1915, a German prisoner-of-war is said to have revealed that he was instructed by the German secret service to follow Diesel and push him overboard to prevent him from passing the secret of his invention to the British. With suicide or accident highly implausible, murder seems the most likely explanation for Diesel's disappearance. The prisoner's story could not be checked, however, so whatever happened to Diesel on board the *Dresden* that night, remains unknown.

Some people have deliberately planned their disappearance, in order to be free of the ties and responsibilities of their old life to start a new one elsewhere. The American detective, William J. Burns recalled the case of a New York toy maker, cursed with a shrewish wife, who vanished while on his way to his factory carrying $10,000 meant as wages for his workers. He left a note in the back of his car saying, 'Has been bumped off. Look for body in the river.' The message would hardly fool anyone, however, since the river was icebound at the time! Eight years later, the man was seen by chance and recognized in a park 1,500 miles away. He had been living a new life in contentment the whole time.

Perhaps a wish to start life afresh also accounts for the disappearance in 1920 of Victor Grayson, a former British Labour politician. Born the son of a carpenter in 1882, he became the Member of Parliament for Colne Valley, Yorkshire, at the age of 25. Much in demand as a public speaker, particularly on matters of social injustice, he was once suspended from the House of Commons for his inflammatory language. After being defeated in 1910 he became a journalist, married an actress, and accompanied her to New Zealand on a tour. There he joined the New Zealand Army, returned to fight in France in World War I and was wounded at Passchendaele.

In August 1920 he boarded a night train from Liverpool, England to Hull, where he was due to make a political speech. When the train arrived, Grayson was not on it. Later his bag was found in a London hotel, having been left there said the manager, by a man whose head was bandaged and whose arm appeared to be injured. The man never occupied his room nor collected the bag.

Over the following years there were several reports that Grayson had been seen by people who had known him. In 1924 and again in 1928, he was thought to have been recognized in England. In 1932 a political colleague, G. A. Murray was convinced he saw Grayson from the top of a London bus. He looked fit and well-dressed but though Murray quickly descended the stairs of the bus to go after the missing man, he was gone by the time he reached the street.

Another former colleague believed he saw Grayson on the London Underground but realized it too late to challenge him. He was accompanied by a woman who called him 'Vic', and when the couple left the train near Parliament, the man had said with a laugh, 'Here's the old firm.' There were persistent reports that he had gone to Australia, one of these as late as 1957 when Grayson would have been 75.

If the person seen on these occasions really was Victor Grayson, he had managed to stay hidden in his own country for years. If those who thought they recognized him were mistaken, he probably disappeared in 1920 on a train between Liverpool and Hull, or in London. Either way his end is a mystery that has never been cleared up.

When adults disappear, there is always the possibility that they have done so voluntarily but this is hardly true of children. When a 12-year-old girl vanishes, as Eliza Carter did in January 1882, the first thought is of abduction. When she never reappears, the mystery deepens. When she is one of a number who disappear from the same area, the mystery defies solution.

Eliza Carter was one of the first to vanish in a 10-year series of such happenings known as the 'West Ham Disappearances', so called because most of them occurred in the West Ham section of London's East End. After a visit to her sister, Eliza failed to return home. When later seen in the street by some of her school-girl friends, she was in a state of fear. They urged her to return to her family but she said she could not. '*They* wouldn't let me,' she said. At 11 pm she was seen in the company of a middle-aged woman, then she disappeared for good. The only trace was her dress, found in the football stadium of neighbouring East Ham. If some harm had come to her, why did her body never show up? What about all the other West Ham residents who vanished? Where were their bodies and why was an ordinary working class area of town the scene of such unexplained events?

An interesting case of someone who disappeared and re-appeared before making a final disappearance, was that of Private Jerry Irwin of the United States army. He was not to be found anywhere for a time, then turned up at camp again. Not long after-ward he disappeared again but reappeared once more. Neither time was the soldier able to say where he had been. On 1 August 1959 he disappeared for good.

The disappearance of the explorer Colonel Fawcett in the Brazilian jungle in 1925 and the Duchess of Bedford – the 'Flying Duchess' – on a solo flight in 1937, were sensations in their time. So was the disappearance of the Austrian Archduke Johann Salvator in 1890, following the climax of a series of quarrels with his cousin, Emperor Franz Josef. The archduke renounced his rank, became a commoner, and took the name John Orth. Having bought a three-masted schooner, he and his wife sailed to Buenos Aires, Argentina. There he took on a new crew and a cargo and set sail for Valparaiso, Chile. The ship was never seen again.

His mother and brothers were reluctant to believe him dead, especially because on his last visit to them before leaving Austria he had said, 'Never, never believe that I am dead, for I will return one day and we shall meet again and talk of this.' It was rumoured that he had not sailed with the ship but had staged a successful disappearance in South America in order to live a private life in peace. But his family never heard from him again. Did he go down with his ship in the treacherous waters around Cape Horn? We may never know. Likewise, although we may assume that Colonel Fawcett was killed by cannibal Indians and that the plane of the 'Flying Duchess' crashed into the ocean, we cannot solve these mysteries for sure.

Sudden disappearances are always intriguing, particularly when the vanished person is someone in the public eye. Generally the disappearance proves to have a rational, if sometimes complicated, explanation, but an element of doubt always persists. It is the absence of a body that keeps the flame of doubt glowing at the back of our minds, no matter how rational and persuasive the arguments for natural death may be. In this respect we show ourselves still close in habit to primitive people – anxious to have our dead buried properly so that their spirits can rest in peace.

CHAPTER 3

THE PUZZLE OF OAK ISLAND

Is there a buried treasure in the Money Pit on Oak Island, Nova Scotia? For nearly 200 years, hopeful prospectors have tried to unearth one. All have been defeated by the ingenious construction that floods the shaft when a certain depth is reached – and a fortune in money and five lives have been lost in the treasure hunt. Did Captain Kidd bury his rich hoard in a seemingly bottomless pit on this insignificant island? Could the unknown engineering genius who built the structure have long ago retrieved whatever was buried? The mystery still remains unsolved today.

Buried treasure is like a magnet to many who get wind of it. They immediately imagine untold wealth, like that described by the French writer Alexandre Dumas in his adventure novel, *Count of Monte Cristo*: 'Three compartments divided the coffer. In the first, blazed piles of golden coin; in the second, bars of unpolished gold were ranged; in the third, Edmond [Dantes] grasped handfuls of diamonds, pearls, and rubies, which as they fell on one another sounded like hail against glass. . . .'

In one real-life treasure hunt, the mere vision of gleaming gold and sparkling gems has kept several generations of hopeful prospectors on the search. But no evidence has ever emerged to link the site of suspected buried treasure with any objects of value. Undeterred by this discouraging record, modern treasure hunters have brought increasingly sophisticated machinery to the task of wresting its secret from the earth. In over 200 years since its chance discovery, an estimated $1½ million has been spent in finding . . . nothing.

The site is on an island, but hardly one associated with dangerous reefs and sharks, as popularly imagined for hidden treasures. Oak Island in Mahone Bay, on the southern coast of Nova Scotia, has long been used by residents on the surrounding mainland simply as a pleasant place for a picnic. It owes its fame to a long ago excursion for that innocent purpose. In the summer of 1795, 16-year-old Daniel McGinnis was paddling his canoe across the bay, intent on going to one of the innumerable uninhabited and unexplored islands. The one he picked was Oak Island, which owed its name to the luxuriant growth of red oaks that thickly covered both ends of it. In shape, the mile-long Oak Island resembled a slightly distorted hourglass, with an area of low swampland linking the two halves.

Daniel beached his canoe in the wide cove on the island's southeastern shore and made his way into the trees. He had not wandered far when he came upon a clearing, in the centre of which stood a gnarled and ancient oak. Fifteen feet above the ground one of the branches had been cut short and the remaining stump showed the marks of scoring by rope and tackle. Directly under the stump the youngster noticed a circular depression in the ground, some 12 feet in diameter. In the clearing, a good deal of wood had been cut down and new growth was springing up to take its place.

Daniel forgot his picnic. He hurried away from the island, convinced that he had stumbled upon the site of buried treasure. Like all the boys on that coast, he had been brought up on tales of pirates. Even the name of the bay is thought to have come from the French word *mahonne*, a swift, low-lying ship much used by pirates in the Mediterranean. Back in his home town of Chester, on the eastern shore of the bay, Daniel shared his discovery with two friends, John Smith, aged 20, and Anthony Vaughan, aged 13. The following day the three of them rowed to Oak Island with picks and shovels and began to dig beneath the tree.

Their excitement mounted when they discovered that they were digging down into a circular shaft with walls of hard clay that clearly bore the marks of picks. Four feet down they found a layer of flagstones, of a kind not found on Oak Island. Ten feet down they came upon a platform made of solid oak logs six inches thick. These extended the full width of the shaft and were embedded firmly in the clay walls. The boys hauled the wood out and resumed digging. At 20 feet they encountered a second oak platform similar to the first, and at 30 feet still another. The earth had settled for about two feet between the platforms.

With the tools at their disposal the three boys could go no deeper. They left sticks to mark the point they had reached, and returned to the mainland to seek help.

This proved more difficult than they expected. Many local people believed the island to be haunted. A woman, whose mother was one of the original settlers in the neighbourhood, recalled that strange lights and fires used to be seen on the island at night. A boatload of men had once rowed to the island and never returned. Not until nine years later, in 1804, did the three treasure seekers manage to persuade someone to come to their aid. By that time John Smith had bought the area surrounding the site. Over the next 30 years he acquired more lots, until he owned the entire east end of the island.

The person they had interested was Simeon Lynds, a well-to-do young man who formed a syndicate of friends 'to assist the pioneers in the search after the treasure and to complete it'. A quantity of mud had settled in the pit during the intervening years but when this was cleared away, the diggers came upon the sticks left in the mud by the three discoverers and they were satisfied that the site had not been interfered with since then.

As the level of the shaft was lowered, a succession of oak platforms was uncovered, some of them reinforced with other materials. There is some confusion as to the exact sequence of platforms but one version gives it like this: at 40 feet, a platform of oak sealed with putty; at 50 feet, plain oak; at 60 feet, oak sealed with coconut fibre and putty; at 70 feet, plain oak; at 80 feet, oak sealed with putty. So much putty was brought to the surface that the amount set aside for reuse served to glaze the windows of 20 houses around Mahone Bay.

At 90 feet, a flat stone was uncovered. Measuring three feet long and one foot wide, it was of a material not found in Nova Scotia. Roughly cut letters and figures were observed on the underside but the treasure hunters could not make sense of them. They seem to have paid little attention to what could have been a valuable clue. Smith fitted it at the back of the fireplace in the house he had built on Oak Island, and there it remained for at least half a century. Some time in the 1860s, it was taken to Halifax and displayed in the window of a bookbinder's shop to help attract people to contribute money for a further search for the treasure. Time and Smith's fireplace had rendered the markings still less legible, although a professor of languages interpreted them to read 'Ten feet below two million pounds.' Sometime in the twentieth century the stone disappeared. In 1935, however, a very old employee of the bookbindery described the stone as resembling 'dark Swedish granite, or fine-grained porphyry, very hard, and with an olive tinge', adding, 'we used the stone as a beating stone and weight.'

The searchers of 1804 didn't see any significance in the stone and ignored it. They pushed a crowbar into the earth, which was by then becoming so waterlogged that they had to remove one cask of water to every two of earth and struck something hard and unyielding, that seemed to stretch across the width of the shaft. All those present agreed it was wood – some said it must be a chest.

This discovery was made near nightfall on a Saturday. The treasure seekers climbed out of the shaft, convinced that their goal lay but a few inches farther down. They occupied the evening happily working out how to divide the treasure. They could not work on the Sunday, so it was Monday morning before they returned – only to find the shaft flooded with water to within 33 feet of the top. They bailed out the water with buckets but no matter how much they removed, the level of water remained constant. A pump was obtained and lowered into the shaft. When it burst, work was abandoned for the year.

In the spring of 1805, the treasure seekers returned and attempted to drain the flooded shaft by digging a second one alongside. At 110 feet they tunnelled sideways toward the first shaft. Suddenly, there was a thunderous roar and a surge of water overwhelmed them so rapidly that they were lucky to escape with their lives. The old shaft had collapsed and water soon filled the second shaft to within 33 feet of the top.

The syndicate had used up its capital and all there was to show for it was two flooded holes and a large quantity of oak logs.

Writing to a friend, Smith said, 'Had it not been for the various mischiefs nature played us, we would by now, all of us, be men of means.' He did not know that this mischief was not of nature's doing, because the incredibly cunning design of the Money Pit, as it came to be called, remained unguessed for many years to come.

No other attempt was made to excavate the Money Pit until 1849, when a group of investors from another part of Nova Scotia formed the Truro Syndicate. There was continuity with the group of 45 years before, however. Dr David Lynds was a relative of Simeon Lynds, head of the first syndicate. Anthony Vaughan, one of the three original discoverers, was then in his late 60s; he helped the new syndicate locate the site of the Money Pit. Of the other discoverers, McGinnis was dead and Smith, who lived until 1857, seems to have taken no active part in the new search.

Both the shafts had caved in, but after 12 days of work on the original shaft, a depth of 86 feet was reached. Flooding no longer appeared to be a problem. Once again, work came to a halt on a Saturday night. The next day the men were relieved to see that hardly any water had seeped into the pit but at 2 o'clock they returned from church 'and to their great surprise found water standing in the pit, to the depth of 60 feet, being on a level with that in the bay.'

On Monday, disappointed but not discouraged, they began bailing out the shaft. Soon they realized that 'the result appeared as unsatisfactory as taking soup with a fork', in the words of a contemporary account. They decided to find out what lay in the depths by employing a pod auger, a horse-driven drill that brought up samples of whatever material it passed through, then used in mining operations. A platform was erected above the water and five holes were bored to a depth of 106 feet. The first two holes were drilled to the west of the centre of the pit and brought up nothing but mud and stones. The statement from the man who directed the drilling shows what was found by the first borings east of the centre:

'After going through the platform [at the level reached by the crowbar in 1804] which was five inches thick, and proved to be spruce, the auger dropped 12 inches and then went through four inches of oak; then it went through 22 inches of metal in pieces; but the auger failed to bring up anything in the nature of treasure, except three links resembling the links of an ancient watch chain. It then went through eight inches of oak, which was thought to be the bottom of the first box and the top of the next; then 22 inches of metal, the same as before; then four inches of oak and six inches of spruce, then into clay seven feet without striking anything.'

The second bore struck the upper platform as before but missed what was thought to be some boxes, although the jerky motion of the rotation chisel suggested that it might be striking the outer edge of a box. Splinters of oak were drawn up with a quantity of what appeared to be coconut fibre. These borings certainly suggested that the Money Pit contained two oak chests, one on top of the other. The nature of the 'metal in pieces' is not recorded as being known. One member of the syndicate later referred to the 'links of a watch chain' as 'a piece of gold chain', but this looks like pure embellishment.

The last boring became an event of the greatest importance. The foreman, James Pitblado, was told to carefully remove every scrap of material brought up to the surface so that it could be examined by microscope. What happened next is confused. Pitblado was accused of taking something out of the auger, studying it closely and putting it in his pocket. When asked to produce it, he refused, saying he would show it to the next meeting of the directors of the syndicate. Surprisingly, no attempt was made to search him – he never appeared at the board meeting. Apparently he had a talk with a local businessman, who then made a determined, though unsuccessful, bid for the east end of Oak Island. What happened to Pitblado is uncertain, but tradition has it that the object he removed from the auger was a jewel.

The Truro syndicate was convinced that two chests of treasure lay in the Money Pit. The problem still was how to get at it. In 1850, they sank a third shaft to the west of the pit and dug through hard clay to a depth of 109 feet, without meeting any water. Like their predecessors in 1805, they tunnelled sideways toward the Money Pit but before they reached it, a flood of water burst in upon them and once again the workmen were lucky to escape with their lives. Within a few minutes, the new shaft was more than half-filled with water.

Only then did someone think of trying to find out where all the water might be coming from. Legend has it that one member of the syndicate fell into the shaft and discovered that the water was salty. Whether or not this really happened, someone at last got around to tasting it and determined that it was sea water. Watching the flood level in the shafts thereafter, they observed that it rose and fell with the tide in the bay. Since there was no possibility of seepage through the impermeable clay soil, the only alternative was that a man-made tunnel connected the Money Pit with the waters of the bay. They hastened to the nearest shore, a beach known as Smith's Cove, 500 feet to the northeast, and there the amazing theory was confirmed. As the tide ebbed, the sand 'gulched water like a sponge being squeezed'.

They dug into the beach and at a depth of three feet found a two inch layer of the same coconut fibre that had been discovered in the Money Pit. Beneath this fibre came a four or five inch layer of eel grass or kelp and beneath this had been placed a quantity of flat stones. For 150 feet along the beach, between high and low water marks, the spongy construction continued. Five box drains , strongly built of flat stones at a depth of five feet, led from it to a funnel-shaped sump set just above the high water mark.

So well built and protected were the drains that on uncovering one of them, it was found that no earth had sifted through to obstruct the water flowing along it. From the sump the water passed along a tunnel for a distance of 500 feet, sinking steadily, until it reached the Money Pit somewhere below the 90-foot level.

The work involved in sinking the Money Pit was impressive but the construction of the flood-tunnel system was unquestionably the work of an engineering genius. As the tide rose in the bay, water was soaked up by the coconut fibre sponge and channelled through the drains and the tunnel into the pit. As long as the pit remained undisturbed, the pressure of earth in the shaft held the water back. As earth was removed, the pressure lessened. Then, when the treasure chests were almost reached, the water broke through from below and flooded the shaft.

These discoveries strengthened the conviction of the treasure seekers that the Money Pit must conceal an immense hoard. Why else go to such trouble to protect it? They began to construct a 150-foot long cofferdam along the centre of Smith's Cove, intending to enclose the area that fed the flood tunnel. Before the structure was completed, it was destroyed by an unusually high tide.

Unwilling to begin another dam, the workmen tried to intercept the tunnel's course across the island. Their first attempt, near Smith's Cove, missed the tunnel. Instead of trying again in that area, where the tunnel was closest to the surface, for some reason they went back to the Money Pit and dug still another shaft – the fifth to that time. At 35 feet they struck a large boulder. When they tried to shift it, a rush of water poured into the shaft. They took this to mean that they had found the flood tunnel, although a moment's reflection should have suggested that it was at too high a level. Heavy timbers were driven down in the hope of blocking the tunnel, and a sixth shaft was sunk 50 feet away from the Money Pit.

At 118 feet, the workmen started tunnelling from this latest shaft toward the original shaft. The tunnel was large, measuring three feet by two feet. At some point during the tunnelling – fortunately when most of the workmen were at lunch – the Money Pit collapsed into the tunnel. The searchers believed that the two chests they sought were dislodged in the general upheaval and fell deeper into the Money Pit, though the evidence for such a conclusion is unknown.

The Truro Syndicate had spent close to $20,000 by then and were obliged to bring their operations to a halt until more money could be raised. They had found no treasure but they had discovered the secret of the flooding.

In 1859, after another nine years had passed, they tried again. Several more shafts were sunk near the original one, all with the aim of draining the Money Pit or diverting the course of the flood tunnel. At one time 33 horses and a work force of 63 men were employed at the pumps. But still the water poured in. In 1861, steam pumps were erected but the boiler burst almost immediately. One man was scalded to death and operations were once more suspended.

As other prospectors tried their luck, the area around the Money Pit became a jumble. There were shafts sunk into the ground on all sides, some filled with water that rose and fell with the tides, others filled with debris. In 1866 operations were taken over by a group known as the Halifax syndicate. They also built a dam in Smith's Cove which was destroyed by the tide. But they managed to locate the point at which the flood tunnel entered the Money Pit. This occurred at 110 feet, 10 feet below the level on which the chests were thought to have rested originally. The mouth of the tunnel was about four feet high by two and a half feet wide, lined with round beach stones. The skill of those who had built it was awe-inspiring.

With the realization of the unique system of protecting whatever might be placed in the Money Pit, people asked themselves the question, 'How had those who buried the treasure intended to recover it?' Some thought they must have planned to make their way somehow through the flood tunnel. Others guessed that some system of floodgates, which could be closed when required, must have been introduced. No one doubted that the treasure must still be there somewhere. Isaac Blair, one of the members of the Halifax company told his nephew Frederick, 'I saw enough to convince me that there was treasure buried there and enough to convince me that they will never get it.'

Frederick Leander Blair later played a big role in the history of the Oak Island treasure hunt. Born in 1867, he was 24-years-old when a new group of prospectors formed the Oak Island Treasure Company in 1891. He drew up the company prospectus, in which it was stated that they intended 'to use the best modern appliances for cutting off the flow of water through the tunnel. . . . It believes that such an attempt will be completely successful and if it is, there can be no trouble in pumping out the Money Pit as dry as when the treasure was first placed there.'

Alas, for such high hopes. Like all but one of the previous syndicates, the new company sank its intercepting shaft not at Smith's Cove but at the Money Pit end of the tunnel. Eventually, like all their predecessors, they returned to the Money Pit itself. Its position was now hard to identify, but the workmen managed to make their way into it through a side tunnel from one of the adjoining shafts. They dug upward till they came to a platform left by one of the previous operations. Money then ran out and work was not resumed for eight years, the next time being in 1897 at Smith's Cove. Blair drilled five holes across the mouth of the flood tunnel there.

Salt water was struck at the third drilling point, a charge of 160 pounds of dynamite was lowered and on being detonated, produced great turbulence in the water of the Money Pit, 450 feet away. Believing the flood tunnel to be blocked, Blair's team returned to the Money Pit but pumping still failed to empty it. The team then proceeded to drill into its depths.

First they sent down a three-inch pipe inside of which their drill would operate more efficiently. This pipe was brought to a stop at 126 feet by an edge of iron and all efforts to force the pipe past it failed. A 1½-inch drill was then put down inside the pipe. This passed the obstruction, went down to 151 feet and struck a layer of soft stone, afterward identified as cement. Twenty inches below the cement, the drill bored through five inches of oak wood. The searchers believed that they were on the verge of learning what lay in the Money Pit at last. But then the drill began to behave oddly. It dropped two inches and rested on something that seemed to be large objects of metal which could be moved slightly from side to side. The movement of these objects hindered the descent of the drill but it finally got below them, only to come in contact with loose metal. This resisted the drill in a different way. At that time, boring was done by raising and dropping the drill rods and small pieces of metal fell into the space left each time the tool was drawn up. At one point, a small piece of a substance identified as parchment was brought up and this fragment still survives. On it, the letters V.I. could be read. Finally, the drill went past the layer of metal pieces into another layer of the large metal objects.

The nature of the metal is not indicated in the report written by William Chappell, one of the men present, but no one doubted that they had located a chest containing small metal pieces that might well be coins, between two layers of metal bars. Edward Hopper, a syndicate member who was at the shaft that day, wrote to a friend in London, 'Never in my life have I known the kind of excitement that gripped us at that moment. We felt we were about to uncover the most cunningly concealed secret on the face of the

earth. The riches down below seemed but of lesser importance, it
was the solution of the riddle that had us all agog.'

The next act was to secure the drill by piping below 126 feet.
Samples could then be obtained of the small pieces of metal.
After the drill was withdrawn, a 1½-inch pipe was lowered
inside the three-inch pipe; but at 126 feet it was deflected by the
iron object and struck the hard wall of the pit. When the 1½-inch
drill was reinserted, it followed the course of the deflected pipe.
The hole down to the chest was lost! Other drills were immediately sent down, one of which appeared to strike the outer edge
of the chest. Another one penetrated a channel of water that
spouted up the pipe at the rate of 400 gallons a minute,
drenching everything within range.

Blair concluded that there must be a second flood tunnel. To
test for it he poured red dye into the pit – and sure enough a red
colouration appeared at three separate places 600 feet from the
pit, this time on the south shore. He sank no fewer than six shafts
– the fourteenth to the nineteenth overall – between the Money
Pit and the shore, in an attempt to intercept the second flood
tunnel. All of them had to be abandoned when water flooded in.
The area soon became a quagmire of clay and mud and the position of the Money Pit became more uncertain. Finally the syndi- '
cate, having spent $115,000, had to call a halt. Blair lacked the
resources to continue on his own but he managed to buy out the
other shareholders and in 1905 acquired a long lease of the
eastern end of the island. Until his death, as a very old man in
1954, he never abandoned hope that the treasure would be found.
One after another, optimistic prospectors appeared on the scene,
sought his advice or enlisted his aid, poured their money into the
bottomless Money Pit and left empty-handed.

In 1909 came Captain Harry Bowdoin, a New York engineer
with rich and powerful friends. Bowdoin cleared out the Money
Pit to a depth of 113 feet and put down a core drill. At 149 feet
they drilled through what appeared to be a layer of cement and
enthusiasm mounted when it was suggested that this could be the
roof of a treasure chamber. But below this layer the drill brought
up only yellow clay; an analysis of the cement showed it to be
'natural limestone pitted by the action of water'. In 1912,
someone tried to freeze the watery mud at the bottom of the

Money Pit but this also came to nothing. Still other attempts were made about this time and in the resulting criss-cross of shafts, the exact location of the Money Pit was once again lost.

In 1931 William Chappell, who had been in the 1897 syndicate with Blair, returned to Oak Island with $50,000 and sank a shaft where the Money Pit was believed to be. He uncovered a pick, a miner's seal-oil lamp and an axe head thought to be 250-years-old. Blair could not understand what had happened to the wood, the cement and the metal pieces that had so tantalizingly eluded him and Chappell, when they had brought up the circle of parchment so many years before. He came to believe that the treasure had dropped further into some natural cavity in the rock as a result of all the activity in the Money Pit. Greater understanding of the geological formation of the island was later to show that, in fact, the underlying limestone contained many cavities and sinkholes.

In 1933 came a British Columbian named Thomas M. Nixon, who believed that the Incas had deposited a treasure on Oak Island. He proposed to enclose the entire Money Pit area within a circle of interlocking steel pilings. If he had carried out this costly operation it might have solved many problems but instead he did no more than sink some bore holes around the Money Pit and depart, like so many others before him, with nothing to show for his trouble.

Nixon was followed by Gilbert D. Hedden, a wealthy New Jersey businessman. In the course of two seasons of digging and drilling, he came to the conclusion that the chests that once held the treasure must have rotted away in the constantly waterlogged soil. He guessed that the treasure lay scattered through the clay. He also took the trouble to explore the island and made a significant discovery in the tangled undergrowth on the edge of the south shore. A triangle of beach stones had been arranged on the ground, with a curved line enclosing the base to give it the appearance of a rough sextant. The sides of the triangle were 10 feet long and an arrow made of stones slanted across the base line to the apex. This arrow pointed due north to the Money Pit.

Hedden did not stumble on this sign by chance. He was led to it by following directions in the book, *Captain Kidd and his Skeleton Island*, written in 1935 by Harold Wilkins. This book included a chart of an island that resembled Oak Island in several particulars and contained the following directions:

18 W and by 7 E on Rock
30 SW 14 N Tree
7 by 8 by 4.

Carrying Wilkins' book in his hands, Hedden searched the ground around the Money Pit and discovered a large granite stone due north of it, in which a hole had been drilled. This reminded Blair, who was still the unofficial advisor for all search operations, of a similar drilled stone he had discovered at Smith's Cove, 40 years before. They rediscovered the second boulder and found that the distance between them was just over 25 rods, a rod being an ancient unit of measure equivalent to 16½ feet. Hedden and Blair called in two land surveyors who calculated a position 18 rods from the drilled stone on the west and 7 rods from the drilled stone on the east. Thirty rods southwest of this brought them to the tangle of undergrowth where lay the arrow pointing north to the Money Pit. The tree that had once grown above it had long since vanished, and in any case it was somewhat more than 14 rods north. What the final line of directions signified Hedden and Blair could not tell, but the first two lines were enough to convince them that the treasure in the Money Pit was Captain Kidd's.

Hedden went to England to consult Wilkins, who was incredulous when told of the Oak Island mystery pit. He denied all knowledge of Oak Island and explained that he had drawn the map in his book from memory after being allowed a glimpse of some apparently authentic Kidd charts in the possession of Hubert Palmer, a collector of antiques. As for the directions, he insisted that they had come out of his head. However, Wilkins was so impressed by the use Hedden had put them to on Oak Island that he later came to believe he himself was a reincarnation of Captain Kidd!

The Kidd-Palmer charts, as they are called, are four in number. They were found secreted in three sea chests and an old oak bureau that had been acquired by Palmer between 1929 and 1934. All had apparently at one time belonged to Captain William Kidd. One is said to have been handed down in the family of his jailer at Newgate prison, where he was hanged in 1701 for acts of piracy in the Indian Ocean. All the charts depicted the same curving island and several bore the date 1669. The charts which are now in Canada, are considered to be genuine seventeenth-century charts and their existence adds another mystery to the Oak Island enigma. The reference to the China Sea in one of them has been held to be a deliberate attempt to mislead, while at the same time making a punning reference to Oak Island by playing on the French for oak, *chene*. Against this theory is the fact that in 1669 Kidd was only in his 20s and though his movements at that time are obscure, it is doubtful that he could have amassed a sizeable treasure so early in his career.

After Hedden came Edwin H. Hamilton, a machine engineer. He drilled down to 180 feet, deeper than anyone before him, located the original Money Pit and made two important discoveries. He found that the second flood tunnel entered the Money Pit at 150 feet and from the same side as the first one, which had been constructed at 110 feet. Both tunnels therefore came from Smith's Cove, one above the other. He also explained why Blair's red dye had appeared on the south shore; at 180 feet a natural stream flowed across the base of the pit from north to south in direction.

Dauntless prospectors continued to turn up. One man appeared equipped with only a pick and shovel. In 1955, a Texas oil drilling syndicate worked on the site for four weeks. Tragedy struck in 1963. Robert Restall, a former circus stunt-rider, had worked on the pit for five years. On 17 August 1963 he was overcome by the exhaust fumes falling into the shaft from his pump. His 22-year-old son John and two other men died in a fruitless attempt to rescue him.

Excavations on a mammoth scale were carried out in 1965 by Robert Dunfield, an American petroleum geologist. He built a causeway from the mainland to bring a 70-foot clam digger to the island and in six weeks he had excavated a vast hole, 80 feet wide and 130 feet deep, where the Money Pit had once been. Another deep crater obliterated the site of the stone triangle and a third, 80 feet wide and 100 feet deep, was dug near Smith's Cove. At the end of the year Dunfield had spent $120,000. He said, 'I'm running out of nerve but I'm damned if I'll quit. I'm going on till I succeed or bust, and I intend to succeed.' He didn't.

Rupert Furneaux, whose book *The Money Pit Mystery* (1972) is an authoritative guide to the chequered history of Oak Island, visited the island after Dunfield's assaults and found the eastern end 'devastated'. As he walked around the island he remembered the old saying that it would only give up its secret when the last oak had gone. He knew that for some years black ants had been causing extensive damage among the oak trees. In his wanderings he found only two oaks, both dead and toppling into the spruces that were taking their place. That was in 1967. Meantime, Furneaux has concentrated on trying to solve the mystery of who constructed the pit. He dismissed the pirate theory completely, on the grounds that the task required special engineering skills. Besides, the construction of the two flood tunnels alone, each more than 500 feet in length, called for the concerted effort of a disciplined body of men for a matter of weeks, if not months. A pirate crew, always eager for the next adventure and more booty, would hardly take such time and make such effort.

Furneaux decided that the pit must have been constructed by disciplined workers under the direction of an able engineer. Putting himself in the position of his mystery engineer, Furneaux realized that his greatest problem must have been to keep the tunnellers working on a straight line from Smith's Cove to the Money Pit. The line of this tunnel is 14 degrees south of the true east-west line. Workmen digging in the dim light of a tunnel would find it easiest to follow the direction indicated by one of the bold cardinal points of the compass, in this case west. This could only have been possible in a year when the magnetic variation from true north, and true west, was 14 degrees.

Such a variation had occurred twice in recent centuries; in 1611, which was clearly too early, and in 1780. Bearing in mind the description by the boys who discovered the pit in 1795 that the clearing had been recently worked and new wood was springing up, the year 1780 looked a likely answer.

It is Furneaux's belief that British engineers dug the pit on Oak Island, possibly on direct instructions from Sir Henry

Clinton, British Commander-in-Chief against the Americans in the Revolutionary War. He was stationed in New York from 1778 to 1782 but he had orders to fall back on Halifax if necessary. Furneaux deduces that Clinton may have felt it wise to prepare a safe place for concealing the large sums of money sent to him from England for the conduct of the war, if he had to fall back on Halifax. In some years these sums exceeded £1 million. Oak Island may have been suggested to Clinton by his close friend John Montresor, principal engineer in the British Army and the man who had surveyed Mahone Bay some years earlier. The soldiers who carried out the work presumably came from Halifax 40 miles up the coast and their lights while working on the island may have given rise to the legend of its haunting. The names of the British military engineer officers serving in America at that time are known but which of them was in charge of the work on Oak Island, if Furneaux's supposition is true, has yet to be discovered.

How did the British hope to recover the money from the pit, protected as it was with flood tunnels? Furneaux's answer is that the money was never intended to be buried deep. After the pit had been dug, but before the flood tunnels had been connected, the officer in charge – possibly accompanied by a few trusted workmen – tunnelled into the sides of the pit at a much higher level, outward and then upward. These high chambers were designed to be the repositories of the money. Recovery might even have been possible from the surface without digging into the pit at all. Anyone not knowing this would expect the treasure to lie at the bottom of the pit and would dig down, eventually to be overwhelmed by the inrush of the tide – which is just what occurred. They would continue to think the treasure lay at the bottom of the pit – as also occurred. Furneaux adds that if the money was actually buried on Oak Island, it must have been recovered shortly afterward or there would have been a big discrepancy in the British Army's accounts.

This solution, attractive though it is in many respects, still leaves some questions unanswered. What were the objects encountered by the pod-auger in 1849 and by the drill operated by Blair and Chappell in 1897? What happened to those objects? How did a fragment of parchment get so deep in the ground?

Many believe a treasure still lies somewhere in the mysterious Money Pit, now a mass of puddled clay and mud on Oak Island. But the attempts to prove it over the past 200 years have cost five lives and a fortune in money.

CHAPTER 4

JINXES AND CURSES

Why do some objects seem to bring misfortune on the people who come into contact with them? What makes them jinxed? How does a jinx, or a curse, work? Why should an ivory stat-uette cause toothache or an unknown force fling coffins around in a family vault? Here are the stories of some of the ships, gems, cars and houses that have been associated with a run of bad luck – and of men and women who, wittingly or not, make things go wrong through the curse of the 'evil eye'.

The year was 1928. The city, Kobe, Japan. A middle-aged English couple, the C. J. Lamberts, stood in front of a junk shop window. 'That's what I'd like', said Marie Lambert, pointing to a tiny statuette of a half-naked fat man seated on a cushion. She recognized the laughing man as Ho-tei, the Japanese god of Good Luck. 'Let's find out what he costs', said her husband, as they walked into the shop. They were pleasantly surprised to find that the figurine was cheap, even though it was made of ivory. It seemed almost too good to be true. Back on their cruise ship the Lamberts examined their purchase closely. The statuette had the creamy colour of old ivory and was beautifully carved. As far as they could see, its only minor imperfection was a small hole underneath, plugged neatly with an ivory peg. If the carver had used the base of an elephant's tusk for the statue, which was possible, the tiny hole would be natural as the point where the nerve of the animal's tooth had ended. Altogether, the statue seemed to be one of those rare bargains that tourists dream about. The Lamberts hoped the presence of the 'Laughing Buddha', as

Ho-tei is sometimes called, would insure good luck for the remainder of their voyage.

Ho-tei was originally a sixth-century Buddhist monk who devoted his life to helping the poor, taking special care of children. Statuettes of Ho-tei, who later became a god, show him holding in his right hand a string of beads or a fan and in his left hand a sack. Sometimes a small child is hanging onto his back or sitting on his shoulder, illustrating a legend that he once carried a child to safety across a dangerously flooded river. The legend of St Christopher, who features on many good luck charms in the West as the protector of travellers, is believed to be a Christianised version of the legend of Ho-tei.

Marie Lambert packed the statuette in one of her suitcases. On the second day out, on route to Manila (the next scheduled stop), Mrs Lambert began to suffer from a toothache. The ship's doctor prescribed painkillers but they did little good. Once in Manila, both Lamberts contracted an unpleasant fever whose chief symptom was pain in all the joints and Marie Lambert had to delay her visit to a dentist. When she finally got to one, his drill slipped during treatment and drove through the nerve of her tooth, increasing her pain instead of curing it.

On the next lap of the voyage, which took the ship to Australia, Mr Lambert in turn was prostrated with an agonizing toothache. While in Cairns he went to a doctor, who told him there was nothing wrong with his teeth. In fact, the ache had stopped while he was at the dentist. It started again as soon as he returned to his cabin. Two days later he consulted another dentist and the same thing happened. Finally, in Brisbane he desperately ordered a dentist to start pulling out his teeth and to keep on pulling until the pain stopped. When the first tooth came out, the pain went away. However, it started again as soon as Lambert returned to the ship. He had not noticed that the Ho-tei figurine was in his suitcase at the time his toothache started.

In Sydney, the Lamberts left their luggage checked and the toothache ceased. On the voyage to New Zealand the luggage was in their cabin only once, when they repacked; Lambert's toothache started again. When the luggage went into the hold, the pain stopped. While on shore in New Zealand, he had no toothache and there was only one bout of toothache on the continuation trip to Chile – when the Lamberts repacked their luggage in the cabin.

In the United States the couple visited Lambert's mother, who was so delighted with Ho-tei that they made her a present of the little god. When her excellent teeth started aching a few hours later, she handed back the gift saying that she felt it was 'bad medicine'. In spite of this hint about the statuette's ill effects on its owners, the Lamberts did not connect Ho-tei with their own toothaches till they were on their way across the Atlantic to Britain. A fellow passenger who was interested in ivory borrowed the figurine overnight to show her husband. In the morning, she mentioned that she and her husband had both had toothaches. The Lamberts then thought about their toothaches, and realized that they had always occurred when Ho-tei was in their cabin. Marie Lambert wanted to throw the statuette overboard at once but her husband was afraid that the god might retaliate by rotting every tooth in their heads. So they brought Ho-tei back to London with them.

Lambert took the figure to an oriental art shop and showed it to the Japanese manager, who immediately offered to buy it. Lambert explained that he could not take money for it and described the troubles it seemed to have caused. The manager sent for an old kimono-clad Japanese man and they both examined the statuette carefully. From what they then told him, Lambert gathered that his Ho-tei had been a temple god. In the East, the statues of such gods are sometimes given 'souls' in the form of small medallions hidden inside them. That probably explained the ivory plug in the base of the figure. The old man placed Ho-tei in a shrine at the end of the shop and lit joss sticks in front of it. Then, with an expression of awe, he bowed Lambert out of the shop.

Colin Wilson, who tells this story in *Enigmas and Mysteries*, adds that C. J. Lambert derived some profit from his uncomfortable adventure. He recounted it in a travel book that sold well. Lambert could never bring himself to revisit the shop in which he had left Ho-tei, however.

Lambert's understandable assumption was that a god had been taking revenge on unbelievers who had removed him from his temple. But is it possible for a god, or a priest following that god, to fix the power to cause harm into an inert substance? Sceptics take the view that all runs of misfortune are caused by the victims, who unconsciously bring disaster upon themselves. We have all known people who seem to attract bad luck – we call them 'accident prone'. They usually appear to be suffering from plain undeserved misfortune. Yet we still have the feeling that there is some connection between their personality and their lack of good fortune. There may be something about the attitude of such people – a certain expectation that the worst will happen – that triggers off the accident. The subconscious attitude may, itself, be capable of causing the accident to occur. On the other hand, the subconscious attitude could affect the quality of attention the accident prone person brings to day-to-day behaviour and so could allow mishaps to occur more frequently. Even with our limited knowledge of the power of the mind, this possibility cannot be ruled out. However, many people (in civilized countries as well as among primitive tribes) would go as far as to call the consistently accident prone 'accursed'.

The idea of being accursed does not extend only to people. The famous ship *Mary Celeste*, found drifting in the mid-Atlantic with all aboard mysteriously missing, had been dogged by bad luck from the moment of its launching. Few sailors doubt that there are such things as jinxed ships, unlucky from the day they were launched or before.

The 26,000-ton battleship *Scharnhorst* was such a ship. Launched in October 1936 as the pride of Nazi Germany, it should have had a long and successful career ahead, but from the beginning there were clear signs that all was not going well. Before the ship was half built, it rolled over on the side crushing 60 workmen to death and injuring over 100 others. It took three months to raise it back into position. Workmen had to be drafted to complete the battleship because the rumour had spread that it was jinxed. Later events seemed to substantiate the rumour. When the time came for the important launching, Hitler, Goering, Himmler and many other top Nazis were present. Unfortunately the *Scharnhorst* was not, having launched itself the night before. In the process, it ground up two barges as it hit the channel.

The exceptionally powerful long-range guns of the *Scharnhorst* were first used in the bombardment of Danzig in 1939, with unfortunate results. During the attack one of the guns exploded, killing nine men, and the air supply to one of the gun turrets broke down, suffocating 12 gunners. A year later, during the bombardment of Oslo, the *Scharnhorst* was hit by more shells than all the rest of the German fleet combined. Fires broke out in over 30 places, and the ship had to be towed out of reach of the shore batteries. In making its way home for repairs, the battleship had to lie hidden from British bombers by day and move by night. At last it reached the safe haven of the Elbe river but immediately ran into trouble again. Unknown to the *Scharnhorst*, the *SS Bremen* lay ahead. The ocean liner was one of the world's largest and the glory of Germany. Too late, the watch sounded an alarm and seconds later the battleship rammed the prize liner. The *Bremen* sank and settled into the mud where British planes bombed it to pieces.

After being repaired, the *Scharnhorst* was sent north in 1943 to cruise the coast of Norway and intercept convoys on their way to the Soviet Union. On the way there it passed and failed to notice a British patrol boat, lying in the water with a disabled engine. When the battleship was safely over the horizon, the patrol boat radioed a warning. Several British warships steamed to the area and located the German battleship but the *Scharnhorst* managed to escape the slower pursuers after a short exchange of fire. One of the pursuers caught a glimpse of the *Scharnhorst* from about 16,000 yards away and the commander decided to fire a last shot. Knowing that the *Scharnhorst* would try to get out of the line of fire, he made a guess as to which direction to aim and gave the order to fire.

Living up to its jinx, the *Scharnhorst* turned directly into the path of the broadside from the British battleship. Flames shot up from the decks and within minutes the German ship had plunged to the bottom of the icy sea with most of the crew. Only 36 survived out of a total of 1,900. Years later it was discovered that two of the crew had succeeded in reaching a small rocky island where they made a windbreak from their raft. But the *Scharnhorst* jinx pursued them even there, for evidence showed that they were killed when their emergency oil heater exploded.

The jinx on the Lockheed Constellation airliner AHEM-4 began the day (in July 1945), when a mechanic walked into one of the plane's propellers and was killed. Precisely one year later, on 9 July 1946, Captain Arthur Lewis died at the controls while the plane was over the Atlantic ocean. Precisely one more year later, on 9 July 1947, a newly installed engine burst into flame shortly after takeoff. The captain, Robert Norman, succeeded in putting out the flames with a fire extinguisher but then found that the plane lacked enough power to climb above the roof of an apartment building directly in their path. Norman switched on the takeoff power and just managed to climb out of danger but when he tried to ease the power off again, the controls remained jammed. He and his co-pilot finally wrestled the controls back by sheer force, and landed without further mishap.

July 1948 passed uneventfully. But on 10 July 1949, the airliner crashed near Chicago, killing everyone on board including Captain Robert Norman. The AHEM-4's jinx was his bad luck.

Besides ships and planes, there are records of cars and houses that seem to have brought disaster to their owners. One example is the car in which the Archduke Franz Ferdinand, heir to the dual monarchy of Austria-Hungary, and his wife were assassinated at Sarajevo in July 1914 – a murder that precipitated the outbreak of World War I. Shortly after the start of the war, General Potiorek of the Austrian army came into possession of the car. A few weeks later he suffered a catastrophic defeat against the Serbians at Valjevo and was sent back to Vienna in disgrace. He could not endure the shame of this and died insane.

The next owner of the car was an Austrian captain who had been on Potiorek's staff. Only nine days after taking over the car, he struck and killed two peasants, then swerved into a tree and broke his neck.

At the end of the war, the Governor of Yugoslavia became the owner of the car. After four accidents in four months, one of which caused him to lose an arm, he had had enough and sold the car to a doctor. Six months later the car was found upside down in a ditch. The doctor had been crushed to death inside it. The car was next sold to a wealthy jeweller who committed suicide only a year later. After a brief spell in the hands of another doctor, who seems to have been all too anxious to get rid of it, the car was sold to a Swiss racing driver. He was killed in a race in the Italian Alps, when the car threw him over a wall. The next owner was a

Serbian farmer. Having stalled the car one morning, he persuaded a passing cart to give him a tow – and became the car's tenth victim in a bizarre accident. Because he forgot to turn off the ignition, the car started up, smashed the horse and cart and over-turned on a bend. The car's final owner was Tibor Hirshfeld, a garage owner. Returning from a wedding with six friends one day, Hirshfeld tried to overtake another car at high speed. He crashed and was killed along with four of his companions. The car was then taken to a Vienna museum, where it has been ever since.

Would anyone dream of a fairytale castle being jinxed? Probably not, but the beautiful castle of Miramar near Trieste seems to have brought bad luck to those who lived in it. Miramar castle was built in the mid-nineteenth century by the Archduke Maximilian, a younger brother of the Emperor Franz Josef of Austria-Hungary. Maximilian had once been blown ashore near Trieste while sailing in a small boat and some fishermen gave him shelter. Inspired by the beauty of the place, he decided that day to make his home there. Later he built a white palace with delicate towers, terraces of granite and flights of marble steps leading down to a landing stage guarded by sphinxes. The garden was planted with firs and flowering trees and visitors described it as one of the most beautiful places on earth. The first owner started the catalogue of misfortunes connected with Miramar. It was there that Maximilian accepted the fatal offer of the imperial crown of Mexico, which resulted in his death in front of a Mexican firing squad three years later. His wife Carlotta, who was only 26, went insane.

The Empress Elisabeth, wife of Franz Josef, was the next resident of Miramar, living there with her son Rudolf. Rudolf came to a tragic end in 1889 by committing suicide with his lover and the Empress was assassinated in 1898, by an Italian anarchist who believed in Italian liberation from Austria. The next to live at Miramar was Archduke Franz Ferdinand, Rudolf's cousin and heir to the imperial throne. He and his wife were assassinated in Sarajevo, starting the jinx of the car as well. At the end of World War I, when Trieste passed from Austrian to Italian hands, the Duke of Aosta, a cousin of the King of Italy, moved into Miramar. He died in a prison camp in Kenya during World War

II. After that, two British Major Generals became residents of the castle of Miramar. Both died of heart attacks.

Sceptics maintain that misfortunes such as these occur either by chance, as in the case of the *Scharnhorst*, or as the result of fears and tensions. For example, the crew of the airliner AHEM-4 knew that a mechanic had walked into the propeller and been cut to pieces. The subsequent owner of Franz Ferdinand's car knew that the Archduke and his wife had met violent death in it. The rationalist view is that the belief in jinxes developed, as early peoples felt the need to discover a pattern in the misfortunes that befell them. Cattle sickened, children died unexpectedly, storms destroyed crops. For a society that believed the human being was the centre of creation and that everything which happened did so for a humanly comprehensible reason, two explanations presented themselves. Either some object associated with the victim contained within itself the power to bring harm or some god or person of evil intent was willing harm on them. The idea of the jinx and the curse was born – the jinx connected with objects, the curse with spirits or humans.

The destructive power of a curse is real and undisputed. People who believe they are under a curse to die will often obediently proceed to die. Those most likely to react in this way are primitive people whose lives are rigorously ordered by ritual and taboo. Such were the Maoris of New Zealand and such, still, are many Amazon Indians of South America. In earlier times, a Maori chief was a sacred figure and it was taboo to touch him or objects that had belonged to him. It was accepted that any transgression would be punished by the angered ancestral spirits of the tribe. Sir James Frazer, in *The Golden Bough*, tells of a Maori warrior who unwittingly ate the unfinished dinner of his chief. When he learned what he had done, he was immediately seized by violent stomach cramps and convulsions. He died of the seizures at sundown the same day. Knowing he was fated to die, his body and mind combined to bring his death about.

A modern story of a curse that was connected with a strange death is that of the so-called 'curse of the Pharaoh'. It struck after the opening of Tutankhamun's tomb in Egypt in 1923. The first of several men to die was Lord Carnarvon, who had financed the dig. Three months after the archaeological discovery, he was bitten by a mosquito and the bite became infected. At five minutes to two on the morning of 5 April 1923 he died. At this precise moment two unusual incidents occurred – all the lights in Cairo went out and remained out for some time and back in England, Lord Carnarvon's dog howled and died. No satisfactory explanation has ever been forthcoming for either of these coincidental events.

The famous blue diamond known as the 'Hope Diamond' brought bad fortune to most of its owners over a long period of time. Gemologists believe that the 'Hope Diamond', a product of the great Golconda mines of southern India, must have been cut from a larger blue diamond that was acquired by Louis XIV and disappeared during the French Revolution nearly 75 years later, with the rest of the French royal treasure. It made its first appearance in its present form in 1830, and was bought by the British banker and gem collector, Henry Thomas Hope. He escaped any evil consequences but the cousin to whom he bequeathed it, Lord Francis Hope, was plagued by problems. His wife, a noted actress, blamed all their marital troubles on the blue stone and prophesied evil for all its owners. Her curse may have added to the unluckiness of the exquisite gem.

In the early 1900s, the diamond was sold by Lord Francis Hope, who was said to be suffering grave financial trouble. Jacques Colot, a French broker, paid more than three times its original price for it and sold it to a Russian noble, Prince Kanitovski. Colot went mad and committed suicide. The prince behaved as if he were mad. He lent the diamond to an actress at the Folies Bergères and then shot her from a box in the theatre the first night she was wearing it. A few days later he was stabbed by revolutionaries. A Greek jeweller by the name of Simon Mantharides was the next to own the 'Hope Diamond'. He is said to have been thrown over a precipice. In 1908, Abdul Hamid II, the sultan of Turkey known as 'Abdul the Damned', bought the gem for tens of thousands of dollars. He was deposed in April 1909 – the last of Turkey's sultans. Habib Bey acquired it next, putting it on exhibition in London in June 1909. In November he was drowned when the French liner *La Seyne* sank off Singapore.

In spite of this ominous record, the diamond was bought by Edward Beale McLean, proprietor of the *Washington Post*, as a gift for his wife. McLean was involved in the Teapot Dome scandal of President Harding's administration and afterward became an alcoholic, losing his mind as well. The eldest of the four McLean children was killed by an automobile at the age of nine. The last owner, said to have paid in the millions for it, contributed the seemingly sinister 'Hope Diamond' to the Smithsonian Institution, where it still rests.

Is it a curse that decrees that every president of the United States, elected in a year divisible by 20 will die in office? History shows that this has been the case since 1840. Three died naturally – William Henry Harrison, who was elected in 1840, Warren G. Harding (1920), and Franklin D. Roosevelt (1940). Assassins killed Abraham Lincoln (1860), James A. Garfield (1880), William McKinley (1900), and John F. Kennedy (1960). The pattern in itself is odd enough but the fact that both assassinations and natural deaths fit into this pattern is odder still. When Roosevelt, first elected in 1932 and re-elected in 1936 and 1940, survived to the end of his third term, it might have been thought that the jinx had been lifted. But it reasserted itself during his fourth term. Re-elected in November 1944, he was dead the following spring.

No one can put a name to an apparent blight that strikes American presidents in given years. But in many countries the cause of a person's misfortunes is easily attributed to the 'evil eye'. The belief that certain individuals possess the power to bring disaster to another person simply by a look, is still widespread today in the countries around the Mediterranean, particularly in Italy and nowhere more so than in Naples and the south. In Florence and Tuscany, this unlovely gift is known as *male d'occhio* (evil eye); in Rome it is called *fascina* (fascination). In the south it is *jettatura*, meaning a spell cast by touch, word or look. Of the three, the look is the most penetrating and potent.

To ward off the dreaded power of the 'evil eye', most people wear amulets most of the time. Some of these charms are grotesque or ridiculous in design, meant to attract the attention of the evil eye and distract it from the person wearing it. Many are indecent or obscene for the same reason, the commonest of all being the phallus or objects suggested by it. Snakes, fish, crescent moons, pieces of coral, closed hands with the thumb protruding between the first and second fingers and horns of all sorts, shapes and sizes.

The horn is believed to have the greatest power of defence. Even to mutter the word *corno* (horn) is better than nothing.

When obliged to speak to someone having the 'evil eye', Neapolitans will hold their hand in a gesture of protection, extending the first and fourth fingers in the sign of the horned hand. Out of courtesy, they may keep the hand behind their back or in their pocket but they will not relax the position of the fingers till they feel safe from danger.

Some people probably trade on their reputation as bringers of bad luck, the jinxes of their community, but others are entirely unwilling agents for the harm they cause and the terror they inspire. Apparently there is no way possessors of the 'evil eye' can rid themselves of their fatal gift. It is as much a curse on them as on their victims – they are born with it and must live and die with it. Aristocrats and churchmen were frequently credited with having the evil eye. The most eminent churchman to have this reputation was Pope Pius IX. It is said that even devout Catholics, while asking for a blessing, would keep the horned hand pointed at him. F. T. Elworthy in *The Evil Eye* quotes this statement about whether the pope had the malevolent gift or not, 'They said so and it seems really to be true. If he had not the *jettatura*, it is very odd that everything he blessed made *fiasco*. We all did very well in the campaign against the Austrians in '48 [1848]. We were winning battle after battle and all was gaiety and hope, when suddenly he blessed the cause and everything went to the bad at once. Nothing succeeds with anybody or anything when he wishes well to them. When he went to S. Agnese to hold a great festival, down went the floor and the people were all smashed together. Then he visited the column to the Madonna in the Piazza di Spagna and blessed it and the workmen; of course one fell from the scaffold the same day and killed himself. . . . I do not wonder the workmen at the column in the Piazza di Spagna refused to work in raising it unless the Pope stayed away!'

The horned hand may or may not help against the 'evil eye'. But there seems no way in which sailors can protect themselves if they sail in a jinxed ship. Many mariners are convinced that spirits of the dead are involved in jinxes and point to the two most notorious jinx ships of the nineteenth century – the British vessels *Hinemoa* and *Great Eastern*.

On its maiden voyage in 1892, the 2,000-ton steel bark *Hinemoa* carried a ballast load of rubble from an old London graveyard. During the voyage, four apprentice seamen died of typhoid. The first captain went insane, the second became a criminal, the third was removed from his command on grounds of being an alcoholic, the fourth was found dead in his cabin and the fifth shot himself. Under the sixth captain, the *Hinemoa* capsized and two sailors were swept overboard when it righted itself. The end came during a storm in 1908 when the bark drifted ashore on the west coast of Scotland, a total loss. Sailors say the vessel was jinxed right from the start by the presence of graveyard bones in the ballast on the maiden voyage.

The *Great Eastern* was built by the famous British engineer, Isambard Kingdom Brunel, starting in 1854 and was one of his few failures. In its day the passenger liner was the largest – and the unluckiest – ship in the world. The vessel was planned to be the wonder of the seas, a floating palace carrying 4,000 passengers in luxury around the world. The six masts and five funnels were more than any other ship had ever carried. Marine jargon did not have enough names for so many masts, so they were referred to as Monday, Tuesday, Wednesday, Thursday, Friday, and Saturday. The colossal hull, 692 feet long, surpassed the dimensions of Noah's Ark. In fact, the *Great Eastern* had two hulls, one inside the other, three feet apart and heavily braced. Inside the hull there was an ingenious arrangement of longitudinal and transverse bulkheads, forming 16 watertight compartments. This was designed to make it virtually unsinkable – and it is true that while nearly every other calamity befell the ship, it never sank.

Hammering in the three million rivets, each one an inch thick and all driven in by hand, took 200 rivet gangs 1,000 work days. Fatal accidents during construction were fewer than average, four workers and a spectator. But one riveter and his apprentice disappeared and there was a rumour that they had been sealed up in a hull compartment and that their screams for help had been drowned in the din of the hammers.

The original backers ran out of money when the price of iron plate increased and work stopped till Brunel had succeeded in raising more money. Launching the heaviest hull in history into the Thames river had to be performed sideways. It took an agonizing three months to get the vessel to move the 330 feet down to the water. Chains snapped, barges sank, innumerable hydraulic rams burst under the strain. Day after day, Brunel worked to inch his giant structure a few feet closer to the water. The *Times* correspondent in London wrote, 'There she lies on the very brink of the noble river which is to carry her to the ocean, but she will not wet her lips'. When the launch was finally made on the last day of January 1858, it had cost £1,000 a foot.

Total expenses had already reached over £1 million. The cost of completing the ship broke the next company but once more Brunel managed to raise the money to carry on. The new board of directors set aside the original plan to take the *Great Eastern* on long voyages to India and Australia – for which the liner was uniquely suitable. Instead, they went after the quick profits of a North Atlantic run. Only the first class cabins were completed for the maiden voyage, the second and third class accommodation left for what turned out to be another nine years. The day before the great ship was to sail, Brunel came down for an inspection. The famous engineer was prematurely aged at 53. Just after posing with colleagues for a photograph, he staggered and collapsed with a stroke. Brunel died a week later as news came through that one of the *Great Eastern*'s funnels had exploded as the liner steamed down the channel because a steam valve had been left closed. Five men were scalded to death and another fell to his death in one of the great paddle wheels. The grand salon with its mirrored walls and sumptuous decoration was wrecked.

Repairs took longer than expected and the planned voyage to the United States was cancelled. In order to get some return on their investment, the directors moved the by-then notorious ship to Holyhead, Wales and opened it to sightseers. Not long after, a howling gale tore it from its moorings and drove it out to sea. For 18 hours the vessel rode the storm while many nearby ships sank, proving how well it was designed. But the recently repaired salon was ruined again. Three months later the captain, the coxswain and the nine-year-old son of the chief purser were drowned when a sudden squall upset their gig as they were going ashore.

Nothing casts a sharper blight over a ship's character than the death of the captain during, or before, a maiden voyage. When the news reached London, the directors of the *Great Eastern*'s managing company resigned. The next board set a definite sailing date of 9 June 1860, but 9 July came and went. Most of the 300 ticketed passengers (all that the ship had beds for) tired of waiting and sailed on one of Sir Samuel Cunard's more reliable ships. When the Great Eastern finally left Southampton on 16 June only 35 paying passengers were aboard. The new captain, commanding a crew of 418, had never crossed the Atlantic before.

During the 12 day crossing, the cheap coal that was being used as an economy measure damaged the funnel casings and made the main dining room so hot that passengers refused to sit there. Otherwise the voyage was uneventful and the huge liner arrived to a sensational welcome in New York. However, sightseers, incensed at the high $1 admission fee charged for visiting on board, tried to get their money's worth by pocketing souvenirs. Later, an announced two-day excursion turned into a nightmare. Two thousand people were faced with the problem of sleeping on only 300 beds. A pipe burst in the storage room and flooded the food supplies, leaving nothing available to eat except dessicated chicken, salted meat and stone-hard biscuits. For this passengers were charged outrageous prices. Most of the passengers had to spend the night on the deck, where they had the unpleasant experience of being covered by cinders raining down from the five funnels. In the morning there was no water to wash off the grit. The passengers thought they could at least look forward to a speedy landing but by some error of navigation, the *Great Eastern* had gone off course during the night and was 100 miles out to sea. There was no food left for breakfast or lunch. When land was at last reached, the hungry, grimy, weary passengers fought to disembark.

A second excursion was announced but not surprisingly, only a handful of tickets were bought. New York was disenchanted with the great ship. Almost unnoticed it left for England with 90 passengers on board. But the return trip was not to be without incident either. In mid-Atlantic a screw shaft gave out. At Milford Haven the vessel fouled the hawser of a small boat and drowned two of its passengers. Then the huge liner crashed into the frigate *Blenheim*.

The next captain, the third, never sailed, resigning rather than sail short-handed when the directors fired one-third of the crew. Under the fourth captain, the ship sailed with only 100 passengers, even though there were 300 emigrants willing to travel steerage. In fact, the *Great Eastern* never carried any emigrants across the Atlantic, although in this respect it could have beaten all competition and made great profits. The owners single-mindedly concentrated on first-class passengers during the nine years before second and third class accommodation was installed – and the ship never came near getting a full complement of such travellers. Profits were also hindered because the vessel was too cold to cross the Atlantic in the winter.

In September 1861, the *Great Eastern* was struck by a hurricane that would probably have sunk any other vessel. Both the side paddles were ripped off. All lifeboats were torn away. The rudder broke and began crashing against the screw. Repairs cost £60,000. The following year in Long Island Sound, the ship struck a tall needle of rock unmarked on the charts – it tore a rip 83 feet long and 9 feet wide in the outer hull. This time repairs cost £70,000.

In 1864, the unlucky ship was put up for auction and bought for £25,000 to begin a new career as a cable layer. Misfortune still hounded it. When 1,186 miles out from Ireland on the way to Newfoundland, an accident caused the cable to slip and the severed end sank three miles to the ocean bed. All efforts to recover it failed, so the ship returned to England. Another try in 1866 was successful and on 27 July the first messages by undersea cable passed between Europe and North America.

As a vessel for laying cable, the *Great Eastern* at last justified its existence. In 1869 it sailed for India (the only time it visited the latitudes it had been designed for) and laid a cable between Bombay and Aden.

In 1874, the launching of the first custom-built cable ships brought an end to the only profitable employment the *Great Eastern* ever enjoyed. A mere 15 years after being launched, the great ship was brought back to Milford Haven where it remained rusting and blocking the shipping lines for the next 12 years. By 1886 the barnacles on the hull were six inches thick. In that year the owners managed to sell the one-time liner for £20,000 and it was gingerly taken around the coast of Wales to Liverpool. There the *Great Eastern* damaged the tug *Wrestler*, the last boat it was to crash into. Then this former 'Wonder of the Sea', this 'Floating Palace', was painted with slogans advertising a Liverpool store. Later the vessel was taken to Dublin to advertise a brand of tea. Finally a firm of metal dealers bought the down-at-heel ship. It had been sold for the last time.

Breaking up the *Great Eastern* proved almost as difficult as building it. In fact, the wrecker's iron ball, suspended on a giant chain, had to be invented for the purpose in 1889. Inside the double hull, demolition experts discovered two skeletons – the riveter and his boy apprentice, who had vanished when the ship was being built. Few people doubted that they had discovered the cause of the ship's jinx.

Is there a more logical explanation? The sailors on board the *Hinemoa* knew that the ballast had been taken from a graveyard; the seamen on the *Great Eastern* during the maiden voyage knew that two workmen might have been sealed up in the hull. Couldn't it be said that they anticipated bad luck and went to meet it half way? Perhaps. But if that explanation satisfies some for jinxed ships, the same kind of reason can hardly account for the restless behaviour of the coffins in the Chase Tomb.

In the churchyard of Christ Church, Barbados, on a headland overlooking Oistin's Bay, stands a small but strongly built stone tomb. It has been empty since 1820 and seems likely to remain so. Designed as a quiet resting place for the dead, it proved to be anything but.

The family vault, built of large blocks of local coral stone firmly cemented together, is recessed two feet deep into solid limestone rock. The floor space is 12 feet long by 6½ feet wide. Originally the entrance was closed by a heavy slab of blue Devon marble, which sealed the tomb between internments. It was built in 1724 by the widow of an English aristocrat whose body does not seem to have been interred there unless his coffin was subsequently removed. The first recorded internment is that of Mrs Thomasina Goddard on 31 July 1807.

In the following year, the tomb came into the possession of the wealthy Chase family, whose head was Thomas Chase. On 22 February 1808, the small lead coffin of Mary Chase, his infant daughter, was interred in the vault. Four years passed and another

Chase daughter, Dorcas, died (of uncertain age but apparently an adult). She was interred in the tomb on 6 July 1812. At that point there was nothing out of the ordinary in the state of the other two coffins.

Matters were very different when, on 9 August the same year, Thomas Chase himself was brought to the tomb. The coffins of both his daughters had been shifted – it looked as though by violence. That of the infant Mary had been thrown across the vault and lay head downward against the far wall.

The black labourers were alarmed at the sight but the Chase family did not seem unduly upset. The coffins were returned to their original places beside the undisturbed one of Mrs Goddard and Thomas Chase's was placed alongside them. His was an exceedingly heavy lead coffin, requiring eight men to lift it. When the marble slab of the vault was put in position, great care was taken to seal it properly.

On the death of Samuel Brewster Ames, a baby who may have been a Chase relative, his coffin was brought to the tomb on 25 September 1816. All the coffins were in confusion, save that of Mrs Goddard. Her coffin, which had been made of wood, had disintegrated but was in its place, the others had been flung about and upended. Thomas Chase's heavy lead coffin was lying on its side several feet to the left of its original spot. This time the Chase family was furious, assuming that the desecration was linked with the abortive slave rising that had been crushed with much bloodshed earlier in the year. But apart from the unlikelihood that the superstitious blacks would be willing to enter a tomb, the sheer weight of Thomas Chase's coffin made it a wellnigh impossible task to have been accomplished unnoticed.

The coffins were rearranged and the marble slab cemented into position. On 17 November of the same year, the tomb had to be opened again to receive Samuel Brewster, who had been murdered during the slave uprising and temporarily buried elsewhere. Once again the coffins were in the wildest disorder. Except for Mrs Goddard's – undisturbed as always – they were leaning against the walls, crossing and overlapping each other. This time the minister of Christ Church, a magistrate and two other men searched the vault thoroughly. They found no crack, no concealed entrance. A fairly big crowd had accompanied the funeral procession and the findings confirmed their worst fears – the Chase Tomb was cursed. The black labourers had to be ordered sharply to enter the tomb and restore. order. Mrs Goddard's bones, which had fallen out of her disintegrating coffin, were wrapped up and placed against the wall. Once again the entrance was sealed.

Three years passed before the next, and last, coffin was brought to the Chase Tomb. The tomb's troubled history had created such sensational interest on Barbados that the governor, Lord Combermere, the commander of the garrison, and many hundreds of spectators walked behind the coffin of Mrs Thomasina Clarke on 17 July 1819. The vault was opened only with difficulty because Thomas Chase's heavy coffin was upended and resting against it, six feet from the place it should have been. The two children's coffins, which had rested on top of two larger ones, were on the floor. Only Mrs Goddard's, the flimsiest of them all, was untouched.

Lord Combermere had been one of the Duke of Wellington's most successful cavalry commanders against Napoleon. It took a lot to frighten him. He personally supervised a meticulous examination of the interior of the vault. When nothing had been revealed by this search, he had the seven coffins put back into position, and ordered fine white beach sand to be sprinkled on the floor. This would show the footprints of any one who entered the vault. The marble slab was put in place and Lord Combermere and several others imprinted their personal seals in the wet cement sealing the slab.

Nine months later, on 19 April 1820, Lord Combermere was in the neighbourhood of Christ Church again. He was due to return to England that year and was curious to know whether anything had happened inside the Chase Tomb. He found the seals on the slab unbroken. No footprints appeared on the sanded floor. The remains of Mrs Goddard's coffin were against the wall where they had been left. But again the other coffins had been flung all over the place. One child's coffin was lying just inside the entrance. Thomas Chase's particularly heavy coffin and another one were upside down.

Experienced campaigner as he was, Lord Combermere knew when a situation was beyond his control. He ordered the coffins to be removed and buried elsewhere. Since then, the tomb has remained empty.

What power disturbed the coffins has never been discovered. Barbados suffers from earthquakes but no quake would overturn a lead coffin and leave fragile wood unmoved. No moisture was ever detected in the vault but even if water had somehow entered it and been able to shift the coffins, the wooden one would have been the first to move – and yet its position remained unaltered. Neither of these natural explanations (which seem to be the only two) are convincing. It also seems impossible that a human agency was involved. What about the supernatural?

Thomas Chase was the most hated man on the island. Both he and his daughter Dorcas were believed to have killed themselves – she, it was said, starved herself to death out of despair over her cruel father. The disorders began after her internment, as though the other corpses resented the presence of a suicide among them. Could some power associated with the corpse of Mrs Goddard, whose coffin always remained undisturbed, have flung the coffins about the vault? Could the arrival of a second suicide and the corpses of three who did not die by their own hand have intensified the power? If the answer to these questions is 'yes' the mystery still remains of what that power is and why it manifested itself in this particular case. The curse on the Chase Tomb is as much a puzzle today as when it confronted the citizens of Barbados in the nineteenth century.

CHAPTER 5

MYSTERIES OF THE SEA

Who or what caused everyone on board the Mary Celeste *to abandon the ship? Why was the seaworthy vessel, with cargo intact, left in apparent haste near dangerous rocks in the Atlantic Ocean? This mystery, unsolved and much discussed since 1872, is the most famous of the unexplained puzzles about crewless ships adrift, crews of corpses and ships that seem to be capable of independent action of their own. No one has yet plumbed the depths of the mysterious seas to find the answers to such riddles.*

The captain of the English brig, *Dei Gratia*, was the first to see the strange two-masted ship sailing an erratic course, with only the jib and the foretopmast staysail set. Though the vessel was on a starboard tack, the jib was set to port – a sure sign to a sailor that a ship was out of control, the crew either injured or dead. Captain Edward Morehouse decided to close in but the sea was running high after recent squalls and two hours passed before he was near enough to read the name. It was the *Mary Celeste*.

Captain Morehouse knew the vessel well. He also knew Captain Benjamin Spooner Briggs, the man in command. Only a month ago their two ships had been loading cargo at neighbouring piers in the East River in New York. The *Mary Celeste* had set sail for the Italian port of Genoa on 5 November 1872; 10 days later the *Dei Gratia* had followed across the Atlantic, bound for Gibraltar. Now Morehouse had caught up, only to find the ship drifting halfway between the Azores and the coast of Portugal. No one was at the wheel, no one on deck.

Morehouse sent Oliver Deveau, his first mate, to see what was amiss. Deveau was a large man of great physical strength, described as 'absolutely fearless'. He and two seamen rowed over to investigate the mystery. The ship seemed deserted. The first thing Deveau did on boarding her was to sound the pumps. He found that one of the pumps had been drawn to let the sounding rod down, so he used the other pump, leaving the first on the deck as he found it. There was a great deal of water between decks, probably as a result of recent storms, two sails that had been set had blown away and the lower foretopsails were hanging by the corners. In spite of these problems, however, Deveau established that the *Mary Celeste* was in no danger of sinking.

Deveau and the second mate, John Wright, searched the vessel; they found no one aboard, alive or dead. They did find that the binnacle had been stoved in, destroying the compass, that two of the hatches were off and that one cask of crude alcohol in the hold had sprung its lid. Otherwise the cargo seemed in good order and the ship's wheel, which had not been lashed, was undamaged. It looked as though the *Mary Celeste* had carried a yawl on deck, lashed to the main hatch. Two fenders were in position on the hatch, showing that a yawl could have been there, and two sets of rails had been removed apparently in order to launch it.

In the cabin, Deveau and Wright discovered that the six starboard windows had been nailed up with planks but there was no way of telling if they had been so fastened before the voyage or during it. The port windows were shut but still let in some light. Much water had entered the cabin through the open door and through the skylight that was also open. The clock had been ruined by the water and much of the bedding and clothing was wet. Because the linen and clothes were difficult to dry out, Deveau concluded that they had been made wet by sea water. He later testified,

'The bed was as it had been left after being slept in – not made . . . I judged there had been a woman aboard. I saw female clothing . . . I noticed an impression in the bed, as of a child having laid there. There seemed to be everything left behind as if left in a great hurry, but everything in its place. There were boxes of clothing. There were also work bags with needles, threads, buttons, books and a case of instruments, a writing desk. A harmonium or melodeon was in the cabin.'

In those days it was not uncommon for a captain's wife to accompany him on a voyage and Sarah Briggs had in fact done so. The couple had also brought their two-year-old daughter, Sophia Matilda. They had left their other child, seven-year-old Arthur, with his grandparents in Marion, Massachusetts to continue his schooling.

Almost as many legends have attached themselves to the *Mary Celeste* as there were barnacles on its hold. One of these is that a half-eaten meal was discovered on the cabin table and that breakfast was still cooking in the galley. Deveau's sworn statement shows otherwise. Though the rack for stopping dishes from sliding off the table was in position, he reported, there were no eatables in the cabin, nor was any cooked food found in the galley. Pots and kettles had been washed up and stowed away. An open bottle of medicine was found, which suggested that whoever had taken it had left in too much of a hurry to put the cork back into the bottle. From the meagre evidence, it was presumed that the ship had been abandoned some time in mid-morning – late enough for breakfast to have been cleared away but not before Mrs Briggs had made the bed. This presumption was partly based on the fact that no New England woman of Sarah Briggs' background would have allowed the beds to remain unmade till late in the morning, even at sea.

Less water had entered the seamen's quarters than the cabin. The seamen's chests were dry and there were no traces of rust on the razors left behind. The crew had evidently gone in a great hurry, leaving behind as they did not only the contents of their chests – everything of value they possessed – but also their oilskin boots and even their pipes, articles no sailor would abandon unless in a state of panic.

Looking for some explanation, Deveau studied the logbook in the mate's cabin. The last entry was dated 24 November and it gave the ship's position as 100 miles southwest of San Miguel Island in the Azores. There was some later information jotted on the log slate, found in the captain's cabin. It showed that the next day, 25 November at 8 am, the ship passed Santa Maria Island. Eleven days had passed since that final entry had been made. In that time the ship had continued for another 500 miles, apparently on course. For some undetermined period of that time, however, it had been unmanned. The date of the last entry on the log slate does not necessarily mean that the *Mary Celeste* was abandoned on the 25th. In small ships the log is not regarded as very important, and is seldom written up every day. For example, in the 18 days that the *Mary Celeste* had been at sea before sighting the Azores, only seven entries had been made in the log. There was no way of telling exactly when Captain Briggs took his wife, child and crew of seven onto the yawl – if he actually did so. Neither was there any indication why they had left a sound and seaworthy vessel in an apparent hurry.

To some, the story of the *Mary Celeste* could be seen as a warning that the name of a ship should never be changed. Long John Silver of Stevenson's *Treasure Island* said, 'I never knowed any luck as came of changing of a ship's name. Now what a ship was christened, so let her stay, I says.' When the future *Mary Celeste* was built on Spencer's Island, Nova Scotia, in 1861, it was christened the *Amazon*. From the start the vessel was an unlucky one. The first captain died 48 hours after the *Amazon* was registered. On the maiden voyage, it ran into a fishing weir off the coast of Maine and damaged the hull. While being repaired, fire broke out amidships. In the Straits of Dover, it collided with another brig, which sank. By that time the ship had had three captains. Under the fourth, the *Amazon* ran aground on Cape Breton Island and was wrecked. It was salvaged, however, and then passed quickly through two or perhaps three other owners, one of whom renamed it the *Mary Celeste*. As such the vessel was bought by James H. Winchester, founder of an eminent shipping firm that still bears his name in New York. On discovering dry rot in the timbers, he rebuilt the bottom with a copper lining. He also extended the deck cabin and generally put the ship in excellent condition. The *Mary Celeste* had exchanged the red ensign of the British merchant navy for the stars and stripes.

Early in September 1872, the newly named vessel was tied up at Pier 44 in New York's East River being loaded with about 1,700 red oak casks of commercial alcohol. In one of her last letters to relatives, Sarah Briggs described her reaction to this cargo, saying that she thought she had gone slightly daft with the 'amount of thumping and bumping, of shaking and tossings to and fro of the cargo.' She also mentioned 'screechings and growlings', which could have been caused by sweating casks of a volatile liquid such as crude alcohol.

At a nearby pier, the *Dei Gratia* was taking on a cargo of petroleum and the two captains, Briggs and Morehouse, dined together the night before the *Mary Celeste* sailed. The curious coincidence that it was the *Dei Gratia* which later found the *Mary Celeste* abandoned was to sow suspicion in the minds of the members of the Board of Inquiry trying to decide what had happened.

Captain Briggs was master of the vessel and part owner, having purchased a few shares of the ship from Winchester. He was an experienced seaman of 37, robust, correct and temperate. Having been brought up among New England puritans, he never allowed liquor aboard a vessel under his command.

In after years, several grizzled sailors claimed to be survivors of the *Mary Celeste* but the names of the crew of seven are all known. The first mate was Albert Richardson, who was married to Winchester's niece. Andrew Gilling, the second mate and Edward Head, the steward-cook, were the other Americans of the crew. The four seamen were all German; Volkert and Boz Lorensen, brothers from Schleswig-Holstein, Arian Martens and Gottlief Goodschaad (or Gondschatt). In one of her letters to her mother-in-law, Sarah Briggs said that she was not sure how smart the crew would prove to be but Captain Briggs was satisfied they were reliable.

When Deveau and White had completed their examination of the drifting ship, they returned to the *Dei Gratia* to report to Captain Morehouse. In spite of his friendship with Briggs, Morehouse apparently did not go aboard the *Mary Celeste* for a personal look. Either he or Deveau proposed taking the abandoned ship into Gibraltar to claim salvage. Deveau returned to the *Mary Celeste* later that afternoon with two seamen, taking their ship's small boat, a barometer, sextant, compass, watch and some food prepared by their steward. In two days the *Mary Celeste* was ready to sail and the two ships set out, remaining in sight of each other till they reached the Straits of Gibraltar. At that point a storm separated them. The *Dei Gratia* reached Gibraltar on the evening of 12 December and the *Mary Celeste* arrived the following morning. Then, unexpectedly, the arguments began.

A claim for salvaging an abandoned ship on the high seas generally presents no problem because in the vast majority of cases the crewless vessel is dismasted, waterlogged or otherwise in bad shape. But the case of the *Mary Celeste* was different. F. Solly Flood, the British Admiralty Proctor in Gibraltar, said in his report to London, 'The account which they [the salvors] gave of the soundness and good condition of the derelict was so extraordinary that I found it necessary to apply for a survey.'

The surveyors reported that the hull of the *Mary Celeste* was perfectly sound and that the ship was not leaking and had not been in a collision. However, they remarked on two curious grooves which seemed to have been cut with a sharp instrument on each side of the bows, several feet back from the prow and a foot or two above the waterline. There was no damage within the ship, no trace of an explosion, no suggestion of a fire. The *Mary Celeste* was said to be in better shape than many of the small ships that did the Atlantic run. How could the captain, mate and crew of the *Dei Gratia* swear that they had come upon this seaworthy and amply provisioned vessel drifting in mid-ocean? The British authorities in Gibraltar found such testimony hard to believe. In their view, it was far more likely to be a case of collusion between the crews of the two ships to claim the salvage money, the cargo alone being worth $30,000. Flood suspected even worse. He believed the case to be one of mutiny, piracy and multiple murder. Described as a fussy and pompous man, Flood's good qualities were the counterpart of such faults – he was a painstaking investigator and he was dedicated to the rule of law. He was not going to let criminals, if so they proved, get away with their crimes.

Flood suggested that the groove on the bows had been deliberately made to look as if the vessel had struck rocks. Horatio J. Sprague, the United States Consul in Gibraltar, hotly disputed this interpretation, and when the *USS Plymouth* put in at Gibraltar, he asked the captain to give his opinion of the grooves. Captain Schufeldt thought that the grooves were 'splinters made in the bending of the planks which were afterward forced off by action of the sea without hurting the ship.'

Meantime, Flood had found brown stains, which might have been blood, on the deck. More such stains were also found on the blade of an ornate Italian sword under the captain's berth. Deveau was closely questioned about these but denied he had cleaned or scraped the decks to remove other similar stains. He maintained that his attention was fully occupied in running the ship and he refused to accept that there was anything remarkable about the sword. It is a measure of the mistrust in which he and his companions were held that when samples of the brown stains were analyzed, the *Dei Gratia* crew was charged with the cost of analysis. Flood not only declined to reveal the report of the analysis but also refused to give Sprague a copy. Even more surprising, he withheld the report from his own government! Could he have been hiding the fact that the results indicated no blood? Not until 1887, fourteen years later, was Sprague able to obtain a copy of the results of the analysis.

Flood also discovered irregularities in the log Deveau had kept while on board the *Mary Celeste*. At Captain Morehouse's instructions, he had written it up after arriving at Gibraltar. One entry stated that Morehouse had come on board the *Mary Celeste* but Deveau insisted that he had made an error and that Captain Morehouse did not step foot on the ship till it had arrived in Gibraltar. Even more suspicious, in Flood's opinion, was the way the ship had continued on course for 11 days after 25 November. He took this as an indication that the *Dei Gratia* crew must have boarded the *Mary Celeste* much earlier than they said they had.

Fortunately for the *Dei Gratia* crew, the members of the Board of Inquiry were experienced naval men. They knew that logs were not always kept without fail and they could appreciate that Deveau, with only two men to help him sail the ship, had enough work on his hands without wanting to bother with paperwork. Unlike F. Solly Flood, they did not find anything untoward in the grooves on the bow or in the stains on the deck and once all the available facts had been presented to them, they were quick to clear Morehouse and his men of any suspicion. In contrast, they spent a long time trying to work out what could have happened to Captain Briggs and his crew. When Winchester came over to Gibraltar from the United States in hopes of speeding the inquiry, he found himself subjected to such close questioning about his ship, the crew, the captain, the history and himself that finally he became angry.

'I'm a Yankee with some English blood', he cried out, 'but if I knew where it was, I'd open a vein and let the damned stuff out!'

When the court eventually handed down its judgment in March 1873, it confessed itself unable to decide why the *Mary Celeste* had been abandoned. This was the first time in its history it had failed to come to a conclusion. It awarded to the *Dei Gratia* a sum equivalent to about one-fifth of the combined value of the *Mary Celeste* and its cargo. The *Mary Celeste* was returned to Winchester and under a new captain and a new crew, sailed to Genoa. There the cargo was unloaded – three-and-a-half months late but otherwise intact. Winchester sold the ship as soon as it returned to New York but its reputation as an unlucky vessel kept seamen from signing on as crew. The *Mary Celeste* changed hands rapidly, bringing little profit to any of its short-term owners.

In 1884, the ship was acquired by a disreputable captain named Gilman C. Parker, who deliberately ran it onto a reef in the West Indies for the sake of the insurance. Even this desperate measure brought no profit. The insurance companies became suspicious, asked awkward questions of the crew and brought Captain Parker and his associates in the scheme to trial. Because the penalty for destroying a ship on the high seas was death by hanging, the jury, mindful of the ship's unlucky history, was reluctant to convict. The defendants were freed on a technicality but within eight months Parker was dead, one of his associates went mad, and another committed suicide. Their association with the *Mary Celeste* brought them nothing but grief.

As to what really happened to the *Mary Celeste* on that morning in late November 1872, somewhere between the Azores and Portugal, there have been many guesses. Surprisingly, interest in the subject was slow to develop and for 11 years the mystery remained relatively unknown outside the seafaring community. Then an impecunious young doctor with an ambition to become an author, wrote a story based on the affair.

Entitled *J. Habakuk Jephson's Statement*, the story appeared in the *Cornhill Magazine* in January 1884 with the ship's name changed to the *Marie Celeste*. In the story, the ship had been taken over as part of what would now be called, a Black Power plot. According to the author's version of events, the lifeboat was still on board when the vessel was found.

When the identity of the writer became known, he was launched on the road to fame. The author was Arthur Conan Doyle and his fictionalization of the Mary Celeste mystery started a flood of books and articles on the subject. Since then, so many books and articles have been devoted to the riddle that the Atlantic Mutual Insurance Company in New York, has an entire room kept as a *Mary Celeste* Museum. One writer imagined that the Mary Celeste was attacked by a kraken or giant squid that picked off the crew one by one, sliding its tentacles through the portholes until it had consumed the last morsel of human flesh. Charles Fort suggested that the crew had been snatched away by a 'selective force' which left the ship untouched. One of the more original theories had it that the crew built a platform under the bow in order to watch a swimming race around the ship between the captain and the mate. This explained the strange grooves. The platform collapsed and all were drowned. This explained the disappearance of everyone aboard. UFOs have also been held responsible.

What are some of the more logical ideas about the mystery?

One fact to be taken into account is that everyone left the ship in obvious great haste. Mrs Briggs left her child's clothing behind, the seamen abandoned their pipes and oilskin boots. Clearly they left in panic, perhaps in deadly fear of something they believed was about to happen. They almost certainly left in the yawl and they appeared to have done so under the guidance of someone responsible – the captain or the first mate – because the chronometer, the sextant and the ship's papers were not found on board and must therefore have been taken along.

There are three credible theories as to what caused the abandonment of the *Mary Celeste*.

The first was believed to be the likely explanation by Captain Morehouse and Captain James Briggs, brother of the mystery vessel's captain. Knowing that on the morning of the 25th the wind had dropped after a night of violent storm, they thought the ship may have been becalmed in the Azores and found itself drifting toward the dangerous rocks off Santa Maria Island. Everyone on board took to the yawl for safety, staying near the ship. But suddenly a wind got up and took the ship away and, though the men in the boat rowed frantically, the *Mary Celeste* drew farther from them. In the gales that again blew up in the afternoon, a single wave would have swamped the little boat.

Against this theory is the widely accepted surmise that the *Mary Celeste* kept to a steady course for several days after the 25th. This makes it more probable that the abandonment took place on a later date.

The second theory with a logical basis was proposed by Deveau and would explain why the pump plunger was found lying on the deck. He pointed out that the ship had been through heavy storms and some of the water between decks had found its way into the holds. This may have given the impression that the ship was leaking, so the pump plunger was drawn and the pump sounded – by someone who misread the depth. He at once spread the alarm that the ship was on the point of going down. Panic followed.

This would be neither the first, nor the last, time a crew had panicked on grounds that later proved unjustified. For example, when Captain Cook's famous *Endeavour* was in difficulties off the East Australian coast, the ship's carpenter was sent to sound the well. He mistook the reading and, in the ensuing hysteria, the crew would have abandoned the ship had Cook not been able to restore calm. In 1919, the schooner *Marion G. Douglas*, which carried a cargo of timber, was abandoned by the crew off the coast of Newfoundland. They had believed their ship to be sinking – but a moment's thought would have reassured them that a ship with a cargo of timber was unlikely to go down. It went on to sail across the Atlantic without them.

The flaw in Deveau's theory is that it means there was a sudden loss of nerve on the part of the captain and this conflicts with what is known of Briggs' character. Some supporters of this theory have circumvented that point by arguing that Briggs could not exert his leadership because he suffered a heart attack during the panic.

The last of the three most likely theories was the one put forward by Winchester and it focuses on the nature of the cargo. Captain Briggs had never before carried crude alcohol and possibly did not know how it would react on the voyage. The change in temperature from wintry New York to the warmer climes around the Azores, would cause the casks to leak and sweat. Then the stormy weather, severely buffeting them, would create vapour and the pressure that built up could have been enough to blow out the forward hatch cover. The sweating would have been accompanied by rumbling noises that must certainly have sounded ominous to men who did not know the natural explanation for such sounds. Captain Briggs may have ordered the hatches opened to let some vapour escape and what looked like smoke emerged. One of the casks had been opened, which indicates that it had been inspected. If there had been a naked light in the vicinity, there could well have been a small explosion – too small to leave a trace but enough to start a panic.

In the wake of this threat, the captain's anxiety will have been increased by the presence of his wife and small daughter. Thinking primarily of their safety, he may have ordered everyone into the yawl until they saw whether or not the ship would blow up. There was no explosion – but a great gust of wind filled the sails, the towline connecting the small boat to the ship snapped and the *Mary Celeste* inexorably sailed away from them. Their little boat could not withstand the waves and winds of the ocean and finally capsized, drowning all of them.

Was this what happened? No one knows for certain and probably no one will ever know.

The *Mary Celeste* is the most famous drifter of the sea but it is only one of many others. Some have the added macabre touch of still being crewed – by corpses. In September 1894, for instance, the British brig *Abbey S. Hart* was found drifting in the Indian Ocean. A boarding party found three seamen dead in their bunks and a fourth man, apparently the captain, delirious or mad. He died an hour later without having uttered one understandable word. The ship had sailed from Java a week previously and it was assumed that some deadly fever had struck the crew down. It is known that in the days of long voyages under sail, tropical diseases could decimate a crew trapped together far from land.

Other killers at sea are less easy to explain than disease. The Dutch freighter, *Ourang Medan*, was overwhelmed by an unknown tragedy in February 1948 while steaming through the Straits of Malacca bound for Indonesia. SOS signals from the ship were heard by other vessels in the vicinity and they hurried to its assistance. The distress calls continued meanwhile, until there came an alarming message, 'All officers including captain dead, lying in chartroom and on bridge . . . Probably whole crew dead.' This was followed by a series of dots and dashes that made no sense and then the words, 'I die'. After this – silence.

When the *Ourang Medan* was located, it was drifting with the current but a thin ribbon of smoke still issued from the funnel. The captain was found dead on the bridge. Throughout the ship – in the wheelhouse, chartroom and on the decks – lay the life-less bodies of the unfortunate crew. The body of the radio oper-ator was found slumped in a chair, his fingers against the transmitter key. Even the ship's dog was found with his lips drawn back in a rictus of death. 'Their frozen faces were upturned to the sun', stated the report in the Proceedings of the Merchant Marine Council, 'the mouths were gaping open and the eyes staring.'

No wounds were discovered on the bodies and the vessel seemed undamaged. The boarding parties were uncertain what to do next, when suddenly flames surged out of the hold and spread rapidly. Everyone hastily returned to their own vessels. Within a short time, the boilers of the *Ourang Medan* exploded and the ship sank. Could the crew have been overcome by carbon monoxide or some other poisonous fumes, generated within the hold or in the boilers? If so, it is hard to see how that could have killed everyone, even those who were in the open air.

In *Invisible Horizons*, a book of sea tales, Vincent Gaddis cites an even more grisly example of a floating morgue. In the summer of 1913, the British ship *Johnson* caught sight of a sailing vessel drifting off the coast of Chile. As they drew near they could see that the masts and sails were covered with green mould. On the prow, faded with the passing of many years, could still be seen the name *Marlborough*. The timbers of the deck had decayed so greatly that they crumbled as the boarding party picked a way across them. A skeleton was discovered beneath the helm, six more were found on the bridge and 13 others elsewhere in the ship.

It was later learned that the *Marlborough* had left Littleton, New Zealand, 23 years before in January 1890, with a cargo of wool and frozen mutton. There were also several passengers aboard, including one woman. Nothing had been heard of the ship since it had been sighted on the regular course passing through the Straits of Magellan 23 years before. What had happened? Where had the ship been to remain undiscovered for nearly a quarter of a century? Could it have been trapped in an ice ocean like the schooner *Jenny* and others?

The unfortunate *Jenny* was discovered by the whaling schooner *Hope* south of Drake Strait in the Antarctic on 22 September 1860. The towering wall of ice parted abruptly and the *Jenny* emerged, the hull battered and encrusted with ice, snow upon the decks, the rigging fallen, the sails in icy shreds. The cold had preserved the corpses of the crew perfectly, in natural attitudes. The captain's body was seated in a chair, a pen in his hand and leaning backward. Examination of the log revealed that the *Jenny* had been imprisoned in the ice for 37 years. The last entry, signed by the captain, read '4 May 1823. No food for 71 days. I am the only one left alive.'

The ice of the Arctic Ocean on the other side of the world proved too much for the *Octavius* in 1762. This vessel left England in 1761 bound for China On the return journey the captain is thought to have decided to look for the elusive Northwest Passage rather than to sail all the way around South America. But they got no further than the north coast of Alaska, when the ice trapped them. Thirteen years later the whaleship *Herald* caught sight of the *Octavius* drifting into open water between icebergs. The crew of the *Herald* sensed at once that this was a ship of the dead and they only reluctantly obeyed their captain's order to lower the longboat in preparation for boarding. Captain Warren led the party.

On the ice-coated deck of the *Octavius* there was no sign of life. Captain Warren made his way to the forecastle and after kicking away the snow, opened the door. He was met by a heavy musky odour. Stepping inside he saw that every bed, 28 in all, was occupied by a dead seaman, perfectly preserved by the freezing air. The men were heavily wrapped with blankets and clothing but the Arctic cold had proved too great for them.

In the captain's cabin, a dank and mustier smell greeted them. A thin green mould had spread over the dead captain's face although his body was otherwise well preserved. He lay slumped at a table, his hands spread out and a pen beside them. Captain Warren handed the logbook to one of his sailors and stepped into the next cabin. There he found the body of a woman in the bunk covered with blankets. Gaddis writes, 'Unlike the captain, her flesh and features were unmarked and lifelike. Her head was resting on her elbow and it appeared as if she had been watching some activity when she died. Following the line of her vision, Captain Warren saw the body of a man cross-legged on the floor and slouched over. In one hand he held a flint and in the other a piece of steel. In front of him was a heap of wood shavings. Apparently he had been attempting to start a fire when death had claimed him. Beside the man was a heavy sailor's jacket. When the captain picked it up, he found the body of a small boy underneath.'

Captain Warren's men got panicky and insisted that he let them return to their ship. Back on the *Herald* the captain settled down to read the log, only to find that the sailor entrusted with its care had dropped the centre pages into the sea while hastening into the longboat. The surviving front pages gave details of the ship's company and recorded the successful start of the voyage to China. The account of the following 14 months was missing and the only remaining page was the final one. Dated 11 November 1762 it read, 'We have now been enclosed in the ice 17 days and our approximate position is Longitude 160W, Latitude 75N. The fire went out yesterday, and our master has been trying to rekindle it again but without success. He has handed the steel and flint to the mate. The master's son died this morning and his wife says she no longer feels the terrible cold. The rest of us seem to have no relief from the agony.'

The most outstanding feature of the discovery of the *Octavius* is that it occurred in Greenland waters, at the eastern end of the Northwest Passage, even though the ship had been locked in the ice when north of Alaska, at the western end. Only one explanation was possible. The ship must have found the Northwest Passage on its own. Season by season it had crept eastward, frozen up each winter and drifting on again during the short summer thaw, until at last it reached the North Atlantic. Ironically, the *Octavius* was the first ship to navigate the Northwest Passage but the crew and the captain never knew it.

Another ship that went it alone in the Arctic is the *SS Baychimo*. Owned by the Hudson's Bay Company, the *Baychimo* is a trim, steel-clad cargo steamer, considered the finest possible craft for battling the pack ice and the floes. The ship joined the far northern fleet in 1921 and made nine annual visits to the bleak Arctic coasts of Canada, buying furs from the trading posts along the Beaufort Sea and the McClintock Channel. No other vessel had managed to make the perilous trip more than two years in succession.

On 6 July 1931, the *Baychimo* left Vancouver, Canada, with a crew of 36 under the command of Captain John Cornwall. Passing through the Bering Straits, the ship entered the Northwest Passage. The captain spent hundreds of thousands of dollars buying furs along the Victoria Island coast. On the return journey the ship was caught in early winter pack ice during a howling blizzard and was unable to move. With the vessel in danger of being crushed, Captain Cornwall and his crew established a camp on safer ice closer to shore and prepared to wait there till the spring. A three-day storm early in November brought a rise in temperature, enabling the men to emerge for a look around. They found that the *Baychimo* had snapped its moorings and disappeared.

Captain Cornwall led his men to the safety of Point Barrow, 50 miles away, where they learned that Eskimos had sighted the missing ship 45 miles southwest of its former position. The crew and a party of Eskimos managed to reach the ship and after 15 days of difficult work, removed the bulk of the valuable cargo. Before they could finish, however the *Baychimo* had vanished again.

The following spring, the ship was observed 300 miles further east near Herschel Island. A young trapper and explorer, Leslie Melvin, found the *Baychimo* while on a journey by dog team. He boarded the drifter and reported that it was in excellent condition.

Since then the *SS Baychimo* has been sighted frequently. A party of Eskimos boarded the ship in 1933, but were trapped by a sudden storm and drifted for 10 days before they could make their way to shore on a raft of ice. In June 1934, Isobel Hutchinson, a Scottish botanist, sighted it and went aboard. Year after year, reports of sightings have come in from whalers, prospectors, Eskimos, travellers. In November 1939 an attempt to tow the ship into port had to be abandoned in bad weather. Still it survived. After a period of no reports on the *Baychimo*, a party of Eskimos saw it in March 1956, moving north in the Beaufort Sea. In March 1962, fishermen found the still apparently seaworthy ship in the same area. The *Baychimo* seems to have disappeared since then but may yet turn up again. There is no parallel in modern times for a ship to sail the seas without a crew for so long a time. For over 30 years the *Baychimo* survived the ice in one of the cruellest seas of the world.

Some ships appear to have a will of their own as well as a sense of survival. Two in particular seem to have been strangely devoted to their owners. One of these was the *SS Humboldt* whose captain, Elijah G. Baufman, was the only master the ship ever knew. The *Humboldt* began its career in 1898 as a passenger and freight carrier between Seattle and Alaska. Captain Baufman reckoned that during the Alaskan Gold Rush, it brought back gold valued at over $100 million. Long after those frantic years were over, the *Humboldt* continued to work the Northwest Pacific ports but in 1934 the time came for Baufman and his beloved vessel to retire. Baufman moved from Seattle to San Francisco and the *Humboldt* was taken farther south to San Pedro, destined for the scrapyard.

On 8 August 1935, Baufman died. That night the crew of the coastguard cutter *Tamaroa* near San Pedro harbour noticed an old steamer making for the open sea. The only light was a red warning light at the stern. No one was aboard, no smoke came from the funnel. It was the *Humboldt*. Somehow the ship had managed to slip its moorings and drift through the harbour as though determined to sail north to join its former captain. It had done this on the very day its old master died.

Seattle has another tale of mysterious rapport between man and boat. Captain Martin Olsen was a seine fisherman and for many years he went out in the *Sea-Lion* to net salmon in the deep creeks of Puget Sound. When he retired he beached the *Sea-Lion* on a sandy point near his home across the sound from Seattle. For 10 years the boat settled deeper into the sand – but on the day Captain Olsen died, a day unmarked by storm or abnormal tides, the boat is said to have floated off the sandspit and begun drifting around the bay. Three days later it attended the captain's funeral, drifting up to the beach on Bainbridge Island at the point closest to the cemetery. After the funeral, the *Sea-Lion* drifted away and a few days later returned to the sandspit on which it had passed the previous 10 years.

Another uncanny tale of a ship seeming to act on its own is the classic story of the *Frigorifique*'s 'revenge'. This ship was the first French vessel to carry refrigeration equipment and it enjoyed eight prosperous years bringing frozen meat from Uruguay to France, before meeting its doom in a thick fog off the French coast on 19 March 1884. Captain Raoul Lambert heard a siren wail but could not tell from what direction the sound came. He ordered the engines stopped and blew three warning blasts. Nothing more was heard, so the *Frigorifique* moved forward again at low speed, tolling the bell continuously.

Danger came suddenly. The dark hulk of another ship emerged through the fog to starboard and though the helm was pulled hard to port there was no escaping the inevitable crash. The rammed *Frigorifiqu*e at once began to list heavily and the captain ordered his crew of 11 men to abandon ship.

The other vessel in the accident was the English collier *Rumney*, bound for La Rochelle from Cardiff. The *Rumney* was undamaged and took the crew of the *Frigorifique* aboard. By then the stricken vessel had disappeared in the fog.

Two miles farther on, Captain John Turner of the *Rumney* noticed a ship bearing down on him through the fog. It was the *Frigorifique*, no longer listing, smoke pouring from the stack and seemingly bent on wreaking vengeance for being rammed. The Rumney's helmsman desperately swung the wheel to starboard to put it on a course parallel to the French ship. He acted just in time. The *Rumney* escaped the prow of the *Frigorifique* by just a few inches. Once more the avenging ship vanished into the fog.

The two captains discussed the mystery. Could it have been

another ship, resembling the *Frigorifique*? Captain Lambert shook his head. He knew his own ship.

Less than a mile later, the *Frigorifique* came at the *Rumney* again, silent, speeding, inexorable, the prow once more aimed to charge.

'Hard to starboard', shouted Captain Turner. Then, 'Reverse engines'. Neither manoeuvre worked; this time there was no escape. The *Frigorifique* rammed the collier with a thundering impact and water began pouring into the hold and engine room. Once more the *Frigorifique* vanished as the *Rumney* began to sink. Two boats, bearing the separate crews, pulled away and watched the English ship go down.

In 15 minutes the lifeboats had rowed out of the fog and sighted the French coast on the horizon. Suddenly, out of the mist behind them they saw the *Frigorifique* yet again, moving in wide circles with the boilers still sending out power. Captain Lambert decided to go aboard and try to make harbour. After some difficulty the two lifeboats managed to pull alongside and the captain and several volunteers went aboard. There they discovered how the *Frigorifique* had been able to pursue and ram the *Rumney*. The helmsman had left the wheel lashed hard over to starboard and had forgotten it in the rush of leaving the ship. This made the *Frigorifique* go around in circles after it had been abandoned. Because the *Rumney* was moving in its straight course at reduced speed, one of the *Frigorifique*'s circular swings brought it head on into the collier.

Although the first ramming had damaged the *Frigorifique*, the engine room was not flooded. But the second collision had doomed the refrigerated freighter. Water was rising quickly. It seems as though the *Frigorifique* had taken that third circle to avenge itself and was then ready to sink in peace. For the second time in an hour, the French captain gave the order to abandon ship and the lifeboats rowed away. The *Frigorifique* rolled over onto its side and slowly went down. The honour of the wounded ship had been satisfied.

Other mysteries of the sea have to do with the sea itself playing strange tricks, extending the long arm of coincidence around the globe. Take the case of the *SS Saxilby*, which left Newfoundland in November 1933 bound for South Wales.

Somewhere in the North Atlantic it vanished. Twenty-nine men were on board.

Early in 1936, a cocoa can was washed ashore near the Welsh village of Aberavon. Inside was a message saying, '*SS Saxilby* sinking somewhere off the Irish coast. Love to sister, brothers and Dinah. Joe Okane.' Joe Okane, a member of the crew aboard the lost steamer, had lived in Aberavon, the message was addressed to his relatives in Aberavon – and the can had drifted ashore less than a mile from their home.

Another example of a message with a strong homing instinct was one sent by the New Zealander, Ross Alexander. In 1952, the troopship he was on ran aground on a reef north of Darwin, Australia, and while awaiting rescue he threw an SOS note overboard in a wine bottle. In 1955, back home in New Zealand, he was walking along the beach one day. There he found the bottle which still contained the message he had entrusted to the sea three years before.

In 1934, Doyle Branscum enclosed a photograph of himself in a bottle and threw it into a river in Arkansas. In 1958, Bill Headstream found the bottle near his home in Largo, Florida. Oddly enough, the two men had been boyhood friends who had not heard from each other for many years. Headstream returned the photograph to Branscum with a letter telling what had happened to him in the 24 years since 1934.

These incidents are astounding enough but the case of Coghlan's coffin seems to make the impossible come true. Charles Francis Coghlan was an actor. Born on Prince Edward Island, Canada, in 1841, he first appeared on the London stage at the age of 18. Over the years he acquired an international reputation as a Shakespearean actor. On his last tour in the United States, he appeared with Lily Langtry. While they were performing in Galveston, Texas, he died on 27 November 1899. His lead-lined coffin was placed in a granite vault in a Galveston cemetery, many thousands of miles from his birthplace on Prince Edward Island, which he always regarded as his true home though he was so often away from it.

On 8 September 1900, Galveston was struck by a hurricane. Six thousand people were killed and thousands of homes were reduced to rubble. Floodwaters poured into the cemeteries, sweeping coffins out of the graves and shattering vaults. A log jam of coffins floated out into the Gulf of Mexico. Many sank or were washed up on the coast but Coghlan's coffin must have drifted southeast until it was caught in the West Indian current which carried it northeastward past Florida into the Gulf Stream. In this mighty current, the coffin was borne northward until it reached the vicinity of Newfoundland. There a storm must have blown it out of the current because for the next few years it drifted around the eastern Canadian coast.

In October 1908, several fishermen from Prince Edward Island sailed out to set their nets in the Gulf of St. Lawrence. They came upon a large box floating in the waves and towed it back to shore. The wood was encrusted with barnacles but a silver plate on the top told the astonished fishermen that it was the coffin of Charles Coghlan. Only a few miles away stood the village where Coghlan had been born and raised. Also nearby was the home in which he had stayed between his long tours abroad. The actor's body was reburied near the church where he had been baptized. Charles Coghlan had at last reached home to stay.

Not so Thomas 'Dusty' Miller, captain of the motorship *Joyita* which has been called the *Mary Celeste* of the Pacific. The *Joyita* was a twin-screw ship that met with disaster in October 1955, some time after leaving Apia in Western Samoa. It was heading for Fakaofo in the Tokelau Islands, a mere 270 miles to the north. On 10 November, more than a month after setting out, the *Joyita* was found abandoned and half-foundering. But the ship was cork-lined and therefore practically unsinkable. Captain Miller had known that perfectly well – in fact, he had often boasted of it. His mate 'Chuck' Simpson, an American Indian married to a Samoan woman, also knew of the five-inch slabs of cork that lined each of the three holds. Why had they abandoned a ship that should stay afloat indefinitely?

Perhaps they had not, for there were signs that two men had stayed aboard. An awning had been erected either to catch water or to keep off the sun. Where had these men gone?

There could be no doubt whatever that the *Joyita* had been in trouble. Only one of the two engines was working, and the radio was defective. Although the ship could stay afloat, it could not be called seaworthy.

The vessel was taken to Suva, Fiji, where it was drydocked and pumped out. The basic cause of the trouble then became apparent. Under the boiler room floor was a badly corroded section of pipe, which explained why the ship had become waterlogged. Four mattresses were found in the engine room, brought there apparently to block the leak if it could be located. The two bilge pumps were blocked with cotton waste and hardly worked at all. The port engine clutch was partly disconnected and into a brass T-piece in the port engine's salt water cooling system had been threaded a galvanized pipe. This had started the corrosion that results when a ferrous metal is joined to a nonferrous metal.

How had a ship in such bad shape been entrusted with the lives of 25 persons, including children?

The *Joyita* had started out well. It had been built in 1931 for Roland West, a movie director and husband of the movie star Jewel Carmen. *Joyita* means 'Little Jewel'. In the war it was used by the United States navy as a patrol ship and after the war it was converted into a fishing boat with cork-lined refrigerated holds. In 1952, Dusty Miller chartered the *Joyita* and began fishing operations in Hawaii. His first success was followed by consecutive failures. Working in Pago Pago in American Samoa, the ship's refrigerating equipment failed and much of the catch went bad. Miller got into debt and the American authorities seized some of the ship's papers.

Dusty left Pago Pago in March 1955 for Apia in Western Samoa, which is under New Zealand trusteeship. It was there that he met R. D. Pearless, recently appointed District Officer of the Tokelau Islands. Miller took him on a combined fishing trip and tour of the islands and Pearless suggested to the Western Samoan government that they charter the *Joyita* to provide regular transport of supplies to the Tokelaus. This would have solved Miller's problems completely. Although he was destitute, he would at least have a steady job sailing the ship he loved. The only snag was his inability to provide the papers still held in Pago Pago. For five months the *Joyita* lay at anchor in Apia harbour and during this period Miller nearly starved, finding food and money where he could. He is described as 'good-natured', a colourful character who liked to wear a sarong at sea.

He was honest and paid his debts when he had the money but the long wait from May till September turned him into a desperate man. Personal matters were also troubling him. Back in Wales, the woman he had married shortly after the war was suing him for divorce on grounds of desertion.

When the *Joyita* was finally given permission to sail it was in poor condition – and Captain Miller knew it. He told the charterers that he would be able to fix the faulty clutch at sea. Even more unwisely, he failed to test the radio transmitter before leaving. A simple check would have revealed a break in the aerial cord above the transmitter that was to prevent the ship's signals from being heard more than two miles away.

Miller saw the journey as his last hope. He hastily found himself a crew that included two Gilbert Islanders, Tokoka, the bosun and Tanini, the engineer, who had worked for him before. Pearless was impatient to go. The Tokelau Islanders needed medical supplies and there were 70 tons of copra in the islands waiting for collection. Among the other passengers were two doctors and two representatives of the chartering company. One of these, G. K. Williams, carried £1,000 in silver and banknotes to buy copra. The remainder of the passengers were local people of the islands.

Before the *Joyita* had left harbour its engine broke down. When Miller finally got it going again at 5 am the following morning, he and his crew had been working through the night and were short of temper. But Miller trusted to luck – the luck that had failed him so often in the past.

Disaster probably struck the *Joyita* the first night out from Apia. Heavy seas broke the corroded pipe below the boiler room floor and water poured in. The pumps were inadequate because of the blocked suction pipes. The port engine may have already stopped. The starboard engine stopped when water reached a height of 18 inches. All lights would then go out. The radio transmitter was tuned to the distress frequency (where the rescuers found it a month later) but the broken cord failed to carry the signals.

Robin Maugham, the novelist who eventually bought the *Joyita*, guesses that at some stage Miller was incapacitated. In view of what they had been through, it would not be surprising if one of the passengers entered into an argument with him. Miller may have fallen or been pushed from the bridge to the deck, suffering severe head injuries. Maugham's support for this theory comes from the discovery in the scuppers of a doctor's stethoscope, a scalpel, some needles and catgut and four lengths of bloodstained bandages. One of the doctors may have given Miller first aid. The other passengers either did not know the boat was cork-lined, or with water clearly rising inside, no longer believed it. The *Joyita* carried no dinghy but her floats were hastily launched, the passengers clambered aboard and drifted away. In the high seas they must soon have capsized.

Someone remained on the vessel and built the awning. Maugham thinks this may have been the Gilbert Islander, Tanini, who was devoted to Captain Miller. But then what happened? At this point another mystery arises. Did some new panic cause Miller and his companion to abandon ship? That is unlikely, since Miller knew his boat was unsinkable. Even if he had died of his wounds, his companion would surely have remained. One theory is that the drifting vessel encountered a pirate ship and that Miller and his companions were murdered. It is true that some of the cargo was missing but it seems more likely that it was thrown overboard in the original panic to lighten the ship. William's strongbox, which contained £950 in Bank of Samoa banknotes and £50 in silver, was missing. It seems unlikely that he took it on the raft with him, knowing the Bank of Samoa would replace at least the banknotes. The crew of the other vessel may not have come as pirates, but may have been unable to resist temptation after boarding the *Joyita* and finding the money.

Even this explanation leaves questions unanswered. Chuck Simpson also knew the boat was unsinkable and would never have chosen the alternative of a raft in shark-infested seas. What happened to him? Was he also thrown from the bridge and injured?

Dusty Miller's wife had to wait till 1961 before her husband could be declared officially dead. The judge granting her a divorce on grounds of desertion and presumption of death said of him, 'Had he reached his destination he might eventually have become a millionaire. But he never got there. Instead he became a corpse.'

The exact manner in which he met his untimely death is unknown. It seems unlikely that the full facts will ever come out now to clear up the mystery.

CHAPTER 6

RIDDLES OF THE AIR

A plane goes down in the South Pacific with a famous aviator and her navigator aboard. Why did no trace of them ever turn up? The disappearance of Amelia Earhart in 1937, is one of the great unexplained mysteries of aviation history but there are many others. A plane landed by two corpses . . . the vanishing crew of a blimp in mid-air . . . the mysterious explosion of the luxury dirigible Hindenburg *. . . the lost trailblazers of the polar flying route. Will such puzzles ever be explained?*

At about 10:45 am on 16 August 1942, a military blimp drifted ashore at Fort Funston, California. The door of its gondola was open – there was no one aboard.

In wartime America on the West Coast, blimps on anti-submarine duty were a common sight, so the hapless airship did not frighten two fishermen on the beach. They simply tried to rescue it. They caught hold of the tie lines in an attempt to pull it down but a sudden gust of wind forced them to let go after they had been dragged across the sand for 100 yards or so. The derelict blimp raked against a cliff along the beach, at which point one of its 300-pound depth charges was released and plummeted onto the earth at the side of the highway below. Lightened by the loss of the charge, the blimp shot up into the air again and drifted southeasterly. About half an hour later, the airship settled to earth in a street in Daly City, just south of San Francisco.

Where was the two-man crew? What had caused them to abandon their vehicle? Why had they failed to complete their mission?

United States military investigators reconstructed the case in an effort to solve the mystery. Blimp L-8 had taken off from Moffett Field at around 6 am that day. Its two officers, Lieutenant Ernest D. Cody and Ensign Charles E. Adams, were experienced and reliable. The weather was cloudy but good and for nearly two hours the airship made regular radio contacts. At 7:50 am, Cody had sent a radio message saying that he had seen a suspicious oil slick. 'I'm taking the ship down to 300 feet for a closer look', he signalled. 'Stand by'.

The L-8's position was about five miles east of Farallon Islands at that point. Two armed patrol boats had been alerted and were observing the blimp. Two fishing trawlers in the area also watched the airship circling lower. Guessing that it might be on the track of a submarine, the fishermen hastily dragged their nets in and retired to a safe distance in case there was a depth charge explosion. Instead of making a bombing run, however, the blimp suddenly shot upward and disappeared into a cloud.

At 8:05 am, three hours before the L-8 came to rest in Daly City, the control tower at Moffett Field had tried to contact the blimp but had no response. After further unsuccessful tries to get in touch, search planes were sent out. At 10:40, one plane briefly caught sight of the airship as it rose above the cloud cover and immediately descended into the cover again. Five minutes later, the blimp had floated onto the beach where the fishermen who tried to catch it had seen it empty.

When the salvage crew investigated the Blimp L-8's gondola, they found all the equipment in position. Parachutes and rubber raft were properly in place. The only missing items were two bright yellow life jackets but that was understandable because the crew was required to wear them when in flight over water, as Cody and Adams had been. Nothing had been damaged. There was no water in the gondola's lower deck. The motors were turned off, although one throttle was open and the other half open. Ignition switches were still on.

The open door and the sudden ascent of the airship after Cody's last message suggested that the two officers fell into the sea. Perhaps, it was conjectured, one officer fell part way out and when the second came to his aid, both fell out. But the position of the throttles contradicts this theory, for why would the pilot leave one throttle on full and the other halfway open when he went to help his companion? Besides, no fall or splash was seen by the fishermen or the patrol boat crews who had observed the blimp as it descended for its inspection of the oil slick, even though both men must have had their yellow life jackets on. Finally, no bodies or life jackets were ever recovered after extensive searching.

The absence of water in the gondola's lower deck showed that the blimp had not touched down in the ocean at any time. This countered any idea that Cody and Adams were surprised by a surfacing Japanese submarine and taken prisoner. The intervention of a submarine had always been considered improbable anyway and Japanese records after the war confirmed that no submarine had been in the area at the time of the Blimp L-8 episode.

To this day, no one has any idea what happened to Cody and Adams and their fate remains an unsolved mystery of the air.

In the less than a century since humans have been flying around the world in airships, planes and other craft, the air already rivals the sea as a source of mysterious happenings. In the early days, odd accidents were only to be expected. Airplanes were light and unstable, airships were difficult to manoeuvre and for many years both could be seriously affected by any sudden change of wind. Many crashes were the understandable teething troubles of a new science and could be laid to mechanical faults that were corrected in subsequent designs. But the fate of the Zeppelin L-50 after a bombing raid over England in 1917 is a mystery. Likewise, the cause of the fire that destroyed the *Hindenburg*, last and greatest of the zeppelins, has never been established. Accidents such as these have never been satisfactorily explained.

What are some of the enigmas of the air? Some aircraft have unexpectedly crashed, others have vanished off the face of the earth. Pilots have disappeared in front of witnesses, passengers have stepped out of planes for no clear reason. There may be an explanation for each of these strange events but so far the answer has eluded everyone. For example, what could have happened to the British Lancastrian airliner, *Star Dust* as it approached the airport in Santiago, Chile on 12 August 1947? A radio message from the apparently doomed plane repeated the word 'stendec' rapidly three times at the end of the last call ever heard from the crew. The *Star Dust* vanished utterly in the next three minutes. No trace of it was found. Was 'stendec' a warning? Did the strange word contain a clue to what was happening? Would knowing its meaning help to explain the plane's disappearance? Perhaps, but the word has never been deciphered.

World War I gave rise to many puzzles about planes and pilots. One of the oddest events occurred on a fine September morning in 1916, when six German fighter planes were returning from a dawn patrol over the French lines. As the squadron was passing a thick cloud bank over Armentieres, a British two-seater reconnaissance plane suddenly flew out of the cloud toward them. The German planes scattered, just managing to avoid a collision, then darted back to attack, raking the small plane with machine gun fire. To their surprise, the British plane did not return their fire. Nor did it alter course but continued in a wide circle to the left. A second attack still failed to down the plane. Cautiously, suspecting a trick, the German squadron leader flew closer until only a few yards separated the two aircraft; then he banked steeply and looked into the open cockpit. A chilling sight met his eyes. Dead, but still strapped into their seats, sat the pilot and the radio operator, their sightless eyes staring ahead, their uniforms smeared with blood from a multitude of wounds. The German pilot dipped his wings in a gesture of respect and ordered the squadron to return to home base.

The pilotless British plane continued to fly for another 40 minutes until the engine ran out of fuel. Even then it did not crash but glided smoothly down to a safe landing in an open field. An autopsy on the two fliers revealed that they had been killed by a single bullet that passed through one's left lung and buried itself in the base of the other's brain. Extraordinary as that may seem, it is equalled by the fact that although hundreds of bullet holes were found on the plane, not one of them had struck a vital part – propeller, engine, fuel tanks and controls were all undamaged. It was as if ghostly hands had brought the plane safely back to land.

In contrast, it was a mysterious crash that killed the German war hero Max Immelmann, the air ace known as *Der Adler von Lille* (the Eagle of Lille). On the morning of 18 June 1916, Immelmann shot down his sixteenth enemy plane. That afternoon he took off again and joined a fierce air battle between four

German and seven British aircraft. German ground artillery was effective and shrapnel was whining dangerously close. Suddenly, Immelmann's plane was seen to nose upward, whipstall, and fall into a diving spiral. At 8,000 feet the plane began to come apart. The tail section twisted free, the rear part of the fuselage ripped away and finally even the engine tore itself loose and hurtled like a stone to the ground. Buried within the twisted mass of steel the Eagle of Lille lay dead. The cause of the crash has never been determined.

Wishing to preserve the legend of Immelmann's invincibility, the German High Command gave out that his plane had failed in mid-air. The designer of Immelmann's fighter plane was not prepared to have his aircraft blamed however. He examined the wreckage and found evidence that the fuselage had been sliced in two by shrapnel. A British report provided a third version of events, when it announced that an Allied plane had shot down a similar plane at the time and place in question. Which account is correct? It will probably never be known.

Mystery also surrounds the last flight of Georges Guynemer, who by September 1917 was the leading French ace with 54 German planes to his credit. Eight times he had been shot down and escaped unharmed. The French people knew him as 'Georges the Miraculous'. But his luck came to an end on 11 September, when he took to the air over Ypres with two other members of his celebrated *Stork Squadron*. Catching sight of a German two-seater in the distance, he signalled to his companions to stay behind as cover and lookout, then banked his plane into a dive and pursued his adversary. Meanwhile a group of German fighters flew up and Guynemer's companions became occupied in luring them away. Some minutes later one of the French pilots returned to see how Guynemer was faring. His plane was nowhere to be seen. A search up and down the lines and in the sky above the clouds revealed nothing. Guynemer never turned up again.

In the ordinary way of things, Guynemer's death would have been claimed by the Germans but no announcement was forth-coming. A rumour came filtering through to the effect that Guynemer had been shot down by a German pilot named Wissemann and after a longer interval than usual, a German communique was received giving details of his death. But the date given was 10 September instead of 11. The French also received word from the Red Cross that Guynemer had been given a military funeral in Poelcapelle, Flanders.

This news later proved to add to the mystery. When Allied infantry captured Poelcapelle a month afterward, they were unable to find Guynemer's grave. The Germans responded by saying that Guynemer's plane had been brought down near Poelcapelle cemetery and that the badly wounded pilot had to be left beside it because an intense Allied bombardment was under way. Guynemer's body and the plane had been shot to pieces in the ensuing barrage.

What this account does not explain is why news of the French ace's death was so long in coming, nor why the Red Cross reported his military funeral at Poelcapelle. If the Red Cross was wrong, whose body was buried in the grave that could not be found? Some believe that Guynemer met a death the Germans thought best to conceal. Perhaps he died in captivity. Whatever the conjectures, no further news concerning him was ever received.

The German pre-war development of rigid dirigibles had given them an immense advantage when war came. Zeppelin airships made many bombing raids over England and if the physical damage they inflicted was slight by the standards of later wars, the psychological effect was great.

On 19 October 1917, a fleet of 11 zeppelins rendezvoused over England for one of the largest bombing raids of the war. They climbed to 16,500 feet, spread out over Hull, Sheffield and Grimsby, dropped their bombs and turned for home. But though the guns far below were powerless to reach them, the zeppelins soon found themselves at the mercy of the elements. The wind changed. Tailwinds that had been assisting their flight back to Germany became violent and at high altitudes reached almost hurricane force. Creaking and rolling, the airships made their way across the English Channel where shore batteries shot fire rockets up toward them. Hastily the commanders dropped ballast and rose out of range to 20,000 feet. But they were scarcely better off. Engines and men struggled to keep working in the thin, icy air. As the zeppelins came over France the gales scattered them across a wide area. For Zeppelin L-50, commanded by Captain Schwonder, the journey ended in tragedy and mystery.

Seven zeppelins managed to make their way back to base but five were still above France the next day and running low on fuel. The L-44 was shot down over the French lines. The L-45 managed to get to the Mediterranean coast where it landed on a sandbank – the crew smashed the engines and set fire to the gasbags. The crew of the L-49 tried to do the same when their airship landed but were too groggy from oxygen starvation to prevent French soldiers from capturing them and the zeppelin. Only the L-50 remained in the air.

Captain Schwonder turned east, hoping to cross the French Alps into neutral Switzerland but the crew could not function properly, as the oxygen supply became shorter. The airship could not even clear the first mountain peak and slumped into it, wiping off the control gondola and one of the engine gondolas. A number of crew members survived the crash but four unconscious airmen remained in the dirigible when it shot up to 21,000 feet and drifted away.

Schwonder and the other survivors watched it disappear into the Alpine fog. Later that day it floated over the captured crew of the L-45 and out to sea. When last sighted it was far out in the Mediterranean. It then disappeared without trace and its fate remains a matter for supposition. It may have descended into the sea, or winds may have carried it across to North Africa, where it slowly drifted down in some inaccessible and unexplored reach of the Sahara Desert.

After World War I, air travel began to establish itself as the modern way of travel. Many wealthy businessmen owned their own planes and hired pilots to chauffeur them. Between England's airport at Croydon and Brussels, the flying time was about two hours. It was a route Alfred Loewenstein travelled often. On 4 July 1928, the plane he had boarded in Croydon reached Belgium, but Loewenstein did not. When he climbed the short flight of steps into the rear of his three-engine Dutch-built Fokker VII, he had embarked on his last journey, leaving an unsolved riddle.

Loewenstein was a well-known international financier who was seldom out of the news. He lived like a prince, making and spending millions in business deals said by some to be dubious.

That summer he was under a blackmail threat regarding his financial dealings. Loewenstein certainly had problems on his mind as he climbed into his Fokker at Croydon. But the previous night, a private detective had discovered the identity of the blackmailer and Loewenstein was preparing his counter-attack.

Those whom Loewenstein spoke to at Croydon airport that afternoon remembered him as being his usual good-humoured self, perhaps only a little tired after a long day in London in the July heat. He gave no indication of depression or despair.

Loewenstein's plane had one unusual feature. When the rear outside door was opened, it exposed the toilet and washbasin area but this compartment could be shut from sight when passengers were boarding by opening the door alongside it that led to the cabin. This was a dual-purpose door, either shutting off the cabin from the toilet and rear of the plane, or shutting off just the toilet to make the whole rear area and the cabin one long continuous space. In flight the door was always closed on the cabin.

In the thickly carpeted cabin, Loewenstein took his place at a table toward the front of the plane. His private secretary, Arthur Hodgson sat at a table alongside. Behind Loewenstein was his diminutive valet, Fred Baxter and in the fourth corner two typists were busy at their typewriters on the table between them. As the plane reached the channel the co-pilot glanced back through the window of the cockpit door and saw Loewenstein with his head halfway out of the sliding window next to him, apparently looking down at the sea. The pilot, remembering that high flying gave his employer attacks of breathlessness, thought Loewenstein might be feeling the need for more air. Although the plane was only 4,000 feet above sea level even the slightly lower oxygen content at that height could make breathing uncomfortable for him.

Halfway over the channel Loewenstein walked down the cabin to the toilet, shutting the door on the cabin after him. It was the last time he was seen alive. Ten minutes later Hodgson became aware of his employer's long absence and spoke to Baxter. The valet knocked on the door to the rear. There was no reply. Hodgson gripped the handle and pushed. The door opened and the two men stared in disbelief. The whole rear area of the plane, including the toilet, was empty. But the outside door was open, shaking slightly. The incredible had happened. Loewenstein had fallen out.

The typists both went into hysterics and the valet collapsed, teeth chattering in fear. Only Hodgson retained some presence of mind. Since the engines were too loud for conversation to be heard, he wrote a brief note to the pilot. The pilot brought the plane down on a stretch of beach north of Dunkirk, in order to try to establish what had happened before they faced airport officials and the press.

Was Loewenstein's disappearance accident, suicide or murder? The first two possibilities seemed to be ruled out when tests on similar planes showed that only by exceptional strength was it possible to open the outside door more than a couple of inches during flight. Murder also seemed unlikely inasmuch as Loewenstein had been in the compartment alone at the time. A fourth possibility was suggested when the announcement of the financier's disappearance led to a sharp fall in the value of shares in his companies. According to this theory, Loewenstein knew that a crash was coming and had laid an ingenious plan for disappearing. It consisted of concealing himself in a secret compartment at the rear of the plane and, on landing on Dunkirk beach by arrangement, slipping away unnoticed by immigration officials.

When Loewenstein's business affairs were examined they were found to be in good shape and when 15 days later his body was picked up by a channel trawler, all the wilder theories had to be abandoned. The autopsy revealed no evidence of a struggle. Loewenstein had been alive when he struck the water. The impact caused multiple injuries but his death was by drowning.

How had it happened? Further tests, this time on Loewenstein's own plane, showed that it was possible to push open the outside door to about 18 inches during flight. Although there can be no certainty about what took place in the rear of the plane that day, it does not seem likely that Loewenstein, even if caught by another attack of breathlessness, would have been so unwise as to open the outside door to get more air. The dual-purpose door looms as a likely cause of an accident that may have occurred like this. Loewenstein leaves the toilet to return to the cabin. With his mind preoccupied by thoughts of the man blackmailing him, he ignores the nearer door. It is the door that opens into the cabin but he thinks of it as the door of the toilet. Instead he turns the handle of the other door, the outside door. As he tries to open it he encounters some resistance but still he does not realize his mistake. He pushes his body against the stubborn door and it opens – not very far but far enough for the slipstream to drag him out. His cry of alarm is lost in the roar of the engines.

Is that what happened? It is only a guess. There can be no certainty.

The decade of the 1920s was an era in which fame and fortune could be won by pilots who broke speed records or were the first to fly over a given route. Several determined contenders vanished somewhere in the Atlantic in the exciting months before and after Lindbergh's nonstop solo flight in May 1927. One of these was young Paul Redfern, who set off in August 1927 on a solo trip from Brunswick, Georgia to Rio de Janeiro, Brazil, 4,700 miles away. He managed to reach the northern coast of South America in his green and gold Stinton Detroiter *Port of Brunswick* and was glimpsed flying toward the impenetrable jungle of Guyana and the Amazon. Then he disappeared. Over the next dozen years, several expeditions searched the jungle for some trace of him. Rumours had come back that relics of his lost plane had been seen in the possession of Amerindians. Some fanciful versions of his fate would have it that he was living among the Indians, venerated as a 'great white god' who had come out of the skies. In all probability, the *Port of Brunswick* crashed in a tropical storm, killing Redfern instantly. But the facts may never be known.

The same must be said of Amelia Earhart, one of the heroines of early aviation. In 1928 she became the first woman to fly the Atlantic. In 1932 she flew the Atlantic solo and broke the speed record in doing so. In 1937 she set off to fly around the world.

'I feel that I've got one more big flight in me', she said.

She was then 39 and had been married for seven years to a successful New York publisher. Though often in the limelight, she was unprepossessing and unspoiled by fame. This was her second try for an around-the-world flight.

On 1 June 1937, Amelia Earhart took off from Miami, Florida in her twin-engined Lockheed Electra. Her navigator was Frederick Noonan, a man with many years of experience with a commercial airline. Forty gruelling days and 22,000 miles later they reached New Guinea by way of South America, Africa, India, and Southeast Asia. From Lae on the eastern coast of New Guinea they faced the most difficult leg of their journey, the 2,556 miles to tiny Howland Island. Howland was a mere speck in the ocean, only 1½ miles long, a half mile wide and a few feet above sea level. A runway had just been built on the island and the Electra would be the first plane to land there if the pair managed to reach it. Even the best navigator would be hard put to locate the pinpoint of land, however.

Because of a slight headwind, the Electra's flight time was expected to be 20 hours. The plane carried fuel for 24. The plan was to leave Lae at 10 am and fly all day by dead reckoning, checking their position as they flew over the Solomon Islands. That night Noonan would navigate by the stars and, as they approached Howland Island the next morning, they would home in on radio signals from the United States Coast Guard cutter *Itasca*, anchored off the island for that purpose. The critical section of the journey was the 500 miles in the middle when they would be out of contact both with Lae behind them and the *Itasca* ahead.

Over 1,000 people watched the silver plane take off from Lae. For nearly 1,200 miles the ground operators at Lae kept track of the Electra's progress, through its half-hourly reports. Then, a half-hour after a very faint message, they could hear nothing. The coast guard cutter took over and, as night came on, the operators on the *Itasca* tried to make contact. Static interference was bad but at 2:45 am they managed to pick up the flier's low voice saying, 'Cloudy and overcast', before the static overwhelmed it again. Garbled messages were heard at 3:45 and 4:45. The first clear message did not come through until 6:15, less than two hours before the plane was due to reach Howland Island.

'We are about 100 miles out. Please take a bearing on us and report in half an hour. I will transmit into the microphone.'

When the radio operators tried to get a bearing, however, there was no signal.

At 6:45 am, Amelia Earhart's voice broke through the static again, urgently asking for a bearing. This try also failed because she had not transmitted long enough for the direction finders to pick up the signals. Not for another hour was her voice heard again.

'We must be right on top of you but we can't see you . . . gas is running low . . . have been unable to reach you by radio . . . we are flying at an altitude of 1,000 feet. . . '

The cutter immediately sent out its homing signal but when the pilot next made contact it was evident that she had heard none of the *Itasca*'s messages. Something seemed to be wrong with her radio on the very part of the journey that she most had need of it. At 8:00 am, however, she spoke again and her message made the men on the *Itasca* think the worst might be over. She was receiving their signals, she said, but was in urgent need of a bearing. She whistled into the microphone but the sound could hardly be heard above the accompanying static.

One last time the *Itasca* heard Amelia Earhart's voice. 'We have only half an hour's fuel left and we cannot see land', she reported. When nothing more was heard it was assumed that the plane had crashed, but this did not necessarily mean that the two occupants were dead. With the tanks empty and the cocks closed, the plane might keep afloat indefinitely in calm weather. Even without a working radio there was still a chance of rescue. For two weeks, ships and planes searched a quarter of a million square miles of ocean – and found nothing. Amelia Earhart and Frederick Noonan were missing, presumed drowned.

Later that year a disturbing rumour arose. It was suggested that the United States government had instructed the fliers to spy on Japanese war preparations, probably in the Marshall Islands. Having deliberately flown off course to spy, the story went, they had fallen into the hands of the Japanese and were prisoners. The Japanese indignantly denied this rumour but when all the Japanese-held islands were captured after the war, an attempt was made to find out if the story had any foundation.

From the Marshall Islands came a report that in 1937 two white fliers, one a woman, had crashed between Jaluit and Ailinglapalap atolls. They had been picked up by a Japanese fishing boat and taken away in another Japanese boat to Saipan, a large island of the Mariana group, which the Japanese were illegally fortifying. From Saipan itself came information that an entire album filled with photographs of Amelia Earhart was discovered.

Other reports from Saipan seemed to contradict those from the Marshall Islands. One said that a plane had been seen to crash in the bay and a white woman and man had been brought ashore from it. The woman was dressed like a man and both looked exhausted and pale. Japanese soldiers led them away into the jungle, after which shots were heard.

These reports of the crash and execution, though collected several years after the event, cannot be entirely discounted. But until more conclusive evidence comes to light, the answer to the disappearance of Amelia Earhart and Frederick Noonan lies in the Pacific Ocean's great depths.

Amelia Earhart had once said to her husband, 'I don't want to die, but when I do, I want to go in my plane – quickly.'

Perhaps her wish was granted.

Surely none of the passengers on the *Hindenburg*, Germany's luxury dirigible, wished to go down with the airship when they boarded it for an Atlantic crossing on 6 May 1937 – nor did they expect to. There had never been a passenger fatality on any of Germany's commercial airships. The *Hindenburg*, largest dirigible ever to fly, was designed for safety as well as beauty and grandeur. There were 70 staterooms, a lounge, a dining room and a bar, all sumptuously decorated. Broad promenades with large windows afforded spectacular views. It was, as it was called, a Great Floating Palace.

The obvious weakness of the *Hindenburg* was its inflammability because of the seven million cubic feet of hydrogen that filled its 16 vast gas cells. This was a flaw created by lack of supply rather than by design, however, since it had been intended to use non-flammable helium. But the only country that produced helium in sufficient quantities was the United States and with Hitler in power and the danger of war increasing, the Americans refused to supply helium in case it was later used for military purposes.

Fire precautions on board the *Hindenburg* were stringent. The crew members wore antistatic asbestos overalls and hemp-soled shoes. All matches and lighters were removed from the passengers before they boarded. The smoking room was especially insulated, pressurized to prevent hydrogen entering and fitted with a double door; a steward lit cigars and cigarettes for smokers and ensured that no fire left the room.

During 1936, the *Hindenburg* safely cruised back and forth

across the Atlantic. Once the captain guided it through a thunderstorm with such ease that many passengers were unaware of the poor weather conditions.

On 6 May 1937 the *Hindenburg* was on another routine crossing. The commander was Captain Max Pruss, an airship officer of long experience, recently commander of the *Graf Zeppelin*. With him in the control gondola was the veteran airship pilot Captain Ernst Lehmann, himself formerly in charge of the *Hindenburg*, who was going to Washington.

When the *Hindenburg* reached the Lakehurst Naval Air Station near Boston, where it was supposed to moor, it was running 10 hours late. Pruss decided to delay the landing still further because of rain, wind and cloud. He swung over New York, circling the Empire State Building. After waiting another hour, Pruss prepared to land. Darkness was coming on, though the rain and wind had slackened. With the mooring mast 700 feet away, the airship's engines reversed and the Great Floating Palace drifted to a standstill. The mooring ties were dropped 200 feet below where the ground party ran forward to pick them up.

Suddenly, the belly of the silver airship glowed red. At the same time flames broke from the tail, just forward of the upper fin. The crowd below screamed and scattered. In the control gondola Pruss had felt only a slight shock and did not realize what had happened until he glanced out and saw the ground below glowing redly. Within seconds huge flames leaped up, bursting one gasbag after another to feed more hydrogen to the already white hot inferno. Explosions were heard 15 miles away.

Before the blazing zeppelin touched ground, some of the passengers and crew jumped from windows, doors – any opening they could find – and hurtled to the ground. Miraculously there were some survivors. Once on the ground, others were saved.

That anyone at all should have escaped the inferno is a wonder. Only 32 seconds elapsed between the first explosion and the final crash of the melting, white-hot framework. Yet of the 97 passengers and crew aboard, 62 lived through the danger. Captain Pruss repeatedly ran into the glowing wreck to help until he was forcibly prevented from re-entering. Captain Lehmann, badly burned, staggered back and forth mumbling, 'I don't understand. . . I don't understand. . . .' The following day he died in great pain.

The commission of inquiry set up to discover the cause of the explosion wanted to consider the possibility of sabotage but crew members, well enough to be called to the stand, were unhelpful on this point. Other possibilities were examined – a spark from the engine, an electrical fault, a sticking gas valve, structural failure, static electricity – but the crew's evidence convinced the commission that none of these could be responsible. Eventually the commission had to fall lamely back on St. Elmo's Fire, a form of atmospheric static electricity, as 'most probably' the cause, even though scientists doubted that St. Elmo's Fire could set light to hydrogen under almost any circumstances.

Not till after the war was it learned that Hermann Goering, chief of the Nazi Luftwaffe, had sent orders to the officers and crew of the *Hindenburg* that 'they should not try to find an explanation.' The destruction of the *Hindenburg* was a serious enough blow to the pride of Nazi Germany. If it had become known at that time that an enemy saboteur was responsible, the repercussions within Germany might have become uncontrollable. So the crew kept their suspicions to themselves and only years later did the survivors talk of the frantic passenger who had been pacing up and down the dining saloon 20 minutes before the explosion. 'I don't want to go round the field again', he had cried out, 'I want to go down!' The FBI discovered that this passenger had claimed in conversation to be an American citizen, although he was using a foreign passport.

There is also the puzzling behaviour of the tall, fair-haired rigger, Erich Spehl. A moody and reserved young man, his hobby was photography. He had full access to the interior of the airship and could have placed an explosive device in the crevices of a gas cell on many occasions. His last watch ended one and a half hours before the explosion and it is significant that at the time of the blast he was as far away from it as possible, one of the few crew in the foremost part of the nose. Two of the surviving crew members who saw the start of the fire said that it began with the sort of flash that could have been caused by a photoflash bulb.

Before the *Hindenburg* left Frankfurt on its last flight, Spehl had been seen in the company of an older woman believed to have communist sympathies. She called at the zeppelin company's offices three times during the airship's flight, to ask about its position. Spehl perished in the tragedy, so his side of the story can never be known. It is always possible that the explosion was timed to occur after the landing, without loss of life and that the more than 11-hour delay before mooring put the plan awry. Sabotage seems to be the most likely explanation but there is little chance of this being established beyond doubt.

There seems to be even less chance of ever explaining the disappearance of six Soviet airmen who were trying to establish an air route over the North Pole. Their goal was to fly non-stop from the Soviet Union to Alaska, starting in Moscow and ending in Fairbanks. They set out in early August 1937, a dangerous time of year for polar flight because the summer thaw made a sea of possible emergency landing zones. But three of the crew members were veteran polar fliers and the other three were exceptionally well qualified. Captain Sigismund Levanevsky was confident of success.

For the first 2,000 miles the flight was on schedule, although a headwind cut the plane's speed and the heavy fuel load prevented it from rising above the cloud. Near the pole the plane did manage to climb above the cloud and, after passing the pole, held steady for the next two hours. Then came a distress call. An oil line had burst from the cold, cutting one of the four engines. This meant that the plane had to descend to 13,000 feet, at which level ice was forming on its surface.

Not long after the danger alert, the radio operator signalled that the plane had to land. He gave the location but the message was too garbled to understand. It turned out to be the last message from the Levanevsky expedition.

The Soviet government, the Explorers Club of New York and private individuals made intensive searches from the day after the disappearance on 13 August 1937 to the next spring. Only one frail lead turned up – some Eskimos living between Aklavik, Canada and Point Barrow, Alaska had heard a plane on 13 August. Its engines had died away south and inland, putting it in the hazardous mountain region. Was it the Levanevsky survey plane ? Even that is not known. Not a trace of the fliers or their plane and not a clue to the mystery of their end, has ever been found by anyone.

If Levanevsky had vanished over the ocean south of Florida

instead of over the pole, he would have been one of a statistically improbable number of air disappearances in recent years. The area is known as the Bermuda Triangle – and its mystery has been much plumbed, as the next chapter reveals.

CHAPTER 7

THE BERMUDA TRIANGLE

Why have so many vessels and aircraft disappeared in that patch of the Atlantic Ocean known as the Bermuda Triangle? Are they swallowed up? Sucked into outer space? Dashed to the bottom of the sea? Why are no bodies or fragments of the ships and planes ever found? For many years the number of unexplained accidents, near accidents and disappearances in the Triangle has been more than can be laid to mere chance. Will we ever have enough data to understand what happens in this mystery region?

'Calling tower, this is an emergency . . . We seem to be off course . . . We cannot see land . . . Repeat . . . We cannot see land.' This was the radio message that alerted the Naval Air Station at Fort Lauderdale, Florida, that something was wrong with Flight 19 somewhere out in the Atlantic between Florida and the island of Bermuda. The speaker was Lieutenant Charles C. Taylor, leader of the five Avenger torpedo bombers making up Flight 19, which had taken off at 2:00 pm that afternoon, on a routine mission. The date was 5 December 1945 and the time was 3:45 pm – the planes should have then been returning to base.

'What is your position?', the tower radioed.

Back came the astounding reply, 'We're not sure of our position. We can't be sure just where we are. We seem to be lost.'

Lieutenant Taylor was an experienced pilot. It was incredible that he should not know his position. The mission of Flight 19 had been to fly due east from the Florida coastline for 160 miles to the Chicken Shoals in the Bahamas, where the planes were to

make practice runs on a target hulk. Afterward, they were to fly
north for 40 miles and then southwest back to Fort Lauderdale.

At the time of the distress call, the first two legs of the flight
had been carried out satisfactorily. Accordingly, the tower
instructed him, 'Assume bearing due west.'

Taylor's reply to this was alarming. 'We don't know which
way is west. Everything is wrong . . . strange . . . We can't be
sure of any direction. Even the ocean doesn't look as it should.'

When the planes had taken off from Fort Lauderdale, flying
conditions had been good – sunny with scattered clouds. If the
planes were now unable to tell whether or not they were flying
west, it must mean the sun was invisible to them. Had weather
conditions deteriorated out there? As for the reported 'strangeness' of the ocean, this detail was to be the subject of much
speculation over the next 50 years. For although the doomed
planes of Flight 19 did not know it, they were flying straight into
a legend. Many stories, articles and books were to tell of their
last flight, theorizing as to their fate. Films were to re-enact their
mission to oblivion. They were to become the most celebrated
victims of that danger area of the Atlantic, known by such
names as 'The Triangle of Death', 'The Hoodoo Sea', 'The
Graveyard of the Atlantic' but most recently and widely as 'The
Bermuda Triangle'.

Vincent Gaddis, American author of a book on sea mysteries,
first coined the phrase in drawing attention to the great number
of ships and planes that have disappeared in this relatively small
area of the ocean. Most of them leave no trace of wreckage or
bodies. They vanish. Gaddis wrote, 'Draw a line from Florida to
Bermuda, another from Bermuda to Puerto Rico and a third line
back to Florida through the Bahamas. Within this roughly trian-
gular area most of the vanishments have occurred.' Others have
taken place in adjacent areas to the north and east in the
Atlantic, south in the Caribbean and west in the Gulf of Mexico.
But the biggest majority of mysterious disappearances have
occurred within the Bermuda–Puerto Rico–Florida triangle.

The Avengers of Flight 19 were well within this triangle when
the unknown misfortune overtook them. Apparently, they found
it increasingly difficult to hear messages from base because of
static interference but Fort Lauderdale was able to hear the

messages passing between the five pilots. There were complaints that their instruments had gone wild and that their compasses were spinning. The tone of these radio exchanges moved from bewilderment to fear. Each Avenger usually carried a crew of three – the pilot, a gunner and a radio operator – but one airman had put in a successful request to be removed from flight duty that day. He was not replaced, so the number involved in this unexpectedly mysterious and fatal journey totalled 14.

The senior flight instructor at Fort Lauderdale picked up a request by one of the pilots to another asking about his compass readings. The reply was, 'I don't know where we are. We must have gotten lost after that last turn.' The same flight instructor was finally able to contact Taylor who reported back, 'Both my compasses are out. I am trying to find Fort Lauderdale . . . I'm sure I'm in the Keys but I don't know how far down.'

The senior flight instructor advised him to fly north, keeping the sun on his portside. If Taylor's plane were over the Keys, the chain of low islands strung out like a loose necklace from the southern tip of mainland Florida, the flight north would bring him within sight of the Florida coastline. Then he heard Taylor say, 'We have just passed over a small island . . . No other land in sight. . . .' It was clear that Taylor could not have been over the Florida Keys and was totally disoriented.

At 4 pm the tower heard Taylor turn over command to one of the other pilots. Since he was the instructor of the flight and the other four pilots were students, this abdication of command was an extraordinary act. It was a terrible confession by Taylor that he could not face up to the hazardous situation. The new flight commander, Captain Stiver of the Marines, sent back a message that Fort Lauderdale managed to hear through the static, ' We are not sure where we are . . . We must have passed over Florida and we must be in the Gulf of Mexico.'

The flight turned east and at once the voices of the pilots began to fade. They were evidently on the Atlantic side of Florida rather than the Gulf side, heading for the open sea again.

Faint messages between the planes were still heard for a time. Once they turned and flew west, a change of direction that would have brought them home if their fuel had lasted. But within a few minutes they were flying east once more, farther and farther from land. Some reports claim that the last words heard from the flight was the mysterious phrase, 'We are entering white water. . . .' After that came silence.

The disappearance of five planes and 14 men produced consternation at Fort Lauderdale. Worse was to follow. A Martin Mariner flying boat, with a crew of 13, was dispatched on a rescue mission. The huge and powerful Mariner, 77 feet long with a wing span of 124 feet, was fully equipped with rescue and survival gear and its specially reinforced hull enabled it to make rough landings at sea. It flew northeast toward the area where the Avengers were presumed to have been. A message received soon after takeoff from one of its officers, reported strong winds above 6,000 feet. Twenty minutes after the Mariner left the base, the tower sent out a message to check its position. There was no reply. Anxiously the tower continued its call, while apprehension mounted among the officers present. The Mariner never answered. It had vanished as completely as the Avengers it had set off to find.

Darkness fell but throughout the night Coast Guard vessels watched for signal flares that might indicate survivors. The next morning a massive rescue operation got under way. There were eight Coast Guard vessels, four destroyers, several submarines and hundreds of private yachts and boats for the surface search. The aircraft carrier *Solomons* moved into the area and added 60 planes to the 240 land-based planes for the air reconnaissance. They meticulously criss-crossed the area, flying in grid search formation. The Royal Air Force dispatched all available planes from the Bahamas and the West Indies to assist in the operation. Land parties combed the shore line of Florida. Low-flying planes checked the swamps and the Everglades. Not a scrap of wreckage was found, not a hint that there had been a single survivor from any of the six lost planes.

The Avengers were capable of staying afloat for 90 seconds, and the crew had been trained to abandon the plane in 60 seconds. They could have obtained life rafts from outside the plane. Yet no wreckage was discovered, despite the long search of over 280,000 square miles of water.

It is this absence of wreckage that gives the Bermuda Triangle its special strangeness. There are several other areas of the world notoriously dangerous for shipping. But the vessels that go down at Cape Horn, the Cape of Good Hope, the Great Australian Bight or Sable Island, produce wrecks and wreckage. The Bermuda Triangle sometimes yields up identifiable wreckage but the number of ships and planes that disappear without trace has created a yet unsolved riddle.

The report of the Naval Board of Inquiry that investigated the disappearance of Flight 19 stated in part, 'A radio message intercepted indicated that the planes were lost and that they were experiencing malfunctioning of their compasses.' The instrument officer at Fort Lauderdale was exonerated of possible blame, however, when it was established that all the instruments had been fully checked before takeoff. What went wrong for Flight 19? An Air Force information officer had to admit in a press interview that, 'Members of the Board of Inquiry were not able to make even a good guess as to what happened.' But theories abounded. One had it that all five planes had collided in mid-air, simultaneously killing all the crew members. Another maintained that a freak waterspout had destroyed the planes. One officer remarked, 'They vanished as completely as if they had flown to Mars.' His comment was hardly intended to be taken seriously but it foreshadowed many later theories that some power unnatural to the earth, possibly involving UFOs, must be operating within the Bermuda Triangle.

Curiously, the area in which the planes disappeared was not at first considered significant. Not until the 1960s did such writers as Gaddis and Charles Berlitz, author of *The Bermuda Triangle*, draw attention to the long list of disasters associated with this part of the Atlantic Ocean. Among his writings, Berlitz has listed 61 known disappearances that occurred before 1945 and 80 other instances in the 31 years between then and 1976.

For example, in December 1947 a United States Army C-54 Superfortress carrying a crew of six, disappeared 100 miles southwest of Bermuda on a routine flight to Palm Beach, Florida. The intense air and sea search covered over 100,000 square miles of sea. Apart from some seat cushions and an oxygen bottle that were not identified as equipment from the lost plane, no wreckage, no survivors, no oil slick was sighted. Some authorities suggested that 'a tremendous current of rising air in a cumulo-nimbus cloud might have disintegrated the bomber.' It is accepted that such clouds can produce turbulence capable of destroying aircraft, particularly jets, but the disintegration of a plane invariably produces debris in the sea.

The next incident, coming a few weeks later, involved a British Tudor IV passenger plan on the Azores–Bermuda run. At 10:30 on the night of 29 January 1948 the *Star Tiger*, carrying 29 people on board, radioed its position as 400 miles northeast of Bermuda. The message commented on the favourable wind and the excellent performance of the plane's engines. The final words were, 'Expect to arrive on schedule.' There was no further word.

About a year later and seeming to establish a pattern that disappearances occurred in the few weeks either side of Christmas, the *Star Tiger*'s sister plane, *Star Ariel*, vanished in the middle of the Bermuda Triangle. The *Star Ariel* left Bermuda for Jamaica on the morning of 17 January 1949 climbing into a clear tropical sky. Fifty-five minutes later the pilot sent Bermuda a radio message on weather conditions ending, 'All's well.' He changed radio frequency to pick up Kingston, Jamaica but neither Kingston nor anyone else heard from the *Star Ariel* again.

The British Court of Inquiry on the case commented, 'It may truly be said that no more baffling problem has ever been presented for investigation.' Did both planes suddenly, without any warning and given no time to send an SOS, dive into the sea and sink to the bottom? Could they crash without leaving a trace of debris? The Court of Inquiry experimented with exact replicas of the vanished planes, sending them crashing into deep water – in all cases fragments escaped to litter the surface. The British Investigators remained baffled by the problem.

About three weeks before the disappearance of the *Star Ariel*, the Bermuda jinx had struck at a DC-3 passenger plane chartered for a night flight from Puerto Rico to Miami. The 32 passengers, including two babies, had been spending Christmas on the island and the atmosphere on the plane was happy.

'What do you know?', Captain Robert Linquist reported by radio at an early stage of the flight, 'We're all singing Christmas carols.'

The time was 4:13 am on 28 December 1948 when the DC-3 approached the end of its 1,000 mile flight. Captain Linquist could see the lights of Miami ahead. 'We are approaching the field . . . One fifty miles out to the south. All's well. Will stand by for landing instructions.'

Whether he heard those instructions will never be known. Nothing more was heard from him or his plane. If it vanished into the water, which is clear and shallow around the Keys toward which he had been flying, his plane left no trace. Search planes would have been able to see an object as large as a DC-3 through the clear water. But though they watched for debris and scanned the sea for tell-tale groups of sharks and barracuda, nothing was ever found.

In the years following the loss of the *Star Ariel*, a succession of aircraft – one or more each year – have vanished in the same mysterious way. In March 1950, a United States Globemaster disappeared on a flight to Ireland while on the northern edge of the Bermuda Triangle. In February 1952, a British York transport carrying 33 passengers and crew vanished at about the same area on a flight to Jamaica. On 30 October 1954, a United States Navy Constellation flying from Maryland to the Azores was lost in the Triangle, never to be heard of again. There were 42 on board, the highest number lost in the mystery area so far. Aircraft of all kinds, light planes and jets, cargo and passenger, vanish abruptly. On two occasions an SOS message is thought to have been heard, but neither gave a clue to the disaster that had overwhelmed the planes. What power is it that, in Gaddis' dramatic words, 'snatches planes from the sky?'

Some have suggested that the planes fall instant victims to the disintegrating rays emerging from a subterranean power source placed on the seabed by former inhabitants of the earth. Others suggest that unknown forces operating within the Triangle create space warps, or time warps, that convey the planes into another dimension from which they cannot return. It has also been suggested that the planes are not forced down into the water but up into space, either through a reversal of gravity or through capture by extraterrestrial beings. The mother of one of the young pilots of Flight 19 stated at the time of the inquiry that she had received the impression that her son 'was still alive somewhere in space'. Manson Valentine, a Miami doctor whose interest in the subject goes back many years, has said, 'They are still here, but in a different dimension of a magnetic phenomenon that could have been set up by a UFO.'

These are modern attempts to provide an answer but the problem goes back long before anyone would have been discussing UFOs and multidimensional space. The area of the ocean now called the Bermuda Triangle, has been a place of disaster for centuries.

Soon after its discovery in 1515, Bermuda became known as 'the Isle of Devils' because of the numerous ships that sank around its shores – some without survivors. In Shakespeare's play *The Tempest*, the sprite Ariel recalls the island's sinister reputation when he says, 'Thou call'dst me up at midnight to fetch dew / From the still-vexed Bermoothes [Bermuda] . . .' And vexed they have remained to this day.

A large part of the Bermuda Triangle falls within that area of the West Atlantic known as the Sargasso Sea, a slow-moving tract of water many hundreds of miles wide, named after the seaweed *Sargassum* that floats in enormous masses throughout the area and particularly around its borders. A sea within a sea, it is bounded by the Gulf Stream and other strong ocean currents, but it itself is nearly stagnant and largely without currents. This seaweed sea was held in dread by mariners in the days of sail. Their ships could be immobilized by the weeds and becalmed for weeks – perhaps forever – by the deadly lack of winds. 'The Graveyard of Lost Ships' and 'The Sea of Fear' are only two of the many names applied by sailors to this accursed sea.

There are other curious phenomena associated with the Bermuda Triangle region and one of the first seamen to take note of them was Christopher Columbus. On the eve of his discovery of the New World, a bolt of fire shot across the sky to plunge into the ocean, terrifying his already fearful and mutinous crew. As his ships neared the Bahamas he observed an inexplicable glowing in the sea two hours after sunset. This is now a well-known phenomenon in the area. Interestingly, the Apollo 12 astronauts reported that these same luminous streaks were the last light visible to them from earth. The cause of this luminosity is not precisely known but possible explanations include the movement of fish, fine particles of marl stirred up by fish, or the movement of organic matter. At sea level, the phenomenon presents itself as a wide-spreading luminosity in the water but from the air it appears strikingly as regular white banding.

The Sargasso Sea was a death trap because it was nearly without currents. In contrast, the area around the Bahamas, where wide banks slope abruptly into abyssal depths, is dangerous and unpredictable – a death trap because of wild currents. Divers exploring the underwater limestone formations of the banks have discovered extensive cave systems called 'blue holes'. Stalactites and stalagmites can be seen in some of these caves, evidence that they were formed when the seabed was dry land. The holes penetrate the substratum for enormous distances, branching into smaller passages of bewildering complexity. Divers have reported that even the fish seem confused and can be found swimming upside down. Extremely powerful currents flow through these holes, funnelled by the tides and fish can be carried along them for considerable distances inland. Berlitz reports that a 20-foot shark once made a sensational appearance in a quiet inland pond 20 miles from the shore, creating great agitation among the local inhabitants.

The currents of the Bahamas waters form such strong whirlpools at the surface of the sea that they are capable of sinking a small boat and dinghies and fishing boats have been found wedged far within the blue holes at depths of up to 80 feet. It is natural hazards, then, that have been responsible for the majority of ships lost in the area.

Certain disappearances, however, have never been satisfactorily explained. When the British frigate *Atalanta* left Bermuda for England in January 1880, there was a crew of 290 aboard, mostly young naval cadets in training. The large ship was never seen again and no identifiable debris was ever found. The British Navy conducted a long search during which six ships from the Channel Fleet advanced in a line, separated from one another by a few miles, over the area in which the *Atalanta* was presumed lost. The search continued until May without success.

The first strange disappearance of a ship within the Triangle in the twentieth century occurred in 1918. This ship was the *USS*

Cyclops, considered at the time it was launched in 1910 to be the last word in marine construction. Its displacement was 19,500 tons and the special superstructure that gave the ship a rather odd silhouette, enabled it to deliver coal to other vessels at sea. On 4 March 1918, the *Cyclops* sailed from Barbados in the British West Indies for Norfolk, Virginia carrying a valuable cargo of manganese ore. There were 57 passengers on board and a crew of 221. The weather was calm. The *Cyclops* had excellent radio equipment but no radio messages were received. No vestige of the ship was ever found.

Because World War I was still in progress, first thoughts were that the American ship had struck a German mine or met a German submarine, but examination of German records after the war showed that no mines were laid and no submarine had been in the area at that time. Another theory cast suspicion on the German-born captain of the ship, who had changed his name to Warley from Wichmann and who had sold his house in Norfolk, before leaving on his last journey. It was suggested that he had steered the *Cyclops* with her valuable cargo to a sympathetic neutral port, or perhaps sailed to Germany. Some initial support for this idea came from the fact that on leaving Barbados the *Cyclops* had turned south instead of north. Another possibility was that the crew had mutinied against their captain. He was undeniably eccentric and may even have been mad, one of his weird habits being to walk the bridge wearing long underwear and a derby hat.

Another and more plausible explanation of the disappearance was based on the ship's high superstructure which, with a shifting of the cargo, may have caused the boat to turn turtle and sink almost immediately. The British battleship *Captain* had sunk in just this manner. However, the Naval Board of Inquiry rejected this theory, arguing that the *Cyclops* had proved its seaworthiness in eight years of service. As for the cargo shifting, it was of the sort that could only have shifted in extremely rough weather. During the time the *Cyclops* was at sea, the weather had been fair and the winds no more than light to moderate.

'The disappearance of the ship', stated a Navy fact sheet, 'has been one of the most baffling mysteries in the annals of the Navy, all attempts to locate her have proved unsuccessful . . .

Many theories have been advanced, but none that satisfactorily accounts for her disappearance.'

So the loss of the *Cyclops* remains an enigma. Forty years later it has been joined by an unusual number of similar enigmas.

What happened to the *Cotopaxi*, an American freighter bound for Havana from Charleston that vanished in January 1925? The cargo tramp *Suduffco*, sailing south from Newark to Puerto Rico in May 1926? The Norwegian freighter *Stavanger*, carrying a crew of 43, lost in October 1931 somewhere south of Cat Island in the Bahamas? What was the fate of the United States frigate *Sandra*? It left Savannah, Georgia in June 1950 with a cargo of insecticide. It was seen passing St. Augustine, Florida. Then contact was lost, never re-established and the ship was never seen again.

John Godwin, an author who was one of the first to gather together details of 'The Hoodoo Sea', points out that all these vessels varied greatly in age, tonnage, cargo and equipment. 'The only similarity about them was the manner of their disappearance', he writes. 'Although all carried radios, none sounded a distress call. Not one of these ships had encountered serious storm conditions. In spite of wide search sweeps, nothing associated with any of them was ever found. The case of the *Cyclops* was repeated over and over again.'

One ship that did send out a brief and tantalizing last message was the Japanese freighter *Raifuku Maru*. It disappeared between the Bahamas and Cuba during the winter of 1924 and the last words heard are reported to have been, 'Danger like a dagger now . . . Come quickly . . . We cannot escape. . .' The nature of the danger remained unspecified. A ship that steamed toward the *Raifuku Maru* on hearing the SOS found no wreckage, no survivors.

One of the most recent ships that disappeared sent no distress signals but did leave three scraps of wreckage consisting of one life jacket, one life belt and one man's shirt – not much to survive from a 425 foot long freighter with a crew of 39. The ship was the *Marine Sulphur Queen* and it left the port of Beaumont, Texas on the morning of 2 February 1963. It carried a cargo of 15,000 long tons of molten sulphur in specially

designed steel tanks. The destination was Norfolk, Virginia and
the route lay through the Gulf of Mexico, past Florida and north
through the Triangle.

The weather was good, the sea calm. On 3 February the ship
reported its position near Key West in the Strait of Florida. No
more was heard. Berlitz reports that the ship was first missed,
not by her owners but by a brokerage house. One of the seamen
aboard the *Marine Sulphur Queen* had been speculating in wheat
future on the stock market and had placed an order to buy before
the ship left Beaumont. The brokerage house carried out his
instructions and cabled him confirmation. Receiving no reply,
they informed the owners and the alarm went out. From 6
February to 15 February, Coast Guard cutters searched the
waters from Virginia to Key West. Five days after the search
was called off, a life jacket from the ship was found bobbing in a
calm sea between Florida and Cuba. A new search was begun
and this brought in the other two items. Nothing more. Did the
ship capsize? Had she struck a mine or been sunk by Cubans?
Did the sulphur explode? The investigation could offer neither
theory nor solution to the disappearance.

As much as anything else, it is the absence of bodies that has
puzzled investigators of the Bermuda Triangle disappearances.
In other cases of shipwreck, in other localities, a few bodies are
usually washed up on nearby beaches even though the floating
corpses become the prey of sharks and barracuda. Since many of
the ships that have disappeared in the vicinity of the Triangle
have done so almost within sight of land, the complete absence
of corpses on the beaches is hard to explain.

Cases of total disappearance are only one aspect of the many
sea mysteries on record. Perhaps equally perplexing are the
numerous discoveries of drifting ships, from which all passengers and crew have vanished. The earliest recorded example is
the French ship *Rosalie*, bound for Havana in 1866. When
discovered, its sails were mostly set and its cargo was intact –
but the only living thing on board was a half-starved canary in a
cage. If everyone had abandoned the ship, they had left no
message explaining why. If they had been forced off, it was by
someone or something unknown, with more interest in human
beings than in the ship or its cargo.

In August 1881, a schooner was found drifting west of the Azores by the American schooner *Ellen Austin*. The abandoned boat was boarded and found to be shipshape, with sails furled and rigging intact. The captain of the *Ellen Austin* decided to take advantage of this seeming piece of good fortune by claiming the derelict ship as a prize and putting a crew aboard her. Almost immediately, a sudden squall caused the two ships to lose sight of each other and it was two days before the *Ellen Austin* sighted the other boat again. Oddly enough, it was drifting once more. On investigation it was discovered that the prize crew had disappeared, leaving nothing to indicate what had happened or where they had gone. It was a strange repeat of the first encounter.

The captain was not to be thwarted of his prize, though he had to use all his powers of persuasion to get a new prize crew aboard the mysterious and possibly dangerous ship. Unbelievable as it may seem, another squall blew up, contact between the ships was lost once more – and this time neither the vessel nor its second prize crew was ever seen again.

It was not stormy when the German boat *Freya* vanished in the early part of the twentieth century. The *Freya* sailed from Manzanilla, Cuba on 3 October 1902, and was discovered 17 days later, partly dismasted, listing and with no one aboard. The date on a calendar in the captain's cabin was 4 October, so the mysterious fate of the crew had been decided on the ship's second day out. Between the 3rd and the 5th only light winds had been reported in the area.

The list of Triangle victims goes on. In April 1932, the two-masted schooner *John and Mary* was found 50 miles south of Bermuda, its sails furled, its hull newly painted – but not a soul on board. The *Gloria Colite*, a 125-foot schooner from St. Vincent, British West Indies was found abandoned in February 1940. Fourteen months before the disappearance of Flight 19, the Cuban freighter *Rubicon* was discovered drifting off the coast of Florida. A dog was the only living thing aboard.

The late Ivan Sanderson, naturalist and writer, was a supporter of the theory that the unexplained disappearance of planes and ships was the result of kidnapping by extraterrestrial beings. He found special significance in the fact that animals have been left behind on ghost ships. He pointed out that when a crew has to abandon ship, it is most unusual for them to leave their mascot or their pets. From this he argued that the crew must have been forcibly removed and suggested this was done by entities who only wanted creatures able to communicate by words. Sanderson made the point that whereas cats, dogs and a canary have been left behind on ships from which the crews have vanished, '. . . parrots seem to vanish with the humans. . .' In his view, this confirms the fact that the ability to talk – even parrot-fashion – is the decisive factor in abductions by outer space creatures.

Berlitz was not the first person to write about the Bermuda Triangle but he was the first to assemble reports from people who had narrowly escaped its strange perils. One of these was Captain Don Henry, owner of a salvage company in Florida. He described how in 1966 he was aboard the tug *Good News* towing an empty petroleum nitrate barge from Puerto Rico to Fort Lauderdale. The tug had reached that area of the Bahamas known as the 'Tongue of the Ocean' a very deep and precipitous trench immediately to the east of Andros Island and the site of many disappearances. The weather was good, the sky clear. Suddenly the tug's compass began to spin clockwise. The sea became turbulent. 'We couldn't see where the horizon was', Captain Henry recalled. 'The water, sky and horizon all blended together.' All electrical apparatus stopped working. The generators continued to run but produced no electricity. 'I was worried about the tow. It was tight but I couldn't see it. It seemed to be covered by a cloud and around it the waves seemed more choppy than in other areas.' Henry signalled full speed ahead but had the feeling that something was holding the tug back. Slowly it moved forward with the emerging 1000-foot towline sticking out straight behind her 'like the Indian rope trick.' Nothing was visible at the end, where it was covered by a concentration of fog, although there was no fog anywhere else and visibility ahead was 11 miles. After further effort on the part of the tug, the barge came out of the mist. In the clouded area where the barge had been, the water continued to be choppy but Captain Henry had no wish to go back and find out what was causing it. The generators of the *Good News* began to work normally again, though all the batteries were dead.

Berlitz also quotes the experience of Joe Talley, captain of the *Wild Goose*, a 65-foot shark fishing vessel being towed south in the 'Tongue of the Ocean' by the 104-foot tug *Caicos Trader*. It was night and Captain Talley was asleep in his bunk below decks on the *Wild Goose*. He awoke to find a flood of water pouring over him. Grabbing a life jacket, he fought his way out through an open porthole. Once outside, he discovered he was still under water but he found a line and followed it to the surface, a distance he estimated to be between 50 and 80 feet. The *Wild Goose* had been submerged about 50 feet when he managed to escape from her.

When he reached the surface he found that the *Caicos Trader* was nowhere to be seen. After a worried half hour, he was relieved to hear his name being called through a megaphone. He was told that the crew of the *Caicos Trader* had seen the *Wild Goose* sink straight down 'as if in a whirlpool.' The force dragging the boat down to the bottom was so powerful that it threatened to capsize the *Caicos Trader* as well. The crew therefore had cut the towline and hastily left the area. They had returned just in case Talley had managed to escape.

Both the *Good News* and the *Caicos Trader* crews talked about a powerful force exerting a tremendous pull. Was this sensation of fighting an unknown power felt by all the ships that sailed into oblivion? It is impossible to know in cases in which no tug crews were present as witnesses.

The reports of individual survivors, however, may lead to a clearer understanding of what happened to those who did not survive. For example, the Avengers of Flight 19 were not the first planes to report malfunction of instruments. In 1928, Charles Lindbergh, flying the *Spirit of St. Louis* from Havana to Florida, recorded in his log, 'Both compasses malfunctioned over Florida Strait, at night. The earth indicator needle wobbled back and forth. The liquid compass card rotated without stopping. Could recognize no stars through heavy haze. Located position, at daybreak, over Bahama Islands, nearly 300 miles off course. Liquid compass card kept rotating until the *Spirit of St. Louis* reached the Florida Coast.'

Since then, it has frequently been reported that electromagnetic instruments 'go crazy' in the area. In 1944, a B-24 piloted by Lieutenant Robert Ulmer, was flying at 9,000 feet in the same locality east of the Bahamas where Flight 19 disappeared the following year. Suddenly the plane went out of control, shook as if it were about to fall to pieces and lost 4,000 feet of altitude in an instant. Since the plane would not respond to any of the controls and was clearly heading for the water, the crew bailed out. The crewless plane then righted itself and flew off in a southeasterly direction for about 2,500 miles, before crashing into a mountain in Mexico. All but two of the crew survived, one of them the navigator. Thirty years afterward, that lucky survivor summed up his recollection of the incident with the words, 'There is just no logical explanation for what happened.'

Electromagnetic malfunction has also been known to occur underwater in the region. When, in February 1955, the submarine *USS Tigrone* crashed into an underwater peak between Puerto Rico and the Virgin Islands, the only such obstacle in the area, its bow was crushed. The vessel would undoubtedly have sunk had it not been the only submarine in the Atlantic Fleet equipped with an icebreaker bow. Despite sophisticated radar and sonar guidance through gyro and compass backup systems that worked perfectly before and after, the submarine was four miles off course when it struck the reef. Numerous smaller craft have had comparable experiences.

The phenomenon affecting instruments has found its way into jokes. One of these is about a group of airline executives on a flight between Florida and Bermuda. Just for fun they send the captain a jerkily handwritten message saying, 'Do you know we are in the Bermuda Triangle?' The captain replies, 'I can't worry about that now. All my instruments are off and my compass is spinning.'

The late Wilbert B. Smith, who headed a magnetic and gravity project for the Canadian government, claimed to have found certain locations in which normal magnetic forces did not apply. He called these 'areas of reduced binding'. The locations were only about 1,000 feet in diameter but extended upward to an undetermined height. Smith's discovery has not been confirmed but if such areas do exist, a plane, ship or submarine would have no advance notice of an approach to one, until all its instruments suddenly 'went crazy'.

Professor Wayne Meshejian, a physicist who has plotted satellite pictures for several years, is reported to have observed that polar orbited satellites at an altitude of 800 miles, frequently began to malfunction when above the Bermuda Triangle. The official explanation for these failures is that they are due to tape rewinding and without further information, it is hard to draw any reliable conclusion from Professor Meshejian's findings. Could it not be, however, that the magnetic field above the Triangle is as peculiar as the sea within it? It is worth remembering that the area of the Bermuda Triangle is one of two places on the earth where a magnetic compass points true north. In all other places, it points toward the magnetic north and the difference between the two can vary as much as 20 degrees in the course of circum-navigating the earth. The Seventh Coast Guard District, which commands the Florida coastline, points out that, 'If the compass variation or error is not compensated for, a navigator could find himself far off course and in deep trouble.' To take that further, no compensation at all could be made if instruments go awry as they seem to, over or in the Triangle. That means trouble for certain.

The other place on the earth where compasses point due north is off the southeast coast of Japan. Known to Japanese and Filipino seamen as the 'Devil's Sea', it exhibits many of the same characteristics as the Bermuda Triangle. Ships unaccountably disappear there without apparent reason and have been doing so for at least a century. Between 1950 and 1954, no less than nine ships vanished without trace. No wreckage, no lifeboats, no bodies. The Japanese government declared the area a danger zone and early in 1955, sponsored an expedition to survey weather and water conditions in the area. A group of scientists set sail aboard the *Kaiyo Maru 5*. The *Kaiyo Maru* itself vanished.

Since there seems to be a parallel between the two danger areas, this works against what believers in the Bermuda Triangle call its 'special and unique danger'. The Seventh Coast Guard District has never minimized the danger of the Atlantic area – it cannot, since it annually receives about 10,000 calls for help.

But the experienced and qualified seamen of the Coast Guard feel that the so-called baffling disappearances all have a natural explanation. In their view, it may never be known exactly why the *Cyclops*, the *Marine Sulphur Queen* and others vanished but enough natural hazards exist to have been the cause.

The coastguards point to the unpredictable Caribbean-Atlantic weather pattern that brings sudden thunderstorms and waterspouts; to the complex submarine topography of the area varying from extensive shoals to deep trenches, and to the swift and turbulent Gulf Stream. They also draw attention to the general lack of seamanship of many who own, or use, small private boats.

Mrs Athley Gamber, president of Red Airways in Fort Lauderdale, is of the same opinion. The widow of a pilot who disappeared on a flight to the Bahamas, she has had ample opportunity to watch the search operations for lost planes. She does not believe that there is anything mysteriously sinister about the Bermuda Triangle. In her estimation, as many as half of the disappearances are due to simple pilot error.

This is also the opinion of Lawrence Kusche, author of *The Bermuda Triangle Mystery – Solved*. Kusche has compiled an exhaustive bibliography of articles and books dealing with the Bermuda Triangle and makes some telling points about the incident that really started it all – the disappearance of Flight 19. He argues that the tragedy came about because Captain Taylor, who had just been transferred to Fort Lauderdale from a station in southern Florida, made a crucial error of observation. When Taylor said, 'I'm sure I'm in the Keys, but I don't know how far down', he assumed he was over the Florida chain of islets. Kusche maintains that he was in fact over the Bahamas, based on Taylor's words that, 'We cannot see land'. Both sets of islets have a similar appearance but those in the Bahamas do not connect with nearby land, as they do in Florida.

Supporters of the mystery theory argue that Taylor must have seen something out of the ordinary when he remarked, 'Even the ocean does not look as it should.' According to Kusche, Taylor was desperately trying to make the sea around the Bahamas fit his memory of the sea around the Florida Keys, which was impossible. Disbelieving what his instruments were telling him,

Taylor altered his course to head in the direction he thought Florida would be. This only took Flight 19 farther away, eastward over the Atlantic toward Africa. After Taylor, by then completely disoriented, had handed over command, one of the other student pilots was heard to say, 'Dammit, if we flew west we'd get home.'

It may have been his misfortune to be led by a commander who, according to Kusche, mistook his position and trusted to his intuition rather than his instruments.

As for the Mariner flying boat sent out to rescue the Avengers, Kusche points out that to keep them flying a long time, the Mariners were so heavily laden with fuel that they were popularly known as 'flying gas tanks', Kusche thinks it possible that some member of the crew, affected by the aura of alarm surrounding the disappearance of Flight 19, in his nervousness disregarded the safety instructions and lit a cigarette. That could have meant the destruction of the fuel-laden aircraft. The merchant ship *SS Gaines Mills* observed an explosion high in the sky at 7:30 pm but this fact is not emphasized by Gaddis and Berlitz, who both imply that the Mariner left 'within a few moments' of the last words heard from Flight 19 at 4:25. In fact the Mariner took off at 7:27 pm, a few minutes before the explosion seen by the crew of the merchant ship.

If there is less mystery to Flight 19 than many writers infer, the absence of bodies from the mission's planes and other planes and ships remains unexplained. The disappearance of the British Tudors, particularly the *Star Ariel* in 1949, is also a genuine mystery. The *Star Ariel* was sound, fully equipped with every navigational device and carried life-saving equipment. It was, moreover, lightly loaded with passengers, carried more than enough fuel for the 5½ hour flight and manned by a skilled and experienced crew. When it took off, the weather was almost perfect for flying and it sent three routine signals all suggesting a perfectly normal flight ahead. Then it vanished.

The messages from the pilots of Flight 19, properly interpreted, give an idea of what must have happened. But no further messages were heard from the *Star Ariel* in the four hours that elapsed before the station at Kingston began to wonder at its long silence. Isaac Asimov, scientist and science fiction author, has said he does not 'think that anything is essentially unexplainable. There are things that are unexplained. They may never be explained because we may have no data to explain them with.' Is this not true of the Bermuda Triangle? Where there is insufficient data, a mystery may always be a mystery.

CHAPTER 8

FIRES FROM NOWHERE

There have been many reports of ball lightning during electrical storms and some of them have a strange twist – the phenomenon seems to have a mind of its own. It also seems to act in a friendly way towards humans. This is in contrast to fireballs, which appear to attack people. Can there be a force that causes fires from nowhere'? Is there such a thing as spontaneous human combustion? Do halos and other cases of glowing, arise from internal fires? Perhaps all of these are tied in with the still mysterious relationship of mind to matter.

In the summer of 1921 the Reverend John Henry Lehn, then a young man of 24, had a strange experience during an electrical storm. He saw a ball of lightning enter his bathroom, roll around his feet and jump up into the wash basin before it soundlessly disappeared.

'It was about the size of a grapefruit and yellow in colour similar in hue to sodium flame, though it did not dazzle my eyes', he later wrote of this odd event. 'It made no sound at any time.'

The ball lightning had somehow managed to get through the wire screen of the open window, without losing its form and without damaging the screen in any discernable way. But that was not all that was surprising about its behaviour It also melted the steel chain holding the rubber stopper of the drain, leaving it in two parts. The whole mysterious episode lasted only several seconds and the young man was left guessing where the bright ball had gone. He thought it must have disappeared 'down the drain'.

A few weeks later during another electrical storm, almost exactly the same thing happened in the same bathroom. The lightning globe entered through the window without melting the screen and circled Lehn's feet as before. Then it again melted a chain holding a rubber drain stopper – this time the one in the bathtub!

Is the phenomenon, called ball lightning, explainable as a natural happening'? Scientists do not even agree that these floating balls of fire are lightning at all, in the strict sense of the word. Although ball lightning is always reported as luminous, it is variously described as to size and colour from a few inches to several feet in diameter and from a dull white to a fiery red. Sometimes the lightning balls disappear with a loud bang, suddenly and sometimes they merely fade away in silence. Ball lightning does not act like lightning, in fact. It moves more slowly, lasts much longer and disregards conductors. It does not seem to harm humans, even when it vanishes with a blast. Most curious of all, it seems to display an independent will. For as John Henry Lehn remarked with good humour, 'maybe the second sphere wanted a chain of its own to melt in two – at any rate, that's what it did.'

Other reports appear to support the theory, formulated by Vincent Gaddis in his book *Mysterious Fires and Lights* (1967), that ball lightning has a definite will of its own and that it is benevolent toward humans. Gaddis cites several examples of what he calls 'socially minded lightning balls' from the collection of incidents recorded by the French astronomer, Camille Flammarion. In one of these, a fiery globe actually pushed open the door in order to get into the house it invaded. Another time, a ball of light stopped at the top of a tree, went down it slowly from branch to branch, and moved carefully across a farmyard. When it arrived at the door of the stable, one of two children standing there kicked it. The ball lightning exploded with a deafening noise but left the children unhurt. Not so the animals inside the barn. Several of them were killed.

Flammarion recounts another instance in which animals suffered death from contact with a lightning ball that did no injury to people. It happened in a village in southwest France. A burning sphere came down the chimney of a farmhouse and, passing through a room with a woman and three children in it, entered the adjoining kitchen. During its progress through the kitchen, it nearly touched the feet of a young farmer, who was not harmed. The ball lightning ended up in a small stable that was part of the house. There, as though it was its intent, it touched a pig as it vanished – and left the animal dead.

No cases have been reported of people being killed by ball lightning. But there is another fiery phenomenon that seems to be malevolent toward human beings. This is the fireball. Unlike ball lightning, fireballs are not connected with electrical storms. They fall suddenly, move quickly and cause intense heat in their vicinity. Something of the power possessed by these strange objects can be seen from the experience of Richard Vogt of Eagle Bend, Minnesota. Driving home on the night of 10 May 1961 he saw what looked like 'a ball of fog, about three feet in diameter and slightly elongated.' It was heading for his car at about a 45 degree angle and came so rapidly that he could not hope to avoid it. Indeed, he did not. The bright ball struck his car just in front of the windshield, exploding as it did. At this, the car became so hot that Vogt had to jump out as quickly as he could. When he touched the windshield, which had been cracked by the impact, he could not leave his fingers on it for more than a second. Asked to give an opinion on the incident, scientists from the University of Minnesota could not offer much help. They were as baffled as anyone that the object fell out of a perfectly clear sky.

'The sky was also clear on 29 May 1938 when a fiery object dropped to earth and burned nine men in a town in England. They described the mysterious menace as 'a ball of fire'. When the barn on a Massachusetts farm was burned down on 19 April 1965, more than one witness said that they saw a sphere that looked like a 'flaming basketball' fall near the barn just before the outbreak of the fire. The local fire chief said that he did not think the fire could have started from a natural cause.

Perhaps the strangest and least understood of all kinds of burning from a seemingly unnatural cause, is that in which the human body is consumed by a heat so great as to turn bones to ash. Some cases of death by burning have been so baffling that the only answer seems to be an impossible one – spontaneous human combustion. How else to explain a body burned to ashes when nothing – or very little – around it has been in any way touched by flames?

The classic case supporting the idea of spontaneous human combustion is that of Mary Hardy Reeser, who died on 1 July 1951 under circumstances that have never been explained. When found in her apartment, almost nothing remained of the 170 pound woman – only her liver still attached to a piece of backbone, her skull, her ankle and foot encased in a black satin slipper and a little heap of ashes. These gruesome remains lay inside a blackened circle about four feet in diameter, which also contained a few coiled seat springs. Nothing outside the four-foot circle had been burned. No flames had been seen to alarm her landlady or neighbours. The landlady had suspected nothing when she went to deliver a telegram to the widow at eight o'clock in the morning. Having found the doorknob too hot to handle, however, she had sought help in getting into the apartment and, with the two workmen who came to her aid, had made the appalling discovery. She remembered that she had looked in on her tenant about nine o'clock the night before and had seen her seated in her armchair, ready for bed but smoking a last cigarette.

Could the cigarette have ignited Mary Reeser's rayon nightgown and burned her and the chair? No fire started in this way could possibly have consumed flesh and bone so completely. In crematories, for example, a temperature of 2500°F or more, sustained for three or four hours, is required to cremate a body; sometimes pulverization is still necessary to reduce the bones to a powder. After long and intensive investigations, no one could come up with a reasonable solution – not firemen, not detectives, not outside experts, including a leading pathologist specializing in deaths by fire. A year after Mary Reeser's death, the detective on the case admitted, 'Our investigation has turned up nothing that could be singled out as proving, beyond a doubt, what actually happened.' The police chief agreed, saying, 'As far as logical explanations go, this is one of those things that just couldn't have happened, but it did.'

Is it possible that spontaneous combustion is the logical explanation, little as people want to believe it? Spontaneous combustion is fully accepted as a natural occurrence in the vegetable and the mineral kingdoms. Haystacks and ricks of corn have frequently been consumed by the heat generated during the fermentation produced from moisture within them. Barns, paper mills, stores of explosives, all have gone up in flames from the same causes. In certain circumstances, a mass of powdered charcoal will heat up as it absorbs air and spontaneously ignite. Bird droppings can produce the same effect – it has even been suggested that some church fires have been caused by the spontaneous ignition of bird droppings, accumulated over the centuries on the roof.

The surface of the earth can also burn, usually because of the presence, beneath the topsoil, of oil-bearing shale or coal. The so-called 'Burning Cliff' near Weymouth, England periodically burns for days and in past centuries did so for years. Around the English village of Bradley, a thick bed of coal lying eight feet below the surface began burning in the 1750s and continued to do so for at least 60 years.

Though doctors and scientists accepted these forms of spontaneous combustion, however, they remained largely blind to any evidence that the same phenomenon could occur in humans. Dr Alfred Swaine Taylor, author of the influential *Principles and Practice of Medical Jurisprudence*, wrote in 1873, 'The hypothesis of such a mode of destruction of the human body is not only unsupported by any credible facts, but is wholly inconsistent with all that science has revealed.' Ignoring the possibility that science had not, by 1873, revealed all the facts of the universe, he went on to say, 'In the instances reported which are worthy of any credit, a candle, a fire or some other ignited body has been at hand and the accidental kindling of the clothes of the deceased was highly probable.'

It is interesting to follow in successive editions of Taylor's great work, a modification of this denunciatory attitude. The editor of the 8th (1928) edition, while still 'absolutely rejecting any doctrine of spontaneous combustion', thereupon adds, 'it must be admitted, on the other hand, that there are cases recorded by credible authorities which require some explanation to account for the unusual amount of destruction (burning) which has been produced in a human body by what are at first sight very inadequate means.'

Doctors of an earlier century found no difficulty in accepting the fact of death by spontaneous combustion, although in nearly all the cases they considered the deaths to be the result of too much drinking. Thomas Bartholin, a seventeenth-century Danish medical writer, described the case of a poor woman of Paris who 'used to drink spirit of wine [brandy] plentifully for the space of three years, so as to take nothing else. Her body contracted such a combustible disposition, that one night when she lay down on a straw couch, she was all burned to ashes except her skull and the extremities of her fingers.'

A celebrated murder case in eighteenth-century France brought about a more scientific study of spontaneous human combustion in Europe. The lawyer in the case got his client acquitted by producing evidence to support the idea of spontaneous combustion of the victim, rather than murder. The fact that the dead woman was an habitual drunkard led to a connection being made between deaths by unexplained burning and alcohol. In 1763, a book dealing with 'the spontaneous burnings of the human body' was published in France. Medical writers in the Netherlands, Germany and elsewhere, followed with their studies. One book of 1832 cited a case of 100 years before in Italy. It had happened in Cesena in 1731, when the 62-year-old Countess Cornelia Bandi died under mysterious circumstances. What was left of her body was found about four feet from her bed – her legs, her half-burned head and a pile of ashes. No other signs of fire were present.

The authorities laid the cause of death to 'internal combustion' – and gossip added that the Countess often washed her body with 'camphorated spirit of wine' when 'she felt herself indisposed.' So alcohol makes its appearance again, if in a discreet way. It would not do to suggest that a countess went to bed drunk but alcohol had to be introduced in some manner. Doctors began to warn their drinking patients to steer clear of flames, and no doubt similarly warned them against cooling themselves with camphorated spirit of wine.

It was not hard to find examples of those who had disregarded such warnings. In 1744, a woman in Ipswich, England who 'had drunk, plentifully of gin', was found burning like a log near the grate – but there was no fire going. A few years later, a woman 'much addicted to drinking' was found dead in similar circumstances in Coventry, England. John Anderson of Nairn, Scotland, a carter known for his indulgence in whisky, was found 'smoul-dering' and dying by the roadside outside his hometown.

Deaths like this were ammunition for the rising Temperance Movement. The abstainers warned of the horror of dying from an inner, self-started fire. It was said that water could not extinguish these particular flames, that they burned from within and destroyed nothing but the drunken victim; even that the smoke which issued from the bodies was unlike other smoke, depositing an oily, sticky soot on whatever it touched.

It was also as the consequence of – and sometimes the punish-ment for – drunkenness that spontaneous human combustion entered the novels of the nineteenth-century. The best known incident of spontaneous combustion in the fiction of the period occurs in Charles Dickens' *Bleak House*, in which the old miser Krook meets this repulsive death. The build-up to the discovery is vivid with horrifying details – the smell like burning chops in the air outside the room, the soot that smears 'like black fat', the 'thick yellow liquor' that drips from the corner of a window sill to lie in a 'nauseous pool'. Once inside Krook's room, 'There is a very little fire left in the grate but there is a smouldering suffo-cating vapour in the room and a dark greasy coating on the walls and ceiling.' And so to the discovery between the chairs, 'Is it the cinder of a small charred and broken log of wood sprinkled with white ashes . . . ?' It is not. It is all that remains of old Krook—a man 'continually in liquor'.

Dickens received many letters from readers who found this death incredible and who took him to task for 'giving currency to a vulgar error'. But Dickens was not merely a sensationalist. He had attended an inquest on just such a case when he was a cub reporter 20 years before and he had followed later developments in the subject.

Searching for a pattern in human deaths by mysterious burning, Michael Harrison in his book *Fire from Heaven* considers the possibility that the better educated are spared from seemingly mali-cious attacks by fire. He cites the case of James Hamilton, who was a professor of mathematics at the University of Nashville, Tennessee. In January 1835, Hamilton was standing outside his house when he felt a stabbing pain in his left leg – 'a steady pain like a hornet sting, accompanied by a sensation of heat.'

When he looked down, he saw a bright flame several inches long, 'about the size of a dime in diameter, and somewhat flattened at the tip.' It was shooting out from his trousered leg. He tried to beat it out with his hands but this had no effect. He did not give way to panic, however. Although what he was seeing was clearly impossible, he accepted that it was taking place. Possibly without consciously recalling the fact, he knew that combustion requires oxygen. He cupped his hands around the flame, cutting off the supply of oxygen and the flame went out.

Hamilton's quick-wittedness saved him from a fiery attack and perhaps even death. But how can some people's apparently natural immunity to fire be explained? The well-known Bible story in which Shadrach, Meshach and Abednego walk around in a fiery furnace without getting a single mark on them or their clothes, depends on a divine agency for protection. What about the many recorded cases of mystics and shamans who walk unscathed across red-hot beds of coal or lava? How can certain people control fire so that it does not burn them?

In Paris in the eighteenth century, two young women demonstrated remarkable ability to submit themselves to what would be torture by fire for others. Gabrielle Molet and Marie Sonet were *convulsionnaires*, the name given to those who claimed miraculous cures after experiencing convulsions at the tomb of a highly esteemed local deacon known for his kindness and humility. Gabrielle Molet astounded onlookers by thrusting her face into a blazing fire and withdrawing it unburned. She would also leave her feet in the fire until her shoes and socks were burned away – and come out without a burn on her flesh. Marie Sonet went even further. She exposed her whole body except her head and feet to a raging fire by lying over it supported on stools at each end. Wrapped only in a sheet, she remained rigid over the flames for hours.

The nineteenth-century medium Daniel Dunglas Home, also exhibited feats of daring with fire. While in a trance or semi-trance, he could handle scorching hot coals as though he had asbestos gloves on. Once he was reported to have picked up a glass lampshade, touching a match against it. The glass was hot enough to ignite the match. Home then put the shade between his lips, which showed no ill effects from the intense heat. This medium, who was never caught in fraud throughout his exceptional career, also had the added quality of being able to transfer his own immunity to fire, to other people and to objects. For example, it was said that he could hand searingly hot coals to someone else without that person feeling any pain or burning. He also put such coals against handkerchiefs or clothing without so much as singeing the cloth.

It is an accepted fact that an increase in body temperature is one of the physical changes sometimes associated with trances and other unusual states. The most celebrated twentieth-century case is that of Padre Pio, a saintly Capuchin friar who lived in the southern Italian town of Foggia and was known for performing miracle cures. His normal body temperature was slightly below normal but during one of the ecstatic states he experienced, it would soar beyond the reach of an ordinary clinical thermometer to the extraordinary figure of 118.4°F. During his trancelike states, it was observed that Padre Pio seemed to glow. This phenomenon is frequently mentioned in the lives of saints and other holy figures. Saint Philip Neri, Saint Ignatius Loyola and Saint Francis de Sales are among the many who are said to have been seen surrounded by a bright light when preaching or saying mass. When Moses came down from Mount Sinai 'the skin of his face shone', and in the presence of other people he had to wear a veil. In Christian religious art, God and Christ care represented as being surrounded by a shining nimbus or glory. The golden haloes shown encircling the heads of saints are stylized expressions of this same glow. Travellers who have climbed to the summits of mountains in stormy weather, have sometimes observed sparks shooting from their clothes and hair. Their heads can even be surrounded by an electric aureole very like that of a medieval saint and it is possible that some people can unconsciously produce a similar effect at ordinary altitudes.

Is there, then, such a thing as a human firefly? Take the case of Anna Monaro, whose strange glowing hit headlines all over the world in May 1934. An asthma patient in the hospital at Pirano, Italy, Mrs Monaro emitted a blue glow from her breasts as she slept. This emanation lasted for several seconds at a time, occurred several times a night and continued for a period of weeks. Many doctors and psychiatrists observed the phenomenon. None could explain it.

Can some of the mysterious fires and lights be connected with the poltergeist phenomenon? There are many well-attested and recent reports of poltergeist activity involving fire, including self-destructive attacks as well as assaults on others. Harrison in *Fire from Heaven* also sees in this an unconscious suicide bid, and most cases of spontaneous combustion as an unconscious suicide bid that succeeded. He theorizes that in a trancelike state, or when half-sleeping, intoxicated or in some other manner 'outside themselves', the victims were able to call forth fires or flameless heat because they were possessed of an unconscious wish to die. Can the mind influence matter so much?

It seems only fitting that this section should end as it began, with the undefined relationship between mind and matter. Just as incomprehensible powers exerted by the one upon the other seem to lie at the roots of coincidence and to give a reality to our beliefs in jinxes and curses, so the mystery of the 'fires from nowhere' may eventually be understood in similar terms. Until this understanding is forthcoming, many phenomena must remain *mysterious* – a word that in the ancient world meant 'a secret known only to initiates'. At some future point, mankind may be initiated into those secrets.

Part Two

'Here Be Dragons'

When a medieval cartographer came to depict unexplored regions on a map – such as the depths of Africa, the distant steppes of Russia or the vast Atlantic Ocean – he would often write the phrase 'Here Be Dragons' across the area. This was more than a map-maker's trick to fill-in embarrassing blanks, the man would almost certainly believe it to be a plain statement of fact – all authorities of the time agreed that monsters lurked beyond the walls of civilization.

At the turn of the twentieth century, despite the invention of orbital satellites that can count the number of tiles on your roof, the belief in monsters remains strong across the globe. The planet may have been mapped to the square-inch but many wilderness regions remain and monster reports emerge from them with striking regularity. Do surviving dinosaurs roam the Congo jungles? Do semi-human Yeti wander the Himalayas or Sasquatch, the North American forests? Do water monsters swim unnoticed beneath our passenger ferries or haunt our inland lakes? And what of the more fantastic monsters – vampires, werewolves and dragons? If they are only fairy-tales, why do they occur in folklore around the planet and why are cases still reported in the modern day?

The word monster comes from the Latin *monere*, meaning 'to warn' – for the ancient Romans, any freakish or strange creature was seen as an omen of ill fortune. Perhaps our continued belief in 'monsters' is likewise, just a childish expression of our fear of the unknown. On the other hand, what if some of the reports in this section are true?

CHAPTER 9

THE LEGEND OF THE VAMPIRE

The famous nineteenth-century novel about Count Dracula has established the modern picture of a vampire as a gaunt, but not unattractive, man with long sharp teeth and blood-red lips. But what is the long-lasting legend behind this relatively recent picture ? According to old folk tales the world over, vampires can take the form of a wolf or a bat or even a misty vapour without shape. Is there any basis for the belief in corpses that maintain a semi-life by sucking the blood of the living? Are vampires all in the mind – devils to be ousted by exorcism ?

One night in January 1973 John Pye, a young British police officer, was called to investigate a death. Within an hour what had seemed like a routine mission turned into one of the strangest cases any policeman can have encountered. Police Constable Pye found the dead man's room plunged in darkness. The man had apparently been so terrified of electricity that there were no light bulbs in his room. But gradually the beam from the policeman's flashlight revealed an extraordinary scene. PC Pye was looking at a fortress prepared against an attack by vampires. Salt was scattered around the room and sprinkled over the blankets. A bag of salt rested by the dead man's face and another was laid between his legs. The man had mixed salt with his urine in various containers. Outside, on the window ledge, he had placed an inverted bowl that covered a mixture of human excreta and garlic.

The dead man was Demetrious Myiciura, a Polish immigrant who had left his country for Britain 25 years earlier. He had worked as a potter in Stoke-on-Trent, in the heart of England's

pottery district. That is where he met his bizarre death. It would
certainly be hard to imagine a place more remote from the traditionally vampire-haunted forests of Transylvania in Romania.
Stoke-on-Trent is an industrial town, set in a landscape mutilated
by factory chimneys and slag heaps. Opposite the station is a
large old-fashioned hotel, in front of which is a statue of the
town's most famous citizen – Josiah Wedgwood, who made
pottery a major industry. There is the usual imposing town hall.
Otherwise the streets of little houses are uniformly black and
narrow. It is all the more surprising, therefore, to come across the
line of large old-fashioned dwellings where Myiciura had made
his home. The houses look gloomy and somehow eerie. They are
simply called 'The Villas', and it was at number 3 that Myiciura
met his death.

The body was duly removed for examination. At the inquest
the pathologist reported that Myiciura had choked to death on a
pickled onion. The coroner thought this unusual but commented
that it was not unknown for people 'to bolt their food and die'.
Meanwhile, the young policeman could not forget what he had
seen. He had gone to the Public Library and read the *Natural
History of the Vampire* by Anthony Masters. His suspicions were
confirmed; salt and garlic are traditional vampire repellents and
the mixture on Myiciura's window ledge was intended to attract
the vampires, who would then be poisoned by the garlic. When
told of this, the coroner ordered a re-examination of the alleged
pickled onion. It was found to be a clove of garlic. As a final
desperate measure to ward off the vampires, this wretched man
had slept with a clove of garlic in his mouth and the garlic had
choked him to death. So in a roundabout way, the vampires did
get him in the end.

What, then, are these vampires that literally scared Myiciura to
death? Vampires are corpses, neither dead nor alive, that rise
from the grave at night and suck the blood of the living. They
gradually drain the blood of their victims, who must then become
vampires in turn. The legendary home of the vampire is in eastern
Europe, notably Romania. It was there, in the province of
Transylvania, that British author Bram Stoker set his famous
story of *Dracula*. His Count Dracula, with arched nostrils, blood-
red lips and long sharp teeth, has come to typify our image of a

vampire. But like the legendary vampires, Dracula could readily change into an animal such as a wolf or a bat. A vampire might even become a vapour to filter around the window frames in search of his or her chosen victim. When their gruesome feast of blood is over, the vampires crawl back into their coffin, where they can easily be recognized by the excellent state of preservation of their body. No matter how long vampires have been buried, it is said, they look as if they were still alive. Garlic, salt, or a crucifix may drive them off but the only way to destroy them is to plunge a stake through their heart – at which time they give a horrible death shriek. They may need to be beheaded and burned as well.

A primitive superstition? Perhaps. Nevertheless, Myiciura believed it. He was convinced that vampires exist – and not just in the faraway forests of Transylvania. Demitrious Myiciura believed that he was being threatened by vampires in a British city in the 1970s.

'This man genuinely believed', remarked the coroner afterward. He denied that Myiciura was mad, although 'obsessed perhaps'. The Pole, who was born in 1904, had lost everything in World War II. His farm had been taken over by the Germans and his wife and family had been killed. He arrived in England after the war with nothing.

'I've been a lawyer for a long time', said the coroner, 'dealing with courtroom cases of all kinds. I've seen all sorts of depravity, all sorts of nonsense, but I can visualize what was behind this man. A lot of evil had happened to him. All right, he thought, I'll cling to evil and he happened to believe in vampires. I am convinced, even after this inquest, that this man genuinely was afraid of vampires and was not trying to kill himself.'

Even in New York, surely a most unlikely hunting ground for vampires, there were in the 1970's, two strange cases reported by writer Jeffrey Blyth. A girl calling herself Lillith told two psychic researchers that she met a young man in a cemetery who tried to kiss her. It is not clear what she was doing in the cemetery in the first place but instead of consenting to the kiss she plunged her teeth into the man's neck with such a surge of strength that she drew blood. 'I never considered myself a Dracula', she said, 'but rather a very evil person who liked the taste of blood.' The second vampire was a young man named Carl Johnson, who crept into his sister's bedroom while she slept, gently pricked her leg and sucked her blood. This gave him a thirst, he said and he could feel himself gaining in strength as he drained his victim.

Such cases indicate that far from being a legend of the past, vampirism exists today, if only in people's minds. Indeed, there has been an amazing revival of interest in vampires on both sides of the Atlantic. There is a Dracula Society in London and another in California. Modern British writers have studied the vampire and professors in the United States and Canada have published learned books and papers on the subject. Countless movies are still made about Dracula and vampires – and so are studies of the movies. In Britain, a national poll revealed that the actor Denholm Elliot was the most 'dreamt of' person in the country after he had portrayed Count Dracula on television. It has also been discovered recently that mental patients tend to identify themselves with Count Dracula as much as with Napoleon.

For the most part, this modern preoccupation with vampires is little more than a harmless fantasy. But there are elements, such as the desecration of graveyards in Britain, that are disturbing. The graveyard activity reached an unpleasant climax with the so-called vampire hunters of Highgate Cemetery in London. Highgate Cemetery was once a place of splendour. It was designed by the best nineteenth-century British architects and landscape gardeners and has graceful avenues of trees for the bereaved families to stroll through. It has deteriorated, however, and is so thickly overgrown that the atmosphere is sinister even on a bright sunlit morning. Reports of black magic are all too believable and the work of vandals is only too evident.

The case of the vampire hunters was again brought to public notice in 1974, with a second trial of David Farrant, president of the British Occult Society, who was described as a 'High Priest' in court. News stories were limited because of the bizarre details of the case but headline writers went as far as they could with lines like 'Capers among the Catacombs' and 'High Priest Lectures Judge on Witchcraft'. When told of girls dancing naked at witchcraft ceremonies, the judge commented with dry legal wit that they must have found it extremely chilly in October.

Here is what happened. After Farrant stated in a television

interview of 1970 that a seven-foot vampire had been seen in Highgate Cemetery, 100 vampire hunters converged on the place. Farrant was brought to trial. The startled jury learned that iron stakes had been driven through mutilated corpses after their tombs had been smashed in. (The bodies were later returned to their graves as discreetly as possible to spare the feelings of relatives.) Photographs of a naked girl in a mausoleum were found in Farrant's home and a police inspector reported that a witness he visited, 'had salt around the windows of the room, salt around the doorway and a large wooden cross under his pillow.' It was also revealed that voodoo dolls with pins through their chests had been sent to the police by Farrant.

Farrant was charged with damaging a memorial to the dead, entering catacombs in consecrated ground and interfering with and offering indignity to the remains of a body 'to the great scandal and disgrace of religion, decency and morality'. Admitting that he frequently held occult ceremonies in Highgate Cemetery, he denied all the charges and conducted his own defence, claiming that a Satanic sect and vandals had been responsible for the damage. He was found guilty on two of five charges and sentenced to jail for almost five years.

It is tempting and, probably correct, to dismiss such cases as a form of unhealthy aberration. Yet not far from Highgate Cemetery lives a man who takes reports of vampirism seriously. The Reverend Christopher Neil-Smith is a leading British exorcist and writer on exorcism. He can cite several examples of people who have come to him for help in connection with vampirism. 'The one that particularly strikes me is that of a woman who showed me the marks on her wrists which appeared at night, where blood had definitely been taken. And there was no apparent reason why this should have occurred. They were marks almost like those of an animal. Something like scratching.' He denies that this might have been done by the woman herself. She came to him when she felt her blood was being sucked away and after he performed an exorcism the marks disappeared.

Another person, who came from South America 'had a similar phenomenon, as if an animal had sucked away his blood and attacked him at night'. Again, the Reverend Neil-Smith could find no obvious explanation. There was a third case of a man who, after his brother had died, had the strange feeling that his lifeblood was being slowly sucked away from him. 'There seems to be evidence this was so', says Neil-Smith. 'He was a perfectly normal person before, but after the brother's death he felt his life was being sucked away from him as if the spirit of his brother was feeding on him. When the exorcism was performed he felt a release and new life, as if new blood ran in his veins'. Neil-Smith rules out the possibility of a simple psychological explanation for this, such as a feeling of guilt by the survivor toward his brother. 'There was no disharmony between them. In fact he wasn't clear for some time that it [the vampire] *was* his brother.'

The clergyman describes a vampire as 'half animal, half human', and firmly refutes the suggestion that such things are 'all in the mind'. 'I think that's a very naive interpretation', he says. 'All the evidence points to the contrary'. Concluding that there is such a thing as vampirism, he identifies this strange belief as a persistent form of devil worship.

Many people will say that Neil-Smith is easily taken in. Most will dismiss reports of vampirism in the modern world as nonsense. And yet, as Hamlet tells Horatio in Shakespeare's play, 'There are more things in heaven and earth, Than are dreamt of in your philosophy.' But do these undreamed of things include vampires? On the face of it, how can anyone believe that corpses can rise from their coffins at night to suck the blood of the living, make new vampires of their victims and return to the grave before daybreak? Sceptical minds find this incredible. Some even say it is the silliest superstition of all.

Yet people have believed in vampires all over the world since the earliest recorded times. Legends reach back many centuries before Christ to ancient Assyria and Babylonia – and always vampirism includes the drinking of blood, the life-giving fluid.

Aztecs poured blood into the mouths of their idols. In India, rajahs drank blood from severed heads. In China, the family would guard a corpse the night before burial lest a dog or cat jump over the body and transform it into a vampire. This belief is echoed in a book called *Antidote Against Atheism* written in the seventeenth century by Dr Henry Moore. He tells the story of Johannes Cuntius of Silesia in central Europe, whose dead body was scratched by a black cat before the funeral. Sure enough,

Cuntius was later reported to have reappeared and to have drunk blood. When his body was duly dug up again, it was said to be in the typical well-preserved vampire condition.

The ancient Greeks and the Romans after them, believed in a type of female vampire called a *lamia* who seduced men in order to suck their blood. Later the Greeks had another word for the vampire – *vrukalakos*, a creature who was able to revive the dead and whose victims would then feast on the living. Anyone – male or female – with red hair, a birthmark, or even blue eyes was suspected of being a vampire. Blue eyes are rare in Greece. But those born on Christmas Day, a seventh son, a person with a hare lip or anyone in the slightest bit unusual were also suspect, so many people would easily fit the description of vampires.

Vampires were so rife on the Greek island of Santorini, now called Thera, that Greeks would say 'send a vampire to Santorini' just as we talk of 'taking coals to Newcastle'. In 1717, a distinguished French botanist, Joseph de Tournefort, stated that throughout 'the whole Archipelago there is no Orthodox Greek who does not firmly believe that the devil is able to re-energize and revitalize dead bodies.'

Closer to home and as recently as 1874, a man in Rhode Island dug up his daughter and burned her heart because he believed she was draining the lifeblood from the rest of his family.

The true home of the vampire, however, lies in eastern Europe and the vampire legend as we know it today, grew up in Romania and Hungary around the start of the sixteenth century. The word itself comes from a Slavonic term and did not exist in English until the 1730s. At that time, reports of vampires were numerous in eastern Europe. These accounts were picked up by travellers whose writings about them spread the vampire story all over Europe. Fiction then made the vampire famous. In the nineteenth century, best-selling horror writers seized on the vampire tale. Even great poets like Byron, Goethe and Baudelaire tried their hand with the vampire theme. It was British author Bram Stoker, however, who finally took the many jumbled strands of the vampire legend and wove them into the classic *Dracula*, published in 1897. His mixture of fact and fiction has dominated our conception of a vampire ever since.

Stoker never went to Transylvania, which is now a province of

Romania and where his story opens. But his research into museum records and guidebooks on the area was extremely thorough and *Dracula* contains a great deal of authentic Slavonic folklore. The choice of Transylvania as Dracula's homeland was an apt one. The swirling mists, the peasants in colourful national costume and the wooden crucifixes beside the Borgo Pass that Stoker described in his book, are all still there. In this part of Europe, vampirism was a part of life -- and death. As the Reverend Montague Summers, a leading historian of vampirism, wrote, '. . . in Romania we find gathered together around the Vampire almost all the beliefs and superstitions that prevail throughout the whole of eastern Europe.'

We tend to think of the vampire as pale, gaunt and emaciated. This is misleading, for after a feast of blood the creature would be replete, red-lipped and rosy-hued. In some ways this image of the vampire as something sleek with blood, is even more horrifying. But, deathlike or robust, do such beings exist? Many early authorities were tempted to think so, including the French monk Dom Augustin Calmet. He was the author of one of the earliest learned studies of vampires, published in 1746. Calmet strived to maintain an open mind, but he wrote, 'We are told that dead men . . . return from their tombs, are heard to speak, walk about, injure both men and animals whose blood they drain . . . making them sick and finally causing their death. Nor can the men deliver themselves unless they dig the corpses up and drive a sharp stake through these bodies, cut off their heads, tear out the hearts, or else burn the bodies to ashes. It seems impossible not to subscribe to the prevailing belief that these apparitions do actually come forth from their graves.'

Other eminent writers had no doubts about the existence of vampires. Jean-Jacques Rousseau the famous French philosopher of the eighteenth century, declared, 'If ever there was in the world a warranted and proven history, it is that of vampires. Nothing is lacking; official reports, testimonials of persons of standing, of surgeons, of clergymen, of judges; the judicial evidence is all embracing.'

In our own time Colin Wilson, author of *The Occult* (1971) agrees. He says, 'There *must* have been a reason that these vampire stories suddenly caught the imagination of Europe.

Obviously *something* happened and it seems unlikely that it was pure imagination.' He, too, refers to the documentation, 'Examples of vampirism are so well authenticated that it would be absurd to try to maintain a strictly rationalist position.'

There is a surprising weight of evidence in support of the vampire legend, much of it collected and endorsed by army surgeons. In the Yugoslavian village of Meduegna near Belgrade, for example, a group of doctors investigated an epidemic of vampirism. On 7 January 1732 Johannes Flickinger, Isaac Seidel, Johann Baumgartner and a lieutenant colonel and sub-lieutenant from the capital of Belgrade, signed the medical report. They testified to an examination of 14 corpses. Only two – a mother and baby – were found to be in a normal state of decomposition. All the others were 'unmistakably in the vampire condition'.

There were so many such reports of vampirism in the mid-eighteenth century that it was said by one surgeon to have 'spread like a pestilence through Slavia and Walachia . . . causing numerous deaths and disturbing all the land with fear of the mysterious visitors against which no one felt himself secure.'

A classic case history of the time concerned a Hungarian soldier, who was billeted on a farm near the Austro-Hungarian frontier. He was eating with the farmer and his family one evening when they were joined by an old man. The soldier noticed that the family seemed extremely frightened of the man, who simply touched the farmer on the shoulder and then left. Next morning the soldier learned that the farmer was dead. Apparently the old man was the host's father and had been dead for 10 years. When he visited and touched his son, he both announced and caused that son's death.

The soldier told the story to other men in his regiment and the old man was soon labelled a vampire. For although he had not taken blood from his son, his coming showed him to be a member of the living dead and he had certainly brought about his son's death. The affair was beginning to spread alarm among the soldiers, so it was investigated by the infantry commander, some other officers and a surgeon. The farmer's family was questioned under oath, testimony was taken from villagers and eventually the old man's grave was opened. His body looked like that of a man who had died recently – not 10 years earlier – and 'his blood was like that of a living man'. The commander of the regiment ordered that the vampire's head be cut off and the body was laid to rest again.

During their inquiry the officers were told of another vampire who returned at 10 year intervals to suck the blood of members of his family. It is a notable feature of vampire stories that the vampire's relatives or lovers are usually the first to suffer attack. One case in a remote village in Yugoslavia, concerned a particularly pernicious vampire who killed three of his nieces and a brother within a fortnight. He was interrupted just as he was starting to suck the blood of his fifth victim – another beautiful young niece – and he escaped.

A deputation, whose members' credentials seem impeccable, was sent from Belgrade to investigate. The party consisted of civil and military officials and a public prosecutor. They went to the vampire's grave as dusk fell, accompanied by the villagers. The man had been buried three years before but when the investigators opened his grave, they found his body intact with hair, fingernails, teeth and eyes all in good condition. His heart was still beating, unbelievable as that seems. When the investigators thrust an iron stake through the corpse's heart, a white fluid mixed with blood burst out. They then cut off the head with an axe. Only when the body was finally reburied in quicklime did the young niece who would have been the vampire's fifth victim begin to recover.

Usually in such cases a terrible smell was reported around the corpse but that is hardly surprising. One body was described graphically as 'puffed and bloated like some great leech about to burst', and when the customary stake was plunged into the breast of another, 'a quantity of fresh scarlet blood issued, and from the nose and mouth as well; more issued from that part of his body which decency forbids me to name.' There was another poignant case when tears sprang from the vampire's eyes as he gave his last scream of anguish.

One of the chief reasons for people's acute fear of vampires is their alleged power to infect victims with their own insatiable lust for blood. According to some traditions, only people who die from loss of blood after repeated vampire attacks will become vampires themselves. Other vampire tales maintain that one or two attacks are enough and that any victim of a vampire will come back as a new vampire after his or her natural death. The vampire is said to hypnotize its victims while it feeds, so that the person remembers nothing of the gruesome experience but simply complains of disturbed sleep and a strange lack of energy. Thus the vampire can safely return night after night to the same victim if it wishes, until that victim grows progressively more anaemic and dies. Sometimes there are tell-tale puncture wounds on the victims' neck. In that case, if they believe in vampires, they may well suspect their plight.

An example of how one vampire creates another was reported to the Imperial Council of War in Vienna in the 1730s. It involved a Hungarian soldier, Arnold Paole. He had been killed when a cart fell on top of him but he was said to have returned from the dead 30 days later and claimed four victims who eventually died 'in the manner traditionally ascribed to vampires' – presumably from the typical weakness attributed to loss of blood. Friends remembered Paole saying that he had been attacked by a vampire himself during military service on the Turko-Serbian border. But he thought he had cured himself of any possible infection by the traditional remedy of eating earth from the vampire's grave and rubbing himself with its blood. This had obviously failed, however, for when Paole's body was exhumed, it 'showed all the marks of an arch vampire. His body was flushed, his hair, nails and beard had grown and his veins were full of liquid blood which splashed all over the winding sheet.' The local Governor ordered the inevitable stake to be thrust through the heart and the vampire uttered the familiar shriek. Then the body was burned. The same procedure was also applied to the four recent victims in case they became active.

All these precautions apparently proved futile. Five years later, there was a further outbreak of vampirism in the same area and 17 people died. One woman claimed that her son, who had died nine weeks earlier, had attempted to strangle her while she slept – she died three days afterward. The governor demanded another inquiry and it was learned that Arnold Paole had attacked animals as well as humans during his reappearance as a vampire. Parts of the flesh of these animals had been eaten and, in due course, had caused the new epidemic. This time all the new infected vampires were exhumed, staked, decapitated and burned. For good measure their ashes were thrown into the river. This seemed to be effective at last and the terror was over.

Local bishops frequently sought the advice of the Pope on the vampire problem but they received little help. The Church maintained, with some justification, that such phenomena were delusions. However, at one point the Vatican issued the cautious advice that suspect bodies should be exhumed and burned. Dom Calmet is one of the few authorities who quelled his occasional doubts and managed to remain objective. He showed a rare compassion for the vampires, especially if they were really innocent victims of superstition, 'They were killed by decapitation, perforation or burning and this has been a great wrong; for the allegation that they returned to haunt and destroy the living has never been sufficiently proved to authorize such inhumanity, or to permit innocent beings to be dishonoured . . . as a result of wild and unproved accusations. For the stories told of these apparitions, and all the distress caused by these supposed vampires, are totally without solid proof.' Ever open-minded, however, he eventually came to the conclusion that, 'This is a mysterious and difficult matter and I leave bolder and more proficient minds to resolve it.'

Dom Calmet rightly uses the word 'mysterious', and this element of mystery may be one simple reason for the lasting fascination of the vampire legend.

There are other vampire stories, however, which are far from entertaining and which stem from genuine fear. It was part of the vampire legend that people who were outcasts of society in life would remain outcasts after death and might return as vampires. This compares to the western European folklore that an evil-doer – or the victim of evil – is often fated to return after death as a ghost. The Church may have found it useful not to discourage this belief that served as a warning to the guilty. In eastern Europe around 1645, it was stated that people who had led a 'wicked and debauched life' or had been 'excommunicated by their bishop' were likely to be condemned to the fate of the vampire, forever searching for the peace that was denied to them. The same threat applied to all suicides, those buried without the proper religious sacraments, perjurers, people who died under any kind of curse and, in Hungary, to the stillborn illegitimate children of parents who were also illegitimate. In other words, anyone who had defied the social conventions of the times might become a vampire after death.

A vampire's grave is reputed to stink and the creature's breath is said to smell foul from its diet of blood. The appearance of a vampire is also often heralded by an appalling odour. Interestingly, an abominable smell is also a frequent element of possession by the devil even today and features prominently in the popular book and film *The Exorcist*. A vampire story that demonstrates this aspect well was recounted by Dr Henry Moore in 1653 and concerns a Silesian. The story goes as follows: 'One evening when this theologer was sitting with his wife and children about him, exercising himself in music, according to his usual manner, a most grievous stink arose suddenly, which by degrees spread itself to every corner of the room. Hereupon he commended himself and his family to God by prayer. The smell nevertheless increased and became above all measure pestilently noisome, insomuch that he was forced to go up to his chamber. He and his wife had not been in bed a quarter of an hour but they find the same stink in the bedchamber; of which, while they are complaining one to another, out steps the spectre from the wall and creeping to his bedside, breathes upon him an exceedingly cold breath, of so intolerable stinking and malignant a scent, as is beyond all imagination and expression.'

This smell sounds like a symbol of impending plague and was frequently interpreted as such. As early as 1196, the historian William of Newburgh told of a 'lecherous husband' who returned from the grave to terrify people in his home town. He said, 'For the air became foul and tainted as this fetid and corrupting body wandered abroad, so that a terrible plague broke out and there was hardly a house which did not mourn its dead, and presently the town, which but a little before had been thickly populated, seemed to be well nigh deserted, for those who had survived the pestilence and these hideous attacks hastily removed themselves to other districts lest they should also perish.'

Two young men, plainly braver than the rest, traced the living corpse to its grave and cut its head off with a spade so that the red blood gushed out. The body was then burned. This destruction of the corpse in the fashion of a vampire succeeded. 'No sooner had that infernal monster been thus destroyed', the story goes on, 'than the plague, which had so sorely ravaged the people, entirely ceased, just as if the polluted air was cleansed by the fire which burned up the hellish brute who had infected the whole atmosphere.'

It is interesting to see how the infernal monster is used as a scapegoat for the plague, with the added condemnation that he was a lecherous husband, as if his behaviour when he was alive was responsible for the whole calamity. It is true that epidemics of vampirism and plague did tend to go together – in 1729 it was said that any plague where 'within a few hours five or six persons fell ill in the village', would automatically be linked to vampirism. But it is not a case of the vampires causing the plague. On the contrary, periods of plague created the perfect atmosphere for a belief in vampires.

There are, therefore, several perfectly reasonable explanations for the proliferation of the vampire legend but nevertheless the doubts remain. As the curtain fell on the first stage production of *Dracula*, the producer Hamilton Deane came out in front of the curtain to warn the audience to take care as they went home. 'Remember', he cried in sepulchral tones, 'There are such things!' Well, are there?

CHAPTER 10

WHY BELIEVE IN VAMPIRES?

Can premature burial be at the root of the widespread belief in vampires? It is known that in the past many people have been mistakenly thought dead and buried before they actually died. What if some awakened and tried to claw their way out of their coffin? Wouldn't their bloody hands and shrouds make people think they were vampires if their graves were later opened for any reason? Along another line of reasoning, couldn't the idea of bloodsucking be a symbol for the way some people seem to live off the energy and vitality of others? Whether arising from the subconscious or the real, vampires are still very much with us.

'Bring out your dead!' That cry was horrifyingly familiar to the people who lived in times of plague. Carts piled high with corpses would trundle by night after night, bound for the burial pit. A red cross marked the doors of the stricken and the sick were often abandoned even by their own family for fear of contagion. Streets became blocked with decomposing bodies as the living left the towns to the dead and dying. It is easy to understand how terrified people must have been by this devastating disease that flared up periodically in Europe, from ancient times right down to the eighteenth century. Never knowing where it might strike, or when it might end, must have made the plague more alarming even than warfare. Such an epidemic would leave an area depressed mentally as well as physically, creating the ideal climate for panic.

The worst plague of all was the Black Death which swept through Europe in the fourteenth century. It claimed millions of victims – a quarter of Europe's population. When the Black Death finally began to subside, a strange delusion took possession of whole communities in the region that is now Germany. It was known as the 'Dance of St. Vitus' and the nervous disorder that is marked by jerky involuntary movements is still known by that name today. The dancers seemed to lose their senses, performing wild leaps screaming and foaming at the mouth. Regardless of the dismayed crowds that watched them, they danced together for hours in this strange state of delirium until they fell from sheer fatigue and heard nothing except for some who were haunted by religious visions. In spite of this, the priests believed that the dancers were possessed by the devil and tried to pacify them by exorcism.

The dancing spread to Belgium and northern France. At one time, streets in the town of Metz, France were choked by over a thousand dancers. The only solution was to encourage the dancing, which was sometimes done with the aid of hired musicians. Then the dancers would reach the final stage of exhaustion more quickly, and collapse on the ground apparently lifeless. Slowly, however, they began to recover.

This frenzied dancing seems to have been a form of collective hysteria – a result of the nervous strain left by the Black Death. In the same kind of hysteria, rumours of vampirism would be especially likely to spread in times of pestilence and would grow in the retelling. Another explanation for stories of vampires is even more convincing – the high frequency in those days of premature burial or of accidental burial alive. This was all the more probable in times of plague when people were terrified of infection and disposed of bodies as hastily as possible.

Strangely enough it has always been difficult to ascertain exactly when death occurs. Far from being rare, premature burial happened frequently in the past and similar accidents can still happen today. In 1974, doctors in a British hospital were dissecting a body for a kidney transplant when they realized to their horror that the corpse was breathing.

This is not an isolated case. In the late 1970's, in a southern state of America, an unmarried mother-to-be became so agitated at the sight of a policeman knocking on her door that she collapsed and was certified as dead. A week after her burial, her mother arrived and insisted on seeing the body for herself. When the grave was opened it was discovered that the baby had been born and that the mother's fingers had been worn down in the effort to scratch her way out of the coffin.

If we can make such mistakes today with all our medical knowledge, imagine how easy errors must have been in the days when such states as catalepsy (a trancelike condition which might last for several weeks), epilepsy, or apparent death from suffocation or poison were not properly recognized. A state resembling death may even be induced deliberately, as by the fakirs of India.

Even those who were simply in a drunken stupor might have awakened to find themselves interred forever in the darkness It is hard to imagine a more appalling fate: first the gradual realization of what had happened, then the panicky and hopeless attempts to get out and finally the slow suffocation. If the grave of someone prematurely buried was broken into by body snatchers seeking a body for dissection or by robbers hoping to find a valuable ring on one of the fingers, it would be discovered that the body had twisted into a different position in the cramped space. The searchers would probably find also that the shroud was torn and bloody, that there was blood on the fingers and nails from the wretched person's efforts to claw a way out and that the mouth was bloody from being bitten in the final agony. How easily these signs could be attributed to vampirism.

Dr Herbert Mayo, Professor of Anatomy at King's College, London, realized this truth in 1851 and wrote, 'That the bodies, which were found in the so called Vampyr state, instead of being in a new or mystical condition, were simply alive in the common way, or had been so for some time subsequent to their interment; that, in short, they were the bodies of persons who had been buried alive, and whose life, where it yet lingered, was finally extinguished through the ignorance and barbarity of those who disinterred them.' In other words, some alleged vampires might still have been alive when the stake was plunged through their heart. Dr Mayo quoted the case of a man who was believed to have become a vampire and who was exhumed. 'When they opened his grave,' Mayo says, '. . . his face was found with a colour and his features made natural sorts of movements, as if the dead man smiled. He even opened his mouth as if he would inhale fresh air. They held the crucifix before him and called in a loud voice, "See, this is Jesus Christ who redeemed your soul from hell, and died for you." After the sound had acted on his organs of hearing, and he had connected perhaps some ideas with it, tears began to flow from the dead man's eyes. Finally, when after a short prayer for his poor soul, they proceeded to hack off his head, the corpse uttered a screech and turned and rolled just as if it had been alive . . . .'

In Moravia, in the eighteenth century, a postmaster was thought to have died from epilepsy. When some years later it became necessary to transfer various graves, his body was disinterred and it was discovered that he had been buried alive. The doctor who had signed the death certificate lost his reason over it.

In 1665, a terrible outbreak of plague decimated the population of England, claiming nearly 150,000 victims. One symptom of the disease was an acute drowsiness that brought an overwhelming desire for sleep. Since bodies were hurried out of the houses at night, it is hardly surprising that those deeply asleep might be taken for dead – as they were buried hastily in communal pits without the proper formalities of a funeral. Some 150 years or more later, premature burial was still so common that it gave rise to this limerick:

> 'There was a young man of Nunhead
> Who awoke in his coffin of lead,
> "It's cosy enough", he remarked in a huff,
> "But I wasn't aware I was dead."'

Even at the beginning of this century, premature burial occurred so often in the United States that there was said to be a case of it every week. In one instance a young woman from Indianapolis was to be buried two weeks after her seeming death, which several doctors had attested to on the death certificate. Her young brother clung to her body as it was removed for burial and in the confusion a bandage around the woman's jaw fell loose. It was then noticed that her lips were quivering. 'What do you want?', the boy cried. 'Water', whispered the woman, who subsequently recovered and lived to an old age.

The director of an American school for orphans was declared

dead on two occasions. She was only saved the second time when the undertaker happened to pierce her body with a pin and saw a drop of fresh blood ooze from the wound. Washington Irving Bishop, a stage thought reader in America, who frequently entered a state of trance, was once considered dead until a cut made at the autopsy revealed he was alive. A similar case concerned a powerful Churchman of Spain whose heart was brought to view and was seen to beat while he was being embalmed. At that moment he regained consciousness and 'even then had the sufficient strength to grasp with his hand the scalpel of the anatomist' before he finally died.

In creating his arch-vampire Dracula, Bram Stoker may well have drawn on stories he had heard as a child of a great cholera epidemic that, like the plague, created an atmosphere of panic and increased the likelihood of premature burial. This epidemic affected the whole of Europe. In 1832, it reached County Sligo in the West of Ireland, where Stoker's mother Charlotte, then a young girl, was living with her family. Her house was besieged by desperate looters among the last survivors in the village and the story was told that, when she saw a hand reaching through the skylight, she took an axe and cut it off. She told Stoker about Sergeant Callan, a giant of a man whose body was too big to fit in his coffin. To make it fit the undertaker took a hammer to break his legs. At the first blow of the hammer the supposed cholera victim sprang back to life and he was seen around for many years afterward.

Premature burial, therefore, is one logical explanation for bodies that have moved and twisted in their graves. Another is that a dead body shrinks naturally and as the corpse shrinks, the hair and nails appear to grow longer. There are also medical explanations for such apparent phenomena as the scream that the body is supposed to utter as the stake is plunged through the heart. Finally, the soil in which a body is buried can explain why it remains so well preserved. For example, on the Greek island of Santorini, where vampires were said to be so abundant, the volcanic nature of the soil would help keep the bodies intact longer.

These explanations do not account for the reports of vampires who have left their graves and are seen outside them at night. Yet even here there is a straightforward answer suggested by Dennis Wheatley, a best-selling writer on the occult. In times of extreme poverty, beggars would take shelter in graveyards and make family vaults or mausoleums their macabre homes. Driven by hunger, they would have to leave these tombs by night to forage for food in the neighbourhood. If such figures were glimpsed in the moonlight, it is understandable that they might be thought of as vampires. An empty grave can be explained simply as the work of a body snatcher who had stolen the corpse to sell for medical dissection.

All these logical explanations fail to account for the persistence of the vampire legend, however. It seems to go a lot deeper into the human personality. Indeed, much of the fascination for vampires lies in the subconscious.

On one level there is the basic desire for reunion with dead loved ones. 'It is believed', wrote British psychologist Professor Ernest Jones in *On the Nightmare*, 'that they [the dead] feel an overpowering impulse to return to the loved ones whom they had left. The deepest source of this projection is doubtless to be found in the wish that those who have departed should not forget us, a wish that ultimately springs from childhood memories of being left alone by the loved parent.' He concludes, 'The belief that the dead can visit their loved ones, especially by night, is met with over the whole world.' It is certainly the case that the majority of reports show alleged vampires returning to their loved ones and families.

What about the traditional symbolism of blood as the vital essence of life? To the vampire, the sucking of blood is a form of transfusion and this life restorer is a remedy that goes back through history. Early Australian tribes used to treat their sick by opening the veins of male friends, collecting the blood in a bowl, and feeding it to the invalid in its raw state.

Bloodsucking may also be an image for the way in which certain people seem to feed on the energy of others, draining them of vitality. Most of us have come across someone whom we might call a parasite, a sponger or a leech. Vampire would be an equally suitable description. An encounter with such a person can leave us feeling absolutely exhausted. It has been noticed in hospitals that some people can even have this effect on machines, causing them to drop in electric current.

The draining of another's energy is particularly likely to happen in a marriage, family, or other close emotional relationship -- traditionally the vampire's favourite feeding ground. There are also real cases of a strong personality exerting an unnatural influence over a weaker one. One example of this is how Ian Brady controlled Myra Hindley in their wholesale torture and killing of children in the British Moors Murders. Another is the power of Charles Manson over the group called his family. In this connection we might recall the vampire's reputed power to hypnotize a victim while draining its strength.

Above all, there is a powerful sexual element in vampirism, which is undoubtedly one of the main reasons for its continuing fascination. This aspect of the vampire theme was played down in the nineteenth century when, although cruelty and violence were acceptable topics for publication, sex was heavily censored. However, some Eastern European vampire tales state quite frankly that bloodsucking was not the only activity the vampire had in mind when he or she chose a victim. It is certainly part of the legend that male vampires prefer beautiful young girls, while female vampires practice their hypnotic charms on handsome young men.

The vampire's biting kiss on the victim's throat in order to suck out blood, has an erotic and sadistic content that has not escaped the attention of psychologists. Ernest Jones says that "The act of sucking has a sexual significance from earliest infancy which is maintained throughout life in the form of kissing.' A bite, according to Freud, is a part sadistic, part erotic kiss. Blood is also deeply linked with sexuality. 'It has long been recognized by medico psychologists', wrote Montague Summers in his history of vampirism, 'that there exists a definite connection between the fascination of blood and sexual excitement.' Modern psychologists also note that blood and bloodletting are frequently associated with the erotic fantasies of their patients.

Freud believed that 'morbid dread always signifies repressed sexual wishes.' British writer Maurice Richardson, a contemporary expert on vampirism, agrees. The vampire embodies repressed sexual desires and sexual guilt that date from infancy, he maintains. Though we may not like to admit it, sex is a major part of the vampire's appeal. Writing about Bram Stoker's

Dracula, Richardson declares, 'From a Freudian standpoint, and from no other does the story really make any sense; it is seen as a kind of incestuous, necrophiliac, oral-analsadistic all-in wrestling match. And this is what gives the story its force. The vampire Count, centuries old, is a father figure of huge potency.'

Christopher Lee, the movie actor who has become famous for his portrayal of Dracula, describes the vampire Count as a 'superman'. 'He offers the illusion of immortality, the subconscious wish we all have for limitless power, a man of tremendous brain and physical strength with a strange dark heroism. He is either a reincarnation or he has never died', says Lee. It is interesting to note that of the two greatest horror novels ever written, one, *Frankenstein*, deals with the creation of life and the other, *Dracula*, *with* perpetuation of life.

Lee continues, 'He [Dracula] is a superman image with an erotic appeal for women who find him totally alluring. In many ways he is everything people would like to be, the antihero, the heroic villain, and, like the much maligned Rasputin, part-saint and part-sinner. Men find him irresistible because they cannot stop him and, to women, he represents the complete abandonment to the power of a man.'

Christopher Lee's best-known predecessor in the role of Count Dracula was the Hungarian actor, Bela Lugosi. His version of Dracula, directed by Tod Browning in 1931, was an early horror film and is the oldest talkie still playing commercially. After the movie, Lugosi received piles of fan mail from women admirers. The appeal of the vampire had already infected Hollywood long before, however, with the creation in 1913 of the *vamp*. This word, still used today especially in advertising copy, was coined deliberately to launch the first movie star created by publicity. This was Theda Bara, whose name is an anagram of 'Arab Death'. She was shown to the public in *A Fool There Was*, in which she had the celebrated line 'Kiss me, my fool', and she was photographed in seductive poses – once crouching over a male skeleton. In *The Kiss of the Vampire* in 1916, the vamp revelled in the destruction of men. It was said of her, 'She just wanted to ruin her victims and then laugh at them. She was bad!'

The erotic female vampire is just as much a part of the classic vampire legend as her male counterpart. She is described as voluptuous and wanton, irresistible, heartlessly cruel. Like the male vampire she has full red lips – supposedly the result of sucking blood but also traditionally regarded in folk belief as a sign of excessive sensuality. Even the pure must succumb to her macabre charms. By day, however, all vampires are powerless. Some legends continued the erotic theme in their instructions for detecting a vampire's grave while the creature was asleep. A virgin boy or girl was supposed to ride naked over the graveyard on the back of a coal black virgin stallion that had never stumbled. The horse would shy when it came upon a vampire's tomb, it was said.

We now see that there are psychological reasons for the appeal of the vampire as well as logical explanations for vampire beliefs. But the big question remains unanswered – are there really such things as vampires – not the living person who drains us of vitality, nor the occasional individual who develops a mania for blood but the bloodsucking cousin of the ghost, the so-called living dead? As an expert on vampires, Montague Summers came to this conclusion, 'Consciously or unconsciously, it is realized that the vampire tradition contains far more truth than the ordinary individual cares to appreciate and acknowledge.'

A century ago, people would not have believed that we would be able to sit in our homes, watch a square box, and through it see a man land on the moon. There may well be another, spiritual world around us of which we are still unaware.

When someone dies, a close friend or relative frequently gets an instinctive feeling that the death has happened, even hundreds of miles away. Sometimes the death is dreamt of. Occasionally, the dying person is seen by another at the very moment of death. In a similar way, the sighting of vampires could be a time lapse, a version of the experience known as *déjà vu* in which one feels one has been in a strange place before. Some people believe that the sighting of flying saucers is a look into the future when such transport will be common. Conversely, alleged glimpses of the Loch Ness Monster may be a look back into the prehistoric past, when monster creatures abounded.

Such a case of time out of joint would help to explain the Irish legend of a funeral cortege which, having just buried their local priest in the neighbouring hills, noticed a clerical figure coming toward them. As he passed, they were shocked to recognize the man they had just laid to rest. Hurrying to his home they found his mother in a state of extreme agitation because her dead son had appeared at the house an hour before. Had this happened in eastern Europe, the priest might well have been dubbed a vampire, particularly if there were any other unusual or mysterious circumstances in the way he died.

A more complex theory concerning the existence of vampires was put forward by the late Dion Fortune, a leading modern occultist. Like many occultists she believed in the astral body – the spiritual, second body that can separate itself from the physical body and take on a life of its own. She maintained that by a trick of occultism, it is possible to prevent disintegration of the astral body after the death of the physical body. She referred to a case she had encountered involving some dead Hungarian soldiers who were reported to have become vampires and to have made vampires of their victims. She suggested that these soldiers 'maintained themselves in the etheric double [astral body] by vampirizing the wounded. Now vampirism is contagious; the person who is vampirized, being depleted of vitality, is a psychic vacuum himself absorbing from anyone he comes across in order to refill his depleted sources of vitality. He soon learns by experience the tricks of a vampire without realizing their significance and before he knows where he is, he is a full-blown vampire himself.'

After death, separation of the astral body from the physical body is permanent. But occultists believe that the astral body can also escape from the physical body during a person's life and that it may take on some other form – that of a bird or animal, for example. Could this provide further grounds for a belief in the existence of vampires? Dion Fortune firmly believed in the ability of powerful feelings to create thought forms that possess a separate existence. Highly charged negative feelings might therefore cause the astral body to assume the form of an evil monster or ghost – possibly a vampire.

Discussing Dion Fortune's theory in *The Occult*, Colin Wilson agrees that 'strange forces can erupt from the subconscious and take on apparently material shape.' He quotes the story of a young Romanian peasant girl, Eleonore Zugun. Eleonore showed a psychical investigator 'devil's bites' on her hands and arms. As he sat with her, she cried out and marks of teeth appeared on the back of her hand, developing into bruises. A few minutes later she was bitten on the forearm and the investigator could see deep teeth marks. Was this a ghost, asks Wilson, or Eleonore's own subconscious mind out of control? Perhaps it wasn't even Eleonore's mind, he suggests. 'It might have been *somebody else's* mind.'

'The subconscious mind is not simply a kind of deep seat repository of sunken memories and atavistic desire', says Wilson, 'but of forces that can, under certain circumstances, manifest themselves in the physical world with a force that goes beyond anything the conscious mind could command.' He feels that this might explain the mystery of vampires, and indeed of all, so-called, occult phenomena.

Can a mental image be projected as a physical reality? Can the subconscious mind create monsters or ghosts that attack and destroy? Can the astral body of a dead person attach itself to a living person, feeding off him as a vampire in order to maintain life?

Many people would say that the only vampires we might possibly encounter are living people whose private fantasy, life and peculiar aberration is that of the bloodsucking vampire. If this side of a person becomes dominant, he might even believe himself to be a vampire. If his fantasy assumes the shape of a wolf, he may act like a wolf. But the nagging question remains – is there ever a moment when that person actually *becomes* a vampire or a wolf, through some external influence we do not yet understand ?

CHAPTER 11

MAN INTO BEAST

A wolf at night, a man by day – that is the old folk belief about werewolves. Is there any foundation, in fact, for the existence of such a half animal half human creature? According to tradition, people actively seek to become wolves or other predatory animals such as leopards, hyenas or bears. The commonest reason, it is said, is for revenge. Does this give us an explanation for the werewolf legends? Is the werewolf the dormant beast in us all, a monster of the unconscious? Stories have come down to us from Roman times and still occur today. Do they answer a psychological need?

In the year 1598, in a remote patch of forest in western France, an archer and a group of armed countrymen came across the naked body of a boy. The corpse had been horribly mutilated and torn. The limbs, still warm and palpitating, were drenched with blood. As the Frenchmen approached the body, they caught sight of what appeared to be two wolves running off between the trees. The men gave chase but to their amazement, they found they had caught, not a wolf, but what proved to be a man – tall, gaunt, clothed in rags and with matted, verminous hair and beard. To their horror they noticed that his hands were still stained with fresh blood and his claw-like nails clotted with human flesh. The man, it turned out, was a wandering beggar named Jacques Roulet and he was brought to trial at the town of Angers in August 1598. And if the discovery of Roulet was a shock to the people of Angers, the trial proceedings were shattering.

Roulet confessed to the court, 'I was a wolf.'
'Do your hands and feet become paws?'
'Yes, they do.'
'Does your head become like that of a wolf?'
'I do not know how my head was at the time; I used my teeth.'

In reaching their verdict the court had to decide whether Roulet was a werewolf, as he claimed, or a lycanthrope, which is related but different. A werewolf is a living person who has the power to change into a wolf. The word comes from Old English *wer*, meaning man and wolf. A *lycanthrope* is someone suffering from a mental illness that makes him believe he is transformed into a wolf. This word comes from the Greek for wolfman. In either case, Roulet could have faced execution. But the court showed a compassion rare for its time. Judging Roulet to be mentally sick – and therefore a *lycanthrope* – they sentenced him to a madhouse for only two years.

A true werewolf was generally believed to undergo an almost complete transformation into a wolf, unlike the werewolf of Hollywood movies who remains basically human in appearance. Much controversy arose in the past over people who were said to disguise the fact that they were wolves, by wearing their fur on the inside. It was claimed that such people looked ordinary enough but that their skin was inside out. When they were torn apart – as hundreds of innocent people were at various times in past centuries – the hair, or wolf fur, could be seen on the other side of the skin.

The werewolf and the vampire have much in common. In fact it was often assumed that a werewolf would become a vampire after death unless special precautions, such as exorcism, were taken. Anyone who ate the flesh of a sheep killed by a wolf was liable to become a werewolf. A person who ate a wolf's brains or drank water from his footprints was certain to become one. In some places, eating certain large and sweet smelling flowers or drinking from a stream where a wolfpack had drunk, was a sure way to turn into a wolf.

Anybody with small pointed ears, prominent teeth, strong curved fingernails, bushy eyebrows that met over the nose, a third finger as long as the second on each hand, or even a lot of hair – especially on the hands and feet – was immediately suspect. However, if you are tempted to take a closer look at your friends next time you see them, remember that the eyes of a werewolf always remain human.

Like the belief in vampires, these beliefs stemmed from peoples' ignorant fear of anyone who was different. In some traditions it was easy to become a werewolf by accident. In others, you had to be especially evil to merit such a fate. Some tales suggest that a bestial person would return after death as a wolf. Ghostly werewolves, however, are extremely rare in folk-lore, which is where the werewolf differs most from the vampire. The vampire is akin to the ghost. The werewolf is very much a living person and more akin to the witch, in that he or she may actively seek to become a werewolf. This can be done by entering into a pact with a demon known as the Wolf Spirit, or with the Devil himself.

Surprising though it may seem, many people actually wanted to become werewolves and, in addition to the magical methods already mentioned, went through elaborate rituals in the hope of doing so. The right moment for such a change was at midnight by the light of a full moon. The would-be werewolf drew a magic circle and built a fire over which he placed a cauldron containing a potion of herbs and drugs. Then he smeared his body with an ointment made from the fat of a newly-killed cat, mixed with ingredients like aniseed and opium. Around his waist he bound a belt made of wolf's skin. Kneeling inside the circle as the magic potion simmered, he chanted an incantation that went something like this:

> 'Hail, hail, hail, Great Wolf Spirit, hail!
> A boon I ask thee, mighty shade.
> Within this circle I have made,
> Make me a werewolf strong and bold,
> The terror alike of young and old.
> Grant me a figure tall and spare;
> The speed of the elk, the claws of the bear;
> The poison of snakes, the wit of the fox;
> The stealth of the wolf, the strength of the ox;
> The jaws of the tiger, the teeth of the shark;
> The eyes of the cat that sees in the dark.'

Such a powerful plea might sound irresistible. To the sceptical mind, however, it is significant that the simmering potion included large amounts of poppy seed and the salve contained opium. This suggests that the initiate may have been in a drugged condition. The incantation concluded with the cry:

> 'Make me a werewolf! make me a man eater!
> Make me a werewolf! make me a woman eater!
> Make me a werewolf! Make me a child eater!
> I pine for blood! human blood!
> Give it to me! Give it to me tonight!
> Great Wolf Spirit! give it to me, and
> Heart, body, and soul, I am yours.'

If the ritual had been correctly carried out, the aspirant would then begin to change into a wolf. Tall and phantomlike, his figure would glow in the darkness until it assumed the 'form of a tall thin monstrosity, half human and half animal, grey and nude with very long legs and arms, and the feet and claws of a wolf.' Once fully transformed, he would indulge in the werewolf's traditional night-time activities of hunting, killing and eating. The commonest reason for wishing to become a wolf was said to be a desire for revenge.

The man or woman who has achieved the power of metamorphosis will change into a wolf at sunset every night until death, reassuming human shape at dawn. Some folk tales say that the werewolf must roll in the dirt or the morning dew in order to change back into a human; others that the transformation occurs automatically at daybreak. A werewolf that is wounded or killed immediately becomes human again. Usually, the creature can be caught or destroyed like an ordinary wolf but the most effective way of killing a werewolf is to shoot it with a silver bullet. The corpse must then be burned, rather than buried.

To most people all this sounds like a welter of primitive superstition and it is significant that reports of werewolves decreased as cities spread into the countryside. Such tales have always been commonest in remote regions where the wolf was the foremost beast of prey. Today, when the wolf has all but disappeared from the United States and many European countries, it may be hard for us to imagine the terror this animal inspired in our ancestors. In northern countries especially, the wolf was a deadly enemy, hated and feared for its ferocious attacks on flocks and people alike. But the wolf also seemed eerie, moving mainly by night, ghostly grey and silent, almost invisible except for the slanting eyes that glowed red by firelight and yellow-green by moonlight. Add to this its spine-chilling howl – said to be an omen of death – and it is not surprising that the wolf came to be regarded as an evil, almost supernatural, monster. Wherever there were wolves there were also reports of werewolves, whom people feared with a panic verging on hysteria.

Nevertheless, there are eminent authorities on werewolves who do not regard the idea of a human turning into a wolf as superstitious fantasy and who take reports of werewolves seriously. Sabine Baring-Gould, author of *The Book of Were-wolves, Being an Account of a Terrible Superstition* (1865), maintained that because the legend was so persistent 'everywhere and in all ages, it must rest upon foundation of fact.' He claimed that 'Half the world believes, or believed in werewolves.'

Writing in this century, Elliott O'Donnell agrees and declares that there is no conclusive evidence that the people who claimed to be werewolves were shams. It was a characteristic of trials for lycanthropy, that the accused seemed eager to confess. He suggests that many of the accused had been victimized and confessed under torture, which is doubtless true. But even if they were shams, O'Donnell thought this 'would in nowise preclude the existence of the werewolf.' He becomes less convincing, however, when he asserts that werewolves were created by 'malevolent forces, the originators of all evil.'

As with vampirism, reports of werewolves have been documented all over the world since ancient times. As early as the fifth century BC, Herodotus, who is known as the 'father of history', wrote, 'Each Neurian changes himself once a year into the form of a wolf and he continues in that form for several days after which he resumes his former shape.' In the second century AD, a Roman doctor observed that 'lycanthropia is a species of melancholy which can be cured at the time of the attack by opening a vein and abstracting blood.'

Petronius, the first century Roman satirist, tells a werewolf story with a universal theme. It concerns a servant who accompanied a soldier on a night's journey out of town and was aghast to see him strip off his clothes by the roadside and change into a wolf. With a howl, the creature leaped into the woods and disappeared from view. When the servant reached his destination, he was told that a wolf had just broken into the farm and had savaged the cattle before being driven away by a man who had thrust a pike into the animal's neck. Hurrying home at daybreak, the servant came to the place where the soldier's clothes had been but he found only a pool of blood. Back home, the soldier lay wounded with a doctor dressing his neck.

This epitomizes a constant theme of the werewolf legend – the wolf is wounded in a fight and a human being is later discovered suffering from the same wound. A story from the Middle Ages tells of a Russian noblewoman, who doubted that anyone could change into an animal. One of her servants volunteered to prove her wrong. He changed into a wolf and raced across the fields, chased by his mistress' dogs which cornered him and damaged one of his eyes. When the servant returned to his mistress in human form, he was blind in one eye.

Another famous case took place in the Auvergne region of central France in 1558. A hunter out in the forest met a neighbouring nobleman who asked him to bring him back some game, if the hunt was successful. The hunter was later attacked by a savage wolf, but was able to drive it away after slashing off one of its paws. He put the paw in his pouch as a memento and set off for home. On the way, he stopped at the nobleman's chateau and told him of his adventure. Reaching in his pouch for the wolf's paw, he was amazed to find a delicate female hand in its place. The nobleman was even more astonished as he recognized the gold ring on one of the fingers. Dashing upstairs, he found his wife bandaging the bleeding stump of her wrist. She confessed to being a werewolf and was burned at the stake.

Just as the vampire has its traditional home in eastern Europe, the forests of France seem to have been the natural home of the werewolf. Reports of werewolves, called *loups-garoux* in French, reached epidemic proportions in the sixteenth century. As many as 30,000 cases were listed between 1520 and 1630.

One of the most famous werewolves in history is a stooping, bushy-browed hermit called Gilles Garnier. On 13 September 1573, authorities in the French town of Dôle gave permission for a werewolf hunt, after several local children had been found killed and partially eaten. The permission read, 'And since he has attacked and done injury in the country to some horsemen, who kept him off only with great difficulty and danger to their persons, the said court, desiring to prevent any greater danger, has permitted and does permit, those who are dwelling in the said places, notwithstanding all edicts concerning the chase, to assemble with pikes, halberds, and sticks, to chase and pursue the said werewolf in every place where they may find or seize him; to tie and to kill without incurring any pains or penalties.' Clearly the peasants were convinced that a werewolf was to blame before they had even started the hunt. It is extraordinary that in all such reports, there is never any suggestion that the victims might have been seized by a real wolf.

Two months later, a group of villagers heard the screams of a child and the baying of a wolf. Hurrying to the spot – expecting to find a werewolf – they discovered a small girl, badly mauled and thought they recognized Garnier in the wolf that raced away. When a 10-year-old boy disappeared six days later, they raided the hut of 'the hermit of St. Bonnet', as Garnier was known and arrested both him and his wife.

Garnier made two immediate confessions. One concerned a 12-year-old boy killed in a pear orchard the previous August. Garnier had been about to eat the boy's flesh when he was interrupted by some men. They testified that Garnier was in the form of a man not a wolf. On 6 October, in a vineyard near Dôle, Garnier had attacked a 10-year-old girl, this time in the guise of a wolf. He killed her with his teeth and claws, stripped her and ate her, enjoying the meal so much that he brought some of the flesh back for his wife's supper. On the evidence of this confession, Garnier was burned alive on 18 January 1574.

Thirty years later, the similarly named Jean Grenier, a handsome 14-year-old shepherd boy, confessed to a series of crimes in the Bordeaux area of southwest France. For what his confession is worth, he admitted to having eaten more than 50 children. Sometimes, he said, he lay in wait in the woodlands until dusk fell and his transformation into a wolf took place. Then he watched for victims from a thicket beside a favourite pool. Once he surprised two girls, bathing naked; one escaped, but he devoured the other. When he was provoked by extreme hunger, he said, he hurled himself fearlessly into a crowd until he was driven off.

Grenier confessed with suspicious eagerness, reciting his crimes with such relish that he even caused laughter in the crowded courtroom when he talked of pursuing an old woman only to find her flesh 'as tough as leather'. He also complained about a child in this way, 'When I lifted it out of its crib, and when I got ready for my first bite, it shrieked so loud it almost deafened me.' There had been killings in the area and three girls testified against Grenier, so his detailed confession was believed. However, Grenier accused other people of being werewolves too and the judge found the evidence so appalling that he sent Grenier to a higher court for further investigation of the strange case.

The houses of the people named by Grenier were searched and although nothing was found, Grenier's father and a neighbour were arrested. Monsieur Grenier impressed the higher court judge with testimony that his son was a well-known idiot who boasted that he had slept with every woman in the village. Nevertheless, Grenier continued to confess with such conviction that his father and the neighbour were re-examined. Under torture, they admitted that they had sought young girls 'to play with, but not to eat.'

Grenier was sentenced to be burned but the case had caused such a stir that it was eventually reviewed by the high court of justice in Bordeaux. Judge de Lancre recorded this testimony by the youth, 'When I was 10 or 11 years old, my neighbour del Thillaire introduced me, in the depths of the forest, to the Maitre de la Fôret [Lord of the Forest], a black man, who signed me with his nail and then gave me and del Thillaire a salve and a wolf skin. From that time I have run about the country as a wolf.' Grenier maintained that he went hunting for children at the command of this Lord of the Forest, changing his shape with the help of the salve and the wolf skin, after hiding his clothes in the thicket.

Like the beggar Roulet before him, this self-confessed were-wolf was treated with a rare degree of understanding. The high court called in two doctors who decided that the boy was suffering from 'the malady called lycanthropy, which deceives men's eyes into imagining such things', although they added that the illness was the result of possession by an evil spirit. Judge de Lancre gave an intelligent summing up, which must apply to many similar contemporary cases of alleged werewolves, 'The court takes into account the young age and the imbecility of this boy, who is so stupid and idiotic that children of seven and eight years old normally show more intelligence, who has been ill fed in every respect and who is so dwarfed that he is not as tall as a 10-year-old . . . Here is a young lad abandoned and driven out by his father, who has a cruel stepmother instead of a real mother, who wanders over the fields, without a counsellor and without anyone to take an interest in him, begging his bread, who has never had any religious training, whose real nature was corrupted by evil promptings, need and despair, and whom the devil made his prey.'

The boy's life was spared and he was sent to a monastery which the judge visited several years later. He found that Grenier's mind was completely blank, unable to comprehend the simplest things, yet the young man still maintained he was a werewolf and that he would eat more children if he could. Also, he wanted 'to look at wolves.' Grenier died in 1610 as a 'good Christian', but it is not altogether surprising that anyone in the region with the name of Garnier or Grenier was regarded with suspicion for a long time afterward.

The case of a whole family of werewolves was recorded in western France in 1598. Two sisters, their brother and his son were known as the Werewolves of St. Claude. One of the girls, Peronette, was plainly suffering from lycanthropic hysteria and ran about on all fours. She attacked two children who were picking fruit in an orchard and when the four-year-old boy tried to defend his sister, she seized a knife and gashed him in the throat. Before he died, he testified that this wolf had human hands instead of paws and the enraged peasants tore Peronette to pieces before she could be brought to trial. Her sister was then accused of also being a *lycanthrope* who had the additional evil gift of producing hail. She was said to sleep with the devil who came to her in the shape of a goat. Their brother Pierre confessed that he turned himself into a wolf and that the three would chase people or animals around the country 'according to the guidance of their appetite' until they were exhausted. His son testified that he covered himself with a magic salve to turn into a wolf, and that he had gone hunting with his two aunts and had killed some goats.

The judge visited the wretched family in jail. 'I have seen those I have named go on all fours in a room just as they did when they were in the fields', he said, 'but they said it was impossible for them to turn themselves into wolves, since they had no more ointment and they had lost the power of doing so, by being imprisoned. I have further noted that they were all scratched on the face and hands and legs, and that Pierre Gandillon was so much disfigured in this way that he bore hardly any resemblance to man and struck with horror those who looked at him.' This last sentence is revealing. If Pierre had been disfigured since birth, he may well have desired the company and guise of animals. The verdict was not merciful this time, however, for the entire family was burned to death.

The most notorious German werewolf was Peter Stubb or Stump, who was tried in Cologne in 1589. An historian has written of his trial, 'It is interesting to note the ease with which otherwise intelligent persons rationalized the impossible and made negative evidence into positive proof.' This is another poignant case of a man destroyed by his own confessions – forced from him under torture – and who was prejudged before his trial began. Stubb claimed he had a magic belt that transformed him into 'a greedy devouring wolf, strong and mighty, with eyes great and large, which in the night sparkled like brands of fire, a mouth great and wide, with most sharp and cruel teeth, a huge body, and mighty paws.'

The accusers searched the valley where Stubb said he had left this belt, but found nothing. However, this did not prevent the magistrates from believing Stubb's confession. On the contrary, they declared 'it may be supposed that the belt has gone to the devil from whence it came.' Their revenge was terrible. Stubb was condemned to have 'his body laid on a wheel, and with red hot burning pincers in ten several places to have the flesh pulled from the bones; after that, his legs and arms to be broken with a wooden axe or hatchet; afterward to have his head struck off from his body; then to have his carcass burned to ashes.'

In surprising contrast to these horrifying real-life stories there are reports of protective werewolves, which sound about as unlikely as 'benign vampires'. In Portugal, there was said to be a type of werewolf that never attacked anyone and fled if approached, whimpering pitifully – a cowardly werewolf if ever there was one. Sometimes a person who had become a werewolf by accident would welcome the wound that transformed him back into permanent human shape again. A case recorded in Britain in 1214 tells of a carpenter who fought off a wolf, severing its paw. The animal instantly turned into a man who, though crippled, expressed his gratitude.

France is the favourite locale for protective werewolves as well as savage ones. One French tale concerns an abbot who drank too much at a country fair and was so overcome with the wine and sun on his journey home, that he fell off his horse. He hit his head on a stone and bled so profusely that the scent attracted a pack of wildcats that lived in the forest. As the wild-cats moved in, a werewolf bounded to the abbot's rescue – and even escorted the tipsy, bleeding monk back to his monastery. There the wolf was welcomed and its wounds were treated. At dawn, however, it resumed human shape – that of a stern Church dignitary who reprimanded the abbot most severely for his conduct, and stripped him of his privileges. A moralistic, if protective, werewolf.

Another story concerns the captain of a schooner employed in attacks on the Huguenots (French Protestants) fighting against Catholic persecution in the sixteenth and seventeenth centuries. After one such raid, the captain's ship foundered in the wide waters of the Rhone estuary and he would have drowned if someone had not come to his rescue and dragged him ashore. Reaching out his hand in thanks, the captain was dismayed to find himself grasping a huge hairy paw. Convinced that this must be the devil, who had saved him as a reward for his atrocities against the Huguenots, the captain fell on his knees and asked for the forgiveness of God. The wolf waited grimly, then lifted the sailor up and took him to a house on the outskirts of a village. Once inside, the captain saw the werewolf's face clearly in the light of a lantern and fell headlong to the floor in an effort to escape. Again, the wolf lifted him gently and then gave him food before leaving him in a locked room. The captain ran to the window but it was barred. Then, he noticed the horribly mutilated body of a woman lying in a corner of the room and he feared that the same fate was intended for him. But the next morning the werewolf returned in human shape. He was a Huguenot minister and he revealed that the woman was his wife, cruelly murdered by the captain's crew when they ransacked the village the day before. He himself had been forced aboard the captain's ship in order to be tortured and drowned.

'Well', said the minister, 'I am a werewolf; I was bewitched some years ago by the woman Grenier [again that name] who lives in the forest at the back of our village. As soon as it was dark I metamorphosed; then the ship ran ashore, and everyone leaped overboard. I saw you drowning. I saved you . . . you who had been instrumental in murdering my wife and ruining my home! Why? I do not know! Had I preferred for you a less pleasant death than drowning, I could have taken you ashore and killed you. Yet, I did not, because it is not in my nature to destroy anything.' Needless to say, the captain was so moved by this act of mercy that he became a devoted friend of the Huguenots until the day of his death.

It is a romantic tale and this may be one reason for the appeal of the werewolf legend. There may even be a fragment of fact behind the tales of protective werewolves. Modern studies indicate that the wolf is not necessarily the voracious monster it is traditionally made out to be. Rescues of a human being by an animal are not unknown and there may have been isolated cases in the past in which a wolf was responsible for saving a man's life. Nevertheless, it is the image of the wolf as a cruel and ferocious beast that prevails. Kindly werewolves are rare and the werewolves of legend are almost always bent on the vicious killing and devouring of their victims.

The concept of a man or woman turning into a wolf is no more outrageous than that of a corpse emerging from the coffin at night to drink human blood. Yet it is somehow even harder to believe in werewolves than in vampires. This may be partly because the werewolf fits so neatly into folklore. The monstrous wolfman made the ideal character for a good horror tale to tell around the fire in remote regions, where there was little to talk about apart from the wild animals of the forest and perhaps the even wilder characters in the village. Werewolves were alleged to be especially partial to small boys and girls, so they would serve as a natural threat for the peasants to their children. 'Don't go out in the woods tonight or the werewolf will gobble you up', they might say, just as London Cockneys warned their children not to roam the streets of the East End after the murders of 1888, 'or Jack the Ripper will get you.'

But the belief in werewolves has deeper roots. The metamorphosis of men into animals is part of primeval legend, a power attributed to the gods and heroes of mythology. The Scandinavian god Odin turned into an eagle; Jupiter, the Roman god, became a bull; Actaeon was changed into a stag by the Greek goddess Artemis. There are counterparts of the werewolf in almost all parts of the world, varying according to climate – were-tigers in India; were-leopards, were-hyenas, and even were-crocodiles in Africa; and were-bears in Russia, which also had its fair share of werewolves. In his book on werewolves, Elliott O'Donnell quotes eyewitness accounts of an Indian youth who changed into a tiger and of two Javanese children who turned into jaguars. Significantly, were-animals are always creatures that inspire fear – you never hear of a were-tortoise!

The *berserkers* – ancient Norse warriors who fought with murderous frenzy – exploited the fearsome reputation of wild animals by wearing bearskins in battle. These gangs of Nordic fighters would work themselves into a state of diabolical madness as they hurled themselves into the attack, howling like animals and foaming at the mouth. Our word *berserk*, meaning violently enraged, comes from the *bear sark* – bearskin – the berserkers wore. Just as the word lives on, so the memory of these barbaric warriors may have contributed to the werewolf legend. To the peaceful villagers whose community was attacked one day by fur-clad berserkers and another by a pack of howling wolves, there can have seemed little enough difference between the two. Both might have seemed like men dressed as animals –

or like men completely transformed into raging beasts.

Others trace the werewolf legend back further still, to the time when prehistoric man began to don animal disguise for the hunt and to invoke the spirit of a powerful animal in the hope of inheriting that animal's strength. In his book *Man Into Wolf*, Dr Robert Eisler, a British writer with a profound knowledge of ancient history and legend, develops a fascinating theory of the origins of the werewolf idea. Eisler's explanation starts with the idea that man was once a peaceful vegetarian but was driven to seek new food by changing conditions – such as the arrival of an Ice Age. He was forced to eat meat, to cover himself with animal skins, to hunt and to imitate the behaviour of ferocious wild animals in his struggle to survive. Gradually man himself acquired the same blood lust, probably even turning to cannibalism in times of extreme food shortage. This traumatic upheaval left its scars that lingered on in man's unconscious, says Eisler, giving rise, among other things, to the werewolf legend.

There are also more straightforward explanations. Furs were worn in winter as a protection against cold and a fur-clad figure might easily be mistaken for an animal. Werewolves might have been children who had been lost or abandoned in the forest, raised by a pack of wolves and therefore practicing all the skills of the wild animal. But Eisler's theory is still the most attractive. Writing about the concept of *metempsychosis* – the passing of a soul from one body to another after death – Baring-Gould refers to 'the yearnings and gropings of the soul after the source whence its own consciousness was derived, counting its dreams and hallucinations as gleams of memory, recording acts which had taken place in a former state of existence.'

To some extent this echo exists in us all. The counterpart of the female vamp is the male wolf—a man who pushes his attentions on women – and he is still with us today, complete with wolf whistle. The werewolf is a monster of the unconscious 'the beast within' that may still emerge in our dream life. American psychoanalyst, Dr Nandor Fodor, has recorded a number of dreams reported by patients in which the werewolf theme figures prominently, complete with all the brutal details of transformation, savage attack and killing.

At its fiercest extreme, however, this primeval instinct is seen most clearly in the secret societies of the Leopald Men in West Africa, who continue to disguise themselves as leopards up to the present day. Although it is most unlikely that man can change into wolf, it is certain that man frequently imitates the wildest of animals, even to assuming their skins.

CHAPTER 12

THE WALKING DEAD

What is a zombie, the corpselike creature that abounds on the island of Haiti? Is it really a dead body without a soul or mind? Is it really in the control of a sorcerer, who has trapped the soul to do his or her bidding forever? Haitians believe in zombies and are terrified of them. Do they exist? Example after example is offered to prove that they do and the whole practice of voodoo reinforces the idea of the walking dead as servants of evil magicians. Even if zombielike creatures are found, are they really walking corpses? Could there be a logical explanation for their strange state?

'The eyes were the worst. It was not my imagination. They were in truth like the eyes of a dead man, not blind, but staring, unfocused, unseeing. The whole face, for that matter, was bad enough. It was vacant, as if there was nothing behind it. It seemed not only expressionless, but incapable of expression. I had seen so much previously in Haiti that was outside ordinary normal experience that, for the flash of a second, I had a sickening almost panicky lapse in which I thought or rather felt, ''Great God, maybe this stuff is really true...''

This was how William Seabrook described his encounter with one of the most horrifying creatures ever to step from the realms of the supernatural. For Seabrook was face-to-face with a zombie – a walking corpse. And in that moment he was prepared to believe all he had heard about zombies since he first arrived on the island of Haiti.

The zombie's fate is even worse than that of the vampire or the werewolf. The vampire returns to his loved ones. He may be recognized and lain to rest. The werewolf may be wounded and regain human form. But the zombie is a mindless automaton doomed to live out a twilight existence of brutish toil. A zombie can move, eat, hear, even speak, but he has no memory of his past or knowledge of his present condition. He may pass by his own home or gaze into the eyes of his loved ones without a glimmer of recognition.

Neither ghost nor person, the zombie is said to be trapped, possibly forever, in that 'misty zone that divides life from death'. For while the vampire is the living dead, the zombie is merely the walking dead – a body without soul or mind, raised from the grave and given a semblance of life through sorcery. He is the creature of the sorcerer, who uses him as a slave or hires him out – usually to work on the land.

Haiti is the home of the zombie and the island abounds with stories of people who have died, been buried and reappeared as a walking corpse, sometimes years later. One of the most famous cases, first recorded by American writer Zora Hurston in 1938, is still recounted in Haiti today. It concerns Marie, a lovely young society girl who died in 1909. Five years after her death, Marie was seen by some former school friends at the window of a house in Haiti's capital Port-au-Prince. The owner of the house refused to allow anyone to investigate and Marie's father was reluctant to push the matter. Later, however, the house was searched but by then the owner had disappeared and there was no trace of the girl. Meanwhile the news had spread all over Port-au-Prince and to satisfy public opinion, Marie's grave was opened. Inside was a skeleton too long for the coffin. Neatly folded alongside the skeleton were the clothes in which Marie had been buried.

People say that Marie had been dug up and used as a zombie, until the sorcerer who had held her captive died and his widow turned her over to a Catholic priest. After her schoolmates had seen her, it was said that her family smuggled her out of Haiti, dressed as a nun and sent her to a convent in France. There she was later visited by her brother.

It is a sad aspect of most zombie stories, however, that no one generally comes to zombies' aid. Family and friends may never learn of the zombie's plight, or if they do, they are much too frightened to intervene. One mother told Zora Hurston about her son who had died and been buried. After the funeral, friends stayed overnight with the grieving woman and her daughter. During the night the boy's sister awoke to the sound of chanting and of blows in the street outside. Then she clearly heard her brother's voice. Her screams awoke the rest of the house and everyone looked out of the windows. Outside a grim procession was wending its way along the street and in its midst was the boy they had buried that very day. As he stumbled sightlessly by, they all heard his anguished cry. 'But such is the terror inspired by these ghouls', wrote Zora Hurston, 'that no one, not even the mother or sister, dared to go out and attempt a rescue.' The procession shuffled out of sight. The boy's sister subsequently went insane.

Why are the Haitians so terrified of zombies? What might happen to relatives who try to free their dead loved one? Do zombies even exist? To answer all these questions we need to look at Haiti's past and in particular, at the beliefs and practices of Haiti's voodoo religion.

Voodoo is a unique combination of African, Roman Catholic and even some American Indian beliefs, plus traditional occult practices from Europe. Its deepest roots are in Africa and voodoo began with the arrival in Haiti of large numbers of African slaves. This terrible traffic in human life, started when Haiti belonged to Spain in the sixteenth century, gathered momentum in the late seventeenth century when the island passed into French hands. Haiti was France's wealthiest colony – and depended on slave labour to stay that way. European traders on the west coast of Africa, already supplying millions of slaves to the plantations of the New World, were only too ready to meet France's growing demands. On the rare occasions when the French authorities needed to justify this trade, they did so on the grounds that slavery was the best means of converting the heathen African to Christianity. Many slaves did become members of the Catholic Church but they adapted the doctrines of Christianity to their own temperaments and needs and blended Christian rites with their own religious rituals – a combination that was to persevere down the centuries. Even today, many Haitians practice both voodoo and Catholicism, despite the disapproval of the Church.

Slaves were brought to Haiti from every part of western Africa but the majority came from areas dominated by the Yoruba-speaking peoples. These groups had a strong belief in possession by the gods. Torn from their homeland and their families, transported under appalling conditions to a strange land, the slaves nevertheless carried with them their traditions, their belief in magic and witchcraft and the memory of the gods and ancestors they had worshipped in the forests of Africa. In Haiti, these were to form the basis of voodoo. The new religion became a solace and a rallying force for a suffering and uprooted people and it was swiftly banned by the French authorities. Driven underground, voodoo grew stronger and more sinister.

Slavery was big business. The thousands who died during, or after, their journey were continually replaced. By the 1750s, 30,000 slaves were being landed in Haiti every year. As one generation of slaves succeeded another, a terrible yearning set in and nostalgia for the past fed the flames of rebellion. The first attempt for independence in Haiti took place in 1757. Macandal was the leader of this rebellion of fanatical fugitives, but he was captured by the French and burned to death. Several revolts followed, forcing the proclamation of Haitian Independence in 1804. With the retreat of the French colonists who were the upholders of the Christian faith, the voodoo religion became firmly established.

Voodoo is a formalized religion with its own gods and forms of worship. But it also has its sinister side – the voodoo of black magic, sorcery and superstition, of monsters, murder and raising the dead. Blood is an essential part of some ceremonies, usually involving the sacrifice of such animals as pigs, hens and cockerels.

Voodoo ceremonies take place in *tonnelles*. These may be either simple, rough huts with mud floors or an elaborate building but they always contain a covered area for ritual dance. It is during the dance that worshippers undergo the central experience of voodoo worship – possession by the gods. The dancing, chanting and throbbing of drums are said to generate an atmosphere in which god and worshipper may become one and, at the height of the dance, the worshippers enter a state of trance – a sort of collective delirium – which ends in collapse.

A dancer may be possessed by any one of a huge number of gods and spirits, many of whom are still known by their African names. During possession the dancer is believed to *become* the god or spirit, adopting not only the god's personality but his or her physical appearance, gestures and behaviour. Thus a dancer possessed by the ancient spirit Papa Legba – guardian of the gateway to the other world and god of crossroads, whose symbol is a crutch – becomes apparently old and lame. Others, recognizing the spirit, run forward with sticks and crutches to help him. A sea god will row with invisible oars. A flirtatious female god will make a possessed man or woman assume mincing, flaunting gestures. A traditional goddess from Dahomey called *Agassa* – a royal union of panther and woman – continues to exert her power in Haiti, causing possessed dancers to stiffen their fingers into claws. Evil spirits might throw a dancer into convulsions. Possession can last for several hours and be so absolute, that the possessed walk on burning coals or hold their hands in boiling water without flinching, just as the members of some African tribes used to cut off their own fingers in a state of trance.

A British visitor to Haiti, Patrick Leigh Fermor, gives this interpretation of how possession – or the supposed incarnation of the gods in their worshippers takes place. In his book *The Traveller's Tree*, written in 1950, he notes, 'Every Haitian . . . from his earliest childhood, is spiritually geared for the event of incarnation; and he knows that the moment of miracle occurs in the dark *tonnelle* where the air is afloat with mysteries and where the drums are already violently reacting on his nerves and brain . . . and so, when he has been brought by the drums, the dance and the divine presence to a state of hysteria and physical collapse, a dormant self-hypnosis, finding no opposition, leaps to the surface of his brain and takes control.'

Certainly it has been established by electrical recordings of the human brain that it is particularly sensitive to rhythmic stimulation. The *hungan*, or voodoo priest, may therefore increase suggestibility by altering the pitch and pace of the ceremonial rhythms. *Hungans* are also known to use magical powders and herbs as aids to possession and it is said that even a substance as ordinary as pepper may be enough to bring on possession in the feverish atmosphere of a voodoo ceremony.

Whatever the trigger that induces possession, voodoo worshippers believe that the god cannot take over their body unless their soul is first displaced. The soul is believed to consist of two spirits

– the *gros-bon-ange* (big good angel) and the *ti-bon-ange* (little good angel). The *ti-bon-ange* is what we might call a person's conscience. The *gros-bon-ange* is his essential soul – everything that makes him what he is.

Without the *gros-bon-ange*, the *ti-bon-ange* and the body lose contact. It is the *gros-bon-ange* that is displaced during possession, so that a person is no longer himself but the god who has taken over his body. Normally possession ends spontaneously and the worshipper's *gros-bon-ange* is automatically restored to him. But sometimes the return to oneself will only happen with the *hungan*'s help. Great care is also taken after a person's death to provide his disembodied soul with an alternative dwelling place. The soul, which first spends some time at the bottom of a river, is recalled by the *hungan* during a special ceremony and placed in a sacred jar – a substitute for the physical body. It then becomes an ancestral spirit who will advise and protect his family.

This idea of the soul lies at the heart of many voodoo superstitions, including the belief in zombies. For a soul that has been displaced for the ceremony of possession may fall into evil hands. Having one's soulless body possessed by a god is devoutly to be wished but it also opens up the possibility of a body being taken over by the evil machinations of the sorcerer.

The voodoo sorcerer, or *bokor*, is a terrifying character who communes with the dead and practices all the darkest arts on behalf of himself and his clients. Sometimes *hungan* and sorcerer are one and the same person, for it is said that a priest must be well acquainted with the techniques of sorcery, if he is to combat them successfully. A *hungan* might fight a curse with white magic one day and cast a spell with black magic the next. *Hungans* can invoke good spirits, or evil ones like the *Zandor* who turn people into snakes or vampire bats. Voodooists maintain, however, that the true *hungan* will have nothing to do with sorcery and there certainly are *bokor* who are not voodoo priests. The *bokor* inspire criminal societies, worship the devil and gather in cemeteries to practice the sinister cult of the dead.

Such sorcerers make powders out of cemetery earth and dead men's bones to 'send the dead' against an enemy. Spreading the powder outside the victim's door, or across some path, he often takes, is enough to paralyze or kill him, unless another *hungan* works some counter-magic in time. Another dreaded custom is the dressing of a corpse in the clothes of an intended victim and concealing it in some secret place to rot away, while the living person goes mad searching for it. As students of Haitian belief have pointed out, if the victim knows what is happening and believes in the force of the magic, it can easily have fatal results.

Haitians tell spine-chilling tales of corpses being dragged from the grave to serve the cruel will of the sorcerer. In his book *The Magic Island*, written in 1936, William Seabrook records this story of a young wife, Camille, and her husband Matthieu Toussel. On their first wedding anniversary, Toussel took his wife to a feast soon after midnight. He insisted that Camille wear her bridal dress and she, being afraid of him, obeyed. As the couple entered a candlelit room laid for a banquet, Camille saw that there were four other guests, all in evening clothes. But none of them turned to greet her. Toussel excused their behaviour, promising that after dinner all four men would drink and dance with her. His voice was odd and strained. Camille could see the fingers of one guest clutched, motionless, around a tilted, spilling wineglass. Seizing a candle she looked into his face – and realized she was sharing a banquet with four propped-up corpses.

The panic-stricken girl ran for her life but she never recovered from her nightmare experience. Friends who returned to the scene later the same day, found everything laid out exactly as she had described – but no trace of the silent guests or Toussel, who is said to have fled the island.

Legend or fact? The machinations of a sorcerer husband or the imaginings of an unbalanced wife? The Haitians who told Seabrook this story believed it was true. They knew other stories like it. Haitian children are raised on tales of black magic, bogies and sorcerers' spells. Their mothers warn them never to play with their shadows and tell them that the *bokor* or the *tonton macoute* (travelling voodoo magician), will get them if they don't behave – a threat that could have proved only too true under Haiti's dictator Dr Francois Duvalier, whose strong private army was dubbed the *tontons macoute*.

It is this atmosphere of fear and superstition that has bred belief in the zombie. From cemetery cults and disinterred bodies, it is but a short step to the idea of a corpse brought back to half-life by black magic. Some would say this was Toussel's intention for his dinner guests. Of all the supernatural horrors that sorcery may reserve for the unwary, becoming a zombie is the most dreaded fate of all and a threat that even the most sophisticated may find hard to shrug off. Alfred Metraux, author of *Voodoo in Haiti*, made a study of zombies in the late 1950s. He says, 'At Port-au-Prince there are few, even among the educated, who do not give some credence to these macabre stories.'

One of the macabre stories that Metraux recorded, concerns a young girl who rejected the advances of a powerful *hungan*. He stalked off, muttering threats about her future. Sure enough, the girl grew ill and died. For some reason, she was buried in a coffin too short for her and her neck had to be bent to fit her in. While this was going on, a candle near the coffin was overturned burning the girl's foot. Years later, people claimed to have seen the girl, apparently alive and clearly recognizable by her stoop and the burn on her foot. It was said that the jealous *hungan* had made her into a zombie and kept her as a servant in his house, until so much attention was drawn to the case that he was obliged to set her free.

This *hungan* was motivated by revenge—a common reason for the creation of zombies. Other times, zombies are made simply to provide cheap and uncomplaining labour when any suitable corpse will do. More rarely, they are the carefully chosen victims of a pact with the forces of evil, who demand payment in human souls for services rendered. For while Christians talk of selling one's soul to the devil, a voodoo follower sells the souls of others. In return for power, wealth or some other favour, he must pledge the souls of those nearest and dearest to him. Each year, the horrible sacrifice must be repeated until there are no more relatives or beloved friends left to give and the person must then give himself. He too surrenders his soul. Then his body, like theirs, becomes a zombie.

Such pacts are made with the help of the *bokor* and only he can create zombies. After dark he saddles a horse and rides, backward, to the victim's house. Placing his lips against a slit in the door he sucks out the person's soul and traps it in a corked bottle. Shortly afterward the victim falls ill and dies. At midnight on the day of burial, the *bokor* goes with his assistants to the grave, opens it and calls the victim's name. Because the *bokor* holds his soul, the dead person has to lift his head in answer. As he does so, the *bokor* passes the bottle containing the soul under the corpse's nose for a single brief instant. The dead person is then reanimated. Dragging him from the tomb, the *bokor* chains his wrists and beats him about the head to revive him further. Then he carefully closes the tomb, so no one will notice it has been disturbed.

Led by the *bokor* and his associates, the victim is first taken past his own house. This is said to insure that he will never again recognize his home and try to return there. He is then taken to the *bokor*'s house or a voodoo temple, and given a secret drug. Some say this is an extract of poisonous plants like datura (jimson weed) or belladonna (deadly nightshade), which were sometimes used by the slaves of colonial days to kill their masters. Others maintain that the potion is made of drops that fall from a corpse's nose.

There are other methods of ensnaring a person's soul. A jar containing herbs and magical objects may be placed beneath a dying man's pillow to draw off the soul, or the soul of an insect or small animal may be substituted for the human soul. In neither case does the victim realize what is happening. It is even possible to take the soul from a person already dead. Whatever the method used, the soul plays the same part in the ritual at the tomb and after the giving of the magic drug, all is complete. The victim has become a zombie – a hideous, mesmerized, walking corpse, ready to do the sorcerer's will.

Elaborate precautions are taken to prevent the sorcerer from raising the dead and creating a zombie. A family that can afford it, may bury its dead beneath solid masonry. Others will make sure that the grave is dug in their own back yard, or close to a busy road, with plenty of passers-by. Since only a fresh or well-preserved corpse will serve the *bokor*'s purpose, relatives may keep a continuous watch at the tomb until the body has decomposed. Sometimes the corpse is killed again, being shot through the head, injected with poison or strangled. Occasionally, it is buried with a dagger in its hand to defend itself. Often the body is placed face downward in the grave with its mouth full of earth, or its lips are sewn together so that it cannot speak to answer when the sorcerer calls its name.

Once people become zombies they can never escape from their deathly trance unless they taste salt (frequently a symbol of white magic). They then become aware of their fate and, knowing they are dead, will return to the grave forever.

In his book *The Invisibles*, British anthropologist Francis Huxley tells a story he heard from a Catholic priest of a zombie who wandered back to his own village in 1959. He was taken to the police station but the police were too frightened to do anything and simply left him outside in the street. After several hours, someone plucked up the courage to give the zombie a drink of salt water and he then stammered his name. Later his aunt, who lived nearby, identified him. According to her, he had died and been buried four years before.

A priest was called and, after he arrived, the zombie revealed the name of the sorcerer for whom he and a band of other zombies had been forced to labour. The police, thoroughly scared now, sent a message to the sorcerer offering him his zombie back. However, two days later the zombie was found, well and truly dead this time – presumably killed by the sorcerer because of his damaging revelations. The sorcerer was eventually arrested but his wife and the other zombies were never traced.

There is a strong element of doubt in many zombie tales. Evidence is often missing or incomplete. Other stories are less easy to dismiss. Catholic priests and Protestant clergymen report having seen people die, conducted their burial service, shut the coffin lid and watched the grave closed – only to see that person days or weeks later not dead but staring, inarticulate and apparently insane.

Zora Hurston notes that such creatures were occasionally brought to a missionary by a *bokor* who had been converted – or by a sorcerer's widow who wished to be rid of them. She was one of the few visitors to Haiti to see, touch and actually photograph a zombie. The zombie was Felicia Felix-Mentor, who had died of a sudden illness in 1907. In 1936, she was found wandering naked on the road near her brother's farm. Both her brother and her husband identified her as the woman they had buried 29 years before. She was in such a wretched condition that she was taken to the hospital and it was there, a few weeks later, that Zora Hurston saw her. 'The sight was dreadful', she wrote later. 'That blank face with the dead eyes. The eyelids were white all around the eyes as if they had been burned with acid. There was nothing that you could say to her, or get from her, except by looking at her and the sight of this wreckage was too much to endure for long.'

So zombies or zombielike creatures do exist. But are they really walking corpses? Is it possible for a dead body to be given the semblance of life? Montague Summers, an authority on witchcraft and black magic, once wrote, 'That necromancy can seemingly endow a dead body with life, speech and action is not to be disputed but the spell is invariably of short continuance and the operation, from the confession of sorcerers, is considered to be one of the most difficult and most dangerous in all witchcraft, a feat only to be accomplished by wizards who are foulest and deepest in infernal crime.'

A spell of 'short continuance' would hardly explain the reappearance, after 29 years, of Felicia Felix-Mentor. A far more likely explanation is that so-called zombies have never been dead at all. Some people have suggested that zombies are simply the doubles of persons who have died. If so, why do such doubles always have the characteristic zombie appearance and gait? Zombies are known for their expressionless and often downcast eyes, their blank faces and shambling walk. They appear not to hear when spoken to and their own speech, uttered in a nasal twang, is almost always incoherent. Often it consists only of grunts or guttural noises deep in the throat.

These are often the hallmarks of the mentally defective and it seems probable that many alleged zombies are in fact morons, concealed by their family and deliberately made out to be dead until they are seen again, perhaps many years later. Alfred Metraux was introduced to a zombie only to find a 'wretched lunatic'. On the next day, this zombie was identified as a mentally deficient girl who had escaped from her home, where her parents normally kept her locked up.

Students of Haiti have pointed out that the harsh treatment meted out to zombies is no worse than the treatment of the mentally sick, who are commonly beaten to cow them into compliance. Once he had recovered from his initial shock at the sight of those 'staring, unfocused, unseeing eyes', William Seabrook too concluded that the zombies he had seen were 'nothing but poor ordinary demented human beings, idiots, forced to toil in the fields', rather than half-alive corpses.

What, then, of the reliable witnesses who have testified to the burial of some so-called zombies? Were they lying? Not all zombies started out as morons. What about the person friends remember as a sane, intelligent individual, who suddenly reappears as a vacant, gibbering wreck of his former self? This has to be a different kind of case.

The answer comes from a surprising source – Article 246 of the old Haitian Criminal Code. 'Also to be termed intention to kill', it states, 'is the use of substances whereby a person is not killed but reduced to a state of lethargy, more or less prolonged, and this without regard to the manner in which the substances were used or what was their later result. If following the state of lethargy the person is buried, then the attempt will be termed murder.'

From this, it can be inferred that a zombie may really be a person buried and mourned by his family and dragged from the grave by the *bokor* as the legend says. But he has been buried alive after being drugged into a deathlike trance, from which he may never recover.

A prominent Haitian doctor interviewed by William Seabrook, was convinced that at least some reported zombies were victims of this kind of treatment. Doctors with whom Zora Hurston discussed the case of Felicia Felix-Mentor agreed. 'We discussed at length the theories of how zombies come to be', she writes. 'It was concluded that it is not a case of awakening the dead but a semblance of death induced by some drug – some secret probably brought from Africa and handed down from generation to generation . . . It is evident that it destroys that part of the brain which governs speech and will power. The victims can move and act but cannot formulate thought. The two doctors expressed their desire to gain this secret but they realized the impossibility of doing so. These secret societies are secret. They will die before they will tell.'

The idea, if not the making, of the zombie almost certainly originated in Africa, where legendary tales are still told of sorcerers who can raise the dead. The true zombie, however, is unique to Haiti. While cynics would say that so-called zombies must be lunatics or people temporarily in a state of trance, there are undoubtedly cases that can only be explained on a deeper and more sinister level. Today, voodoo is often exploited as a tourist attraction and spectacular displays of black magic may be mounted for the entertainment of foreigners and natives alike. Francis Huxley tells, for instance, of a magistrate who saw a *hungan* take a body from the grave and apparently reanimate it. Inside the grave, the magistrate found a tube leading out to the air. The 'corpse' was really the *hungan*'s accomplice and had been able to breathe in comfort while awaiting his resurrection.

Haitians know about hoaxes like this. Yet many of them still believe in zombies and have a deep-rooted fear of joining their ranks. For while zombies may not be raised from the grave, they may well be people reduced by drugs to a state that is scarcely distinguishable from death. Who would say which fate is the worse? In either case, the zombie is truly one of the walking dead.

CHAPTER 13

WILD MEN OF THE FOREST

Did the wild men who so frightened our medieval fore-bearers, exist? Could the idea of huge, hairy dwellers of the forests have come from a folk memory of the days when the Neanderthals – an early and apelike form of human – still roamed Europe? The evolution of the wild man from a fearsome demon to a symbol of strength and fertility, to the 'noble savage' is an interesting one. Tarzan of the apes is a modern counterpart, as is the Abominable Snowman and Bigfoot or Sasquatch. Are the wild-haired pop stars another manifestation of the wild man in us?

'All of a sudden, a grown up wolf came out from one of the holes . . . This animal was followed by another one of the same size and kind. The second one was followed by a third, closely followed by two cubs one after the other . . .

'Close after the cubs came the ghost [in this case a hideous looking being of Indian folklore] hand, foot and body like a human being; but the head was a big ball of something covering the shoulders and the upper portion of the bust, leaving only a sharp contour of the face visible and it was human. Close at its heels there came another awful creature like the first but smaller in size. Their eyes were bright and piercing, unlike human eyes.'

This excerpt is from the diary of Reverend J. A. L. Singh, a missionary in Bengal in the first part of this century. It describes the discovery of two-feral children – little girls who had been reared in the wild by wolves. Very rare in real life, children reared by animals is a fairly common theme in mythology and popular literature.

In Rudyard Kipling's *Jungle Book*, the story of Mowgli gives this idea fanciful expression. As a toddler, Mowgli, a woodcutter's child, is nearly killed by a tiger and is rescued by a family of wolves. Mother Wolf immediately becomes fiercely protective of the 'man cub', and manages to persuade the pack, which shows a high degree of social organization, to let him stay. As he grows up, Mowgli learns the ways of the jungle and, like the animals, becomes acutely sensitive to 'every rustle in the grass, every breath of the warm night air, every note of the owls above his head . . .' He seems to enjoy a harmonious relationship with the pack but secretly the young wolves sense and resent his superiority. Eventually, he is forced to leave them and return to his human family – promising Father and Mother Wolf to return for a visit some day. ' "Come soon", said Mother Wolf, "little naked son of mine; for listen, child of man, I loved thee more than ever I loved my cubs." '

Our ambivalent attitude toward the wolf – part fear and part admiration – also emerges in the legend of Romulus and Remus, the twins who supposedly founded the city of Rome. Their mother, the princess Rhea Silvia, had been made a Vestal Virgin by order of her uncle, the usurper of her father's throne of Alba Longa. She claimed that the god Mars was the father of the children but this distinguished, supernatural parentage was of no immediate help to them. The king, fearing their claim to the throne, had them thrown into the Tiber River. They were rescued and suckled by a she-wolf, an animal sacred to Mars and later cared for by a herdsman and his wife. When they grew up, the twins slew the usurper, restored their grandfather to the throne and founded the city of Rome.

Although the legend claims that the city's name is derived from the names of the brothers it is almost certain that the true story is the other way around – that Romulus and Remus were invented later in the history of Rome to provide an appropriately picturesque and mysterious origin for the great city. Stories of children brought up in the wild are fairly common in Greek legend and the Romans, familiar with Greek literature, may have adapted this theme for their purpose. The role of Mars in the story – both as the alleged father of the twins and as the patron of wolves – is clearly an attempt to link Rome with the god of war.

However interesting their stories may be, Mowgli, Romulus, and Remus are, after all, definitely human beings, capable of adapting to human society when and if the necessity arises. Their wildness is artificially imposed. More intriguing is the idea of a creature who is man and yet not man, living in the wild, a perpetual threat to the community, possessed of man's baser, aggressive instincts and of a beast's strength – in short, a creature much like Neanderthal Man.

Today we know that before man in his present form appeared on the scene, more primitive forms inhabited various parts of the earth. In some areas, two species may have co-existed for thousands of years, perhaps in a state of intermittent conflict until one of them died out. For example, although we have no proof of this, it may be that Neanderthal man, who inhabited central and south-eastern Europe up until 32,000 to 35,000 years ago, was known to Cro-Magnon man, our ancestor who emerged about 28,000 to 32,000 years ago. If Neanderthal man was not already extinct and if our ancestors knew him, it is possible that true stories of a man, who wasn't quite man, could have survived as a folk memory long after his type had disappeared. Similar overlappings of species, giving rise to similar stories, may have occurred in other parts of the world. It may seem far-fetched to propose that a species that has not been seen for thousands of years, could survive in people's minds as a threat today but fears and superstitions have deep psychological roots and are more complex than usually thought.

Of course, it was not a *conscious* knowledge of evolution that kept the legend of the wild man alive. The people who believed it in the past, like most of those who believe it today, knew little or nothing about Neanderthal Man and his position in the theory of evolution. Medieval Europeans assumed that men had always looked as they did, stories and pictures of Adam and Eve proved it. If their belief in a wild man stemmed from a prehistoric source, the source itself had long since been forgotten. Perhaps the *unconscious* memory of prehistoric life and its dangers had somehow been transmitted from one generation to the next, in what the psychologist Carl Jung called the 'collective unconscious'. The readiness to believe in the wild man would then be lying hidden in everyone, requiring only certain conditions to keep the legend alive. These conditions are a body of mythology, scientific ignorance and an occasional event that apparently backs up the myth.

The best-known modern example of the wild man legend is the Abominable Snowman or Yeti of the Himalayas, whose existence is stubbornly believed both by local people and by foreign explorers of the region. No one ever manages to capture a Yeti or even to photograph one, although photographs exist of alleged Yeti footprints. But plenty of people claim to have seen one. Their descriptions vary widely and range from five-foot-tall vegetarians to 15 foot meat eaters. The Yeti is often credited with prodigious strength, being able to rip up trees and throw boulders around like pebbles.

North America has its own version of the Yeti, called the Sasquatch in Canada and the Bigfoot in the United States. Long known to the American Indians, the Bigfoot is feared by the non-Indians as well. Every now and then, even today, an accident or a murder in remote mountainous parts of the continent are attributed to this formidable creature. He is generally described as being about eight feet tall with huge feet, as the name suggests. The animal he most closely resembles is the ape – which, however, is not native to North America.

If, with our present knowledge of natural history, we can believe or half believe stories of semi-human creatures roaming the forests, it is not surprising that the people of the Middle Ages, who knew little about zoology, believed in the wild man. In fact, long after the Middle Ages, the Swedish botanist Linnaeus included the *Homo ferus*, wild man, in his *System of Nature* published in 1735. Linnaeus described this distinct human species as 'four-footed, mute and hairy', and cites several cases of feral children as evidence. A vivid description of the Alpine subspecies of the European wild man, appears in Richard Bernheimer's book *Wild Men in the Middle Ages*,

'Huge and hairy and mute . . . he may be so large that his legs alone have the size of trees. His temper when aroused is terrible and his first impulse that of tearing trespassers to pieces. When moved to revenge, he may make lakes disappear and towns sink into the ground. He abducts women and devours human beings, preferring unbaptized children and – according to a belief held in the Italian Tyrol and in the Grisons in Switzerland – makes a practice of exchanging his own worthless progeny for human offspring.'

Belief in this formidable creature has all but disappeared in Europe, except for certain small isolated communities in and around Switzerland. During the Middle Ages, however, the wild man myth in various forms flourished in most parts of the Continent and in the British Isles. His image and those of his mate and offspring as well, appeared in tapestries, on pottery and in engravings, woodcuts and stone carvings. The main portal of the Church of San Gregorio in Valladolid, Spain, built in the late fifteenth century, is adorned with statues of hairy men instead of the expected figures of saints. At first glance this appears to be an astonishing glorification of a mythical beast by the Church. But in fact, the portal taken as a whole is a heraldic representation of King Ferdinand and Queen Isabella, whose coat of arms is carved above the doorway. In their period, the wild man was often represented as a protector or supporter of a family's coat of arms – and, therefore, of the family's honour. Like other creatures shown defending a heraldic shield, such as the lion, unicorn and griffon, the wild man represented strength. He also represented fertility.

It is ironic that the wild man should eventually achieve respectability as the symbolic defender of monarch and faith, for throughout most of his history he had been regarded by the Church as, at best, an unfortunate, spiritually blind creature condemned to a sort of limbo-on-earth and at worst as a demon. He seems to have been left over from pagan beliefs in woodland gods and demons. The Greek woodland god, Silenus was depicted as hairy and said to have superhuman strength. Roman writers including Virgil and Juvenal referred to a race of primitive man born from tree trunks. Somewhat more believably, the Roman historian Pliny states that in India, there was a race of wild semi-human creatures with hairy bodies, yellow eyes and canine teeth. He may have acquired this information from writings on the Indian campaign of Alexander the Great. It seems likely that the source of this wild man myth was some species of large ape, such as the eastern gibbon. Unable to speak in the human sense of the word, the apes nonetheless exhibit many human characteristics. It is not too difficult to understand how reports of large apes grew into wild men stories, as they passed from one person to another.

The myth of the hairy wild man received a boost from the Bible itself, which contains a prophecy in Isaiah of forthcoming desolation in Palestine. It says, 'the hairy ones will dance there.' The Hebrew word *se'erim* is believed to have denoted a kind of hairy monster that lived in wild, deserted areas. The translator, St. Jerome, was of the opinion that these 'hairy ones' were possibly *incubi* – evil spirits who descend on sleeping women and ravish them – or satyrs, who have similar habits but attack women who are awake. In any case, the existence of the hairy wild man and his characterization as a lustful, immoral creature, were fairly well established early in the Christian era.

The fact that no one actually ever saw one of these creatures naturally resulted in a variety of descriptions. Some wild men were depicted as giants that could joust with tree trunks and carry the carcass of a lion slung over the shoulder. Others are described as dwarf. Often they seem to be human size.

Nor were all wild men hairy. In England, particularly, the wild men were leafy covered with moss and ivy. A humourous drawing of the fifteenth century shows two fighting wild men who are covered with a mixture of fur and scroll-like leaves. There is even a feathered species.

The wild man was a familiar part of many medieval festivals and even today, the wild man cavorts in the Carnival and Twelfth Night festivities in some parts of Europe. The villagers of Oberstdorf in Germany perform a wild man dance, in which they wear costumes of hay and lichen and fierce-looking masks carved of wood. Fur-clad wild men dance in Carnival celebrations in the Balkan countries and in Morocco. They are usually accompanied by other figures representing animals, including one wearing a female mask to represent the wild man's bride.

In some of the wild man dances and plays that are still performed, we can discover how the people of the Middle Ages regarded this elusive but powerful being. One of the commonest plots of a wild man play – still enacted in the Balkans – involves a hunt for the wild man, his capture and killing and often his resurrection. The story of the capture of the wild man seems to have been greatly popular during the Middle Ages. Normally the play would begin with the creature ranting and snorting around to the horrified delight of the audience. Eventually a group of villagers would catch up with him and either kill him on the spot or lead him away in chains to face some court of justice. In some of these wild man plays, generally those performed in late spring or early summer, the wild man is brought to life again, apparently suggesting his importance as a symbol of fertility and the renewal of life. In Carnival performances he is usually left dead – possibly because, in this context, he represents the Carnival season itself, which ends with the arrival of Lent. In other words, the killing of the wild man represents the suppression of lust.

The wild man also figured in a riotous revel called a *charivari*, popular in France in the late Middle Ages. This was a kind of brawl combined with dance, performed on the occasion of the marriage of an unpopular person. Some of the participants in this malicious spectacle wore animal skins, while others cavorted in the nude. With their identities concealed under various bizarre masks, the dancers gave vent to their primitive instincts. *Charivaris* were occasionally performed at court and on two occasions at least, the revellers included King Charles VI.

In other plays, the wild man was the leader of the Wild Hunt or Wild Horde. This group of demons, who with their hounds rode through the sky on dark nights, created a terrifying spectacle. The Wild Horde is one of the most widespread of European legends. The original leader of the Wild Horde is supposed to have been the Germanic god Wotan, but as the legend evolved, this role was sometimes taken by the wild man.

To complicate matters further, there was also a female version of the Wild Horde, led by a goddess such as Diana and including a vast company of female demons.

The identity of these female demons of the Wild Horde, became confused with the wild woman – who is not merely the mate of the wild man but a distinct being who occurs in regions where the male of the species is unknown. She varies considerably in size and appearance and as in the case of the wild man, the Alpine version, called *Faengge*, is among the most formidable. Richard Bernheimer reports that she is 'a colossal ogre of great strength and appalling ugliness. Bristly all over, she has a mouth forming a grimace that reaches from ear to ear. Her black, untended hair is interspersed with lichen and according to a report from Switzerland, she has breasts so long that she can throw them over her shoulders [a characteristic shared by the female Yeti]. She is prone to eat human children.'

Ugly as most wild women are reported to be, they nevertheless have the power to bewitch men – first transforming themselves into beautiful young women if necessary. They also seem to have a love of combat, sometimes fighting the wild man for leadership of the Wild Horde.

Yet the tapestries and woodcarvings of the late Middle Ages often show the wild woman in a gentler mood, living companionably with the wild man in a pleasant woodland retreat. 'Her appearance', says Bernheimer, 'if exception be made of her shagginess, is distinctly human and even moderately attractive, and her behaviour is usually that of a faithful housewife operating efficiently under the primitive conditions of a camping trip.'

Such naive and charming representations of the wild man and his household, show how people's attitude toward him had undergone a transformation, at least in more sophisticated circles. He was no longer the demonic creature feared by the peasantry but a rather harmless, even ridiculous figure.

By the end of the Middle Ages, another attitude toward the wild man had emerged, that of admiration and envy. Among some writers, notably the German Hans Sachs, the wild man represented a healthy alternative to the artificiality and corruption, the strife and cruelty of society. Sachs' poem 'The Lament of the Wild Man about the Unfaithful World', includes a detailed catalogue of the vices of the world, followed by the wild man's extolling of the simple life he and his mate lead in the forest. 'We feed on wild fruit and roots, drink the clear water of springs and warm ourselves by the light of the sun. Our garment is mossy foliage and grass which serve also as our beds and bedspreads . . . Company and pleasure we find in the wild animals of the woods, for since we do them no harm, they let us live in peace . . . We exult in brotherly love and have never had any strife among us, for each does to the other as he would want him to do to himself.'

This theme of the noble savage was not new. It had been popular in Greek and Roman writings and was to surface again in the latter eighteenth century. Apart from the question of its truth or falsity, this idea has probably never been widespread in any serious sense. Most people of Hans Sachs' day, or any other day, were much too involved in the world to give serious consideration to the advantages of living in the wild. It may be, however, that belief in the wild man satisfied some unconscious need to believe in such a possibility. Even the terrifying, bestial version of the wild man may have served a psychological purpose by exposing those aspects of human nature that society and religion tried to suppress.

Certainly the role of the wild man as our second self comes across strongly in stories of courtly love. Among the aristocracy, marriage and romantic love were kept separate. A lady might be married and yet also have a spiritual lover whose behaviour toward her was marked by extreme respect, even worship. He performed brave actions to win her approval, offered her songs and poems but never dared to approach her sexually.

Obviously maintaining such an artificial and idealized relationship would have been a strain on both parties. The interior struggle between courtly ideal and natural inclination found expression in innumerable stories and pictures of the knight subduing the wild man for the sake of the lady. Often the lady is abducted by the wild man and carried off to his cave. The knight appears on the scene just in time and, after a battle, slays the wild man.

A variation on the theme shows the lady herself subduing the creature. The wild man approaches the lady with his usual savagery but is captured by her, tamed and civilized by the power of her love. This is clearly intended both as a tribute to the lady and as a plea from the suitor, that she recognize his honourable intentions and grant him her love, thus making him a better man.

Often the aspiring lover pretended to go wild – that is, temporarily insane – until the lady smiled on him. 'The greater the warrior thus brought to grief', says Bernheimer, 'the greater the implied prestige of the lady who had caused his fall. Indeed, some of the most renowned knights of romance, Yvain, Lancelot and Tristan, fell victim to this strange occupational disease of knight–errantry.'

This idea of pretended madness brings us to one of the factual bases for the myth of the wild man – namely, lunacy. The Book of

Daniel tells us that King Nebuchadnezzar 'was driven from men and did eat grass as oxen, and his body was wet with the dew of heaven, till his hairs were grown like eagles' feathers, and his nails like birds' claws.' In the Middle Ages, it was the custom to let some lunatics go free and some of them went to live in the woods. It is easy to see how the fact of an irrational, perhaps violent, outcast leading a crude existence in the forest could perpetuate the legend of the wild man.

The magician Merlin, best known as advisor to King Arthur, had another identity as a madman. A twelfth century epic, 'Vita Merlin' by Geoffrey of Monmouth, describes how Merlin, first driven insane by the death of his brothers in battle, periodically reverts to madness and returns to the woods where he becomes a 'sylvan man' – that is, a wild man.

To the Middle Ages, then, the wild man had many meanings. He could be an actual monster, an unfortunate lunatic, a demon, a symbol of physical love, an embodiment of the pure and simple life or simply a decoration on a coat-of-arms. In one form or another he seemed to fill a need, for he flourished for several hundred years. And in parts of the world he continues to exist today – in people's minds, if not in reality.

Modern man is still fascinated by the wild man and wants to believe in him. In 1913, a man named Joe Knowles emerged from several months of wandering in the wilderness of Maine claiming to have hunted and killed animals with his bare hands This self-styled wild man was given an enthusiastic welcome by the citizens of Boston and other New England towns, who clearly were eager to believe in the possibility of living by one's wits alone in the wild. Later Knowles' claims were proved untrue, no doubt causing widespread disappointment.

A current example of the appeal of the wild man image is the hairy look favoured by some young men. It is not merely a matter of wearing the hair long, which was fashionable and acceptable in society until the last century. It is a matter of leaving long hair uncombed and unwashed to suggest an intentional rejection of civilization and an affinity with raw nature.

Similarly, in listening to some of the more extreme types of rock music popular in the last three dacades and in observing modern dancing, with its tacit rejection of form and its celebration of the primitive, we are tempted to think that the wild man has been absorbed into modern man's self-image. Our ancestors, engaged in building a society and formulating rules of conduct (which, of course, did not prevent their behaving with savagery in good causes sanctioned by Church and State), may have needed to express their own primitive tendencies in an imaginary wild man. Now that psychology has forced us to acknowledge the wild man that dwells within us, we are free to give him expression – at least in harmless, symbolic ways such as unkempt hair and screaming pop stars. In time, the current wild man vogue will probably fade, just as the mythical forest-dwelling wild man of Europe has retreated into obscurity. But it is hard to imagine a day when the wild man, in some form, will have disappeared entirely from our imagination.

CHAPTER 14

MAN AS MONSTER

From Goliath of the Bible to the Greek Titans, to the Norse Ymir and the many huge creatures of British folklore, giants have figured in the beliefs of people. Was it the desire for superhuman power that nurtured such ideas or was there once a race of giants upon the earth? In any case, the giant was clearly human – a monster man. Perhaps, then, the most frightening monster of all is man himself. History is full of inhuman people who, like the Marquis de Sade, went beyond the bounds of imagination in their bestiality. Will we ever completely control the monster within us?

Running through the stories of vampires, werewolves, zombies and all the other mysterious and sinister creatures that resemble living humans, is a mystery that is fascinating and terrible. This is the mystery of the human mind – an infinitely complex structure of fears, desires, repressions, aggressive tendencies and ideals. We like to believe today that we approach the world with a scientific eye and that our ideas follow the rules of logic. Most of us look back with horror at the superstitions that bound and limited the people of earlier times. In fact, some of the most vehement sceptics of the supernatural proclaim their scepticism with an almost fanatical fervour. They are seemingly terrified at the thought that there may, after all, be some truth in occult beliefs. Their repugnance is understandable, for when we look at the desperate lengths to which people's supernatural beliefs have driven them (terrible witchcraft trials, for example), we may feel that it would be a good thing to ignore certain aspects of the supernatural, in hope that they might eventually shrivel up under the bright light of science.

To ignore the supernatural, however, would be to deprive ourselves of an important key to the mysterious workings of the human mind. In our myths we reveal ourselves.

Consider, for example, the fairly straightforward myth of the giant. There is nothing deeply profound about the fascination of giants. They simply represent our desire for superhuman power and strength and, less obviously, our awe of nature. In many cultures, we find that the creation of the world is attributed to a giant and it is easy to see how this explanation seemed plausible. The enormous size of many of the earth's natural features – oceans, mountains, canyons – would suggest, according to primitive logic, a gigantic creator. Similarly, the more violent moods of nature, such as thunderstorms and torrential rains, would naturally be interpreted as demonstrations of the god-giant's displeasure or simply as reminders of his power. On a subtler level the forces of nature – or signs of the giant's activity – may symbolize the forces that man feels within himself and to some extent fears. The folklore of the British Isles is full of fanciful accounts of how hills, valleys and other features of the landscape were formed by giants throwing around spadefuls of earth or flinging enormous rocks into the sea. In their poetry, the Anglo-Saxons referred often to 'the giants' who supposedly inhabited Britain before their own arrival. In this case, the myth seems to have rested not so much on natural phenomena as on the structures erected by the Romans during their 400-year domination of the island. To the Anglo-Saxons, the remains of Roman temples, fortifications and aqueducts must have seemed beyond the ability of ordinary mortals. Hence, they assumed that the people who had constructed them were a race of giants.

It is interesting to note the widespread belief in such a race of giants. The book of Genesis alludes to such a people – the offspring of angels and earth women. In the Apocrypha, there is a reference to a conflict between these giants and God. This myth eventually became transformed into the struggle between God and Satan and the banishment of Satan and his cohorts from Heaven, described in Milton's *Paradise Lost*.

In Norse mythology, the first living creature was a giant named Ymir. He begot both the human race as we know it and a race of frost giants. The Amerindians of northwestern United

States and Canada have many legends of primeval giants with cannibalistic tendencies. Ancient Greek mythology gave us the huge Titans and the equally huge Gigantes, who had serpents for feet. British legend holds that the island was once inhabited by a race of giants who were vanquished by Brutus, the founder of the British race (no connection with the Roman Brutus). The two remaining giants of this breed, Gog and Magog, were brought to the newly established city of London and made to serve as porters at the gate of the royal palace.

In this story we find another theme common to many myths about giants – that of the normal-sized being conquering the giant. Time and again we discover stories of the ferocious giant who terrorizes the community, until a fearless and ingenious young man gets the better of him. The children's story of 'Jack and the Beanstalk' is one familiar example of this theme. Somewhat more realistic is the Bible story of David and Goliath.

The champion of the Philistines, Goliath, is supposed to have measured 'six cubits and a span' in height (about 10 feet). His coat of mail weighed 5,000 shekels of brass (208 pounds) and his spear's head weighed 600 shekels. He challenged the Israelites to produce a man to fight with him as a way of deciding the outcome of the conflict between the two peoples – confident that through him the Philistines would surely win. As everyone knows, the boy David came forward and slew Goliath with one small stone from a slingshot.

An amusing variation on the theme of man as the outwitter of giants, is a tale from the west of England. It seems that a Welsh giant bore a grudge against the mayor of Shrewsbury and so decided, one day, to dam up the Severn River, flood that town and drown its inhabitants. He set off with a great shovelful of earth and walked many miles. Somehow, he managed to bypass the town. Wandering around near Wellington, some 15 miles farther on, he met a cobbler who was returning from Shrewsbury. The cobbler carried a bag full of old shoes and boots to be mended. The giant called down to ask how far it was to Shrewsbury, adding that he intended to drown its citizens. The cobbler, not wishing to lose his good customers, assured the giant that he would never make it to Shrewsbury that day or even the next. 'Why look at me! *I'm* just come from Shrewsbury and

I've had time to wear out all these old boots and shoes on the road since I started.' So saying, the cobbler showed the giant the bag filled with footwear. By now thoroughly fatigued, the giant decided to give up the project. He dropped the spadeful of earth on the ground beside him and stomped home. The earth he dropped created the Wrekin, a prominent hill in the area.

This legend illustrates the tendency to defuse the giant myth by showing him as stupid – easily deterred by a spur-of-the-moment deception by a simple, but quick-thinking, craftsman. Taken all together, the various giant legends seem to suggest that we created the giant, partly in order to account for the natural world and partly to express our unconscious yearning to believe in and identify with, larger-than-life humans. Having created this terrifying monster, we then had to create an accompanying myth in which we conquer the giant through our dexterity, or our superior intellect.

In our complex relationship with animals, we reveal even more about our self-image, fears, and frustrations. An animal need not be fierce, strong or poisonous to arouse strong feelings of antipathy. A common example is the domestic cat, a creature harmless to man and generally considered beautiful, which nevertheless arouses irrational fear and loathing in some individuals.

Conversely, people often have strong feelings of identification with certain animals. In his book *The Naked Ape*, the zoologist Desmond Morris describes a study of children's preferences among animals. It revealed that the top 10 favourites were all mammals and that all of them had one or more humanlike characteristic, such as flat faces, vertical posture as in the bear and the apes and hair rather than feathers or scales. The lion appeared both in the 10 favourites list and in the 10 most disliked animals list. Morris suggests that the ambivalence of the response to the lion is due to 'attractive anthropomorphic characteristics' of expressive face and mane of hair on the one hand and its violent predatory behaviour – and great strength – on the other.

Some people identify with certain animals in an out-and-out way. Historically there is good reason for this. Primitive man, throughout the world, adopted animal disguise in order to hunt successfully. In Africa, a continent that must have seen some of the first and fiercest clashes between human and beast, animals assumed a special and lasting importance in African societies' approach to the supernatural. The hunter depended on the hunted and man respected the strength of the animal, to such an extent that he tried to form special bonds with it and even to emulate it.

Some African tribes developed the concept of the 'bush soul' – an animal with which a man identifies so completely that the two are one, inseparable and interchangeable. 'The theory of an external soul deposited in an animal appears to be very prevalent in West Africa', wrote Sir James Frazer in *The Golden Bough*. 'Every wizard is believed at initiation to unite his life with that of some particular wild animal.' This bond was forged by means of a 'blood brotherhood'. By the ritual mingling of their blood, the sorcerer was believed to acquire the animal's strength and apparent invulnerability, while the animal became his familiar, ready to do his bidding and swift to kill those who offended his master. Frazer adds that such a blood relationship was never formed with a domestic animal, 'but always a dangerous and wild beast, such as a leopard.'

Identification with leopards produced a sinister result – societies of leopard men. Dressed in leopard skins and wielding three-pronged knives that simulate the claw marks of the leopard, these bands of killers terrorized the population of west Africa. Most of their victims were women. After killing the woman by slashing her jugular vein, the leopard man would cut off her breasts and eat them. This bloodthirsty cult has endured in to the twentieth century. In 1938, 400 local women were killed around Wamba in the Belgian Congo, now Zaire. One leopard man when caught took the police to 38 dead female bodies, all with their breasts cut off.

Africa also had its panther men who, like the leopard men and the werewolves of Europe, were believed to transform themselves into animals to kill and devour parts of their victims. During a visit to West Central Africa in the late 1920s, American author William B. Seabrook talked at length with an African clerk, who had been caught wearing a panther skin with iron claws after murdering a girl on a jungle path. Tei, as the clerk was called, insisted that he really *became* a panther on such occasions, that the disguise was merely an aid to his transformation and that being a panther was 'nicer than being a man'. As Seabrook pointed out, when Tei leaped howling from a tree in his panther garb and tore the girl's throat with his claws, he must certainly have seemed like a real panther to her – as he did to those who witnessed the killing.

Another kind of power that we have desired throughout our history, is the power to live forever. Among most people this has taken the form of religious beliefs in the immortality of the soul and perhaps a life in some other body after the death of the earthly body. In the myth of the vampire, this desire appears in a grotesque and perverted form. The vampire is able to preserve his own body by feeding on the blood of the living. Of course, the tellers of vampire tales profess abhorrence of such an idea and those who really believe in vampires are genuinely terrified of them. Yet, to some people, the idea has its attractions. The recently discovered fact that as many psychotics identify with Count Dracula as identify with Napoleon, suggests that this parasitical form of power is as alluring to some disturbed mentalities as military and political power is to others.

With some disturbed people, the vampire fantasy is not a matter of imagining themselves to be Count Dracula but of having a real pathological thirst for blood. For such people, as for the supernatural vampires who rise from their graves, the sucking of blood is a way of revitalizing themselves, if only symbolically or psychologically.

Blood has always had great significance for us apart from its obvious physical importance. Many people have identified blood with the soul – clearly an idea drawn from the fact that if a wounded person loses too much blood he will die. Some peoples ritually drink the blood of certain animals, in the belief that by doing so, they will acquire the qualities they admire in the animal. In early times, for example, Norwegian hunters drank the blood of the bear in order to acquire its great strength.

Many people suppose that the human vampire was named after the vampire bat but in fact, the naming was the other way around. The vampire bat, a native of Mexico and South America, was not discovered by scientists until the nineteenth century, long after the human vampire had become part of European mythology. The bat does not actually suck the blood of its victims – usually cattle or humans – but laps up the blood with its tongue after having pierced the skin with its teeth.

The vampire bat represents vampirism in a purely natural form. The bat simply requires a diet of blood in order to live. Of course, its behaviour is dangerous because it can spread rabies. But the sinister and repulsive character of its attack is largely projected onto it by humans – partly as a reaction to the animal's ugly looks, which also make perfectly harmless bats cause a shudder and partly because of associations with human vampirism.

Leaving aside extreme cases, such as people who have a taste for blood and psychotics who are convinced they are Count Dracula, we are still confronted with the enormous popularity of vampire stories – and the popularity of the vampire himself – among perfectly sane people. The appeal of the stories can be explained on one level as the fun of being frightened. Any horror story, no matter how badly written, is almost guaranteed a certain amount of success. But the appeal of Dracula and his kind lies deeper. The desire for immortality, supported by the occasional discovery of a healthy looking corpse, may have created the vampire myth but the continued appeal of the fictional vampire has more to do with sex than with immortality.

Any vampire story or film contains an obvious sexual element. Dracula's victim is usually a beautiful young woman; female vampires go for attractive men. The setting is usually the victim's bedroom. The attack itself is a perversion of the harmless love bite – or, from a different point of view, the love bite is a harmless version of the vampire's attack. In any case, the sexual connotations are clear. Moreover, they are clearly sado-masochistic – the vampire dominates, wounds and eventually kills in an erotic situation. This seems to strike a responsive chord in many readers and film addicts. The prevalence of such sexual feelings can be inferred from the enormous amount of fan mail the actors who play Dracula receive from women.

It is also interesting to note the popularity of vampire stories in late nineteenth century England. In that repressed society, the adventure, violence and spookiness of the stories were played up, while the sexual element was played down. Even so, the

sexual aspect was still very much present and could be unconsciously enjoyed by respectable readers, under the impression
that they were just reading a good horror story.

By the end of the nineteenth century, some of the less socially
acceptable aspects of the human character were beginning to be
recognized – thanks largely to the pioneering work of Sigmund
Freud. Today's educated adult takes for granted such concepts as
infantile sexuality and the conflicts within our conscious and
unconscious minds. Clinical psychology has even shown us
actual cases of multiple personality, in which two or more
distinct personalities inhabit the same body, coming out at
different times. The true story of *The Three Faces of Eve* is such
a case. Cases of more than one personality are apparently the
result of conflicting elements within a person's psyche. The
conflicts make the psyche split into separate personalities so that
the contradictory drives can be expressed. Yet the complexity of
human nature has been recognized by intelligent writers in every
age. The most intriguing story of multiple personality, in fact, is
a work of fiction written by Robert Louis Stevenson in the late
nineteenth century.

The Strange Case of Dr Jekyll and Mr Hyde is, first of all, a
superb horror story. As a horror story, it lies roughly in the werewolf tradition inasmuch as the leading character had the power
to transform himself into a dangerous and evil creature, altering
his appearance and even his size in the process.

The physical differences between the respectable Dr Jekyll
and his fiendish other self Mr Hyde, have psychological significance. This is apart from the need of the writer to make them
appear totally different to the other characters in the story.
Hyde's smaller size and lightness of step seem to suggest the
'easiness' of evil. At the same time there is the implication that
Jekyll's stature and his heavier step indicate his morality. The
hairy wild man theme appears in the descriptions of the hands,
which says, '. . . the hand of Henry Jekyll . . . was professional in
shape and size; it was large, firm, white and comely. But the
hand which I now saw, clearly enough in the yellow light of a
mid-London morning, lying half-shut on the bedclothes, was
lead, corded, knuckly, of a dusky pallor, and thickly shaded with
a swart growth of hair.' Some film versions of the story have

shown Hyde with a hairy face as well, giving him a strong resemblance to the werewolf. But the author points out several times in the story that Hyde's face is not repulsive in any physical way. 'He's an extraordinary-looking man', says one of the characters, 'and yet I really can name nothing out of the way. He gave an impression of deformity without any nameable malformation.' It is the expression in Hyde's face and particularly in his 'displeasing smile' that makes other people react to him with revulsion. Jekyll comments on this when talking about his second personality. '. . . none could come near to me at first without a visible misgiving of the flesh. This, as I take it, was because all human beings, as we meet them, are commingled out of good and evil: and Edward Hyde, alone in the ranks of mankind, was pure evil.'

It is, as a psychological thriller, that the book achieves its greatness. Jekyll brings about his own destruction through his effort to separate the good and evil aspects of his own personality. He had wanted to do this to relieve the tension he experiences in trying to conquer his moral weaknesses and become the entirely serious, upright gentleman he thinks he should be.

The fatal flaw in Jekyll's experiment is that he first tries the separation of good and evil,when the baser aspects of his character are dominant. 'At that time my virtue slumbered; my evil, kept awake by ambition, was alert and swift to seize the occasion; and the thing that was projected was Edward Hyde.' When Hyde swallows the mixture Jekyll has concocted, he is transformed back into Jekyll – but it is the same old Jekyll with all his vexing inner conflicts. Because Hyde – the abstraction of Jekyll's unconscious and repressed aggressive tendencies – is 'all of a piece', he is stronger than the uncertain Jekyll. Gradually Hyde destroys Jekyll.

Within six months of its publication in 1886, the book had sold 40,000 copies. It was the subject of dinner conversations and Sunday sermons. With its moral tone to offset the violence, it could hardly miss, but its popularity endures in our less moralistic age. It has been filmed several times and no doubt someone will one day make a musical out of it.

In the years since *Dr Jekyll and Mr Hyde* was published, psychologists have approached the problem of our contradictory nature in a variety of ways, and have come up with a variety of explanations. For the average person, however, the problem remains something of a mystery – a mystery that continually shows new aspects of itself. There may be plausible sociological and psychological reasons why, for example, a Mafia killer or the commandant of a Nazi concentration camp, can at the same time, be an affectionate husband and father but this seeming inconsistency still fascinates and appalls us.

Many people who believe themselves incapable of inflicting pain on another person are content and even eager, to see pain inflicted. The public executions that entertained our ancestors have largely disappeared but the mangled bodies from a plane crash will attract hordes of horror seekers from miles around. The publishers of the American tabloid *The National Enquirer*, know what they are doing by publicizing the most nauseating atrocities in huge type on the front page. The newspaper sells. When readers gasp and cry, 'How awful', do they really mean what they say? Or is there something in the story that secretly appeals to them? It is interesting to note that the trailers for films containing violence often consist mainly of the violent scenes. The brutality is assumed to be the most attractive aspect of the film – and this assumption is more than likely made on the basis of market research. A would-be suicide, hesitating on the ledge of a tall building, will attract a large crowd of the curious and often there are a few who urge him on with 'Jump! Jump!'

Of course, the mob as a monster is almost taken for granted. Riots do not surprise us anymore and in any case, we can account for them by explanations of pent-up resentment, racial hatred, fear – motivations that may not be excused but may at least be understood.

Understanding fails us, however, when we approach stories of real human monsters – people for whom the infliction of pain on others is actually a source of pleasure. One such person was Vlad Tepes, ruler of Walachia (now part of Romania), from 1431 to 1477. He was partly famed for his courage in battle. When Vlad won a great victory over the non-Christian Turks, the bells of Christendom rang out in celebration as far away as the Island of Rhodes.

Vlad was known as Dracula, meaning devil or dragon. This

was the name used by Bram Stoker for the bloodthirsty Count of his famous novel but Vlad himself was not a vampire. Compared to the real Dracula's crimes, the bloodsucking habit of his fictional namesake seems like playfulness. It was Vlad's pleasure to impale his enemies on wooden stakes. 'Tepes' means 'the impaler'. On one occasion, the triumphant Vlad impaled 20,000 of his enemies. The slightest provocation would serve as an excuse. After one victory Vlad and some guests sat down to dine, surrounded by his slowly dying victims. When one guest dared to comment on the screams and the stench, he was immediately impaled on a particularly tall stake so that he would be above the smells to which he had so unwisely objected.

In Gilles de Rais or Retz, a Marshal of France who lived at the same time as Vlad, we find a more complex character. Not only a brave soldier who fought alongside Joan of Arc, de Rais was also a cultured and apparently pious man. In 1440, however, he was brought to trial and accused of the murder of some 140 children. Moreover, it was charged that the murders were done with the utmost cruelty and accompanied by sexual perversions. A contemporary account states, 'The most monstrously depraved imagination never could have conceived what the trial reveals'. Among other things, he was charged with having sat on the bowels of a dying boy while drinking his blood. He apparently had an obsession with blood and ordered his servant to stab the children in the jugular vein so that their blood would shoot over him. After being tortured himself, de Rais confessed publicly to all the charges and begged forgiveness of the parents of his victims. He was burnt after first being strangled to death – an act of mercy granted to him for not recanting his confession.

Nearer to our own time, is the case of Fritz Haarman, the Hanover Vampire. He was given this name because he killed so many of his victims with one fatal bite in the throat. He then cut them up and either ate the flesh himself or sold it as sausage meat. This was just after World War I, when meat was scarce and butchers were none too fussy. Haarman was brought to trial in 1924 for the murder of 50 boys.

John George Haigh, the English acid-bath murderer hanged in 1949, is reputed to have been a vampire. He himself claimed that he drank the blood of his victims, although this claim may have been an attempt to escape hanging by being certified insane. Basil Copper, one biographer of Haigh, says, 'There is no doubt in my mind that John George Haigh was a vampire in the classical tradition, possibly the only true monster in this field in the twentieth century.'

Still alive in prison are two of the most infamous murderers of modern times, Ian Brady and Myra Hindley. Called the 'Moors Murderers', this couple tortured and killed a number of children and recorded their screams on tape for future listening pleasure.

These horrifying examples of sadism bring us to the man who gave us the very word for such acts, the Marquis de Sade. De Sade never performed mass torture on the scale practiced by Vlad the Impaler but this was due to lack of opportunity rather than squeamishness. De Sade's belief was that sexual pleasure not only can be achieved, but in fact is best achieved, through inflicting pain. He developed this theme at wearisome length and in excruciating detail in novels such as *Justine* and *120 Days of Sodom*.

During the period of his life, when he was not in prison for his actions, he enacted his fantasies with various victims, some unwilling but some surprisingly willing. His last years were spent in the asylum of Charenton where he was accompanied by the young actress, Marie-Constance Quesnet.

A philosophy of a kind underlies de Sade's hideous practices. In an article for *Horizon* magazine entitled 'Our Bedfellow, the Marquis de Sade', writer Anthony Burgess summarizes this philosophy. According to de Sade, he says, there is no God but there is a goddess who is Nature. 'We are wholly subject to her, being part of her, and we must fulfil in our own actions her most terrible and monstrous impulses. Nature is creative . . . but she is also destructive, revelling in earthquakes, in storms, floods, volcanic eruptions. But this destructive urge is in the service of creating new forms of life. A huge melting pot is always on the boil, and her old creations are thrown into it, to re-emerge transmogrified. The devices of cruelty that man develops are a manifestation of quite impersonal, or rather prepersonal energy. Personal guilt is irrelevant, since the first law of life is to accept the world as it is.'

Burgess points out that de Sade's image of man is, unfortunately, well supported by actual events. 'In the depraved France of the pre-revolutionary era, in the ghastly actions of the Terror, de Sade could see ample evidence that man's appetites for pleasure were most satisfyingly fulfilled through the exercise of power and cruelty. His own private orgies, the extravagant fantasies of his books – what were these but reduced reflections of the conduct of the great world outside the chateau?'

De Sade's contemporary Jean-Jacques Rousseau, believed that man's depravity was due to the corrupting influence of society and that he would be virtuous if he lived in a 'state of nature'. Returning explorers who brought tales of primitive tribes that not only fought each other like Europeans but that also practiced cannibalism, shot a hole in this comforting theory of the noble savage. Savagery, it seems, is a kind of endemic disease that breaks out in various forms wherever humans live – in the forests of wild New Guinea as well as in the laboratories of academic New Haven.

We have explored the unpleasant truth that man is *potentially* a monster. As if this were not cause enough for despair, writer Oscar Kiss Maerth has advanced a theory that man is *essentially* a monster.

In his book *The Beginning Was The End*, he says that the evolution of man was due to cannibalism. He bases his argument partly on evidence that cannibalism was once practiced by humans in all parts of the world. According to Maerth's theory, this practice began among man's ape forebears who mainly ate the brain, as do the few head hunters still found today in some areas. The brain of humans was first prized by our forebears because it increased sexual activity, says Maerth. Only much later was it discovered that eating brain increased intelligence and that this increased intelligence was permanent and hereditary. Various other biological changes, notably our loss of body hair, are attributed by the author to the chemical imbalance resulting from the eating of the pituitary gland of our own kind, thousands of years ago.

Without going further into the details of this unusual theory, we may consider its fundamental meaning. It says that man did not evolve naturally, as modern science teaches, either accidentally or as part of a divine plan. He is a freak of his own making. All of his actions – not only his cruelty to his own kind and his ruthless exploitation of the natural world, but even his great intellectual and artistic achievements – are the actions of a monster.

Whatever arguments a scientist or a theologian might use to refute this theory, we are still left with the nagging thought that there is something monstrous about our species. There is more evil in the world than our minds can cope with. Most people probably try to ignore it as much as possible and concentrate on the mundane problems of living. Others devote themselves to humanitarian pursuits and many of them succeed in curing some of the symptoms of the disease of savagery, if not the disease itself.

It may be that the supernatural monsters, in which many of us believe, are another way of coping with this all-pervasive evil. Subconsciously, we may want to give our fears a form that is different from the real horrors we read of in the papers or, in earlier times, saw performed in the market square and is in some sense more manageable. A vampire, terrifying though he may be, can be dealt with in a variety of approved ways. The zombie and the werewolf, as well as the blustering giant, express those evil tendencies we fear in ourselves and in others. By giving them a name and a shape, however grotesque, we get the illusion of having some degree of control over them.

The pathetic man in Stoke-on-Trent who died from choking on a clove of garlic intended to ward off vampires, may really have been afraid of something else. Demetrious Myiclura had seen his native Poland overrun by the Germans in World War II. His farm was appropriated by the invaders and his family was killed. Many people have survived similar experiences with their mental balance relatively undisturbed but in Myiciura's case, the senseless violence of the war may have been more than he could stand. An individual is virtually helpless against such a juggernaut of evil. Who knows where it may strike again? No evasive action, no preventive measures are possible. But Myiciura did know how to deter vampires. They were an evil against which he could protect himself.

CHAPTER 15

DRAGONS IN MYTH AND MIND

From China to Britain, in terms of distance and from perhaps as far back as 5000 BC in terms of time, the dragon has appeared in story and myth. If the dragon is a symbol of Christian victory over the powers of evil, why are there so many dragon tales from the years before Christianity was born? Is the modern idea of the creature as a symbol of our internal struggle between unconscious drives and demands of conscience, a better explanation for the myth of the lizard-like animal that snorts fire? Why is the dragon a benevolent creature in the East and an evil one in the West?

The dragon is probably the most widely known of all monsters and mythic beasts. For centuries, all over the world, it has played a role in art, in myth and in religion. St. George and the dragon is only one of many legends about this symbolic creature. One version of the St. George myth has it that the people of the North African city of Silene, in what is now Libya, had lived for a long time in fear of an evil dragon outside their gates. At first they had placated it each day with several sheep but soon it was demanding both a man and a sheep. Then, not content with this, it wanted more delectable flesh and insisted on the sacrifice of young virgins. The king decided that the young girls of the city should draw lots each day to determine who would be the next victim. One day, to his horror, the lot fell to his daughter, the beautiful Princess Sabra. In vain the king pleaded with his subjects for her life. They were adamant. He must abide by the rule that he himself had made.

Sick at heart, the king saw his beloved daughter led off to the spot where the dragon was eagerly waiting. But at that moment a strange knight appeared on horseback. It was George of Lydda, on his way to see the Roman Emperor Diocletian and plead for the lives of Christian slaves. Making the sign of the cross with his sword, he spurred his horse against the dragon. They fought until the beast fell wounded to the ground. George told the princess to fasten her belt around the dragon's neck and lead it into Silene. The people honoured George as a hero and when he told them he had been made powerful by the Christian God, they accepted Christianity. George then took his sword and cut off the dragon's head. By an odd coincidence, the town of Silene is near the place that Perseus, a hero of Greek mythology, is said to have rescued the beautiful Andromeda from a terrifying sea dragon.

The fight between St. George and the dragon is usually interpreted as an allegory, showing the triumph of Christianity over the powers of darkness. But legends and traditions found in many different places show that this struggle had an earlier and more universal symbolic significance. In countries as far apart as China and England, we find that the dragon, from early times, represented the principle of fertility. He was born each spring from an egg underneath the water and, like Nature at that season, he grew and flourished. Each year as Nature waned, the old dragon had to be killed to make way for the new dragon that would be born the following spring. When in the Western Christian tradition the dragon became synonymous with evil, the killing came to symbolize not merely the end of the year but also the victory of God over Satan. The slaying of the dragon for this reason has been associated with many Christian saints besides St. George and with secular figures as well.

Modern psychology takes still another view of the dragon myth. The struggle with the dragon has been interpreted as symbolizing our own internal struggle between deep-seated lusts and unconscious drives on the one hand and the demands of conscience on the other. The fertility legend is likewise given a new slant. The dragon is seen as the old man or father whose sexual potency has diminished and who must be killed by the vigorous young sons, so that they can take over the sexual role and enable life to continue. Another psychological interpretation springs from the role the dragon has in many legends as guardian of treasure. In this case, the treasure is seen either as the son's sexual drives, to be guarded or restrained by the mother in the role of dragon, or as the daughter's virginity, to be preserved by her father in the dragon role.

In contrast to the West, the dragon in China is the embodiment of gentleness and goodwill. The Chinese dragon legends and interpretations therefore differ greatly. But whatever the symbolism, why should these strange hybrid creatures exert such power and fascination over our minds? There are land dragons, water dragons, flying dragons, fierce and timid dragons. There are dragons of many shapes in nearly every part of the world. Where do they spring from? Were they created to fulfil some deep need in humans, to personify the otherwise inexplicable forces of Nature, to provide some explanation for arbitrary fate? It seems that this might have been so. But while the West took the dragon to symbolize the evil, ungovernable and destructive side of Nature, the East used it to portray the life-giving, benevolent and restorative side. Both aspects were equally incomprehensible and mysterious and lent themselves to interpretation by symbols that made them easier to understand for ordinary people.

Just as our early ancestors endowed many of the gods with a mixture of human and animal attributes to make them more powerful than either humans or animals, so they may have conceived of dragons as a mixture of different creatures, in order to suggest their supernatural power. It seems that, just as different peoples interpreted the character of dragons to fulfil their own needs, so they concocted the appearance of the dragon from the beasts they found most significant. Thus, in India we find an elephant dragon, in China a stag dragon and in western Europe – where the dragon myths stem from those of the serpent – we find a reptilian dragon. The Western dragon is so reminiscent of prehistoric reptiles, that one is led to wonder whether the conception stems from folk memories of giant dinosaur fossils or even a late freak survival of a prehistoric monster.

Since the serpent was in many civilizations the ancestor of the dragon, we find that in many myths the identity of the two creatures overlaps. The serpent sometimes becomes a dragon in later phases of the same legend. One of the first dragons to appear in myth is thought to be Zu. He arises in the legends of the

Sumerians who settled in Mesopotamia, possibly as early as 5000 BC. The dragon Zu was said to have stolen tablets setting out the laws of the universe from the chief god of the Sumerians, Enlil. As a punishment, Enlil ordered the sun god, Ninurta, to kill the dragon. This battle between the dragon and the sun god is repeated in the myths of many later civilizations and seems to symbolize the struggle between light and darkness, between good and evil.

When in about 1800 BC the Babylonians gradually replaced the Sumerians as a leading power, they took over many of the Sumerian myths. Their story of creation is the story of the struggle between order and chaos, good and evil. The forces of chaos are personified by the sea goddess Tiamat, who adopted a dragon for her symbol. She led a fierce army that included serpents and dragons with crowns of flame and attacked the gods, who stood for order. The dragon, representing Tiamat, was therefore associated with forces of destruction. Marduk, the chief god of the Babylonians and god of the sun, was determined to fight Tiamat in single combat. He used the winds as his main weapon. When Tiamat opened her mouth to consume him, he drove the winds into her mouth and body. Her body became distended and she was unable to close her mouth. Marduk then shot an arrow down her throat, killed her and severed her body in half. One half became the earth and the other the heavens. Thus the dragon is involved in the myth of creation.

Babylonian and Sumerian ideas spread to Egypt and probably inspired the legend of the enormous serpent Apophis, the enemy of the Egyptian sun god. Later this serpent became identified with the ocean, which in Egyptian myth held the world together but constantly threatened to destroy it. Then the myth developed into the struggle between night and day, light and darkness. In some versions, the serpent or dragon (representing night) swallowed the sun at sunset and disgorged it the next morning. In others, the sun went down to the underworld each night to fight the dragon and, having each time succeeded in hacking him to pieces, came up to earth again in the morning. Throughout the West and Middle East, dragons were generally regarded as carriers of evil and bad luck. They might vary greatly in appearance – some resembling serpents, others being formed from such unlikely combinations as a lion, a crocodile and a hippopotamus – but they nearly all have a common characteristic, an endless hostility against human beings.

Some Western medieval scholars believed that the majority of dragons lived beneath the earth, in an area honeycombed with caves. Dragons preferred to be underground and the only ones seen above ground were those that had somehow become lost and strayed into the world of sky and sunshine. Unable to find their way back, they vented their frustration on any person nearby. In psychological terms, the dragons from the dark depths become the evil thoughts dwelling in all of us which, once they are allowed out into the open, bring trouble, pain and sometimes death to our fellow beings.

It was an early dream expert, the second-century Greek Artemidorus, who first mentioned dragons in connection with guarding treasure. He believed that dragons were to be found where treasure was hidden and that therefore, dreams about dragons signified riches and wealth. The link between dragons and treasure and the caves where treasure was usually hidden, is found in many legends in different countries. It became a popular theme in the early Christian and the medieval periods, probably because it lent itself to many symbolic interpretations. In the Teutonic legend of Siegfried, for example, the dragon watches over a hoard of treasure that is the source of life. Siegfried acquires invulnerability by bathing in the dragon's blood after he has killed it. Also by drinking the dragon's blood he learns the language of the birds. In other words, he gains a new understanding of Nature. In many other legends, the heroes gain new kinds of power from killing and eating parts of the dragon.

The English writer J. R. R. Tolkien, gives a vivid picture of a dragon as treasure keeper in his modern fable of the struggle between good and evil, *The Hobbit*. He calls the beast Smaug and describes him this way, 'There he lay, a vast red-golden dragon, fast asleep; a thrumming came from his jaws and nostrils, and wisps of smoke . . . Beneath him, under all his limbs and his huge coiled tail . . . lay countless piles of precious things . . .'

Britain has many dragon legends. One they owe to the Danish invaders of the mid-sixth century, who brought with them their epic of King Beowulf. Although he beheads the murderous monster Grendel, Beowulf is killed by a dragon whose treasure has been stolen. An even earlier folk story concerns the legendary British monarch King Lludd, who lived happily in the city he had built in the southeast of the island – a city later called Londinium by the Romans and London by the Saxons. Suddenly peace was destroyed by an evil that 'went through people's hearts, and so scared them, that the men lost their hue and strength, and the women their children, and the young men and the maidens lost their senses, and all the animals and trees and earth were left barren.'

King Lludd sought the advice of his older brother, King Llevelys of France. 'The plague in your kingdom is caused by a red dragon', King Llevelys said. 'Another dragon of a foreign race is fighting with it, and striving to overcome it. And therefore does your dragon make a fearful outcry.' King Llevelys gave King Lludd careful instructions about how to rid his land of the monsters. King Lludd returned home and, following his brother's directions, had a pit dug in the exact centre of his domain. As Llevelys had predicted, the dragons grew tired of battling one night and fell exhausted into the pit. They drank the mead that had been poured in and fell asleep. This made it easy to take them in two stone chests to the Welsh mountain of Snowdon for burial. The red dragon later became one of the war symbols of the ancient Britons and Welsh and today is one of the symbols of Wales.

Among Britain's other dragon legends, are those in which the monster takes the form of a giant worm. England is rich in stories of such creatures. Of these, the most renowned is the Lambton Worm, which was discovered by John de Lambton in the fast-flowing Wear River near his ancestral home in northeast England. It was a Sunday and Lambton, the heir to the estate, should have been attending church. Instead he defiantly went fishing. It was not much fun for him when he hooked a great worm with nine holes on either side of its mouth. Foot by foot he dragged the huge, grotesque monster onto dry land, cursing the thing's size and ugliness. He thought he had caught 'the Devil himself', and to get rid of it he threw it into a deep well nearby. He then went back home hoping that he had seen and heard the last of the worm. He shortly resumed his 'God-defying' habit of Sunday fishing.

Some weeks later, the worm reappeared. It crawled out of the well, coiled itself round a rock in the middle of the river and lay there all day long. At night, however, it snaked ashore and pillaged the district. It attacked cattle, mangled cows and drank their milk, swallowed lambs in a single bite and terrorized the local women and children. On witnessing this and on seeing how the beast froze its victims on the spot with its 'great big goggly eyes', Lambton confessed his responsibility for the worm's presence. In an attempt to lessen the monster's fury by good works, he joined one of the crusades to the Holy Land and was away for seven years. On his return to England, he learned from his father that the beast had increased its plunder. It uprooted trees in the area, killed all who tried to destroy it and paid a daily visit to Lambton Hall to drink a large amount of milk it demanded as tribute. The heir to the estate determined to kill the worm and visited a local sage, the so-called Wise Woman of Brugeford, to get advice on how to win the battle. 'You will succeed', she told him, 'but remember this. You must vow to kill the first being or person you meet as you recross the threshold of Lambton Hall. If you fail to do so, then none of the Lambtons for the next three-by-three generations will die in his bed.'

Lambton agreed to the condition, put on a special suit of armour studded with blades and went out to face his enemy. A desperate battle ensued. After an hour or more of savage fighting, in which the worm wound itself tightly around the knight's body, Lambton slew the monster. He then waded ashore and walked wearily to the Hall. Before entering the great manor he blew three notes on his bugle – a prearranged signal for the release of his hound Boris so that it would be the first to greet him as he entered. However, the plan misfired and it was old Lord Lambton who reached the warrior before the rest. As the father started to embrace his son, the heir avoided him, called for Boris and ran the hound through. But it was too late, for the vow had been broken. The Wise Woman's prediction came true and the next nine generations of Lambton men died away from their beds. The first to die according to the prophecy was the monster-killer himself, who was slaughtered while on another crusade. The ninth Lambton to meet an unnatural death was Henry Lambton, Member of Parliament who represented the city of Durham. He was killed in June 1761, when his coach was in an accident on a bridge over the Wear River.

In China, the dragons that stalked the land created no need for the country's heroes to kill them, eat their hearts, or drink their blood in order to become as strong, mighty or keen-sighted. Dragons were regarded as benevolent rather than baleful. Far from gobbling up infants, violating virgins and tangling with knights, they were gentle, charming creatures that brought happiness and plenty. They could be found in rivers, lakes and even – when they magically shrank themselves – in raindrops. Along with three other wholesome and well-intentioned creatures of legends – the tortoise, the phoenix and the unicorn – they enjoyed lolling and basking in the sun. Occasionally they snacked on a swallow that flew into their jaws while pursuing flies. They were honoured as the makers of humanitarian laws and were held in particular esteem during the Ch'ing dynasty (1644–1912), when the emperors sat on dragon thrones, travelled by dragon boats, ate at dragon tables and slept in dragon beds.

The Chinese affection for the beasts was made clear in this dictionary definition of around 1600, which stated, 'The dragon is . . . the largest of scaled creatures. Its head is like a camel's, its horns like a deer's, its eyes like a hare's, its ears like a bull's, its neck like a snake's, its belly like a frog's, its scales like a carp's, its claws like an eagle's, and its paws like a tiger's. Its scales number 81, being nine by nine, the extreme odd and lucky number. Its voice is like the beating of a gong . . . When it breathes the breath forms clouds, sometimes changing into rain, at other times into fire . . . it is fond of beautiful gems and jade. It is extremely fond of swallow's flesh; it dreads iron, the *mong* plant, the centipede, the leaves of the Pride of India [the azedarac tree] and silk dyed in five different colours. When rain is wanted a swallow should be offered; when floods are to be restrained, then, iron; to stir up the dragon the *mong* plant should be employed.'

In spite of the help dragons gave, they were occasionally used for food and medicine. According to legend, a tasty soup was made of one particular dragon that fell into the palace grounds of the Emperor Hwo during a heavy shower around 100 BC and the hot liquid was served to the emperor's ministers. Dragons were also chopped into mincemeat and served at the tables of other emperors. In parts of China today, pharmacies sell powdered and dried alligators (which are said to be descended from dragons) to cure anything from warts to lovesickness. However, even in the Far East the dragon was sometimes a malicious and predatory beast. Whenever upset or insulted, it could gather up all the neighbourhood's water in containers and cause a drought. It could also turn on its old enemy the sun and cause an eclipse. The Japanese version of the monster often behaved more in keeping with the Western image. Some Japanese dragons demanded the sacrifice of a virgin once a year.

Legends from all over the world and, in particular, the legend of St. George and the dragon, once inspired a booming trade in fraudulent dragons and monsters throughout Europe. Imitation dragons were manufactured and sold as being straight from the caves and sandy banks of the Middle and Far East. The bogus monsters were displayed as early as the sixteenth century, when the renowned Italian physician and mathematician Hieronimus Cardanus saw some in Paris. 'They were two-footed creatures with very small wings, which one could scarcely deem capable of flight, with a small head . . . like a serpent, of a bright colour, and without any feather or hair', he recorded. The fake dragons were no larger than a kitten, so their sellers tried to pass them off as dragon babies. In fact, they were probably made by mutilating specimens of small flying lizards found in the Malay Peninsula and the East Indies. A scholar who examined one of the ugly specimens felt that all was not right. 'Its head is serrated', he wrote, 'and its crest comes to a peak . . . It has a flexible tail, two feet in length, and bristling with prickles. The skin is like that of a skate.' Other false specimens were made by using parts of a giant ray fish or by adding bat's wings to the dried-up body of a lizard.

Reports of dragons continued throughout the centuries and many of them were included in various respected books. A seventeenth century collection of fables, *Historie of Serpents*, told how dragons killed elephants by dropping on them from trees. In *The Subterranean World*, published in Amsterdam in 1678, the author Father Athanasius Kircher wrote that, 'All the world's volcanoes are fed by one great main fire situated in the very bowels of the earth. Down in this area is a labyrinth of passageways, all running into each other, and most filled with lava, liquid fire, and water. Some of these caves and passageways, however, are empty, and it is here that you will find dragons, the kings of the underground beasts.'

One of the most startling of dragon reports came from the small island of Komodo in the Malay Archipelago as recently as 1912. The pilot of a plane that crash-landed on Komodo afterward spoke of the 'giant, lizard-like creatures' he had encountered. Although most people dismissed his story as 'preposterous', the curator of the Botanical Gardens on Java decided to investigate the aviator's claims. He asked the Dutch Civil Administrator of the district to visit Komodo and see what he could find out. The administrator came back with the skin of a seven-foot-long creature, reporting that the local people swore there were similar beasts of up to 30 feet in length. On receipt of the skin and the information, the curator sent a Malay animal hunter to the island in search of a live monster. A local rajah provided special assistants and dogs. The hunt party captured four dragon-like animals, the biggest of them almost 10 feet long. They were later classified as belonging to a new species of giant monitor lizard and are now known popularly as Komodo dragons.

In the summer of 1960, dragons again made the news. The place was New Guinea. The story was that local residents in an area of the island under Australian administration had been attacked by dragons some 20 feet long. Rumours flew that the monsters belched smoke and fire and sucked the blood from their victims' bodies. Some corpses also had wounds of more than a foot in length, said to have been made by the dragons' claws. There was so much panic that the government authorities moved people into police stockades and posted a substantial reward for the capture of one of the beasts, dead or alive. Perhaps not surprisingly, no one tried to collect the reward. Whether from boredom or overfeeding, the dragons themselves appeared no more.

The dragon is now considered by most people as a purely mythical beast. But its history and symbolism are so rich and diverse that the creature fascinates us more than many a real animal.

CHAPTER 16

MERMAIDS AND UNICORNS

Mermaids – the alluring half-woman, half-fish creatures of the deep – are found in lore all around the world. The roots of the legend go back to ancient Babylon. Why did it endure so long? Can it truly be the symbol for a sexual lust that brings self-destruction, as modern psychologists see it? Most people today do not accept the existence of mermaids, just as they deny the existence of unicorns. That mythical creature – always with a long single horn, whether it resembles a horse or other animal – has had an important place in folklore. Did the unicorn simply meet some imaginative need in the mind of man?

On a warm summer day in the late 1890s, William Munro, a teacher, was walking along the beach in the county of Caithness, Scotland. Suddenly he spotted a figure that resembled a naked woman seated on a rock jutting out to the sea. If he had not known that it was too dangerous to swim out to the rock, Munro would have assumed the figure to be human. But realizing that something was odd, he examined the figure closely. The lower part of the body was covered by water but the creature was using her exposed arms to comb her long, light brown hair. After three or four minutes the figure dropped into the sea and vanished from view.

As the result of an argument 12 years later, Munro wrote to *The Times* of London. In the published letter he described his earlier experience in careful and unemotional language. 'The head was covered with hair of the colour above mentioned [brown] and shaded on the crown, the forehead round, the face plump, the cheeks ruddy, the eyes blue, the mouth and lips of natural form resembling those of a man; the teeth I could not discover, as the mouth was shut; the breasts and abdomen, the arms and fingers of the size of a full-grown body of the human species, the fingers, from the action in which the hands were employed, did not appear to be webbed, but as to this I am not positive.'

Munro went on to say that, although other reliable people had reported seeing the figure, he had not believed them until he had seen it himself. Having seen it, he was convinced that the figure was a mermaid. He finished by saying that he hoped his letter might help to establish 'the existence of a phenomenon hitherto almost incredible to naturalists, or to remove the scepticism of others, who are ready to dispute everything they cannot comprehend . . .'

This clear account shows that a belief in mermaids was not held only by half-crazed sailors on lengthy ocean voyages. In fact, the mermaid – like the dragon – seems to be a nearly universal symbol. She is found in most countries of the world and where there is no sea, she adapts her home to a lake or river. Like the dragon, she seems to answer some deeply felt need in man. She is the unobtainable enchantress, seemingly sexual and voluptuous but underneath cold and elusive. With her eternal youth and beauty, her magical voice and seductive power, she lures unresisting sailors to their doom. She seems, in modern psychological interpretation, to symbolize the mingling of sex and death, the desire by man to lose himself totally even when he knows it means his own destruction.

Behind the mermaid legend lies a long sequence of romantic yearning, the longing for an ideal, if unattainable, woman whose favours were like those of no mere mortal. The very spot on which Munro had his 'arresting experience' was the scene of an earlier and even more eventful happening. According to local stories, a mermaid had given a young man gold, silver and diamonds that she had gathered from a wrecked ship. The youth took her gifts but gave some of the jewels to young women he desired. Worse than this, he failed to meet the mermaid a number of times as planned, so arousing her jealousy and wrath. One day, she met him in a boat and rowed him to a nearby cave, saying it held all the treasures ever lost in the estuary. Once there, the youth fell asleep. He awoke to find himself tied to a rock by gold chains that allowed him to walk only as far as a mound of diamonds at the mouth of the cave. Although he had riches and a mate who satisfied his lust, he was but a prisoner. He was trapped, a victim of his own greed.

Mermaids were well-known for taking ruthless revenge if thwarted or slighted in any way and there are many stories that illustrate this characteristic. This theme may stem from man's sexual fantasy of a wild, untameable creature bent on fulfilling her own desires. Even more sinister, in terms of sexual symbolism, is the idea of the mermaid as a fallen angel who could only eat living flesh. She captured sailors by her singing and sweet music. If this technique failed – which it rarely did – she relied on a unique body smell that no man could resist. Once she had snared her victim and lulled him to sleep, she tore him to pieces with her spiky green teeth.

Slightly less savage as a fantasy, was the myth that mermaids and mermen lived in a kingdom of great riches beneath the sea, to which mermaids took their victims and kept them prisoner. From this tale grew the seaman's belief that it means bad luck to see a mermaid. It was supposed to foretell death at sea by drowning.

The roots of the mermaid legend go back to the powerful Babylonian fish deities, associated with the sun and the moon. Oannes, who represented the sun, had a human form but wore a fish head as a cap and a fish skin as a cloak. He was gradually replaced by the fish god, Ea, who was half man and half fish and can be seen as the ancestor of the merman. The moon goddess Atargartis, half woman and half fish, was the precursor of the mermaid. The Babylonians believed that when they had finished their respective journeys through the sky, the sun and moon sank into the sea. So it seemed appropriate that the gods of the sun and moon should have a form that allowed for life both above and below the water. The strange form of these gods, part human and part fish, and their power to vanish into the unfathomable oceans, gives them a mysterious, elusive quality. This mystery and elusiveness was inherited by mermaids. The mirror the mermaid often holds is thought to represent the moon, which also seems to add to her power because of the way the moon influences the tides. Because the fish deities were accorded enormous power in pre-Christian times, their link to the mermaids helped strengthen the mermaid legends.

Other forerunners of the mermaids were the tritons of Greek mythology. Also half human and half fish, the tritons calmed the waves and ruled the storms. The sirens of Greek mythology, although half bird and half woman, like the mermaid, lured men to destruction by their beautiful singing. When the Greek hero Odysseus was forced to sail past them, he plugged the ears of his sailors with wax and had himself bound securely to the mast in order to be able to resist them.

The Apsaras of India were beautiful water nymphs but despite their human shape, they had much in common with mermaids. Besides their beauty and 'fragrance' they were skilled musicians, especially on the lute and shared the mermaid's power of prophecy. However, though promiscuous and always eager for new conquests, they were friendly toward man and intent on giving happiness.

With the establishment of Christianity, the mermaid legend took on a new aspect in which the mermaid longed to have a soul. According to Christian thought, the mermaid could only gain a soul by promising to live on land and giving up all hope of returning to the sea. This was impossible for the half-fish creature, so it doomed her to an unhappy struggle with herself. Thus the mermaid, who had been a simple figure representing the most elemental urges and desires, became far more complex, with her own internal conflicts. There is a sad and charming story of a mermaid in the sixth century AD who daily visited a monk in the holy community of Iona, a small island off Scotland. She begged to be given a soul and the monk prayed with her, to give her the strength to abandon the sea. But despite her desire for a soul and despite the fact that she had fallen passionately in love with the monk, she was unable to give up the sea. In the end, weeping bitterly, she left the island forever. It is said that the tears she shed became pebbles and to this day, the grey-green pebbles found on the shore of Iona are known as mermaid's tears.

The seal, with its sleek form and human characteristics, has long been linked with the mermaid. Many believe that reports of mythical mermaids are based on glimpses of real seals. In mermaid lore, however, the seal is known as the constant companion of the mermaid. There is a story that a fisherman once stunned and skinned a seal and then threw it back live into the sea. A mermaid, taking pity on the animal, volunteered to search for its skin. However, she was captured by the fisherman's companions and died from exposure to the air. Ever since then, in gratitude for her bravery, the seal has been the special guardian of the mermaid.

The Scandinavians, Scots and Irish had many stories about seal people who were forced to live as seals at sea but who could, at certain times, assume their true human shape on land. Some thought seals were fallen angels, others that they were the souls of drowned people or humans under a spell. Certain Irish families claimed descent from seals and an entire nation in Asia Minor traced their ancestry back to a seal maiden mentioned in Greek mythology. In the myth, a water nymph transformed herself into a seal to evade the unwelcome attentions of the son of Zeus. However, her precautions were too late, for soon after her transformation she gave birth to a son. He was named Phocus, which means seal. The Phocian people commemorated their descendance from the seal maiden by showing a seal on their earliest coins.

Seal maidens had much in common with mermaids and the two creatures became inextricably mixed in many legends. Mermaids and seal maidens both liked to dance and sing. They also both shared the gift of prophecy. There are stories of both seal maidens and mermaids marrying humans and remaining on land for many years. It was said that a mermaid had an enchanted cap without which she could not return to sea. If a man managed to steal her cap and hide it, he might marry her but if she ever found it she would immediately vanish into the waves. In the same way, a man could marry a seal maiden if he could steal and hide her sealskin. An old story from the Scottish highlands is one of many on this theme. A man fell in love with a beautiful seal maiden, stole her sealskin and hid it carefully and married her. They had many children and were happy. But one day, one of her sons discovered where the skin was hidden and told his mother. She eagerly put it on and, leaving her children forever, swam joyfully out to sea.

In 1403, a mermaid reportedly floated through a broken dyke near Edam in Holland and was taken into captivity. Her fate was different from most other captured mermaids. She spent the next

15 years in Haarlem, where she was taught to spin and to obey her mistress. On death she was given a Christian burial.

In some areas the mermaid legend survived a long time. As recently as 1895, the inhabitants of the Welsh seaport of Milford Haven believed that mermaids or underwater fairies regularly shopped at the town's weekly market. They got to the town by means of a covered road on the sea bed, quietly made their purchases, such as tortoiseshell combs for their hair and vanished till next market day.

Most sightings of mermaids, however, have been by sailors. For instance, during his first voyage, the previously sceptical Christopher Columbus recorded seeing three mermaids leaping high out of the sea off the coast of Guiana. Mermaids were regularly seen by sailors suffering from months of boredom and sexual frustration at sea. Could sexual fantasizing have made them see a beautiful half-woman in sea mammals such as graceful seals, or even ungainly dugongs or manatees? Who knows ?

The famous English navigator Henry Hudson, told his mermaid story matter of factly. On 15 June 1625, while sailing in search of the North West Passage, he wrote in his diary, 'One of our company, looking overboard, saw a mermaid. From the navel upward, her back and breasts were like a woman's . . . her skin very white, and long hair hanging down behind, of colour black. In her going down they saw her tail, which was like the tail of a porpoise, speckled like a mackerel.' There are reports of sightings from Russia – where the mermaids were 'tall, sad, and pale' – from Thailand and from Scotland. In the last country in May 1658, mermaids were found at the mouth of the River Dee and the *Aberdeen Almanac* promised visitors that they 'will undoubtedly see a pretty Company of Mermaids, creatures of admirable beauty.'

As the fame of mermaids spread, so the inevitable fakes and frauds began to appear. Usually, false mermaids were carefully constructed from the top half of a monkey joined to the tail of a fish. One of these, probably made in the seventeenth century, was shown in an exhibition of fakes mounted by the British Museum in London in 1961. Most of these so-called mermaids were extremely ugly but they seemed to have aroused great interest.

In a book published in 1717, there is a picture of a supposedly genuine mermaid. The description with the picture said, 'A monster resembling a Siren caught on the coast of Borneo in the administrative district of Amboina. It was 59 inches long and in proportion like an eel. It lived on land for four days and seven hours in a barrel filled with water. From time to time it uttered little cries like those of a mouse. Although offered small fish, molluscs, crabs. crayfish, etc., it would not eat . . . '

As the fame of this mermaid spread, Peter the Great, Czar of Russia became interested and tried to obtain more information from François Valentijn, a Dutch colonial chaplain who had written on the subject. Valentijn didn't add much but reported on another Amboina mermaid. This time, the creature was accompanied by her mate and was seen by more than 50 witnesses. The writer was convinced that the mermaid story was true. 'If any narrative in the world deserves credit', he wrote, 'it is this . . . Should the stubborn world, however, hesitate to believe it, it matters nothing; for there are people who would even deny the existence of such cities as Rome, Constantinople, or Cairo, simply because they themselves have not happened to see them.'

Despite the fact that mermaids were supposed to be wanton and cruel, they were sought after by seamen as if they were virginal and kind. Such was the enthusiasm to find a mermaid – and then presumably keep her for private pleasure – that the ships' look-outs began to see the heroine of their erotic dreams everywhere. As one writer later put it, 'These hauntingly beautiful goddesses of the sea, full of mystery and danger, were surely conjured from the chaos of the water in answer to some primal human need.' But the great eighteenth-century German naturalist, G. W. Steller, seemed to have a rather different image of the origin of mermaids. Up to the time that he joined an expedition seeking a sea route from Siberia to Alaska, sightings of mermaids had been dismissed by some experts as being distorted glimpses of the dugong or manatee. Such water mammals suckled their young and, ran the explanation, a sight of mother mammal suckling her baby gave rise to tales about beautiful sea maidens with shapely naked breasts.

On the expedition's return voyage, Steller's ship was wrecked. He and others were washed up on Copper Island in the Commander Group near Bering Island. It was there at high tide that Steller saw some 'hump-backed' objects in the water. At first they reminded him of capsized boats. On seeing them again, however, he realized that they were seal-like animals of a previously unknown class. He gave them the name of *Rhytina stelleri*, or Steller's sea-cow and claimed that it was these somewhat unfortunately named creatures that had for so long been taken for mermaids. He was the first trained observer to have seen this animal alive. He estimated that they were an average of 30 feet long and weighed some 3½ tons each. They had small heads and large forked tails. Subsequent investigation proved that they mated like human beings – especially in the spring on evenings when the sea was calm.

'Before they come together', he wrote, 'many amorous preludes take place. The female, constantly followed by the male, swims leisurely to and fro, eluding him with many gyrations and meanderings until, impatient of further delay, she turns on her back as if exhausted and coerced, whereupon the male, rushing violently upon her, pays her the tribute of his passion, and both give themselves over in mutual embrace.'

Throughout the Middle Ages, carvings and stone and wooden representations of mermaids adorned churches and cathedrals in almost every part of Europe. But by the middle of the more scientific nineteenth century, belief in them was ebbing. As steamships replaced sailing ships and the duration of voyages grew shorter, seamen less and less claimed to have been seduced, tempted or taunted by the lethal sirens. In spite of this, the mermaid had not yet completely submerged. One was seen again in 1900 by Alexander Gunn, a landholder in the far north of Scotland. While he and his dog were out rescuing a sheep that had become stuck in a gully, he glanced up and locked eyes with a mermaid reclining on an adjacent ledge. With red-gold wavy hair, green eyes and arched eyebrows she was extremely beautiful. She was also of human size. It was hard to tell who was the more startled – she, Gunn or his dog. However, it was the dog which, with a terrified howl, gave vent to its feelings first. It fled with its tail between its legs, followed close behind by the landholder who had seen anger as well as fear in the mermaid's expression. 'What I saw was real', he told a friend later. 'I actually encountered a mermaid.'

More than 50 years later, two girls sauntering along the same shore also chanced upon a mermaid stranded by the tide. Her description fitted that of Gunn's. Shortly after this, in a completely different part of the world, the adventurer Eric de Bisschop added to the relatively few twentieth-century accounts of mermaids. His experiences occurred shortly after midnight on 3 January 1957, when he was sailing his reconstruction of an ancient Polynesian raft from Tahiti to Chile. In his book, *Tahiti-Nui*, published two years later, he told how one of the sailors on watch suddenly began to act like he had gone mad. The man claimed he had seen a strange creature leap out of the water and onto the deck. The being, with hair like extremely fine seaweed, stood upright on its tail. The sailor approached and touched the intruder, which immediately knocked him flat and then jumped into the sea. It was the shining fish scales on the seaman's arms that convinced de Bisschop the man was telling the truth and that he had been in contact with a mermaid. Four years later, in 1961, the Isle of Man Tourist Board introduced an angling week and offered a prize to anyone catching a live mermaid in the Irish Sea. This followed several reports of red-headed water nymphs sporting in the foam. However, the Gaelic mermaids proved as elusive as their sisters of centuries before and none was caught.

Though there are probably only a few people today who would genuinely subscribe to a belief in real mermaids, it might be said that mermaids have attained a degree of reality. The legend is so powerful and universal that, like the dragon, the mermaid has become a symbol – part of man's unconscious imagination. The same can be said for the unicorn.

This mythical creature is based on a variety of animals but is always distinguished from others by its long single horn. Like the dragon, its general appearance and characteristics varied according to place and legend. Sometimes, it strongly resembled one animal such as a goat, a horse or even a serpent and sometimes it combined the features of different animals. In the West it tended to be fierce and untameable, a lover of solitude but in China it was peaceful and gentle and heralded good fortune.

Like other mythical beasts, the unicorn provides a rich field for symbolic interpretation, both of a specific and of a generalized kind. The single horn indicates both virility and kingly power and is also, in some legends, a sign of purity. The unicorn combines both male and female elements with its masculine horn and female body. Its Chinese name, *ki-lin*, means male-female. This reconciliation of the opposing forces of male and female in one creature meant, in symbolic terms, that the unicorn stood for the reconciliation of other opposites. The harmony of opposites was the greatest ideal of Western magicians and alchemists and the unicorn, therefore, has an important place in the history of magic.

The first mention of the unicorn in the West was in a book on India written by the Greek historian Ctesias in about 398 BC. Part of his description went, 'There are in India certain wild asses which are as large as horses, and larger. Their bodies are white, their heads dark red, and their eyes dark blue. They have a horn on the forehead which is about a foot and a half in length.' The description seems to be based on conjecture and travellers' tales. The unicorn appears to be a mixture of the rhinoceros, the Himalayan antelope and the wild ass. Its horn was said to have come to a long sharp point and to be white at the base, black in the centre and crimson at the tip. It is probable that Ctesias had seen drinking cups made of horn and decorated in these colours inasmuch as such drinking horns were often used by Indian princes. He reports that dust scraped from the horn was an antidote to poison and that those who drank from the horn would be protected from convulsions and from poisoning. This belief persisted up to the Middle Ages and the rich and powerful paid enormous prices for drinking vessels believed to be made from the horn of the unicorn.

Apothecaries often claimed to keep a unicorn's horn in their shop in order to cure ailments. Some even thought it had the power to raise the dead. Even in the seventeenth and eighteenth centuries, alicorn, a powder allegedly made from unicorn horn, was featured on the drug lists issued by the English Royal Society of Physicians. It was extremely expensive, and gave rise to the saying 'weight for weight alicorn for gold'. The druggists explained the high costs by the fact that unicorns were mostly caught in India and that the powder had to be shipped from there.

In 1641, a French marquis visiting London wrote that he had seen a unicorn's horn on display in the Tower of London. It had been the property of Queen Elizabeth I and was said to have then been worth about £40,000. He wanted to test its authenticity by placing it on a piece of silk and putting both articles on a hot coal fire. If the horn was genuine, he said, the silk would not burn. However, perhaps fortunately, the presence of the guards prevented him from carrying out this test.

The purifying nature of the unicorn's horn is apparent in a famous medieval legend. In this story, many animals gather at dusk by a pool to quench their thirst but the water is poisoned and they are unable to drink. Soon they are joined by the unicorn who dips his horn into the water and cleanses it. In some Christian versions, the horn stands for the cross and the water for the sins of the world.

Another famous and symbolic medieval legend, is the capture of the unicorn by a young virgin. The unicorn, a small goat-like creature, was too fierce and swift to be captured by hunters. It could only be tamed by a virgin seated alone in a forest under a tree. Attracted by her perfume of chastity, the unicorn would approach and lay its head in her lap. She would stroke its horn and lull it to sleep. Then she would cut off his horn and betray him to the hunters and dogs. The sexual symbolism of this story is fairly obvious and it gave rise to many erotic elaborations. There was also an attempt to put a Christian interpretation on it. In this case the virgin is the Virgin Mary, the unicorn is Christ and the horn signifies the unity of father and son. Christ, as embodied in the unicorn, is slain for the sake of a sinful world.

For centuries, naturalists suggested that it should be possible to produce a unicorn by genetic engineering and in March 1933 it was done. An American biologist, Dr Franklin Dove, performed a simple operation on a day-old male Ayrshire calf at the University of Maine. By transplanting the animal's two horn buds and placing them together over the frontal bones, he forecast that a single unicorn-like horn would grow. His experiment was a total success and he was able to show the world a one-horned bull. It was nothing like the unicorn of the Middle Ages, which through courtly literature had gradually assumed the sleek lines of a horse. But it was not bullish in character. Could people, centuries ago, have performed the same experiment and produced a one-horned creature, with characteristics that differed from its two-horned brethren? And could these creatures have inspired the original legends of the unicorn ? Or did the unicorn, a mysterious and magical creature, spring purely from man's mind, meeting some psychological and imaginative need?

CHAPTER 17

MONSTERS OF THE DEEP

Are all the monsters that have been said to beset seafarers a figment of the imagination? Could some huge prehistoric sea animals have managed to survive deep under the ocean? Sea monsters have long been part of sea lore but have gained little acceptance among the wider population. Yet sightings have persisted through the years and many reports have been from naturalists or observers other than active seamen. Recent underwater explorers have come upon some previously unknown species of sea life, in at least one case of giant size. Will future exploration uncover the sea monster of old?

In 1938, a strange fish was picked up in the nets of a South African trawler. It turned out to be a *coelacanth*, a fish that had been in existence about 300 million years ago and was believed, by scientists, to have been extinct for about 70 million years. The *coelacanth* had no special protective features, so its survival all these millions of years was particularly remarkable. If the lowly *coelacanth* had such powers to survive, why not other ancient marine species? Might there be a few survivors somewhere in the depths of the ocean?

The sea is vast and incredibly deep. Ships travel over only a small portion of the surface and trawlers normally sink their nets to a depth of about 60 feet. Until recently, scientists believed that fish could not survive at great depths but a research vessel has now brought up a fish from a depth of over 26,000 feet. Although the ocean at that level is totally black, that fish still retained two small eyes – evidence that it had once lived far closer to the surface. We know that marine creatures are amazingly adaptable. Salmon leap rapids. A variety of lung fish can live out of water for four years. It is not impossible that certain prehistoric sea monsters have adapted to living in the ocean deeps.

At one time, perhaps as long as 200 million years ago, the sea was filled with giant monsters. There were massive sharks far larger than any we know today, enormous crabs, sea serpents of fantastic lengths and huge lung fish, skates and rays. Many of these creatures developed body armour and protective devices such as stings to insure their survival. In 1930, Dr Anton Brun caught the six-foot-long larva of an eel at a depth of only 1,000 feet. On the assumption that it would mature to 18 times its length – although some eels reach 30 times their larval size – this eel would grow to a mammoth 110 feet. Perhaps there are still larger species existing at still greater depths.

But whether they exist or not, sea monsters have long been a part of mariners' tales. Among the many stories is one that took place in the late eighteenth century, when a Danish sailing ship had been becalmed off the coast of West Africa. Her captain, Jean-Magnus Dens, decided to put the time to good use and ordered the crew to scrape and clean the outside of the boat. To do this, the men worked from planks on the ship's side. Suddenly, without warning, a giant sea monster emerged. Wrapping two of its enormous arms around two of the men, it dragged them into the sea. A third arm went around another sailor, but, as he clung desperately to the rigging, his shipmates freed him by hacking off the monster's arm. Despite repeated attempts to harpoon the monster, it sank out of sight into the water. The bodies of the first two victims were never recovered and the third sailor died that same night. The captain later described the part of the arm that had been hacked off. He said it was very thick at one end and tapered to a sharp point at the other. It was about 25 feet long and covered with large suckers. Judging from the size of the cut-off portion, the captain estimated that the whole arm must have been between 35 and 40 feet in length.

This is a typical seaman's story of a monstrous sea creature – exaggerated, fantastical but fascinating. Such stories were often believed in earlier times. However, even in the late eighteenth century, Captain Dens could find few to credit his tale. The big exception was the young French naturalist, Pierre Denys de Montfort, who was determined to prove to the sceptical scientific world that octopuses of colossal size existed. Choosing to believe that Dens' monster was a huge octopus, he included Dens' account in his unfinished six-volume work, *The Natural History of Molluscs*. These books were published in Paris between 1802 and 1805 and, unfortunately for Denys de Montfort's reputation, he included a mixture of science and imagination in which fact was hard to distinguish from fiction. The Frenchman's one scientific supporter was the German naturalist Lorenz Oken, who, for all his renown, was slightly suspect because he also believed there were more and stranger things beneath the surface of the sea than had ever been seen above it. Despite great ridicule and criticism, Denys de Montfort continued to compile reports of 'the sightings of monsters and serpents of the sea by mariners whose sincerity I do not and will not doubt.'

True to his word, he followed every lead to find his giant octopus. Sometime in the 1790s he journeyed to the northern port of Dunkirk, where a group of American whale fishers were living and working. He wanted to interview the seamen and hear, at first hand, the experiences that few people apart from himself would credit. For example, here is a report he repeated, 'One of these captains, named Ben Johnson, told me that he had harpooned a male whale, which, besides its very prominent penis placed under the belly, seemed to have another one coming out of its mouth. This surprised him greatly and also the sailors, and when they had made the whale fast to the ship, he had them put a hook through this long round mass of flesh which they hauled in with several running nooses . . . They could hardly believe their eyes when they saw that this fleshy mass, cut off at both ends and as thick as a mast at the widest point, was the arm of an enormous octopus, the closed suckers of which were larger than a hat; the lower end seemed newly cut off, the upper one . . . was also cut off and scarred and surmounted by a sort of extension as thick and long as a man's arm. This huge octopus's limb, exactly measured with a fishing line, was found to be 35 feet long and the suckers were arranged in two rows, as in the common octopus. What then must have been the length of arm which had been cut off at its upper extremity, where it was no less than six inches in diameter?' It seemed to Denys de Montfort that at least 10 feet had been sliced off the upper end and a further 10 to 25 feet off the lower – making a total length of some 80 feet.

During his stay in Dunkirk, he found that the whale fishers were eager to speak of their encounters with monsters. He gave an account of what was told by an American captain named Reynolds. 'One day', Denys de Montfort recorded, 'he and his men saw floating on the surface of the water a long fleshy body, red and slate coloured, which they took to be a sea serpent and which frightened the sailors who rowed the whaleboats.' However one sailor noticed that the supposed snake had no head and was motionless, so they found the courage to haul it aboard. They then discovered from the suckers that it was an octopus or squid arm – one that measured 45 feet in length and 2½ feet in diameter.

The arm, which would have been a convincing piece of evidence, was nowhere to be found by the time Denys de Montfort heard about it. Although disappointed at not seeing it, the naturalist's hopes rose when he heard of an extraordinary painting of a sea monster on view further along the coast in St Malo. He hurried to go to St Thomas' chapel where the picture, given in thanksgiving for their survival by a ship's crew, was hanging. Before inspecting it, however, he quizzed several of the port's fishermen about its story. They related how a local sailing ship had run into trouble off the West African coast and how her crew had been set upon by a 'monster straight from Hell'. As Denys de Montfort told it from the accounts he heard,

'The ship had just taken in her cargo of slaves, ivory and gold dust, and the men were heaving up anchor, when suddenly a monstrous cuttlefish appeared on top of the water and slung its arms about two of the masts. The tips of the arms reached to the mastheads and the weight of the cuttle dragged the ship over, so that she lay on her beam-ends and was near to being capsized. The crew seized axes and knives and cut away at the arms of the monster; but, despairing of escape, called upon their patron saint, St Thomas, to help them. Their prayers seemed to give them renewed courage, for they persevered, and finally succeeded in cutting off the arms, when the animal sank and the vessel was righted. Now, when the ship returned to St Malo the crew, grateful for their deliverance from so hideous a danger, marched in procession to the chapel of their patron saint, where they offered a solemn thanksgiving, and afterwards had a painting made representing the conflict with the cuttle, and which was hung in the chapel.'

On hearing this story, Denys de Montfort rushed into the chapel as eagerly as the seamen themselves had done and gazed up at the fantastic and fearsome scene that the painting depicted. The monster, whose arms were wound around the tops of the three masts, was as gigantic and hideous as the naturalist could have yearned for and he was grateful for the boost it gave to his theories. He took the painting to be an exact description of a real event, which his obsessional belief in monstrous octopuses made entirely plausible to him. He had a copy of the painting made by an artist who had not seen the original and who, therefore, made it seem even more fantastic. On publication of the copy, critics called it an even bigger fake than his books. He was branded 'the most outrageous charlatan Paris has known', and no one accepted his challenge to travel the 200 miles to St Malo to see the original for themselves. The picture was later taken from the chapel and either hidden or destroyed. Denys de Montfort sank into disrepute and obscurity. He wrote a phrase book and a book on bee-keeping and, on their failure, became a pedlar of sea shells. Having fallen into deep poverty, he was found dead in a gutter in 1820 or 1821. His reputation as an eccentric overshadowed his fine early work on mollusc shells and it was too soon forgotten that he had created 25 new genera still in use today.

For some decades after, no naturalists were prepared to risk their career by writing about marine monsters, whether or not they thought some of the tales might have a basis in fact. A more recent author views the whole subject in more perspective, however, and writes, 'The sea serpent – or at any rate his cousin, the sea monster . . . is at least as ancient, and therefore as respectable, as the fairies, and a good deal older than the modern ghost.' Tales of the Norwegian monkfish, for instance, go back to medieval times. The first one was caught off the coast after a great tempest. It 'had a man's face, rude and ungraceful with a bald, shining head; on the shoulders something resembling a monk's cowl; and long winglets instead of arms. The extremity of the body ended in a tail.' According to the historian who described it, the peculiar-looking monkfish was given to the King of Poland who took pity on it and had it placed back in the sea.

In 1680 a frightful kraken, which is a legendary giant sea monster, swam too close to the shore of Norway, became jammed in a cleft of rock and remained there until it died. The stench from the kraken polluted the entire neighbourhood and it was months before the local people could go within miles of the rotting carcass. More than 50 years later, in 1734, another kraken was observed by the celebrated Danish missionary Hans Egede – this time near Greenland. He recorded the experience in his diary stating, 'The monster was of so huge a size that, coming out of the water, its head reached as high as a mainmast; its body was as bulky as the ship, and three or four times as long. It had a long pointed snout, and spouted like a whalefish; it had great broad paws; the body seemed covered with shellwork, and the skin was very ragged and uneven. The under part of its body was shaped like an enormous huge serpent, and when it dived again under the water, it plunged backward into the sea, and so raised its tail aloft, which seemed a whole ship's length distant from the bulkiest part of its body.'

Another eighteenth-century writer on the kraken was the Norwegian Bishop of Bergen, Erik Pontoppidan. He wrote a book about the natural history of Norway in 1752 and, although he did not see a sea monster himself, he believed the scores of fishermen who told him that they had. He described the kraken as it was described to him. 'Its back or upper part, which seems to be about an English mile-and-a-half in circumference, looks at first like a number of small islands surrounded with something that floats and fluctuates like seaweed . . . at last several bright points or horns appear, which grow thicker and thicker the higher they rise above the water. . . . After the monster has been on the surface for a short time it begins slowly to sink again, and then the danger is as great as before, because the motion of his sinking causes such a swell in the sea and such an eddy or whirlpool, that it draws everything down with it. . . .'

In 1765, the same year that Bishop Pontoppidan's book appeared in English translation, *The Gentleman's Magazine* in London stated that, 'the people of Stockholm report that a great dragon, named Necker, infests the neighbouring lake, and seizes and devours such boys as go into the water to wash.' This did not stop the Bishop of Avranches from swimming there on a sunny summer day, although the onlookers 'were greatly surprised when they saw him return from imminent danger'.

With some three-fifths of the earth's surface covered with water, it is hardly surprising that stories of sea monsters arose. Sightings were reported in many parts of the world, including North America after it was settled by Europeans. The coast of New England soon became a popular place for serpent encounters, and between 1815 and 1823, hardly a summer went by without someone meeting up with a sea monster. In June 1815, a strange animal was observed moving rapidly south through Gloucester Bay. Its body, about 100 feet long, seemed to have a string of 30 or 40 humps, each the size of a barrel. It had a head shaped like a horse and was dark brown in colour. Two years later it was again seen the bay, and the *Gloucester Telegraph* reported, 'On the 14th of August the sea serpent was approached by a boat within 30 feet, and on raising its head above water was greeted by a volley from the gun of an experienced sportsman. The creature turned directly toward the boat, as if meditating an attack, but sank down. . . .'

The following year, the same or a similar creature was observed in Nahant. One of the clearest accounts was given by Samuel Cabot of Boston. Mr Cabot was standing on the crowded Nahant beach when he noticed that a number of boats were speedily making for the shore. 'My attention', he wrote, 'was suddenly arrested by an object emerging from the water at the distance of about 100 or 150 yards, which gave to my mind at the first glance, the idea of a horse's head. It was elevated about two feet from the water, and he depressed it gradually to within six or eight inches as he moved along. His bunches appeared to me not altogether uniform in size. I felt persuaded by this examination that he could not be less than 80 feet long.' The horse-like monster reappeared again the next summer and it was watched by dozens of vacationers. 'I had with me an excellent telescope', declared one knowledgeable witness, 'and . . . saw appear, at a short distance from the shore, an animal whose body formed a series of blackish curves, of which I counted 13 . . . This at least I can affirm . . . that it was neither a whale, nor a cachalot [sperm whale], nor any strong souffleur [dolphin], nor any other enormous cetacean [water mammal]. None of these gigantic animals has such an undulating back.'

Within a short while, the creature had shown itself to the crew of the sloop *Concord*. The captain and the mate made a deposition of what they had seen before a local Justice of the Peace as soon as they reached shore. In his sworn statement the mate said in part, 'His head was about as long as a horse's and was a proper snake's head – there was a degree of flatness, with a slight hollow on the top of his head – his eyes were prominent, and stood out considerably from the surface. . . .' The same animal was later seen and identified by Reverend Cheever Finch, who said he spent a half-hour watching its 'smooth rapid progress back and forth.'

Many lakes are immensely deep and could provide suitable habitats for large monsters. In fact, the next North American area to be infiltrated by sea serpents was British Columbia, where deep-water lakes are spaced between the Rockies and the Pacific. It was while taking a team of horses across Lake Okanagan in 1854 that an Indian halfbreed claimed to have been 'seized by a giant hand which tried to pull me down into the water.' He managed to struggle out of the grip, but the horses in his charge were not so lucky. The monster – which apparently had several long and powerful arms – got a hold on the animals and pulled them under the surface; all of them drowned. The sea serpent was known as Naitaka to the Indians and Ogopogo to the settlers. It was seen regularly from then on and a pioneer named John McDougal later recounted an experience similar to the halfbreed's. Again the man escaped with his life and again the horses were the victims. By the 1920s, the 'thing in the lake' was internationally famous and a London music hall ditty immortalized it with the words, 'His mother was an earwig / His father was a whale / A little bit of head / And hardly any tail / And Ogopogo was his name.'

From Canada, the story of the serpents moved south to the Mormon settlement of Salt Lake City. In July 1860, the newspaper there, the *Desert News*, offered new testimony about the monster of Bear Lake. Up to that time, the Shoshone Indians of

Utah had been the principal witnesses of the 'beast of the storm spirits' and they were seldom taken seriously. The newspaper story, however, recounted the experience of a respected local resident who had been going along the east shore of the lake. 'About half-way', wrote a reporter, 'he saw something in the lake which . . . he thought to be a drowned person . . . he rode to the beach and the waves were running pretty high. . . . In a few minutes . . . some kind of an animal that he had never seen before . . . raised out of the water. He did not see the body, only the head and what he supposed to be part of the neck. It had ears or bunches on the side of its head nearly as big as a pint cup. The waves at times would dash over its head, when it would throw water from its mouth or nose. It did not drift landward but appeared stationary, with the exception of turning its head.' The next day, 28 July, the creature was seen by a man and three women but this time it was in motion and 'swam much faster than a horse could run on land'.

Reports of the Bear Lake serpent continued for several decades, but were temporarily eclipsed in 1941 with the advent of Slimey Slim, the serpent that inhabited Lake Payette in Idaho. During July and August that summer more than 30 people – most of them boaters on the lake's seven miles of water – saw the monster. For a while, they kept quiet about it. Then Thomas L. Rogers, City Auditor of Boise, Idaho, decided to speak up. He told a reporter, 'The serpent was about 50 feet long and going five miles an hour with a sort of undulating movement. . . . His head, which resembles that of a snub-nosed crocodile, was eight inches above the water. I'd say he was about 35 feet long on consideration.'

With the publication of this story, the lake was inundated with camera-wielding tourists hoping for a glimpse of Slimey Slim. After an article about him appeared in *Time* magazine, the monster seemed to turn shy and little more was heard or seen of him. With Slim's disappearance, attention returned to Ogopogo, which, having been seen by a captain in the Canadian Fishery Patrol, had been described as being like 'a telegraph pole with a sheep's head'. An American visitor to Canada was struck 'dumb with horror' on catching sight of the monster. On 2 July 1949, Ogopogo was seen by the Watson family of Montreal together with a Mr Kray. Newsmen reported of their experience, 'What the party saw was a long sinuous body, 30 feet in length, consisting of about five undulations, apparently separated from each other by about a two-foot space . . . The length of each of the undulations . . . would have been about five feet. There appeared to be, a forked tail, of which only one-half came above the water.'

Three summers later, Ogopogo presented himself to a woman visitor from Vancouver, swimming within a few hundred feet of her. 'I am a stranger here', she said shortly afterward. 'I did not even know such things existed. But I saw it so plainly. A head like a cow or horse that reared right out of the water. It was a wonderful sight. The coils glistened like two huge wheels . . . There were ragged edges (along its back) like a saw. It was so beautiful with the sun shining on it. It was all so clear, so extraordinary. It came up three times, then submerged and disappeared.'

Reports of the sea serpent mounted until 1964, when Ogopogo apparently went into retirement. However, one of the most graphic accounts of the creature was featured in the *Vernon Advertiser* of 20 July 1959. The writer, R. H. Millar, was the newspaper's owner-publisher and the sighting of 'this fabulous sea serpent' was clearly the highlight of his journalistic life. 'Returning from a cruise down Okanagan Lake, travelling at 10 miles an hour, I noticed, about 250 feet in our wake, what appeared to be the serpent', he recorded. 'On picking up the field glasses, my thought was verified. It was Ogopogo, and it was travelling a great deal faster than we were. I would judge around 15 to 17 miles an hour. The head was about nine inches above the water. The head is definitely snakelike with a blunt nose. . . Our excitement was short-lived. We watched for about three minutes, as Ogie did not appear to like the boat coming on him broadside; [he] very gracefully reduced the five humps which were so plainly visible, lowered his head, and gradually submerged. At no time was the tail visible. The family's version of the colour is very dark greenish . . . This sea serpent glides gracefully in a smooth motion . . . This would lead one to believe that in between the humps it possibly has some type of fin which it works . . . to control direction.'

The publicity given to Ogopogo brought eye-witness versions of serpents in other North American lakes, including Flathead

Lake in Montana; Lake Walker, Nevada; Lake Folsom, California and Lake Champlain, Vermont. From Monterey in southern California came reports of the so-called 'monster of San Clement' who was also known as the Old Man of Monterey. Further north, on Vancouver Island, a serpent nicknamed 'Caddy' made a rival bid for the headlines. The most sober and authentic sounding account of Caddy goes back to 1950, when he was seen by Judge James Thomas Brown, then one of Saskatchewan's leading members of the judiciary. He was spending a winter holiday on the island when he, his wife and daughter spotted Caddy some 150 yards from shore.

'His head [was] like a snake's [and] came out of the water four or five feet straight us', stated the judge. 'Six or seven feet from the head, one of his big coils showed clearly. The coil itself was six or seven feet long, fully a foot thick, perfectly round and dark in colour . . . It seemed to look at us for a moment and then dived. It must have been swimming very fast, for when it came up again it was about 300 yards away . . . I got three good looks at him. On one occasion he came up almost right in front of us. There was no question about the serpent – it was quite a sight. I'd think the creature was 35 to 40 feet long. It was like a monstrous snake. It certainly wasn't any of those sea animals we know, like a porpoise, sea-lion and so on. I've seen them and know what they look like.'

Monsters of the lakes and seas continued to make appearances in the present century. Passengers and crews of the *Dunbar Castle* in 1930 and the *Santa Clara* in 1947, sighted such monsters in the Atlantic. It must have been an added thrill for the passengers as they spotted the serpents swimming nearby. In the summer of 1966, while rowing across the Atlantic in their boat *English Rose III*, Captain John Ridgway and Sergeant Chay Blyth were nearly rammed by one of the marine monsters. It was shortly before midnight on 25 July and Blyth was asleep. Captain Ridgway, who was rowing, was suddenly 'shocked to full wakefulness' by a strange swishing noise to starboard.

'I looked out into the water', he recounts in their book *A Fighting Chance*, 'and suddenly saw the writhing, twisting shape of a great creature. It was outlined by the phosphorescence in the sea as if a string of neon lights were hanging from it. It was an enormous size, some 35 or more feet long, and it came toward me quite fast. I must have watched it for some 10 seconds. It headed straight at me and disappeared right beneath me. I stopped rowing. I was frozen with terror . . . I forced myself to turn my head to look over the port side. I saw nothing, but after a brief pause I heard a most tremendous splash. I thought this might be the head of the monster crashing into the sea after coming up for a brief look at us. I did not see the surfacing – just heard it. I am not an imaginative man, and I searched for a rational explanation for this incredible occurrence in the night as I picked up the oars and started rowing again . . . I reluctantly had to believe that there was only one thing it could have been – a sea serpent.'

As far back as 1820, the English naturalist Sir Joseph Banks, who had sailed around the world with Captain Cook, had given scientific credence and his 'full faith' to 'the existence of our Serpent of the Sea.' He was followed in this a few years later by the botanist and director of Kew Gardens, Sir William J. Hooker, who said of the sea serpent that, 'It can now no longer be considered in association with hydras and mermaids, for there has been nothing said with regard to it inconsistent with reason. It may at least be assumed as a sober fact in Natural History. . . .'

Since that time, much has been learned about life underneath the ocean and about the ocean bed itself. In 1865, a Frenchman descended to a depth of 245 feet. Within a hundred years that record was smashed by Dr Jacques Piccard and Lieutenant D. Walsh of the US Navy. On 23 January 1960, these two men took the bathyscaphe *Trieste* down to a depth of 35,802 feet at Mariana Trench in the Pacific. This is the world's deepest trench and, measured from top to bottom, is higher than Mount Everest. They described the bottom as a 'waste of snuff-coloured ooze'. Being able to go so far into the ocean's depths has increased the chances of an encounter with a deep-sea monster, that may date from prehistoric days.

Explorers such as Piccard and the world-famous Captain Jacques Cousteau have seen species of fish that were previously unknown to or unseen by man. Swimming through the deep troughs, trenches and ridges that make the ocean bed a kind of underwater mountain area are millions of hitherto unclassified creatures. 'I was astounded by what I saw in the shingle at Le

Mourillon', writes Cousteau of one of his expeditions, '. . rocks covered with green, brown, and silver forests of algae, and fishes unknown to me, swimming in crystal clear water. . . I was in a jungle never seen by those who floated on the opaque roof.' In 1969, the world's largest research submarine – the electrically powered *Ben Franklin* designed by Jacques Piccard – drifted to a depth of 600 feet below the Gulf Stream. Its six-man crew surfaced with numerous reports of sightings made through one or another of the craft's 29 viewing ports, including the observation of the tiny purple coloured hatchet fish.

From these and other expeditions, it is obvious that man is determined to explore and chart the world beneath the sea. Scientists state that before long some 98 per cent of the ocean floor will have been explored and that such exploration could mean the discovery of any monster or monsters which have been living in the ocean ridges. The US Navy is developing a Deep Submergence Search Vehicle, which will be prepared to encounter more dangerous inhabitants than the prawns, starfish and copepods already found to be living in the low-level oozes. Underwater television, sonar sensing equipment and electronic flash lamps and floodlights will compensate for the lack of light.

Men like Cousteau have pioneered in building underwater houses and villages – such as the US Navy's Sealab machines – in which aquanauts can live beneath the oceans for periods of up to 30 days. In Switzerland today, there is a special tourist submarine that takes visitors beneath the surface of a lake for a view of the wonders down below. From that it is just another large step to underwater cruise liners which are being planned to take tourists under the waters of the ocean. In recent years, giant sharks whose heads measure some four feet from eye to eye have been photographed on the sea bed. This suggests that even bigger fish – the traditional monsters – are waiting to be found. In their places of so-called eternal darkness, the oceans go down six miles or more – and it is there that the kraken survivors or descendants may lurk. In the late 1970s, a giant pink squid was captured off the coast of Peru. Its 35-foot-long tentacles and eyes of a foot in diameter, caused a sensation. Scientists suggest that the pink squid is nothing compared to the creatures that have yet to be caught. To back up their argument, they point to certain pieces of squid that have been taken from the stomach of whales. Projecting the size of the whole squid from the pieces, they say it would be more than 100 feet in length.

It is an often quoted fact that over two-thirds of the earth's surface is covered by water. Being creatures that generally inhabit only two dimensions, we often forget to multiply the area of the lakes, seas and oceans by their depths. The result is an almost unimaginably vast region for water-dwelling creatures to occupy. In this light, it seems hardly surprising that underwater explorers regularly discover new species of sea-creatures – it also seems highly likely that some yet to be detected and recorded will be, what we might call, monstrous.

CHAPTER 18

THE LOCH NESS MONSTER

Many people, including some scientists, take seriously the possibility that a monster lives in Scotland's Loch Ness. Known affectionately as 'Nessie', the huge creature has been reported by watchers from all over the globe. Was Saint Columba one of the first to see Nessie back in the year 565, as the story goes? Did any, or all, of the 3,000 or so people claiming to spot the Loch Ness monster between 1933 and 1974, actually see such a creature? Or were they deceived by logs, the light or small animals swimming in a group? The debate goes on. But Nessie remains tantalizingly elusive.

The African python, which is capable of swallowing a goat, has been seen swimming in the Indian Ocean, sometimes travelling from island to island in search of food. Attempts by large snakes such as this to board passing ships in search of a resting place, have naturally given rise to tales of sea monsters. Bits of floating timber or shipwreck may account for other monster stories. But it is possible that some accounts of sea monsters are genuine. They are disbelieved mainly because the creatures seen have not yet been identified by scientists, or are thought to be long extinct.

About 80 to 90 million years ago, giant reptiles roamed the earth and scoured the oceans in search of food. For survival they depended on brute strength, adaptation to changing environments and hiding from any danger they could not cope with. For many millions of years, the seas were dominated by the fish-eating *plesiosaurus* with its barrel-shaped body and serpentine neck and the sharklike *ichthyosaurus*, or fish lizard. Gradually these animals were displaced by the aggressive 40-foot-long sea lizard, the *mosasaurus*. We know that giant land animals began to disappear from the earth, but we do not know what happened to species of animals that were equally at home in the water. Could they have used their skills of adaptation and hiding to penetrate the depths of oceans and lakes and find a way to survive? It is not entirely impossible. After all, huge sea animals really did exist. They are not a figment of our imagination as some sceptics seem to imply. Let us explore the possibilities that may defy the sceptics.

Many of the Scottish lakes, or lochs as they are known in Scotland, are extremely deep. One of the deepest ones, Loch Ness, has become almost legendary because of its associations with repeated sightings of a monster. A dramatic sighting took place in July 1933. Mr and Mrs George Spicer were driving home to London along the south bank of Loch Ness, when they saw a strange creature emerging from the bracken. It appeared to have a long undulating neck little thicker than an elephant's trunk, a tiny head, a thick ponderous body and four feet or flippers. Carrying what seemed to be a young animal in its mouth, it lurched across the road, lumbered into the undergrowth, and disappeared with a splash into the lake. The whole startling incident lasted only a few seconds, but it left an indelible impression on the couple. Mr Spicer later described the creature to a newspaper reporter as a 'loathsome sight'. He said it looked like 'a huge snail with a long neck.'

Despite the scorn heaped on Mr Spicer by the leading scientists and zoologists of the day, there were many who believed his story of the 25 to 30-foot-long monster. Indeed, Spicer was not the only nor the first person to have seen – or claimed to have seen – the beast from the deep. Ever since the early 1880s, there had been regular sightings of 'Nessie', as the Scottish lake monster affectionately became known. Unaccountably, Nessie was popularly regarded as being female. At various times she was seen by a stonemason, a group of schoolchildren and a forester working for the Duke of Portland. Further appearances were noted in 1912, 1927 and 1930 and descriptions of her personality and activities appeared in newspapers from Glasgow to Atlanta. However, it was not until the summer of 1933 – the same summer that the Spicers reported their experience – that Nessie became an international pet. In that year, a new road was built on the north shore of the beast's lake home between Fort William and Inverness. According to local inhabitants, Nessie was roused from her sleep hundreds of feet beneath the surface of the lake by the noise of the drilling, the vibrations from the explosions and the boulders that every now and then crashed down the banks. Annoyed at having her slumber disturbed, she broke water, clambered ashore and proceeded to roam through the surrounding bracken feasting on any young animals she could get her teeth into.

It was around this period that an Automobile Association patrolman also spotted the sea serpent. He too described it as 'a thing with a number of humps above the water line. . . It had a small head and very long slender neck.' Shortly after this a third person – local resident Hugh Gray – actually took a photograph of Nessie and it was reproduced in newspapers and magazines throughout the world. This photograph, like many that were subsequently taken, was not well-defined. Doubters dismissed the object in the picture as a floating tree trunk or log. For those who accepted this theory, the explanation for the Loch Ness phenomenon was clear: some careless road construction workers had thrown a large piece of wood into the loch. Other disbelievers in the monster's existence preferred to think that someone was trying to pull the public's leg.

In order to seek the truth, journalists from all parts of the globe descended on the area – feature writers and photographers from New York, Rio de Janeiro and Tokyo among them. They were joined in their watch for the monster by a troop of Boy Scouts. When an old lady disappeared from her home nearby, some said that she had become Nessie's latest victim and declared that the beast was an agent of the devil. Others asserted that she wouldn't attack a human and was timid and unaggressive by nature. However, both camps agreed that the monster could change shape at will, that she could rise and sink in the loch vertically and that her body was iridescent, which made her colour vary with the light. To support their view that Nessie was alive, well and dwelling in the lake, her fans produced statistical and historical evidence.

First of all they pointed out that Loch Ness – the largest mass of fresh water in Great Britain – was 22¹/₂ miles long and 734 feet deep in the middle. This meant it could easily be the watery home of any huge monster, serpent, or 'thing from the deep'. They then delved back to the year 565 when a sighting of Niseag – to give Nessie her Gaelic name – was noted by the Irish Saint Columba. For two years previously, Saint Columba had been working to convert the heathen Picts, Scots and Northumbrians to Christianity from his new monastery on the island of Iona, off the west coast of Scotland. His mission took him throughout the north of the country. When he came to Loch Ness, he found some of the local people burying a neighbour who had been badly mauled by the lake monster while out swimming and who afterward died of his wounds. The corpse had been brought to land by boatmen armed with grappling hooks, but this did not deter one of the missionary's followers from swimming across the narrows at the head of the loch in order to bring over a small boat moored on the other side. Clad only in his loin cloth, the man was making good headway when he was suddenly confronted by a 'very odd looking beastie, something like a huge frog, only it was not a frog.'

After surfacing and gulping in some air, the monster proceeded to make an open-mouthed attack on the swimmer. She bore down on the defenceless man and would undoubtedly have swallowed him alive had it not been for the intervention of Columba. Used to dealing with the 'irreligious savages', he thought nothing of addressing a monster equally in need of God. With head raised and arms outstretched he commanded, 'Go thou no further nor touch the man. Go back at once!' Then, according to an eighth-century biography of the saint, 'on hearing this word . . . the monster was terrified and fled away again more quickly than if it had been dragged on by ropes, though it approached Lugne [the swimmer] as he swam so closely that between man and monster there was no more than the length of one punt pole.' This feat was hailed by the potential converts as a manifestation of holy power and the saint – who was noted everywhere for his 'cheerfulness and virtue' – recruited scores of new believers.

From then on, the Loch Ness monster became as much a part

of Scottish lore as the teachings of Columba himself. At the beginning of the nineteenth century, children were warned against playing on the banks of the lake because it was rumoured that Nessie was once again restless and about to pounce. Even such a level-headed, no nonsense person as the novelist Sir Walter Scott perpetuated monster stories. On 23 November 1827, he wrote in his journal, 'Clanronald told us . . . that a set of his kinsmen – believing that the fabulous "water-cow" inhabited a small lake near his house – resolved to drag the monster into day. With this in view, they bivouacked by the side of the lake in which they placed, by way of nightbait, two small anchors such as belong to boats, each baited with the carcass of a dog, slain for the purpose. They expected the water-cow would gorge on the bait and were prepared to drag her ashore the next morning when, to their confusion, the baits were found untouched.'

Perhaps the lake monster cleverly avoided the trap. In any case, she seems to show herself only when she wants to, often unexpectedly. A few decades later, in 1880, a diver named Duncan McDonald came across the beast while attempting to salvage a boat wrecked on Loch Ness. 'I was underwater about my work', he said, 'when all of a sudden the monster swam by me as cool and calm as you please. She paid no heed to me, but I got a glance at one of her eyes as she went by. It was small, grey and baleful. I would not have liked to have displeased or angered her in any way!' By then the major feeling about Nessie was that although ugly of face and bad-tempered when aroused, she did not go out of her way to trouble or frighten people.

Another nineteenth-century account of the Loch Ness monster gives an entirely different view of the lake inhabitant. It said, 'A noted demon once inhabited Loch Ness and was a source of terror to the neighbourhood. Like other kelpies [water-spirits in the shape of a horse] he was in the habit of browsing along the roadside, all bridled and saddled, as if waiting for someone to mount him. When any unwary traveller did so, the kelpie took to his heels, and presently plunged into deep water with his victim on his back.' The teller of this tale mustered up few believers, perhaps because of the great disparity between his description and the more generally accepted ones.

Coming up to the 1930s period when Nessie was at the peak

of her popularity, hotelier John Mackay sighted the lake serpent on 22 May 1933. He said that he saw the lake animal make the water 'froth and foam' as she reared her ludicrously small head in the air. Although Mackay beat the Spicers by two months in his encounter with Nessie, it was George Spicer's story that was most listened to and believed in nonprofessional quarters.

Before the year 1933 was out, Loch Ness and its celebrated inhabitant had become one of the principal tourist attractions of Great Britain. Holiday makers by the thousands got into their cars and headed north to park along the shores of the lake and gaze out over the water. Between 1933 and 1974, some 3,000 people attested to having spotted Nessie as she surfaced, dived, or swam tranquilly along. Claims were also made that the monster made a sound – a cry of 'anger and anguish' when nearly run down by a car. Waiting for Nessie rivalled watching flagpole squatters and marathon dancers, which were big vogues of the mid-30s. Hundreds of sun-dazzled or fog-smeared photographs – with an indistinct blur in them – were offered as Nessie at play. The eager Nessie-hunters were given short shrift by E. G. Boulenger, Director of the Aquarium in the London Zoo. He wrote in October 1933 that,

'The case of the Loch Ness monster is worthy of our consideration if only because it presents a striking example of mass hallucination . . . For countless centuries a wealth of weird and eerie legend has cantered around this great inland waterway . . . Any person with the slightest knowledge of human nature should therefore find no difficulty in understanding how an animal, once said to have been seen by a few persons, should shortly after have revealed itself to many more.'

Another reason for so many sightings was suggested by the more cynical, who pointed to the rewards being offered for the capture of Nessie alive. The money prizes included one for $500 from the New York Zoo, £20,000 from the Bertram Mills circus and a mammoth £1 million from the makers of Black and White Whisky. The whisky firm stipulated that the monster, if taken, had to be declared genuine by officials of the British Museum. Debate on Nessie even reached the British House of Commons, and, on 12 November 1933, a member of Parliament called for an official investigation to settle the 'monster matter' for once and all. The Government spokesman who replied stated that such an endeavour was 'more properly a matter for the private enterprise of scientists aided by the zeal of the press and photographers.'

It was on the same day of the government debate that Mr Hugh Gray took the famous picture mentioned before. It was published first of all in the Scottish *Daily Record* and then reproduced throughout the world. That was all the confirmation Nessie's admirers needed. According to Gray, he was walking along the loch shore near Foyers, camera in hand, when, from his vantage point on a 30-foot-high cliff, he saw the quiet water beneath him 'explode into commotion'. A huge form reared in front of him and a long neck stretched out. During the few seconds that the monster was on the surface, Mr Gray took five hasty shots of her. Due to the spray that was thrown up, the 'object of considerable dimensions' was not clearly discerned. Later, four of the five negatives proved to be blank. The good negative was shown to technical experts of the Kodak camera company, who testified that it had not been tampered with in any way and once again only the professional zoologists remained dissatisfied. Mr J. R. Norman of the British Museum stated that 'the possibilities levelled down to the object being a bottlenose whale, one of the larger species of shark, or just mere wreckage.' Professor Graham Kerr of Glasgow University considered the photograph to be 'unconvincing as a representation of a living creature.'

A local bailiff, Alexander Campbell, held centre stage in June 1934 when he told his Nessie tale. According to him, he had been out fishing in a row boat with two friends when a 'dark grey, rocklike hump' rose from the water, stayed there for a moment and then submerged without causing more than a few ripples. (Campbell was persistent if not consistent. In 1958, he said that Nessie had again appeared before him, but this time she created a 'small tidal wave' that sent him toppling into the lake.)

In 1934, too, came the first of the numerous books about the celebrated Loch Ness monster. It listed 47 sightings complete with drawings and photographs. In January, a newsreel film said to be of Nessie was shown in London to a private audience. The camera caught her about 100 yards away as she swam past. Of this event *The Times* on 4 January said, 'The most clearly evident movements are those of the tail or flukes. This appendage is naturally darker than the body. The photographers describe the general colour of the creature as grey, that of the tail as black. Indeterminate movements of the water beside the monster as it swims suggests the action of something in the nature of fins or paddles.' Unfortunately, this film disappeared before any study of its authenticity was made.

Three months later, Nessie reached the attention of royalty, when the Duke of York – who became King George VI – addressed the London Inverness Association, and told members, 'Its [Nessie's] fame has reached every part of the earth. It has entered the nurseries of this country. The other day, I was in the nursery, and my younger daughter, Margaret Rose [now Princess Margaret], aged three, was looking at a fairy-story picture book. She came across a picture of a dragon, and described it to her mother, "Oh, look Mummy, what a darling little Loch Ness monster !"'

The Abbot of the Monastery in Fort Augustus, at the foot of the loch, added his opinion to the controversy with his announcement that, 'the monster is a true amphibian, capable of living either on land or in water, with four rudimentary legs or paddles, an extraordinarily flexible neck, broad shoulders and a strong, broad, flat tail, capable of violently churning the waters around it.'

How can a creature of Nessie's size hide out so well in a lake, even one as large as Loch Ness? Part of the answer is that this lake is the receptacle of peat particles from 45 mountain streams and five rivers. Little is visible below a depth of six feet and underwater exploration by lung divers is stymied by the dense, impenetrable murk. For the most part, Nessie has been seen as a series of humps when she came up from the depths for air. This proved the case with the investigation backed by the insurance tycoon Sir Edward Mountain, who kept an intense five-week watch on the loch in the summer of 1934. Of the 17 monster sightings reported, 11 of them were of humps. This was also true when a Glendoe sawmill worker saw Nessie at 9 am that same summer. He reported a series of 12 humps 'each a foot out of water.' He said in an article in the Scotsman of 6 July 1934, 'The day was so clear that I could distinguish drops of water as they fell when the monster shook itself. It reached Glendoe Pier and stretched its neck out of the water where a stream enters the loch. It did not actually come ashore, but seemed to be hunting about the edge, and I cannot see how it could move as it did without using flippers or feet.'

The start of World War II in 1939 put an end to speculation about lake serpents for a time and it wasn't until the early 1950s that Nessie made news again. Then came the usual spate of sightings and photographs. An account of one of the sightings appeared in *Harper's Magazine* in 1957. The witness, Mr David Slorach, told how he had been driving to Inverness for a business appointment on the morning of 4 February 1954. On looking to his right to admire the view of Loch Ness, he saw something unusual in the water. Its shape reminded him of a 'comic orna- ment popular at one time – a china cat with a long neck. The thing ahead of me looked exactly like the neck and head part. One black floppy "ear" fell over where the eye might be, and four black streaks ran down the "neck" . . . The object [was] travelling through the water at great speed, throwing up a huge wave behind. I slowed to around 35 miles per hour, but the object raced ahead and was soon out of sight behind a clump of trees.'

Inspired by the renewed interest in Nessie, the BBC sent a television team equipped with a sonic depth finder to the loch in an attempt to prove or disprove the legend. Obligingly, a 'myste- rious object' came into range, was recorded some 12 feet below the surface and was followed to a depth of 60 feet, before it lost the depth finder. Experts of the British Museum and the Zoological Society of London were asked their opinions, but they scoffed at the idea of an unfamiliar beast. Instead they spoke of sturgeons, fin whales, sperm whales and that old standby, the tree trunk. One man was not convinced by the scoffing professionals, however. This was the author and jour- nalist, F. W. Holiday. As he put it, his 'consuming interest in the problem of the Loch Ness Orm or monster began in 1933 when I was 12 years old.' One morning 29 years later, in August 1962, he settled himself on a hillside near Foyers, and, with his binocu- lars, waited for the monster to make an appearance. He described what happened in his book *The Great Orm of Loch Ness*, 'A dozen or so yards into the loch, opposite the leat [a water channel] an object made a sudden appearance. It was black and glistening and rounded, and it projected about three feet above the surface. Instantly it plunged under again, violently, and produced an enormous upsurge of water. A huge circular wave raced toward me as if from a diving hippopotamus . . . Just below the surface, I then made out a shape. It was thick in the middle and tapered toward the extremities. It was a sort of blackish-grey in colour . . . When a chance puff of wind touched the surface, it disappeared in a maze of ripples; but when the water stilled, it was always there. Its size – judging from the width of the leat – was between 40 and 45 feet long.'

Holiday also recorded that a film taken at the loch in 1960, was later shown to specialists at the Ministry of Defence's Joint Air Reconnaissance Intelligence Centre. After carefully studying and analyzing the images which showed the customary humped object moving through the water – the experts decided that something, if not Nessie, existed in the deep. They came to the conclusion that the subject of the film 'probably is an animate object'. However, Nessie came the nearest to getting a certificate of authenticity in 1963, when on the evening of 2 February, Grampian and Border Television, an independent British station, transmitted a programme about her. The programme was presented as a panel discussion and one of the participants was David James, a Highland laird and a Member of Parliament at the time. He had a few months before kept a two-week, round-the-clock watch on the shores of the loch. Mr James, founder of The Loch Ness Phenomena Investigation Bureau, told viewers that his watch had been successful. He said,

'On 19 October [1962], in the middle of the afternoon, we had seven people at Temple Pier, and suddenly everyone was alerted by widespread activity among the salmon. After a few minutes the salmon started panicking – porpoising out in the middle of the loch – and immediately we were aware that there was an object following the salmon which was seen by practically everyone there for three or four minutes.' On hearing that – and after sifting through years of recorded evidence – the panel announced that, 'We find that there is some unidentified animate object in Loch Ness which, if it be mammal, reptile, fish, or mollusc of any known order, is of such a size as to be worthy of careful scientific examination and identification. If it is not of a known order, it represents a challenge which is only capable of being answered by controlled investigation on carefully scientific principles.'

Six years after this television programme, in August 1968, a team from the Department of Electronic Engineering of Birmingham University mounted a sonar system on one of the piers on the loch. The scan was directed at the southeast corner and, according to author Holiday, the scientists achieved 'dramatic success'. The cathode display screen was photographed every 10 seconds by a movie camera but for some days, nothing of interest was seen. Then, at 4:30 on the afternoon of 28 August, there occurred a remarkable 13-minute sequence. 'A large object rose rapidly from the floor of the loch at a range of 0.8 kilometre, its speed of ascent being about 100 feet a minute', Holiday wrote. 'It was rising obliquely away from the sonar source at a velocity of about 6.5 knots, and was soon 1 kilometre away. Its upward movement had now slowed to about 60 feet a minute. This object then changed direction to move toward the pier at about 9 knots, keeping constant depth. Finally, it plunged to the bottom at about 100 feet a minute before rising again at 0.6 kilometre range, when it apparently moved out of the sonar beam and was lost to record. Meanwhile, a second large object had been detected at 0.5 kilometre from the pier which finally dived at the astonishing velocity of 450 feet a minute. Both objects remained many feet below the surface.'

One of the leaders of the team, Dr H. Braithwaite, later wrote a magazine article on the sonar experiment in which he stated that, 'the high rate of ascent and descent makes it seem very unlikely [that the objects were shoals of fish], and fishery biologists we have consulted cannot suggest what fish they might be. It is a temptation to suppose they must be the fabulous Loch Ness monsters, now observed for the first time in their underwater activities.'

There the matter rested and there – admired or maligned, sought-after or ignored – lies Nessie. Among those who have tried to explain her away is Dr Roy Mackal of the Biochemistry

Department of the University of Chicago. On visiting Loch Ness in 1966, he suggested that the monster was most likely some kind of 'giant sea slug'. Four years later another American, Dr Robert Rines of the Massachusetts Academy of Applied Science, took a Klein side-scan sonar to the banks of the loch. In the deeper water he detected several large moving objects, and said afterward in a radio interview, 'We wouldn't have been here if we didn't have the suspicion that there is something very large in this loch. My own view now, after having personal interviews with, I think, highly reliable people, is that there is an amazing scientific discovery awaiting the world here in Loch Ness.'

However, Loch Ness is far from being the only fresh-water lake with a quota of monsters. Loch Morar, some 30 miles to the west and completely separated from Loch Ness, has its own Great Worm. At the beginning of 1970, a scientific team headed by the British biologist Dr Neill Bass began a survey of the site. The team's efforts were rewarded on the afternoon of 14 July when Dr Bass and two colleagues went for a walk on the north shore of the loch. It started to rain and, while his companions sheltered under some nearby trees, Bass gazed out over the rain-flecked water. Then, just as the weather improved and a breeze came up, the surface was broken by a 'black, smooth-looking hump-shaped object'. It was some 300 yards away, and by the time his fellow scientists had joined him, the creature had submerged vertically. Thirty seconds later, however, there was another disturbance in the water. It was followed by what the survey's final report called 'a spreading circular wake or ripple which radiated across the waves to about 50 yards diameter.' For a while Bass thought the object might have been a giant eel, but then realized that the movement was uncharacteristic of such a fish. In the end the report declared it to be 'an animate object of a species with which he [Bass] was not familiar in this type of habitat.'

The following month a zoology student, Alan Butterworth, also spotted the monster through binoculars while keeping watch on Loch Morar. The water was calm, and visibility was good. The watcher observed a 'dark-coloured hump', dome-shaped and similar to a rocky islet. The object was about 1½ miles away. Butterworth left to get his camera and when he returned with it the Great Worm had disappeared. So the most important goal – to obtain authentic film of the monster – was not fulfilled.

Not to be outdone by Scotland, countries from France to Australia to Argentina have claimed that their inland lakes contain their own mysterious and outsized monsters. Ireland, whose legends of lake monsters go back to ancient times, easily heads the list.

Another region with a long tradition of lake monster stories is Scandinavia. It was while visiting Scandinavia and Iceland in 1860 that the English clergyman and author Reverend Sabine Baring-Gould heard of the Skrimsl, a 'half-fabulous' monster said to inhabit some of the Icelandic lakes. Although he didn't see any of the beasts himself, he spoke to educated and respectable lawyers and farmers who told of one particular Skrimsl. It was almost 50 feet long and apparently looked much like the more famous Nessie. 'I should have been inclined to set the whole story down as a myth', wrote Baring-Gould, 'were it not for the fact that the accounts of all the witnesses tallied with remarkable minuteness, and the monster is said to have been seen not in one portion of the lake (the Lagarflot) only, but at different points.'

The clergyman also learned of a similar creature in Norway – a slimy, grey-brown animal that terrified the people living around Lake Suldal. Its head was said to be as big as a rowboat. The story was told of a man who, crossing the lake in a small craft, was set upon by the monster and seized by the arm. The attacker let go only when the victim recited the Lord's Prayer. But the man's arm was mangled and useless thereafter.

In Sweden itself, Lake Storsjö has long been associated with monsters and a turn-of-the-century zoologist, Dr Peter Olsson, spent several years analyzing and sifting through 22 reports containing numerous sightings. The Lake Storsjö monster, or leviathan, was said to be white-maned and reddish in colour, more like an enormous seahorse than anything else. It was first spotted in 1839 by some farmers and reports of it continued well into the twentieth century. The creature differed from its fellows by virtue of its speed, which was estimated at a rapid 45 mph. Olsson regarded it as 'the fastest and most fascinating of lake dwellers', a view which was shared by the *New York Times* in

1946. Under the heading, 'Normalcy?' an article in the paper stated that, after the insanity of World War II, things were getting back into their old familiar and comforting routine because monsters were being seen again.

Shortly afterward, a Stockholm newspaper reported that a group of three people had seen the Lake Storsjö monster when the lake's 'calm, shining surface was broken by a giant snakelike object with three prickly dark humps. It swam at a good parallel to the shore, on which thè waves caused by the object were breaking.' More sightings were reported in 1965. This inspired the local tourist board to use a colour picture of the monster in its brochure and to boast that the beast was Sweden's answer to the Loch Ness monster.

Ireland is Scotland's nearest rival in the 'creature in the lake' stakes, however. There are innumerable reports, accounts and twice-told tales about such beings. In recent times, the stories have proved as vivid and interesting as ever. For example, there is the one of three Dublin priests. On the evening of 18 May 1960, Fathers Daniel Murray, Matthew Burke and Richard Quigly went trout fishing off Lake Ree – called Lough Ree in Ireland – on the River Shannon. They were exceedingly pleased with the warmth, the calmness of the water and the way the fish were biting. All at once, the tranquillity was shattered by the approach of a large flat-headed animal they couldn't identify. It was about 100 yards from where they sat. When it swam up the lake toward them, the startled priests jumped to their feet. ' Do you see what I see?', one of them cried out, and the other two nodded their heads in amazement. 'It went down under the water', stated one of the priests later, 'and came up again in the form of a loop. The length from the end of the coil to the head was six feet. There were about 18 inches of head and neck over the water. The head and neck were narrow in comparison to the thickness of a good-sized salmon. It was getting its propulsion from underneath the water,and we did not see all of it.'

Lough Ree, where this sighting took place, is one of many small lakes in Ireland, whose west coast is dotted with them. Each lake, it seems, has its own particular inhabitant. It was this fact which in the 1960s inspired Captain Lionel Leslie, an explorer and cousin of Sir Winston Churchill, to mount his own investigation of the monsters. In October 1965, he went to Lough Fadda in Galway, and exploded a small charge of gelignite against a rock. He hoped that this would bring a *Peiste*, or lake monster, to the surface. Sure enough, a few seconds later a large black object appeared some 50 yards from the shore. Dismissing the possibility of it being a piece of wood or debris, Captain Leslie later told a reporter from *The Irish Independent*, 'I am satisfied beyond any doubt that there is a monster in Lough Fadda.' A subsequent netting operation failed to capture the creature. Captain Leslie tried again in 1969. In the company of author F. W. Holiday, he plumbed the depths of Loughs Shanakeever, Auna and Nahooin, but came up with nothing. Television cameras were on hand to record the hoped-for event, but all they were able to film was Captain Leslie, his disheartened band of monster hunters and the constant rain.

Such experiences – even though they make ready fodder for newspapers and TV – tend to lessen scientific belief in the existence of lake creatures. John Wilson, warden of the bird sanctuary operated by the Royal Society for the Protection of Birds in Lancashire, England, is another sceptic. Writing in the Society's journal in the summer of 1974, he says that Nessie, and presumably those like her, could well be a group of otters at play. 'Four or five otters swimming in line with heads, bodies, and tails continually appearing and disappearing combine to look like a prehistoric monster', he states.

For the steady line of Nessie-spotters since George Spicer hit the headlines in 1933, the Loch Ness monster is very much a reality. For the disbelievers, explanations like Dr Mackal's sea slug or Mr Wilson's otters are perfectly logical and satisfactory. What is the real truth? No one knows . . . yet!

CHAPTER 19

DID THE DINOSAURS SURVIVE?

There have been tales of encounters with monsters, espe-
cially dinosaurs, in just the last 40 years – and they have
been reported by respected scientists. Such reports have
often come out of Africa, continent with many still uncharted
and virtually impenetrable areas. Can we believe that a
prehistoric animal like the dinosaur could have survived?
We are told that they died out because they could not adapt.
Are we to change our ideas on the basis of unverified
reports, even though some originate with reputable people
of science? Perhaps the proof is yet to come.

Because most of the world has been mapped out, we tend to
forget that much still remains to be explored. Geographers may
take bearings from distant mountain ranges, follow a river along
its banks or photograph regions from the air. However, they will
not usually penetrate huge areas of swamp or forest, climb inaccessible peaks or plumb the depths of lakes. Even discounting the
vast wastes of Antarctica, nearly a tenth of the earth's land
surface remains almost totally unexplored. Who can guess what
lies in the unknown?

In the last 150 years, many new large animals have been
discovered. Some, like the king cheetah, have been found in areas
close to habitation and well-travelled by zoologists and big-game
hunters. They had, for some reason, escaped notice. Others, such
as the okapi, had taken refuge in remote and difficult country.
Because they were believed to be extinct, descriptions of them by
local residents had at first been discounted. It is always exciting to
find a new species – but to discover that an animal, thought to

have been long vanished, still survives is even more thrilling. It is as if, in a reassuring way, it had somehow managed to overcome both the forces of nature and our technological world.

If there is any likelihood of finding other living animals that we thought would never be seen again, it is in unexplored and diffi- cult territory where they may have fled from the competition of newer and more successful species. We know that huge dinosaurs and giant reptiles became extinct about 60 million years ago, probably due to climatic changes that affected their food supply. But what happened to their smaller relatives needing less food? Were they able to find a better area and slowly adapt to changes? Perhaps so. For, although most of the world has undergone violent geological changes in the last 60 million years, Central Africa, hot and swampy, has remained geologically stable. It is essentially the same land mass it was when the giants roamed the earth, much of it almost impenetrable and unexplored. If any creature has survived from the age of dinosaurs, it is here that it would be found. It is certainly here that tales of dinosaurs and other massive monsters abound and persist. Those who tell the tales are often respected scientists.

The well-known naturalist and writer Ivan T. Sanderson, for example, recounts a harrowing adventure on the Mainyu River in the heart of West Africa. The river ran 'straight as a man-made canal', and Sanderson's canoe glided along with the paddles hardly being used. Ahead of him, in the lead canoe, was his fellow explorer and animal collector, Gerald Russell. A hundred feet of water separated the two boats as they approached a deep shadowy gorge, hemmed in by sheer high walls and huge black caves. The two explorers had only recently ventured that far inland and their two African aides – Ben and Bassi – were equally strange to the area. The adventurers were near the middle of the winding mile-and-a-half-long gorge, when their smooth progress was abruptly disturbed. 'The most terrible noise I have heard short of an oncoming earthquake or the explosion of an aerial torpedo at close range, suddenly burst from one of the big caves on my right', declared Sanderson in his book *More "Things"*. 'Ben, who was sitting up front in our little canoe . . . immediately dropped backward into the canoe. Bassi in the lead canoe did like- wise, but Gerald tried to about-face in the strong swirling current, putting himself broadside to the current. I started to paddle like mad, but was swept close to the entrance of the cave from which the noise had come.'

A few moments later, when both canoes were opposite the mouth of the cave, an ear-splitting roar came out of it. In Sanderson's own words, 'Something enormous rose out of the water, turning it to sherry-coloured foam, and then, again roaring, plunged below. This "thing" was shiny black and was the *head* of something, shaped like a seal but flattened from above to below. It was about the size of a full-grown hippopotamus – this head, I mean. We exited from the gorge at a speed that would have done credit to the Harvard Eight, and it was not until we entered the pool (from which the Mainyu stretched north) that Bassi and Ben came to.'

Sanderson and Russell asked the two Africans about the monster, but, not being river people, they could provide no answer. Finally, however, they both yelled, 'M'koo-m'bembo', grabbed their paddles, and sped across the pool. The group soon rejoined the rest of its 20-strong party. The other Africans were all local men and showed great concern over their leaders' frightening experience. The river people among them confirmed Bassi and Ben's opinion that the dreadful creature was one of the M'koo. Said Sanderson, 'These animals lived there all the time, they told us, and that is why there were no crocodiles or hippos in the Mainyu. (There were hundreds of both in the pool, the other river, and the Cross River.) But, they went on, M'koo does not eat flesh, but only the big liana fruits and the juicy herbage by the river.'

Ivan Sanderson's fantastic encounter with a monster occurred in 1932 and he never did find out the exact nature of the gigantic thing that had so dramatically displayed itself. It is difficult to dismiss his experience as the product of an overstimulated imagination, for Sanderson's story has been accepted by a number of experts in the monster field. Among them is the reputable zoologist and author Dr Bernard Heuvelmans, who refers to the incident in his wide-ranging and definitive book *On the Track of Unknown Animals*. In this book, Heuvelmans stresses that the sighting of the M'koo and other monster evidence came from 'a first-rate naturalist whose works are authorities all over the world.' Indeed, as a well-travelled and well-informed expert in such matters, Sanderson knew that there had been a 'very curious going-on in Africa for more than a century'. What he had seen and heard led him to ask – could there still be dinosaurs living in some remoter corners of the African continent and in other isolated parts of the earth?

To Sanderson, this idea was not too startling – even though dinosaurs are one of a group of huge reptiles that lived during Mesozoic times some 70 to 220 million years ago. After all, he and others had seen what could have been a monster left over from prehistoric times and he felt that Africa was still a relatively unexplored continent. 'Its vast jungle and swamplands have been by-passed in all the modern hubbub', he stated in *More "Things"* in 1969, 'and thousands of locations that were fairly well known 50 years ago have now been virtually lost. The mere size of the place is quite beyond comprehension to those who have not visited it, so it is quite useless to suggest that there is not room in it for all manner of things as yet unknown.' For proof of this, Sanderson and his fellow explorers did not need to go back further than 1913, when the German government sent a special expedition to its colony in the mountainous Cameroons. The expedition was led by Captain Freiherr von Stein and its purpose was to make a general survey, map the area and pinpoint the whereabouts of its vegetable and mineral fields.

Because of the outbreak of World War I, the report was never published but the contents of the manuscript were later made available to those in search of sensational monster material. Captain von Stein, a disciplined and hard-headed soldier, wrote in the report that the people who lived by the rivers told him of a 'very mysterious thing' that dwelt in the water. In his book *Exotic Zoology*, scientist Willy Ley quotes from the von Stein report. He points out that the captain recorded the experiences of respected guides who, without knowing each other, gave the same details and 'characteristic features' about the water beast.

The creature – which at the time of the expedition was spotted in a section of the Sanga River previously said to be non-navigable – was described as of a 'brownish-grey colour with a smooth skin, its size approximately that of an elephant . . . It is said to have a long and very flexible neck and only one tooth, but a very long one; some say it is a horn. A few spoke about a long muscular tail like that of an alligator. Canoes coming near it are said to be doomed; the animal is said to attack the vessels at once and to kill the crews, but without eating the bodies. The creature is said to live in the caves that have been washed out by the river ... It is said to climb the shore even at daytime in search of food; its diet is said to be entirely vegetable.'

The fact that the monster was a vegetarian convinced von Stein that it was more likely to be a factual beast than a mythical one. The outsized animals of mythology showed no such reluctance to tear human flesh, drink blood and crunch bones. His belief was strengthened when he was shown the creature's favourite food, 'a kind of liana with large white blossoms, with a milky sap and apple-like fruits'. He was also taken to a spot by another river, where the monster had apparently trampled a fresh path in order to reach the food it liked best. Twenty-five years later, in 1938, the captain's findings were confirmed by another German, Dr Leo von Boxberger. He was a magistrate who had spent many years working in the Cameroons. 'The belief in a gigantic water-animal', he wrote, 'described as a reptile with a long thin neck, exists among the natives throughout the Southern Cameroons wherever they form part of the Congo basin, and also to the west of this area ... wherever the great rivers are broad and deep and are flanked by virgin forest.'

However, neither man was the first European to have experiences of monsters on the so-called Dark Continent. This distinction probably lies with two others of their countrymen, Carl Hagenbeck and Hans Schomburgk. Their adventure took place in 1909.

Hagenbeck and Schomburgk were two renowned wild animal dealers. For years they had heard identical stories from locals and travellers about the existence of what Hagenbeck in his book *Beasts and Man* called 'an immense and wholly unknown animal.' Known as the King of the Zoos because of his work in supplying wild animals, Hagenbeck was fascinated by the creature reported to be half-dragon and half-elephant. It was said to have a single horn like the rhinoceros but as Dr Heuvelmans later points out, 'an animal may look like a rhinoceros without being one.' Hagenbeck believed the beast to be a dinosaur, one that was 'seemingly akin to the brontosaur'. At 'great expense' he later sent out an expedition to find the beast. Unfortunately, the party was forced to return without having discovered any evidence for or against the monster's presence.

It was not until ten years later – and after Captain von Stein had written his report – that the monsters of central Africa again made news. In the London *Times* of 17 November 1919, a story stated that an 'extraordinary monster' had been encountered in, what was then, the Belgian Congo. In October, it had charged a Monsieur Lepage, who was in charge of railway construction in the area. Lepage fired on the beast and then fled with the creature in full pursuit. Only when the animal tired and gave up the chase was he able to examine it through his binoculars. The animal, he told *The Times* correspondent in Port Elizabeth, was some '24 feet in length with a long pointed snout adorned with tusks like horns and a short horn above the nostrils. The front feet were like those of a horse, and the hind hoofs were cloven. There was a scaly lump on the monster's shoulder.'

Soon afterward the animal – by then said to be a dinosaur – rampaged through a nearby village, killing some of the inhabitants. Despite this, the Belgian government prohibited anyone from hurting or molesting the beast. Officials told a hunt that was organized that the animal was 'probably a relic of antiquity', and therefore must not be harmed. 'There is', added *The Times*, 'a wild trackless region in the neighbourhood which contains many swamps and marshes, where, says the head of the [local] museum, it is possible that a few primeval monsters may survive.'

The Times' account made a particular impression on Captain Leicester Stevens, who was even more excited when on 4 December, he read a report from Africa that the monster had been seen in another part of the Congo. This time the beast, said to be a brontosaur, had been trailed by a Belgian big game hunter. He had followed the 'strange spoor' for some 12 miles and had then come across an animal 'certainly of the rhinoceros order with large scales reaching far down its body.' He fired at the monster, which then threw its head up and lumbered off into a swamp. 'The American Smithsonian expedition', the report ended, 'was in search of the monster . . . when it met with a serious railway accident in which several persons were killed.'

After the fatal accident, the Smithsonian Institution offered a
$3 million reward for the monster, dead or alive. On learning this,
Captain Stevens decided that he would hunt the dinosaur down.
With his mongrel dog Laddie, which was part wolf, he set out by
train from London's Waterloo Station on the first stage of his
journey to central Africa. Laddie, a 'barrage dog' which had been
used as a front line message carrier in France in 1914-18, was
prepared, according to Stevens, to take on anything from a tank to
a dinosaur. 'I am leaving for Cape Town on Christmas Eve', the
captain told a newspaper reporter on the train. 'From Cape Town
I shall go 1,700 miles north to Kafue, where my expedition will
be organized.'

Armed with a Mannlicher rifle, Captain Stevens claimed that
he knew the location of a 'vital spot' on the monster, which was
especially vulnerable to bullets. 'Where that spot is', he said
mysteriously, 'is one of my secrets.' His venture fired the imagination of both the general public and expert animal hunters. One
of the latter, the American Walter Winans, supplied the London
Daily Mail with a picture he claimed to have taken of a brontosaur in the central African swamps. This was followed by a
letter to the paper from another experienced big game hunter, R.
G. Burton, in which he advised Captain Stevens to take a 'more
effective battery of guns' with him.

'If the animal is anything like the monster conjured up by Mr
Walter Winans', he wrote, 'the hunter had better take a tank
instead of his "barrage dog". To receive the charge of 80 feet of
primeval monster, armour-plated and exuding poison from fangs
and skin . . . Mannlicher and repeating Winchester rifles are quite
inadequate. I would be sorry to face even a charging tiger with
such weapons, while the shotgun, unless it is for the purpose of
scattering salt on the tail of the creature, will prove worse than
useless. He should take nothing less than a field gun – say an 18
pounder. Armed with a tank, with heavy artillery and with a
supply of poison gas, the modern St George might make "merry
music" against this "dragon of the prime" and have a fair chance
of taking the £1 million offered by the Smithsonian Institution
when he comes galumphing back with the skin.'

It would appear that Burton's warning was a sound one. A
single report came out that Captain Stevens had encountered his

monster 'crashing through the reeds of a swamp, and that it was the brontosaur – a, huge marsh animal, ten times as big as the biggest elephant.' Nothing more was publicly heard of the hunter. The Smithsonian's reward went unclaimed and in February 1920, a member of the Institution's expedition dismissed the monster stories as a practical joke. Whether or not this was true, there was no denying the fact that, from then on, the search for and sighting of dinosaurs was to be a regular feature of the central African scene.

One of the most dramatic dinosaur sightings took place 12 years later in February 1932. J. C. Johanson, a Swedish rubber plantation overseer, was out on a shooting trip in the Kasai valley when he and his African servant suddenly saw an incredible sight – a 16-yard-long monster with the head and tail of a lizard. The beast disappeared almost at once, but reappeared again in a large swamp that the two men had to cross to get home. Just 25 yards separated the hunters and the creature. The African fled. Johanson fainted but just before he passed out, he managed to put his camera to use. The experience left the overseer ill for eight days.

The photographs taken by Johanson were later printed in Germany in the *Cologne Gazette* and this was reported in the *Rhodesia Herald*. 'The photos', the newspaper story went, '. . . were anything but clear, yet they revealed a discovery of great importance. Johanson stumbled on a unique specimen of a dinosaur family that must have lived milleniums ago.' It was similar to an outsized lizard seen a few months later in the summer of 1932, by a young South African hunter. Even so, accusations of fake were once again made. Support for the possibility of such sightings came from the Swiss zoologist Dr A. Monard who, also in 1932, accompanied a dinosaur expedition to Angola.

'The existence of a large saurian descended from the reptiles of the Mesozoic era [the third major geological era] is by no means theoretically impossible,' he wrote in a Swiss scientific journal. 'Though every continent has been crossed and recrossed, most travellers follow much the same track, and there are still holes in the net to be explored. There have been several reports that some kind of "brontosaurus" survives, and several expeditions have even gone to look for it; the fact that they have failed may merely prove that this prehistoric beast is very rare or that it lives in country as inaccessible as the great swamps are. There are some reasons, based on the history of the continents and of the great reptiles, for thinking that they could survive . . . While it is not scientific to be too credulous, it is no better to be incredulous; and there is no reason for saying that the survival of some types of Mesozoic saurians is impossible.'

Dr Monard's optimism, however, was not borne out when he and his companions reached Angola later that year. They were hoping to find a *lipata*, an enormous and 'very voracious' amphibian. It was much larger and fiercer than a crocodile and was only seen at the end of the rainy season from July to September. In spite of paddling for days through the marshes in the sun and rain to follow up every lead, the animal was not found.

Seven years afterward, Mrs Ilse von Nolde, who had lived in eastern Angola for 10 years, had better luck. She actually heard the 'water-lion' roaring at night and knew that the local hippopotami fled the district whenever they heard the fearsome sounds. 'All the people dwelling along the tributaries of the Kuango know about the "water-lion"', she wrote in an article published in a German colonial gazette. 'They had heard it roar during the night, but none of them has ever seen one – at least none of those I talked to – and they say it will come ashore during the night only, and hide in the water during the day.'

After this partial anticlimax in 1939, the next decade was mostly taken up with stories and articles about World War II and its aftermath. It wasn't until the publication in London in 1950 of explorer Charles Miller's book, *Cannibal Caravan* that the monsters of the unknown made news again. The material for the book had been gathered when Miller and his society bride had spent their honeymoon among the head-hunting cannibals of New Guinea. There they heard of a 40-foot-long lizard known among local people as *row*, because of the noise it made. The beast lived on the top of a high grassy plateau and the couple decided to make their way up and take pictures of the animal. They reached the summit and looked over the edge of a cliff, where they saw a large triangular-shaped marsh. As they gazed, the reeds below them began to stir and a long yellowy-brown neck swayed up toward the sky. Miller froze on the spot and his wife, who came over to join him, fell to the grass and lay there too scared to lift her head. Then Miller pointed his camera at the creature.

'As if in obedience to my wishes', he wrote, 'the colossal remnant of the age of dinosaurs stalked across the swamp. Once its tail lashed out of the grass so far behind its head I thought it must be another beast. For one brief second I saw the horny point. I heard it hiss – roooow, roooow, roooow . . . It was a full quarter mile away, it couldn't possibly hear the camera, but I found myself cowering back as if that snapping turtle-shaped beak would lash out and nab me. I gasped with relief when the creature settled back . . . Twice more the row reared up, giving me a good view of the bony flange around its head and the projecting plates along its backbone. Then with a click my camera ran out just as the row slithered behind a growth of dwarf eucalyptus.'

Miller's book had numerous illustrations but there was none of the row that had so frightened him and his wife. He offered his dinosaur film to several producers, but it was never commercially shown. However, as Dr Heuvelmans stresses in his retelling of Miller's adventure, 'it would be rash to assert that such an animal is impossible – zoology and palaeontology [the study of fossils] are full of surprises . . .'

Despite this further disappointment, professional and amateur monster lovers refuse to believe that such creatures do not exist except in controversial books. Ivan Sanderson, who had first-hand experience of a monster in Africa, asserts that much of our present-day world is unknown and he attacks the popular notion that there is little left to be fully explored and mapped. 'There was never a greater misconception', he writes. 'The percentage of the land surface of the earth that is actually inhabited – that is to say, lived upon, enclosed, farmed or regularly traversed – is quite limited. Even if the territory that is penetrated only for hunting or the gathering of food crops be added, vast areas still remain completely unused. There are such areas in every continent, areas that for years are never even entered by man. Nor are these only the hot deserts of the torrid regions or the cold deserts of the poles . . . There might easily be creatures as big as elephants living in some profusion in, say, the back of the Guyanas, which are now only a few hours' flight in a commercial plane from Miami. Such animals might have been well-known to several thousand people for hundreds of years but their presence would still be unsuspected by us, for few of the Amerindians – who from aerial surveys are known to exist in that area – have ever come out, or even been seen by anyone from outside.'

That creatures we call monsters exist somewhere today, is not totally impossible. This was demonstrated in 1938 with the discovery off the coast of South Africa of a live *coelacanth* – a huge fish dating from millions of years ago – and naturally assumed to be extinct long since. The fossils of other *coelacanths* showed the species to be some 70 million years old. Scientists were further amazed and delighted when, in 1952, a second live *coelacanth* was caught off Madagascar. Since then, close to 100 more of these hardy survivors from the past have been discovered and studied, although most live for only a few hours in captivity. Their home is in the Indian Ocean, near the Comoro Islands. These discoveries now make it logical to ask, 'If prehistoric coelacanths are still living today, why not dinosaurs?'

It is possible that dinosaurs exist in spite of all the doubters and, like the coelacanth, are a link in the long chain of living beings. But, unlike the fish, they are savage, huge, lumbering monstrosities not so easily captured.

CHAPTER 20

THE ABOMINABLE SNOWMAN

Giant footprints in the snow of Mount Everest were discovered by world-famous British mountaineers in 1951. Was that proof that the Yeti, popularly known as the Abominable Snowman, exists? Further investigators threw doubts on the report and the controversy goes on. Is there a giant hairy creature, looking somewhat like an earlier form of human, living in the icy confines of the Himalaya mountains? One of the first such reports came in the early part of the nineteenth century and others have followed consistently up to the present. Does the Yeti offer us a riddle that we don't really want to solve?

It was around teatime on a cold November afternoon in 1951. British mountaineers Eric Shipton and Michael Ward, returning from the Everest Reconnaissance Expedition, were making their way over the Menlung Glacier, some 20,000 feet above sea level between Tibet and Nepal. Suddenly, they came across a giant footprint in the snow. It measured 13 by 18 inches! As they saw it, the two men stopped and stared at each other. They knew the imprint had been recently made because it had not had time to melt. This meant that it was closer to actual size than a melted print which appears larger. Therefore its size was all the more amazing. Had the footmark been made by a giant human or a huge snow monster? As they speculated and before they could recover from their initial surprise, they noticed a set of fresh looking tracks in the deep snow lining the lip of the glacier. Almost too excited to speak, they followed the trail for nearly a mile before the snow became thinner and the tracks disappeared.

The two seasoned mountain climbers realized that they could be on the verge of a major anthropological discovery and quickly set about taking photographs of their find.

Using Ward's ice axe and snowboots to show scale, Shipton took two photographs in which the footprints were well defined and perfectly in focus. These photographs were to cause controversy, doubt and sometimes downright disbelief, in every country in which they were later reproduced. Despite those who called the photographs everything short of fake, there was no disputing the fact that the prints had not been made by monkeys, bears, leopards or ordinary human beings. In that case then, what kind of creature had preceded the explorers across that remote section of the Himalayas? Whatever it was, it had five distinct toes with the inner two toes larger than the rest, the smaller toes pressed together and the heel flat and exceptionally broad. If Eric Shipton was in any doubt at the time he photographed the footmarks in 1951, he had certainly made his mind up 10 years later. In a foreword to Odette Tchernine's book *The Snowman and Company* he wrote,

'Before 1951, though like other travellers I had seen several sets of inexplicable tracks in the snows of the Himalayas and Karakoram and had listened to innumerable stories of the "Yeti" told by my Sherpa friends, I was inclined to dismiss the creature as fantasy. But the tracks which Michael Ward . . . and I found in the Menlung Basin after the Everest Reconnaissance Expedition, were so fresh and showed so clearly the outline and contours of the naked feet that I could no longer remain a sceptic. There could be no doubt whatever that a large creature had passed that way a very short time before, and that whatever it was it was not a human being, not a bear, not any species of monkey known to exist in Asia.'

The newspapers of the day – and indeed those since then – seized upon the story as eagerly as they had earlier publicized the newsworthy Loch Ness Monster. Playing down the Tibetan name 'Yeti' – meaning 'magical creature' – they popularized the name 'Abominable Snowman' – which got across the idea of horror associated with the being that was said to exist in the valleys, gaps and glaciers of the Himalayas. The London Zoological Society and the Natural History department of the British Museum, examined the photographs and came to the conclusion that the prints had been caused by a langur monkey or a red bear. The creature's stride alone – a length of some 2¹/₂ feet – made nonsense of the monkey theory. But these austere authorities remained unconvinced and it was left to the highly regarded British medical journal *The Lancet*, to give credence to Shipton's Abominable Snowman claims. In an article published in June 1960, and headed 'Giants with Cold Feet', it stated,

'Even in the twentieth century there are many thinly populated and almost unexplored regions of the world, and in several of these there have arisen rumours of the existence of large animals still awaiting scientific discovery and classification. The publicity accorded to the 'Abominable Snowman' of the Himalayas is no doubt a tribute to the aura of mystery and endeavour surrounding the highest mountain on earth. It may also be due in part to the beguiling name bestowed upon the creature, almost certainly as a result of a losing battle with the local dialect.'

Although the Yeti was big news in the 1950s and early 1960s, it was already old news, with sightings dating back to 1832. According to the well-known anatomist and anthropologist Dr John Napier, the source of the Abominable Snowman stories was the 'military and Civil Service pioneers in the last century, and the high mountaineers in this.' Because of them, Napier says, 'the eastern Himalayas are better known than most of the other mountain ranges where most monster myths are prevalent.'

It was in 1832 that B. H. Hodgson, the British Resident in Nepal, published an article about a strange mountain creature in a scientific journal. He wrote that some Nepalese porters of his had 'fled in terror' from an erect, tail-less being with shaggy black hair that had ambled up to them. They called the creature a *rakshas*, the Sanskrit word for 'demon', and informed him that references to such wild men went back to the fourth century BC. In those early times, *rakshas* appeared in the Indian national epic, *Rama and Sita*. Hodgson derided his servants' talk of a demon creature and explained the intruder away as a stray orang-utan. Fifty-seven years later however, in 1889, Major L. A. Waddell of the Indian Army Medical Corps became the first European to see footprints presumably made by one of the mountain monsters. He discovered the tracks 17,000 feet up in northeast Sikkim but was reluctant to ascribe them to the, then unnamed, Snowman. In his book *Among the Himalayas*, he stated,

'The belief in these creatures is universal among Tibetans. None, however, of the Tibetans I have interrogated on the subject could ever give me an authentic case. On the most superficial investigation it always resolved into something that somebody had heard tell of.' In his conclusion, Waddell insisted that the 'so-called hairy wild men' were simply vicious, meat-eating, yellow snow bears that frequently preyed upon yaks.

The next recorded sighting of tracks by a European came in 1914 when J. R. P. Gent, a British forestry officer stationed in Sikkim, wrote of discovering footprints of what must have been a huge and amazing creature. 'The peculiar feature', he said, 'is that its tracks are about 18–24 inches long, and the toes point in the opposite direction to that in which the animal is moving . . . I take it that he walks on his knees and shins instead of on the sole of his foot.'

It was only a matter of time before the inevitable encounter between a European and a mysterious Yeti. It came in 1921, when Lieutenant-Colonel C. K. Howard-Bury led the first Everest Reconnaissance Expedition. He and his team were clambering over a ridge some 21,000 feet up. Suddenly one of his Sherpa guides gripped his arm excitedly and pointed to a dark upright figure moving rapidly through the snow. The Sherpas immediately jumped to the conclusion that this must be 'the wild man of the snows'. On his return to his own country, Howard-Bury read up on the ways and customs of the Himalaya wild man. He learned that naughty little Tibetan children are threatened into good behaviour by warnings about him. 'To escape from him they must run down the hill, as then his long hair falls over his eyes and he is unable to see them', Howard-Bury said.

There is also a female of the species and the Sherpas say that Yeti women are hampered by the size of their breasts. One investigator of the creatures was told by a Sherpa, 'We followed the track of two Yeti, they were both females – their breasts were so large they have to throw them over their shoulders before they bend down.'

In the spring of 1925, a sighting was made by the British photographer N. A. Tombazi. He observed one of the elusive beings 15,000 feet up the Zemu Glacier and, as a Fellow of the Royal Geographical Society, his testimony was not to be laughed aside. Again, it was a Sherpa who drew attention to the Snowman's presence but to begin with, the bright glare of the snow prevented the photographer from seeing the newcomer. Then, as his eyes grew accustomed to the dazzle, he spotted the creature some 200 or 300 yards away in a valley to the east of the camp. In his book *Big Foot*, John Napier quotes the photographer as follows,

'Unquestionably the figure in outline was exactly like a human being, walking upright and stopping occasionally to uproot or pull at some dwarf rhododendron bushes. It showed up dark against the snow and, as far as I could make out, wore no clothes. Within the next minute or so it had moved into some thick scrub and was lost to view. Such a fleeting glimpse, unfortunately, did not allow me to set the telephoto-camera, or even to fix the object carefully with the binoculars; but a couple of hours later, during the descent, I purposely made a detour so as to pass the place where the 'man' or 'beast' had been seen. I examined the foot-prints which were clearly visible on the surface of the snow. They were similar in shape to those of a man . . . The prints were undoubtedly biped, the order of the spoor having no characteristics whatever of any imaginable quadruped. From enquiries I made a few days later at Yokson, on my return journey, I gathered that no man had gone in [that] direction since the beginning of the year.'

By now belief in the Yeti was growing from country to country and reports of the creature's habits and behaviour were coming from men of prominence and responsibility. The English mountaineer Maurice Wilson, who died in 1934 while attempting to climb Everest alone, was convinced that the Snowmen existed and that they were mystical hermits rather than wild beasts. This theory was shared by the German missionary-doctor, Father Franz Eichinger. He told the London *News Chronicle* that the Yeti were solitary monks who had withdrawn from the pressures of civilization and who lived in cold but contemplative peace in their mountain caves. In 1938, the Yeti emerged as creatures of kindness and sympathy according to the story of Captain d'Auvergne, the curator of the Victoria Memorial near Chowringhee in Calcutta. Injured while travelling on his own in the Himalayas, and threatened with snowblindness and exposure, he was saved from death by a 9-foot-tall Yeti. The giant picked him up, carried him several miles to a cave and fed and nursed him until he was able to make his way back home. Captain d'Auvergne concluded that his saviour was a survivor from some prehistoric human tribe or sect. Like Father Eichinger, he believed that the Snowman and his fellows belonged to an ancient people called the A-o-re, who had fled to the mountains to avoid persecution and who then developed into beastlike giants.

All this was sensational enough but an even more vivid, explicit and dramatic encounter was to take place. It occurred in February 1942 but was not made public until the following decade, when Slavomir Rawicz's best-selling book, *The Long Walk* appeared. In it Rawicz, a Pole, tells how he and six friends escaped from a Siberian prisoner of war camp and crossed the Himalayas to freedom in India. The book came under widespread attack as being more fiction than fact, many critics citing the physical unlikelihood of weakened escapees being able to make such a journey – which included a 12-day hike across the Gobi desert with little food and no water. There was also extreme scepticism about Rawicz's story of meeting two 8-foot-tall creatures somewhere between Bhutan and Sikkim. For two hours, according to the author, he and his companions watched the outsize animals or men from a distance of 100 yards. He gauged the monster's height by using his military training for artillery observations.

In 1953, the Yeti again made international news when New Zealander Edmund Hillary and Sherpa Tenzing Norgay spotted giant prints during their conquest of Mount Everest. In some quarters, their feat was practically eclipsed by their discovery of the Yeti footmarks. Such prints were a familiar sight to Tenzing, who had grown up in a village in the Khumbu Glacier and who told Hillary that his father – 'who was no teller of lies' – had once almost been killed by one of the Snowmen. The older Tenzing had come across the creature while it was eating and had been chased by it down a steep slope. He escaped by running downhill 'for his life'.

It was such anecdotes that led the London *Daily Mail* to organize its own Abominable Snowman Expedition in 1954. Two years before, Yeti tracks had also been seen by Dr Eduard Wyse-Dunant, the leader of a Swiss Everest Expedition. Because he found 'no trace of meals, nor yet of excrement', Dr Wyse-Dunant believed that the 'animal is only passing through and does not frequent these heights.' His view was confirmed by the experience of the *Daily Mail* team, which came up with nothing more positive than a few hairs from a 300-year-old alleged Yeti scalp kept in a Buddhist temple. This scalp, conical in shape, was about 8 inches high and had a base circumference of 26 inches. It was photographed by *Mail* journalist Ralph Izzard, who later had the hairs analyzed. He was told they belonged to 'no known animal'.

In his book about the expedition, *The Abominable Snowman Adventure*, Izzard asserted that their effort, though a stunt to boost circulation, had not been worthless. 'I am personally convinced', he wrote, 'that sooner or later the Yeti will be found, and that it will be sooner rather than later because of our efforts. One must, however, add a word of warning to future expeditions. I think it is the opinion of all of us when we review our own experiences that the Yeti is more likely to be met in a chance encounter round say, a rock, than by an organized search . . . In such country there is no question of stalking an animal in the accepted sense of the term. For miles at a time there may be only one safe path used by men and animals alike, for to deviate from it would mean taking unacceptable risks from crevasses, avalanches and other hazards. Often such a path . . . may cross the dead centre of a snowfield where a party is as conspicuous as a line of black beetles on a white tablecloth and where, from the surrounding cliffs, a lurking animal can hold one under observation for hours at a time with freedom of choice to lie low or steal away across the next horizon . . . That we failed to see a Yeti signified nothing, either for or against its existence . . . There are, I know, many who rejoice that we failed in our main objective – that a last great mystery remains in this much picked-over world to challenge adventurous spirits.'

Just as Izzard had observed, the 'great mystery' inspired three American safaris in 1957, 1958 and 1959. They were financed and headed by the tycoons Tom Slick and F. Kirk Johnson. The expeditions carried hypodermic rifles and bullets, which the Yeti wisely stayed miles away from and the nearest the well-equipped parties came to success, was when the two millionaires took some excellent plaster casts of Yeti prints. Other well-substantiated reports of sightings continued to appear in books and interviews. Mountaineer John Hunt, in his account of the 1953 scaling of Everest, told about a story he heard from the dignified Abbot of Thyangboche Monastery. It seems that a few winters previously, the religious leader had seen a Yeti. Hunt reports the Abbot's story as follows,

'This beast, loping along sometimes on his hind legs and sometimes on all fours, stood about five feet high and was covered with grey hair . . . The Yeti had stopped to scratch . . . had picked up snow, played with it, and made a few grunts . . . instructions were given to drive off the unwelcome visitor. Conch shells were blown, and the long traditional horns sounded. The Yeti had ambled away into the bush.'

During the 1950s, several Soviet scientists took the Yeti seriously. Dr A. G. Pronin, a hydrologist at Leningrad University, for instance, sighted one of the creatures in 1958 in the Pamir Mountains in Central Asia and was duly impressed. Odette Tchernine gives an account of Pronin's encounter in her book *The Yeti*. 'At first glance', he wrote, 'I took it to be a bear, but then I saw it more clearly, and realized that it was a manlike creature. It was walking on two feet, upright, but in a stooping fashion. It was quite naked, and its thickset body was covered with reddish hair. The arms were overlong, and swung slightly with each movement. I watched it for about ten minutes before it disappeared, very swiftly, among the scrub and boulders.'

Despite being attacked in some newspapers, the doctor's story was listened to in official circles. As a result, a professor of Historical Science, Dr Boris Porshnev, was appointed head of a Commission for Studying the Question of the Abominable Snowman. His on-the-spot investigations convinced him that the Yeti was not just another traveller's tale but actually existed. 'In the fifteenth century such wild people lived in the mountain fastnesses near the Gobi desert', he stated. 'They had no permanent homes. Their bodies, except for hands and faces, were covered with hair. Like animals they fed on leaves, grass, and anything they could find.' A third Soviet authority who refused to discount the Snowman, was Professor Stanyukovich. Around 1960, he went to the Pamirs with a Yeti expedition that included some of his country's most expert zoologists, archeologists, botanists and climbers. After nine months of patient endeavour, during which cameras with telescopic lenses were at the ready in concealed observation posts, the creatures had still not been seen – either in person or by way of footprints. The Yeti had prudently ignored the 20 goats and rams put out as bait and avoided the dozens of snares, nets and the team of snow-leopard hunters, who spent more than three months lying in cunningly hidden dugouts.

The professor took it philosophically, however. 'Farewell, you fascinating riddle', he wrote. 'Farewell, inscrutable Snowman, ruler of the heights and snows. A pity, a thousand pities that you are not to be found. What, not at all? Not anywhere? Perhaps you are yet to be found in the remotest mountains of Nepal. Perhaps!'

Edmund Hillary led his own commercially backed Yeti expedition in 1960-61. Although he returned with a Snowman scalp lent to him by the Khumjung monastery, the Yeti remained as evasive as ever. Zoologists classified the scalp as that of a serow, or goat antelope, which is a native of eastern Asia – and only some unfamiliar parasites found among the hair were new to them. At this time, information about the Abominable Snowman had been systematized and it had become clear that there are three distinct types: the *Rimi*, which can be up to 8 feet tall and dwells at the comparatively low level of 8000 feet; the *Nvalmot*, an improbable 15 feet in height and a meat-eater that feeds on mountain goats and yak; and the *Rakshi-Bompo*, a mere 5 feet in stature and a vegetarian that lives on grain and millet. A shy and retiring being, the Yeti of all three types prefers to come out at night and is rarely seen in more than twos. It also appreciates it if bowls of water and food are left where it can find them. The Nepalese and Tibetans will not kill or harm the beast, in the belief that to do so will result in bad luck and general misfortune. The creature is usually described as having long reddish hair and feet that, according to the Sherpas, are placed back to front. They get this idea from its prints, which appear to be going in a contrary direction.

The Yeti is reputed to have a body odour that makes a skunk smell good and to possess such strength that it can throw boulders around as if they were marbles and uproot trees as if they were flowers. Descriptions of the Yeti's voice range from shrill whistles to high-pitched yelps to lion-throated roars. It is also said to be fond of any kind of alcohol.

As more evidence about the Yeti piled up, the Nepal government took a definite stand in 1961. The Yeti, it claimed, positively existed and was to be found in an S-shaped area incorporating Siberia and southeastern USSR, India, Alaska, Canada and the USA. Therefore, the Nepalese granted licenses at a cost of $10,000 to hunters dedicated and rich enough to stalk the beast through the Himalayas. Special triangular stamps were issued by the enterprising Bhutanese Post Office, which depicted the Snowman as a being peculiar to the mountains of Bhutan.

Some experts believe not only that the Yeti exists, but also that it will sooner or later be caught and brought down to civilization – and, presumably, to a caged life in one of the world's leading zoos. The latest theory about the Snowman's origins comes from a team of three zoologists who, toward the end of 1972, set out to hunt the fabled beast. They believe that the Yeti may be a descendant of the giant ape *Gigantopithecus*, which 500,000 years ago retreated to the mountains of southern Asia. At that time the Himalayas were rising by as much as 2400 to 3000 metres. Because of this increase in the height of the mountains, the Snowman may have become isolated. In March 1970, Don Whillans, deputy leader of the triumphant British Annapurna Expedition, discovered and photographed Yeti footprints near the Machhapuchre peak in Nepal – and, by the light of the moon, saw a Yeti-like being 'bounding along on all fours'.

In his best-selling book *Annapurna South Face*, team leader Chris Bonington quotes Whillans as saying, 'The following morning I went up to make a full reconnaissance to the permanent Base Camp site, and I took the two Sherpas along. I thought I'd see their reaction at the point where I'd photographed the tracks the day before. The tracks were so obvious that it was impossible not to make any comment, but they walked straight past and didn't indicate that they had seen them. I had already mentioned that I had seen the Yeti, not knowing exactly what it was, but they pretended they didn't understand and ignored what I said. I am convinced that they believe the Yeti does exist, that it is some kind of sacred animal which is best left alone; that if you don't bother it, it won't bother you.'

Whillans also had the British Medical Association magazine, *The Lancet* on his side, for in a 1960 article the journal concluded, 'Now that the Himalayas are more frequented by mountaineers than formerly, information is likely to accumulate more rapidly, and this most popular of mysteries may become a mystery no more.'

Why has our imagination been so captured by the Yeti? It cannot just have been the kind of news coverage it got. Publicity could have been responsible for a Seven Days' Wonder, but not for the fact that in the 25 years since the publication of Eric Shipton's photographs, the Yeti has become firmly established in people's minds – almost part of folk history. It may be that we have a desire to discover lost peoples or creatures akin to humans. But, although the discovery of unknown tribes of about 100,000 people in New Guinea in 1954 created interest, it did not capture public imagination in the same way as the Yeti. The people of New Guinea are now a fact. The Yeti is still a mystery. We do not know whether it exists or not. The only evidence we have is footprints and occasional sightings – not enough to form a scientific theory but enough to stimulate our curiosity.

Perhaps this is the function that the Yeti serves for most of us. We need creatures to inhabit that strange borderland between fact and fantasy and our interest lies not so much in whether they really exist but in the possibility that they may exist. It is as if the very uncertainty, the remoteness and the scanty evidence on which our ideas are based, increases the hold on us and gives life an extra dimension it would lose if final proof came. These large creatures hovering between man and ape, grappling with nature to survive, satisfy a psychological need for many of us – just as dragons and mermaids did for our ancestors.

CHAPTER 21

NORTH AMERICAN MONSTERS

Like the Abominable Snowman of the Himalayas, there is an elusive giant creature that looks like a hairy human in North America. It is called Bigfoot in the United States and the Sasquatch in Canada – and it has been a figure of American Indian folklore for centuries. According to some of the reports, which started among non-Indians in 1811, Bigfoot can be aggressive and hostile. It has even been accused of murder. Can this manlike giant, kin to the Yeti, be a reality?

North America has its own equivalent of the Yeti, which is known as the Bigfoot in the United States and the Sasquatch in Canada. Like the Yeti, these creatures are said to be hairy, to walk on two feet and to resemble humans in appearance. For centuries, the American Indians had passed on stories of the Bigfoot, whose footprints were said to measure anything from 16 to 20 inches and whose height, when fully grown, was thought to be from 7 to 12 feet. The creature also featured in the folklore of South and Central America. This fact is emphasized by Dr John Napier, curator of the primate collection of the Smithsonian Institution, who writes in his book *Bigfoot*, published in 1973, 'Although in the last 20 years there has been a tremendous revival of public interest since these creatures have come to the attention of the "white settlers", it is a reasonable assumption, from what we know of early written records that, like Peyton Place, the story of Sasquatch has been continuing for a great many years.'

The first recorded sighting of a Sasquatch track by a non-Indian occurred in what is now Jasper, Alberta in 1811. While crossing the Rockies in an attempt to reach the Columbia River, the explorer and trader David Thompson came across a set of strange footprints measuring 14 inches long by 8 inches wide. Four toe marks were shown in the deep snow. This was unlike the five-toe print of a bear and convinced those who heard of the track that it did not belong to a grizzly. About 70 years after this, on 4 July 1884, an account of the capture of a supposed Sasquatch appeared in the *Daily Colonist*, the leading paper of British Columbia. The creature – subsequently nicknamed Jacko – had been spotted by the crew of a train travelling along the Fraser River between the towns of Lytton and Yale. The railmen had stopped the train, given chase to the gorilla-like being with coarse, black hair and, on catching it, had placed it safely in the guard's van. After being on show for the citizens of Yale and the surrounding country for a time, Jacko was sold to Barnum and Bailey's Circus.

As time went on and more and more giant 'wild men of the woods' were seen and written about, it became clear to experts that these creatures were more violent and dangerous than their kin the Yeti. This was confirmed in 1910 when two prospectors, brothers named MacLeod, were found in the Nahanni Valley in the Northwest Territories of Canada with their heads cut off. The Sasquatches who had been seen in the area, were blamed for the double murder and from then on the area became known as Headless Valley. Eight years later, the fearful Bigfoot struck again with an attack on a prospector's shack in Mount St. Lawrence, Washington. According to the *Seattle Times*, which reported the incident, the assailants were about eight feet tall, were 'half-human, half-monster' and were able to hypnotize people, to use ventriloquism and to make themselves invisible at will.

Throughout the next few decades, the Sasquatch and Bigfoot made frequent and much-publicized appearances in British Columbia, Northern California and the state of Washington. One of the most fully documented accounts took place in 1924, in the Canadian province of British Columbia.

At first, the few people who heard it refused to believe lumberjack Albert Ostman's story of being kidnapped in the mountainous hinterland of British Columbia, of being kept prisoner in a remote 'cliff-enclosed' valley for more than a week and of

escaping from his 'relentless captors' and making his way thank-
fully back to civilization. What caused his friends and family to
doubt his tale was the fact that his kidnappers, so he said, were no
ordinary hoodlums or gangsters. They were a family – father,
mother, teenage son and young daughter – but a family of 'near-
human hairy beasts'. According to Ostman, he fell into their
clutches in the summer of 1924 while on vacation. Having
decided to mix business with pleasure, he had travelled to the
head of Toba Inlet, near Vancouver Island, to look for traces of
the gold that had formerly been mined there. Equipped with a
rifle, cooking utensils and cans of food, he spent some six or
seven days roaming through the district. He got farther and
farther off the beaten track. Finally he came across a secluded
glade, surrounded by cypress trees and containing a tempting
freshwater spring in its centre. Tired but contented, he resolved to
spend some time there and pitched his sleeping bag beneath the
stars. On the second night in the glade, however, he woke up to
find himself being carried 'inside my bag like a sack of potatoes,
the only thing in sight being a huge hand clutching the partly
closed neck of the bag.'

Ostman's kidnapper walked rapidly and the journey was rough
and painful for the bagged lumberjack. He was glad when the bag
was suddenly dropped on the ground and he was able to crawl out
of it. Dazed and bruised he looked around him and met the
curious stares of a weird family – all huge, hairy and beastlike.
Ostman feared for his life, but his giant captors did not bother
him. In fact, they even allowed him to prepare his own meals
from his supply of canned provisions. They turned out to be vegetarians who ate sweet grass, roots and spruce tips from the ever-
green forests. They also gave him a certain amount of freedom to
explore his new valley home. Ostman noticed that it was the
mother and son who did the family chores, wandering off into the
trees and returning with tubers and hemlock tips. The father and
daughter kept a careful watch over him.

Ostman feared he might be meant for the daughter later. It was
this consideration, plus the obvious fact that he did not want to
spend the rest of his life as the family's pet, that made Ostman
resolve to escape. He got away one day, when his kidnappers had
become so used to him that they seemed to think he was as happy

in the wilds as they were, and so let their vigilance slip temporarily. On his return home, Ostman was at first reluctant to tell of his unique and unsettling experience. Those whom he did mention it to regarded him as a crank – or worse. So he said no more about it until 33 years later in 1957. Only then did he come forward and tell newspapermen and anthropologists of his enforced stay with the monstrous family. Asked why he hadn't made a public statement earlier, he understandably replied that he had thought no one would take him seriously – or even that they might question his state of mind. In a belated attempt to gain credence, he swore the truth of his story before a Justice of the Peace at Fort Langley, British Columbia, on 20 August 1957 and later agreed to be interviewed by experts.

Ostman's account appeared honest in most respects, but his report of the creatures' eating habits did cause doubt. Considering that the Sasquatch family in all must have weighed more than 2000 pounds – as much as five male gorillas or fourteen adult humans, for example, it seemed unlikely that such outsize beings could have kept alive and active on the kind of low-calorie diet Ostman described. The province's Minister for Recreation and Conservation received a report from Frank L. Beebe of the British Columbia Provincial Museum in 1967. In it the expert stated that the type of vegetation used by Ostman's giants 'produces the very poorest quality of low-energy food and the least quantity of high-energy food of any forest type on the planet.'

A look back at the year that Ostman actually claimed to have met up with the Sasquatches revealed that 1924 had also provided another version of the monsters' activities. This time the incident took place in Ape Canyon, Washington. It was there that a group of coal miners were attacked by a 'horde of Bigfeet' after one of the workers, Fred Beck, had met a Bigfoot at the edge of a canyon and, terrified, had shot it three times in the back. A running battle then ensued between the dead monster's companions and the miners. It ended with the Bigfeet driving the panic stricken men from the area forever. Beck's version, as told to two well-known Bigfoot investigators, was given by Dr John Napier in his book *Bigfoot*,

'At night the apes counter-attacked, openlng the assault by knocking a heavy strip of wood out from between two logs of the miners' cabin. After that there were assorted poundings on the walls, door, and roof, but the building was designed to withstand heavy mountain snows and the apes failed to break in . . . There was . . . the sound of rocks hitting the roof and rolling off, and [the miners] did brace the heavy door from the inside. They heard creatures thumping around on top of the cabin as well as battering the walls, and they fired shots through the walls and roof without driving them away. The noise went on from shortly after dark until nearly dawn . . . The cabin had no windows and of course no one opened the door, so in fact the men inside did not see what was causing the commotion outside. Nor could Mr Beck say for sure . . . that there were more than two creatures outside. There were that many because there had been one on the roof and one pounding the wall simultaneously. However many there were, it was enough for the miners, who packed up and abandoned their mine the next day.'

In 1940, a Bigfoot male that was eight feet tall raided a farmstead in Nevada. The farmer's wife had to grab her children and flee. When she came back later, she found the house encircled by huge footprints. A large barrel of salted fish had also been knocked over and its contents spilled. In 1958, a truck driver named Jerry Crew found some impressively big tracks in the California mud. He followed them up hill and down into low ground, before sensibly taking a plaster cast of one of them. He had himself photographed holding the cast up and the picture caused a sensation in the newspapers and periodicals in which it appeared. Five years later, Texas oil millionaire Tom Slick died in a crash in his private plane while trying to get at the truth about the Bigfoot. The findings of the various expeditions he financed have never been made public. However, the stories about his Bigfoot searches kept the interest in the monster alive. Between June 1964 and December 1970, 25 Bigfoot sightings were reported, bringing the grand total of eye-witness reports of footprints and monsters to more than 300. In 1969, in Canada alone, there were no less than 60 different accounts of Sasquatches and their doings.

Toward the end of the 1960s came a publicity stunt involving the Bigfoot. It was known that the monsters were usually seen in midsummer or fall. Operating on this knowledge, a one-time rodeo worker Roger Patterson, announced in October 1967, that he and a half-Indian friend had encountered a female Bigfoot near Bluff Creek, California and had taken 20 feet of film of her as she ambled along the outskirts of a dense forest. Patterson said he operated the camera while on the run and that explained why the opening frames of his 16mm colour movie jumped about so much. The film was of a creature some seven feet high and weighing between 350 and 450 pounds. It was shown to Dr Napier, who duly noted its heavy build, reddish-brown hair and prominent furry breasts and buttocks.

Dr Napier viewed the movie six times at a private screening in Washington DC on 2 December 1967, before forming an opinion about it. He was dissatisfied with the alleged Bigfoot's 'self-conscious walk', which seemed to him to be that of a human male. He felt that the cone-shaped top of the skull was 'definitely nonhuman', but was suspicious of the being's centre of gravity – as he said, 'precisely as it is in modern man' – and could only accept the buttocks as a 'human hallmark'.

'The upper half of the body', he went on, 'bears some resemblance to an ape, and the lower half is typically human. It is almost impossible to conceive that such structural hybrids could exist in nature. One half of the animal must be artificial. In view of the walk, it can only be the upper half. Subsequently, I have seen and studied the film, frame by frame, a dozen times or more . . . I was [also] puzzled by the extraordinary exaggeration of the walk: it seemed to me to be an overstatement of the normal pattern, a bad actor's interpretation of a classical human walking gait . . . There is little doubt that the scientific evidence taken collectively points to a hoax of some kind. The creature shown in the film does not stand up well to functional analysis. There are too many inconsistencies . . . Perhaps it was a man dressed up in a monkey-skin; if so it was a brilliantly executed hoax and the unknown perpetrator will take his place with the great hoaxers of the world.' By the time Dr Napier had reached this last conclusion, the film had been shown commercially to audiences both in Canada and the United States.

A couple of years after the Patterson film, a sensational headline in the *National Bulletin* screamed, 'I Was Raped by the Abominable Snowman'. The rape victim, a young woman by the name of Helen Westring, claimed that she had met her assailant some three years earlier while on a solo hunting trip in the woods near Bemidji, Minnesota. Hypnotizing her with its pink eyes, she said the monster, with huge hairy hands and long arms, had ripped her clothes off 'like one would peel a banana'. It then stared at her intently, particularly at 'the area between my legs', threw her to the ground and went about its 'beastly purpose'. Fortunately for the victim she fainted; on coming to she took her rifle and shot the rapist through the right eye.

As the story unfolded, it was clear that Helen Westring was not talking about a Bigfoot and that the newspaper was capitalizing on the wide interest in the Himalayan Abominable Snowman by using such a headline. The gory rape-murder story referred instead to the Minnesota Iceman, who was famous in his own right as a monster – and, possibly, as the biggest hoax of the century.

In the late 1960s, the Minnesota Iceman was taken around the carnivals and fairgrounds of the United States and shown to vast audiences for 25 cents admission. The 'mysterious hairy body' was in the possession of Frank Hansen who, in May 1967, first exhibited the so-called 'man left over from the ice age' to the American public. Hansen claimed that the body on display had been found preserved in a 6000-pound block of ice in the Bering Straits.

For more than 18 months the monster was taken from area to area. News of its existence spread, until it was heard by the well-known Belgian scientist and writer, Dr Bernard Heuvelmans and his associate, Ivan Sanderson. The two men journeyed to inspect the Iceman at Hansen's farm near Winona, Minnesota out of their interest in monsters, for by then the creature's identification as a prehistoric man had seemed to evaporate. They found him encased in a block of ice and enclosed in a refrigerated coffin. The monster's right eye had been penetrated by a bullet and the back of his skull shattered. Hansen said he had been murdered. Their examination began on 17 December 1968 and, although it lasted for two days, they had only restricted access to the creature. The coffin was kept in a small poorly lit trailer and in order to sketch the Iceman, Sanderson had to lie on top of the plate glass lid of the coffin, his nose almost touching that of the monster's.

Photographs were also taken. Heuvelmans later wrote a paper for the Royal Institute of Natural Sciences in Belgium, which he called 'Preliminary Note on a Specimen preserved in ice; an unknown living hominid.' From this, it seemed that the two scientists had accepted the Iceman as fact and Hansen's explanation as to the bullet wound on the monster as truth. Heuvelmans' statement was given by Odette Tchernine in her book *The Yeti* as:

'The specimen at first sight is representative of man . . . of fairly normal proportions, but excessively hairy . . . His skin is of the waxlike colour characteristic of corpses of men of white race when not tanned by the sun . . . The damage to the occiput [back of the head], and the fact that the eyeballs had been ejected from their sockets, one having completely disappeared, suggests that the creature had been shot in the face by several large-calibre bullets. One bullet must have penetrated the cubitus [forearm] when he tried to protect himself. A second bullet pierced the right eye, destroying it, and causing the other to start out of its cavity. This caused the much larger cavity at the back of the cranium, producing immediate death.'

With the Iceman's acceptance both in popular and academic circles, Hansen then announced that the creature, nicknamed 'Bozo' by Sanderson, was not his at all: he was merely its keeper. Its real owner was a mysterious 'Mr X', a millionaire Hollywood film maker who had brought the Iceman from an emporium in Hong Kong and had had it flown to the United States. If Hansen was to be believed, Bozo had been shuttled around the Far East from Soviet sealers, to Japanese whalers, to Chinese dealers, all the while causing consternation of Customs and other officials. The Hollywood tycoon was said to be interested only in allowing ordinary people to view their 'Neanderthal ancestor', and so, in 1969, the Iceman returned to the carnival circuits. This time he was billed as a 'Creature frozen and preserved forever in a coffin of ice', in a return to the prehistoric man idea. It was apparent to those who saw it that the second exhibit was no fossil.

As it happened, Sanderson had approached Dr John Napier just before the carnival tour to see if he might be interested in having the monster fully and scientifically investigated. At first Napier was enthusiastic to undertake a study. But then a number of things happened to squash his enthusiasm. First, the Secretary of the

Smithsonian, S. Dillon Ripley, learned from Hansen that the creature about to go on exhibition was a latex model, which, Hansen was careful to say, resembled the original Iceman. Second, after the murder theory was put forward, Ripley immediately wrote to the FBI to see if the Bureau would co-operate in tracing the original exhibit. As no federal law had been broken, the Bureau would not intervene – but this did not stop Hansen from preparing a new display sign for his monster, calling it 'The near-Man . . . Investigated by the FBI.'

The Smithsonian then withdrew its interest in the Iceman, which only seemed to spur Hansen on. He held a press conference at his ranch, timing it prior to taking the Iceman to St. Paul. He admitted to reporter Gorden Yeager of the *Rochester Post-Bulletin* that the monster was 'man-made, an illusion.' From St. Paul, the exhibit moved to Grand Rapids where it was filmed by a team from *Time-Life*. This film showed distinct differences between the model then on display and the Iceman as drawn and photographed by Heuvelmans and Sanderson. The original creature had only one yellowish tooth, while this one boasted at least four.

After the Helen Westring story of the murder of the Minnesota Iceman, Hansen came up with a final version of how the monster had met his death. In *Saga* magazine in 1970, he declared that it was he, not Helen Westring, who had shot the monster in the woods. He had done so while in the US Air Force on a hunting trip with some fellow officers in the north of the state. The creature had fallen mortally wounded in the snow and had stayed there for two months until Hansen removed the body to the deep-freeze at his camp quarters. 'Let's not tell a single person about this', he warned his wife. 'We'll just leave it there until Spring.' After seven years, Hansen took the corpse to his nearby farm. Later, for reasons never explained, he had a latex replica made of it by special technicians in Hollywood. From then on, he simply switched the exhibits when necessary and talked as fast as he could in order to fool the press, the public and the experts.

One person who didn't believe Hansen's 'transparently dubious' confession is Dr Napier, who is as close to the story as anyone. But however sceptical he is about the Iceman, he feels that the 'North American Bigfoot or Sasquatch has a lot going for it . . . Too many people claim to have seen it, or at least to have seen footprints, to dismiss its reality out of hand. To suggest that hundreds of people at worst are lying, or, at best, deluding themselves is neither proper nor realistic.'

Part Three

'All in Your Mind...'

It would be fair to say that many of the cases dealt with in the previous sections might be the result of hallucinations or delusions. Indeed, some sceptics insist that all unexplained events are reducible to 'tricks of the mind'. Such a view tacitly implies the working of the human mind to be something less fantastic than unicorns or fish falling from the sky.

For the scientists of the nineteenth century, this was generally believed to be the truth – to them the brain was a biological mechanism much like an adding machine – it seemed only a matter of time before medical science discovered all its functions and secrets. Yet many of these same doctors were members of 'magical' orders such as the Freemasons, the Rosicrucians and the Order of the Golden Dawn. To them the existence of magic was also self-evident. They were faced with a difficult dilemma – if the brain is just a mechanism to produce thought, then how does the mind produce wonders like thought transference, telekinesis and mesmerism?

Down through recorded history, people have tried to harness the mind's apparent ability to transcend the laws of physics. Whether we call such a power magic or psychic phenomena, the fact remains that evidence of its existence is almost overwhelming. Yet it is only over the last few decades that the science of parapsychology has managed to define even the outer boundaries of such abilities. The answer to much that is unexplained in the world seems to lie between our ears – and there too, parapsychologists believe, is the key to the evolutionary future of the species.

CHAPTER 22

WILD TALENTS

In our rational, scientific world, do people exist who are capable of mysterious feats? What do we know, for all our science, of the energies within our minds? There are many well-authenticated accounts of strange happenings we cannot explain by the natural laws which we believe govern our universe. Are these stories then fakes, or is it possible that there is a dimension of existence which we have not yet recognized? There seems to be evidence that telepathy is possible, that mind can speak directly to mind. Poltergeist activity apparently indicates that mind can act directly on matter. What can we learn from these strange abilities?

Few of us would flatly deny that the universe is a stranger place than the generally accepted natural laws can account for. Most of the time, we choose not to think about it. When we discover that some people appear to have strange powers – powers that apparently enable them to ignore the normal physical laws that contain the rest of us – we prefer not to think about it because we have no easy explanation. It makes life more complicated and it is a subtle threat to our own sense of safety in a known world. When we do think about it, we hunt for the trick, the deception, the proof that everything is as we would like it to be, so that we can return, safely, to not thinking about it. But these wild talents tug at our sleeves, whisper in our ears. Throughout all recorded history, people have been fascinated and have felt threatened by these unexplained abilities. In our recent history we have conducted complicated tests and formulated sophisticated explanations – and then a young Israeli comes along and stops clocks and bends spoons – trivial accomplishments in themselves but how do we explain them? Then we find we have started to think about strange powers and extraordinary events.

Witnessing evidence of such events and powers can be striking, even for those intent on maintaining a strictly unbiased and scientific frame of mind. In the book *Mysteries of the Mind*, author Colin Wilson describes his first meeting with one of the most renowned psychics this century,

'I met the young Israeli wonder worker Uri Geller one morning in the summer of 1974 in the office of a London business tycoon. The meeting had been arranged with a view to my working on a film about Geller's life. A secretary showed me into the inner office. Uri, a good looking but seemingly quite ordinary young man, appeared to be a little nervous or preoccupied. We chatted briefly, after which the three of us went to lunch at a nearby restaurant. We sat at a table in the corner, the woman and I side by side and Uri opposite us with his back to the room. When we had ordered, he offered to try to demonstrate his powers, but said, "I don't know if it will work. Sometimes it doesn't."

'We began with an experiment in *telepathy* (the transmission of thoughts by means other that the five senses). Uri handed me one of the restaurant cards on the table and, turning away from me, asked me to make a drawing on its blank side. I made a sketch of a creature I had invented some time ago to amuse my children. It took only a few seconds, as I had drawn it many times before. I glanced at Uri as I did it. He was staring out across the restaurant, and he could not have watched me without being seen to do so by the secretary beside me. When I had finished, he asked me to cover the drawing with my hand. Then he turned back to the table and took another of the cards. He asked me to concentrate hard and to try to transmit the thought of what I had sketched. A minute went by with no result. Uri shook his head. "It seems very complicated; is it a kind of amoeba?" Slowly and hesitantly he began to draw the creature's right ear – the spot where I always begin the drawing. "You've got it," I said. "Go on!" He completed the drawing quickly. I had carefully redrawn the picture in my mind as I tried to transmit it – which probably accounts for the identical starting point.

'Uri then demonstrated other powers. He caused a restaurant spoon to bend by stroking it gently. He made the hands of my watch turn back two hours and the date go forward two days by stroking a coin placed over its face, explaining afterward that he derives power from metal. He had a little trouble trying to break my American Automobile Association key. Ideally, he said, the key should have more personal associations. However, he placed it against a metal radiator, and after a few seconds said, "It's starting to go." The key snapped in two.

'Finally, he tried to transmit a picture to me by telepathy. I attempted to make my mind receptive, but no image came into it. Feeling rather embarrassed, I just drew the first thing that came into my head : a check mark. Uri showed me the piece of paper he was holding away from me. It contained a mirror image of the symbol I had drawn. It could be significant in this connection that Uri is left-handed.

'After I left Uri Geller I immediately began to sift my impressions. Only the day before, a highly sceptical scientist had warned me to watch carefully for conjuring tricks, especially as Uri had earlier been a stage conjuror. I had to admit that most of the things he had done could have been tricks. For instance, snapping the key with his fingers, and altering the hands and date on my watch with the winder would have been well within the ability of a skilful conjuror. But how could he have faked the drawing of what I had drawn? And if that feat was due to genuine telepathic powers, the other demonstrations could also be genuine.

'A couple of months after this Ted Bastin, a quantum physicist, and I appeared on a television discussion show about supernormal powers – a subject about which Ted is distinctly sceptical. When I mentioned Uri Geller, however, Ted told me he had conducted extensive tests and was convinced that Uri was genuine. A few days later Ted rang me up to announce that Uri had just performed a most spectacular feat in his laboratory. He had dematerialized half a crystal that had been sealed in a metal container. Bastin said that there was no way in which Uri could have touched the crystal.

'Assuming that Uri Geller possesses extraordinary powers, where do they come from? I think the answer must be from his subconscious mind. In recent years psychologists have come to the conclusion that *poltergeists* (ghosts or spirits that make noises or fling objects) originate in the subconscious minds of teenagers who have been seriously disturbed by the problems of adolescence. On the other hand, some investigators believe that poltergeists have a separate existence – that is, that they are real ghosts – but that they have to borrow energy from disturbed adolescents before they can become active. Whatever the truth of the matter, it seems probable that the subconscious mind provides the energy that causes heavy objects to rise and fly across a room or doors to open and bang shut. If this is so, it is reasonable to assume that the energy which causes spoons to bend and broken watches to tick originates in Uri Geller's highly active subconscious mind.'

If these strange powers exist in some hidden depths of the mind, what are they doing there? Are they common to all of us, and are they available to anyone who knows how to use them? We may find part of the answer in an experience of John G. Bennett, the foremost living disciple of the remarkable Russian mystic, Georgei Gurdjieff.

In 1923, Bennett was at Gurdjieff's Institute for the Harmonious Development of Man at the Prieuré in a suburb of Paris. For some days, Bennett had been suffering from almost constant diarrhoea and each morning he felt weaker and found it harder to get up. One morning he woke up shaking with fever and decided to stay in bed. But in the instant of making this decision, he found himself getting out of bed and dressing. It felt, he said, as if he was being 'held together by a superior Will that was not my own.' After a morning's work, he felt too ill to eat lunch. Nonetheless, he joined a dancing class in the afternoon. Gurdjieff's dances involved movements of great complexity, requiring tremendous concentration and physical coordination. As the exercises continued Bennett felt an immense lassitude descend on him. It became agony even to move, but he forced himself to go on. Gurdjieff introduced new exercises which were so complex that the other students began to drop out one by one. Bennett, however, felt Gurdjieff's eyes on him as if commanding him to go on, even if it killed him.

'Suddenly, I was filled with an influx of immense power. My body seemed to have turned into light. I could not feel its presence in the usual ways. There was no effort, no weariness, not even any sense of weight. . . .' When the lesson was over he decided to test the power that had entered his body. He took a spade and began to dig at a rate that would normally have exhausted him in two minutes. In spite of the summer heat, he continued digging for over an hour.

Later, Bennett went for a walk toward a nearby forest where he met Gurdjieff. Without preliminaries, Gurdjieff began to talk about energies. 'There is a certain energy', he said, 'that is necessary for work on oneself . . . we can call it the Higher Emotional Energy . . . There are some people in the world, but they are very rare, who are connected to the Great Reservoir or Accumulator of this energy. . . .' Gurdjieff implied that he was one of those who can tap the Great Reservoir and permit others to borrow its energy.

Bennett continued his walk in the forest, still filled with a tremendous sense of power. He recalled that Peter Ouspensky, another Russian mystic and associate of Gurdjieff's, had once said that if we wish to prove how little control we have over our emotions, we have only to try to be astonished at will. Bennett said to himself, 'I will be astonished.' Instantly he felt overwhelmed with amazement. 'Each tree was so uniquely itself that I felt that I could walk in the forest forever and never cease from wonderment. Then the thought of "fear" came to me. At once I was shaking with terror. Unknown horrors were menacing me on every side. I thought of "joy" and I felt that my heart would burst from rapture. The word "love" came to me, and I was pervaded with such fine shades of tenderness and compassion that I saw that I had not the remotest idea of the depth and range of love. Love was everywhere and in everything. It was infinitely adaptable to every shade of need. After a time it became too much for me; it seemed that if I plunged any more deeply into the mystery of love, I would cease to exist. I wanted to be free from this power to feel whatever I chose, and at once it left me.'

What is this strange power that Gurdjieff was able to evoke in his disciples? It is not as mysterious as it sounds. We are all familiar with its commonest form, which we call 'second wind'.

In most energetic sports, such as long distance running, we force ourselves beyond the normal point of exhaustion. Then sometimes, quite suddenly, we feel a resurge of energy that enables us to continue for longer than usual. On rare occasions we can even force ourselves to continue until we get our third wind. The American philosopher and psychologist William James wrote about this in his essay, 'The Energies of Man'.

'Everyone is familiar with the phenomenon of feeling more or less alive on different days. Everyone knows on any given day that there are energies slumbering in him which the incitements of that day do not call forth, but which he might display if these were greater. Most of us feel as if a sort of cloud weighed upon us, keeping us below our highest notch of clearness in discernment, sureness in reasoning, or firmness in deciding. Compared with what we ought to be, we are only half awake. Our fires are damped, our draughts are checked. We are making use of only a small part of our possible mental and physical resources.

'Stating the thing broadly, the human individual thus lives unusually far within his limits; he possesses powers of various sorts which he habitually fails to use. He energizes below his *maximum* and he behaves below his *optimum*.'

In other words, for everyday purposes human beings have certain predetermined limits. It is like the thermostat on a central heating system. When the temperature rises above a certain point it automatically switches off the heating. When our tiredness reaches a certain limit, we also switch off automatically and allow ourselves to sink into a passive state. But if some crisis arises, we refuse to allow ourselves to remain passive. We become alert and suddenly, as our thermostat readjusts itself, we discover we have become fully alive again.

The implication seems to be that each of us contains a vast reservoir of energy. William James also asks what it is that gives a Leonardo or a Beethoven his creative energy. His answer is excitement, determination, a sense of purpose. He adds, 'We live subject to arrest by degrees of fatigue which we have come only from habit to obey. Most of us may learn to push the barrier further off, and to live in perfect comfort on much higher levels of power.'

This was the aim of Gurdjieff's work. He forced his students to keep pushing the barriers farther and farther back. One of his followers, Fritz Peters, has described how Gurdjieff gave him the task of mowing the lawns at the Prieuré. At first the work took Peters several days. Gradually Gurdjieff accustomed him to doing more and more in a day, until finally Peters could mow all the lawns, which consisted of several acres, in one day. What Gurdjieff called his 'dervish dances' were also designed to break the chain of habit. Try rubbing your stomach with one hand while patting yourself on the head with the other, or tapping the toes of one foot on the floor while rubbing the other foot back and forth like a pendulum. Most people find such movements difficult. Yet Gurdjieff trained his students to do something different with feet, arms and head at the same time. He would also suddenly order them to break off whatever they were doing and to freeze in some complicated attitude.

As Gurdjieff recognized, even exercises as difficult as these can become a habit. Fritz Peters tells a story which reveals that Gurdjieff himself could forget how to establish contact with his own reservoir of energy. At the end of World War II Peters, then a soldier and suffering from battle fatigue and nervous strain, called on Gurdjieff at his Paris apartment. Gurdjieff was busy and asked Peters to wait for him in another room. After a minute or two alone, Peters felt so miserable and desperate that he interrupted Gurdjieff again. Gurdjieff instantly saw the seriousness of the situation and set his work aside. As he sat with Gurdjieff, Peters experienced a sudden trickle of power flowing into him like a spring. It slowly increased until all his tiredness had vanished. But Gurdjieff himself now looked completely exhausted. Peters had no doubt that Gurdjieff had somehow given him his own energy. A crowd of people then arrived at the house and Gurdjieff dragged himself away to entertain them. Five minutes later he returned to the kitchen radiating vitality and remarked to Peters that the experience had been good for both of them. In other words, the effort of revitalizing Peters had awakened Gurdjieff to a recognition that he had lost touch with his own 'source of power, meaning, and purpose'. He promptly re-established contact and recharged his own batteries.

There is nothing mystical or occult about this. We all have within us a robot, akin to the automatic pilot in an airplane, whose task is to simplify our lives by handling a series of routines. Learning to type or speak French or drive a car requires considerable effort and concentration, but once we have mastered it, our robot takes over and does it far more quickly and efficiently than we could do it consciously. The trouble is, the robot can become so efficient that it takes over most of our life. We begin to live like a robot. We automatically drink our martini, eat our dinner, watch TV. It takes a holiday or some sudden crisis to jar us out of this automatic living, to allow our real selves to take over from the robot.

There can be no doubt that Gurdjieff helped Bennett overcome his fatigue, just as he helped Peters. But at a certain point, Bennett's own inner dynamo took over and he wrested control from his robot. He was suddenly dazzled by vistas of possible feeling. For, like our bodies, our feelings are also controlled by the robot. We seldom experience new feeling. For the most part, we play the same old phonograph record over and over again – a record that, except in times of crisis, is full of bland harmonies. What Bennett had realized was that he could experience new intensities of feeling every day; that he could experience a compelling feeling for every tree and every blade of grass.

Our minds contain a vast unused library of 'phonograph records'. And not just our minds. The world around us is full of an infinite number of interesting things that the robot has been trained to ignore. This is perhaps the most important insight that arises from Bennett's description of his experience, '. . . I was pervaded with such shades of tenderness and compassion that *I saw that I had not the remotest idea of the depth and range of love.*' We accept the universe around us as stable and normal, just as a child who knew nothing about water might accept the surface of a pond as a glittering mirror, unaware that there are green depths below, teeming with innumerable forms of life. How many other things is this true of? How much mystery and complexity and reality is hidden from us by ignorance and habit?

Human beings live within arbitrary limits. Not only do we have an arbitrary idea of our powers and capabilities, but we also have an arbitrary idea of the complexity and interestingness of the world around us. Habit has confined human beings in a thoroughly stale universe.

A word of caution should be offered, however. Why should Bennett get tired of the power to see and feel more widely than ever before? Why does he say, 'I wanted to be free from this power to feel whatever I chose . . .?' The reason is that these arbitrary limits to our powers are also safety limits. Our habits, which can become so oppressive, are also intended to protect us. Bennett could have achieved many of the same effects of power and perception by taking a psychedelic drug such as mescalin or LSD. These also destroy the robot and disconnect our habit mechanisms so that the world appears new and strange. Psychedelic drugs also release the capacity to feel whatever we choose – the thought of love can produce a tidal wave of love.

On the other hand, a negative thought produces equally powerful results. One man who had taken LSD under medical supervision described how the thought of death produced the hallucination that peoples' faces had become grinning skulls, and the air seemed thick with the smell of earth and decaying flesh. Some people who have had bad trips have become permanently unbalanced mentally. The power of the mind can be highly dangerous and meddling with it simply for kicks, is as irresponsible as allowing a child to drive a high-powered car. Bennett realized that it would be wiser to learn to extend the range of his consciousness step by step and to consolidate each step before moving on, rather than to take a sudden leap into powers that were beyond his understanding and almost certainly beyond his ability to control.

Once we know the world is not as dull and ordinary as it may seem, we have taken a major step toward doing something about it. The real objection to habit is that it makes us lazy, paralysing the will. Once we realize that our robot is insulating us against much that is rich and rewarding in the world around us, we can begin to organize the will to resist the power of habit.

While we know enough about second wind to understand Bennett's experience, it is altogether more difficult to grasp how Gurdjieff could have projected energy into Bennett and Peters. What is the nature of this energy? The following may throw some light on it.

In 1919, Bernard Kajinsky, a Russian electrical engineer, was awakened in the night by a ringing sound like that of a spoon hitting glass. The next day he learned that his closest friend had died of typhus. When he called on his friend's mother, he discovered that she had been about to give him a dose of medicine at the moment he died. Kajinsky, suddenly excited, asked her to show him exactly what she had done. She took a silver spoon and dropped it into a tumbler. It made the same ringing sound that had startled him awake.

Kajinsky was a scientist with no interest in telepathy or extrasensory perception. But he had no doubt that his friend had thought of him at the moment of death and that the sound of the spoon striking glass had somehow been conveyed to him. He thereafter made an exhaustive study of telepathy and reached the conclusion that, 'the human nervous system is capable of reacting to stimuli whose source is not yet known.'

Kajinsky's work came to the attention of a famous Russian animal trainer, Vladimir Durov, who was convinced that his animals could read his mind. Durov began to conduct experiments in association with Vladimir Bekhterev, a distinguished neurologist. Under Bekhterev's supervision, Durov gave complicated telepathic orders to his animals. Usually the animals would carry them out. For example, Bekhterev wrote instructions on a sheet of paper and handed it to Durov. Durov looked into the eyes of his German shepherd dog Mars for several seconds without speaking. Mars went into the next room, looked on three tables and, finding what Bekhterev had asked for on the third – a telephone directory – carried it to Durov in his mouth.

Many animal lovers have noticed that their pets seem to possess some telepathic power. Edward Campbell, a British newspaper editor who studied this question, tells an interesting story about a German animal trainer, Hans Brick. Brick's favourite lion was a man eater named Habibi and Brick's bond with the lion was a strange one. It was tacitly agreed between them that the lion – which was savage and unbroken – was entitled to kill Brick if it could find a moment when his attention lapsed. While Brick maintained his full attention the lion never attacked him. But on several occasions when his attention had wavered, an attack came instantly. Brick insisted it was his own fault. 'I know the rules; so does he', he said.

During World War II, Brick was interned in England for a while and Habibi was looked after by a zoo. When Brick was released, a British film company asked him to supervise some wild animal sequences in a film using Habibi. A problem arose because the owner of the zoo wanted payment for having tended Habibi and Brick could not afford the fee. According to Campbell, at six o'clock on Sunday morning Brick walked into the zoo, went to Habibi's cage on an upper floor, released the lion and looped a whip loosely around his neck. Brick then made a mental pact with the animal – Habibi was not to attack him while they were making their escape from the zoo.

The animals in other cages were in an uproar as the lion walked out. Rabbits and peacocks were ranging freely about the floor but Habibi made no attempt to attack them. Brick walked to the door, Habibi following. They went down a flight of stairs and into the street. The lion walked quietly behind Brick and entered a travelling cage that he had parked in the next street. In effect, Brick had told the lion telepathically, 'These are special circumstances. You want to get out; I want to get you out. No tricks. . . .' And the lion had kept to his side of the bargain.

So far we have been speaking of telepathy which, most investigators agree, seems to depend on some form of waves. They are generally known as *Psi* waves (Psi is a Greek letter used in parapsychology for psychic ability or phenomenon.) At present, we have no idea of the nature of such waves. We might compare Psi waves with radio waves. But radio waves can be used only to communicate, whereas when Gurdjieff used Psi power on Bennett and Peters, he seems to have been doing much more than merely communicating.

In 1940, not long before the invasion of the USSR, Joseph Stalin ordered an investigation into the powers of a psychic named Wolf Messing, who appears to have possessed Psi powers to an extraordinary degree. Messing described these experiments in a Soviet science magazine. His first test was to walk into a bank, present the cashier with a note and will him to hand over 100,000 roubles in cash. Two official witnesses went with Messing when he did this. They saw the cashier take packets of banknotes out of the safe and hand them over. Messing put them in a briefcase and left. Then, with the two witnesses he re-entered the bank and handed back the money and the note – which was in fact a sheet of blank paper. The clerk looked at it, suddenly realized what he had done – and collapsed with a heart attack.

The stories about Brick and Messing may make one conclude that Gurdjieff simply used his Psi powers to suggest certain feelings to Fritz Peters. But it is difficult to see why, in that case, the effort should have exhausted Gurdjieff – and even more difficult to see how Peters could have been so genuinely re-invigorated. For the moment, it may be best to acknowledge that we do not even begin to understand the possibilities of Psi, and leave it at that.

Psi powers are not as rare as we might suppose. In fact, there are a number of simple experiments that anyone can do to verify that they are more than merely auto-suggestion. The simplest test requires four or five people. One of the group, the subject, stands in the centre of the room with the others around him. The subject closes his eyes tightly and the others place their fingers gently against his chest, shoulders and back, making sure not to exert pressure. The aim of the experiment is to make the subject sway in a particular direction, which the others can decide upon by movement of the eyes or a nod of the head. They concentrate hard on willing the subject to sway in the chosen direction. He usually feels a force pulling him in the chosen direction, as if he were a compass needle and someone had brought a magnet close to him. It usually takes only a few seconds, depending on the suggestibility of the subject.

The second experiment, which also takes five people, is lifting a seated person using only index fingers. It is familiar to most schoolchildren. The chosen subject sits in a chair and the the other four attempt to lift him by placing a finger under his armpits and knees. It is, of course, impossible. Then the four place their hands, one on top of the other, on the head of the seated person. No person should have his own two hands next to each other. All concentrate hard for about 20 seconds. Then they quickly remove their hands from the head, place their index fingers under the subject's knees and armpits – and the seated person is lifted effortlessly into the air. The glib explanation of this is that the hands piled on the subject's head operate as a kind of Psi accumulator. The interesting question is why and how they do so – and at present we have no answer.

The third experiment can be performed with a sheet of paper about two inches square. Fold it from corner to corner, from top to bottom, and from side to side. By pinching the corner folds, it can now be turned into a kind of paper dart, its point at the intersection of the fold lines. Take a needle and stick it blunt end first into a cork. Balance the paper dart on the needle point so that it looks like a partly opened umbrella. Making sure that you do not breathe on it, try to will it to rotate about the needle point.

Author Colin Wilson – 'psychically deaf' by his own description – gives this account of his own attempt at the above experiment:

'The first time I attempted this, nothing happened – which is what I expected. However, I kept the dart by my typewriter, and every now and then I tried to make it turn, cupping my hands around it. Eventually I stopped trying to make it move by sheer will power, and imagined that it was moving. Immediately, it began to rotate. I thought for a moment that this was due to the heat from my hands, so I tried stopping it. It stopped. Then I made it turn in the opposite direction. Once I had acquired the trick, I found it easy to make it rotate in either direction, even without my hands cupped around it.

'The original paper model for this experiment was sent to me by Robert Leftwich, a water diviner who also claimed to be able to dispel clouds by concentrating on them. Although I later met Leftwich, I never saw him dispersing clouds. However, a well-authenticated experiment in cloud dispersal was filmed by a British television program in June 1956 on Hampstead Heath in London. This kind of Psi power is known as *telekinesis* (making objects or bodies move without visible force). Many experiments on this subject were carried out by Soviet researchers.'

It seems possible, then, that thought can exert some form of pressure quite distinct from powers of telepathic suggestion. This, in turn, suggests that stories of the power of blessings and curses may have a foundation in fact. If Gurdjieff could make Peters feel better, he could also, presumably, have made him feel worse. Ira Levin's novel, *Rosemary's Baby* has an episode in which a black magic group wills a man to death. If thought pressure is a reality, such telekinetic homicide may be possible. Donald Omand, a Church of England clergyman who has performed many exorcisms, believes that if a group of people determinedly brood on someone they dislike, they can inflict psychic damage. Directing mental forces may be as harmful as physical assault.

Gurdjieff tells this story about a station master in a small Russian town. Early every morning as he rang the bell announcing the arrival of the mail train, the station master would also shout curses. Asked why he did this, he explained that whenever he rang the bell, people all over the town woke up and invoked curses on his head. In order to fend these off, he redirected the malevolence back against the townspeople.

By the beginning of the twentieth century, scientists knew a great deal about the nature of light waves. One of the things they thought they knew was that light is an imponderable, that if it consisted of waves of radiation it could have no weight and would exert no pressure. Einstein's Theory of Relativity predicted that, on the contrary, light particles have weight and should be subject to gravitation. During the 1918 eclipse of the sun, he was proved spectacularly right. Measurements showed that the light rays actually bent as they passed through the sun's gravitational field. Nowadays, scientists design spaceships with 'light sails' to exploit the pressure exerted by light waves.

Orthodox science has yet to accept the idea of thought pressure and decrees that thought is supposed to be an imponderable. There are many scientists who, in the face of much evidence, decline to accept the reality of telepathy. Nevertheless, evidence has continued to accumulate until the point has now come when the only way to deny telepathy is to ignore the facts, or to refuse to examine them closely. The only way to explain many of these facts is to assume that thought, like light, can exert its own kind of pressure.

A final question – if we are higher up the evolutionary ladder than other animals, why is it that Brick's lions, like many dogs and other pets, seem to possess more highly developed telepathic powers than we? The answer may be that we have allowed just as powerful faculties in us to fall into disuse. In our most primitive form, our capacities may have been as highly developed as those of other animals – more highly developed, probably, or we might not have survived against predators. As we developed tools, the use of fire, and other techniques, we had less and less need for such innate powers. We needed reason and conscious awareness rather than instinct and subconscious awareness.

Humankind seems always to have been more interested in

power than in inner awareness. This desire for power is the scarlet thread we shall find running through the history of men of strange powers.

CHAPTER 23

THE WILL TO POWER

History reveals that some have learned to control the myste-
rious powers of their minds. The impulse to wield power
over fellow human beings seems to be a universal one and
perhaps no power is so tempting as the ability to control the
thoughts and actions of others. Old Testament prophets
arranging duels with pagan gods, Simon Magus challenging
St. Peter, and the half-legendary figure of the medieval
magician Faust, are examples of men using their psychic
powers to influence others – with widely differing motives.
The great magicians appear to share common traits –
egoism and the need to impress.

In the mid-1930s, a young American psychologist named
Abraham Maslow, spent most of his vacation in the monkey house
of New York's Bronx Zoo. The thing that impressed him most
about the animals' behaviour was that they all seemed to be sex
maniacs. Every minute of the day, males were mounting females,
males were mounting other males, females were mounting other
females. It looked like a simian Sodom and Gomorrah. Maslow's
first conclusion was that this behaviour was proof of Sigmund
Freud's view that sex is the most important of all animal urges. It
was only much later that another solution dawned on him – the
animals were demonstrating dominance behaviour.

Zoologists have grasped the full importance of the concept of
dominance only in recent years. Farmers, however, have known
·about it for centuries. In the farmyard, the most dominant
chicken can peck all the others; the second most dominant can
peck all except the most dominant, and so on down to the

weakest, who has no other to peck and may be pecked by all the others. The same pecking order can be seen everywhere in nature among jackdaws, baboons, wolves, rats, mice and other animals that live in groups.

What about human beings? Civilization has made us appear to be less obsessed with dominance, but anyone who has worked in a large office or factory knows this is untrue. The pecking order and the concern with status are still there, even if they are partly hidden by conventions of social behaviour. In primitive societies, the dominance hierarchy is absolutely clear, for it is part of the social structure. The ruler seems to wield a mysterious, almost divine power that is seldom if ever challenged. The young men submit themselves to all kinds of painful tests to establish their right to a place in the dominance hierarchy.

Our primitive ancestors knew all about the pecking order and the will to power, but when people began to live in cities, the old, carefully graduated society structure gave way to the disorganized scramble for status. Nowadays, we refer to such a scramble as the 'rat race', but this is unfair to the rats. Of all creatures, none is so obsessed by the will to power as man. From what we know of magicians, it seems likely that magic developed as an instrument of this will to power.

It seems certain that primitive man was familiar with what we have called 'thought pressure'. Palaeolithic cave paintings, some of them 20,000 years old, show tribal shamans (magician-priest-doctor) performing magical operations to aid the hunters. The anthropologist Ivar Lissner, has described how modern shamans still perform these operations. The shaman makes a drawing or clay model of an animal that is to be hunted. Then, by means of spells, he summons it to a certain place. The following day the hunters go to that place – and find the animal there. In his book *Patterns of Islands*, Sir Arthur Grimble describes the ceremony of 'calling the porpoises', which he witnessed in the Gilbert Islands. The shaman fell asleep in his hut and entered a trancelike state in which he invited the porpoises to a feast. When he awoke, he rushed out of the hut. All of the villagers ran into the sea and stood there armed with clubs. Shoals of seemingly hypnotized porpoises then swam gently into shore, where they were dragged onto the beach and killed by the villagers.

Modern man finds it impossible to understand how this magic works, but it is obviously only one step away from Messing's Psi power over the bank clerk that enabled him to rob a bank unarmed. Primitive man also used magic against other human beings. We are not sure, precisely, when this began to happen but we are reasonably certain that it did happen because at a certain. point in history, some of our distant ancestors suddenly stopped making models and drawings of other men. Why? Because they realized that if magic was potent against deer and bison, it could be effective against people. The mind power that could lure animals to their destruction could also destroy human beings. So anybody who made a drawing or model of a person immediately became suspect. This suspicion still applies among some primitive people today. They generally refuse to be photographed in the belief that the camera is capable of stealing the soul.

Slowly, over the course of many thousands of years, the tribal shaman evolved into the modern sorcerer. That is, he ceased to be what is called a white witch – a benevolent and helpful worker of magic – and became more interested in obtaining power for himself. We can see this transformation beginning in the Old Testament prophets, such as Moses, Joshua, Elijah and Daniel. It is true that they are men of God and that their power apparently comes from God. But it is significant how often they are engaged in magical contests in which they demonstrate their power at the expense of competing magicians. Aaron throws down his rod in front of the Pharaoh and it turns into a snake. The rival Egyptian magicians do the same thing and their rods also become snakes. But Aaron's snake eats up all the other snakes. Elijah challenges 450 priests of Baal to a test of magic in which they are to call on their god to light the fire under a sacrificial bullock. Their god fails them. Elijah, with great dramatic flair, tells his people to drench his bullock and firewood with water three times. Then he calls upon Jehovah. The God of the Jews sends down a fire that consumes the bullock, the wood and the water. After this, Elijah orders the people to kill all the priests of Baal. The will to power swaggers through the whole story.

The desire to dominate, to assert themselves, to humiliate or destroy those who oppose them, is something that can be observed again and again in the lives of the great magicians. Moreover, the magical contest – the battle with a rival – is a standard feature of the lives of the magicians. In the first century AD, the Greek magician Apollonius of Tyana engaged in a contest with a rival named Euphrates. Simon Magus, the magician of Samaria referred to in the Acts of the Apostles, was supposed to have been challenged by St. Peter. The legend is that Simon conjured up huge black hounds that rushed at Peter. The apostle held out a loaf of holy bread and the hounds vanished into thin air. In one version of the legend, Simon then rose into the air, hovered for a moment and flew through a window. Peter fell to his knees and prayed, whereupon Simon plummeted to the ground. He died from his injuries in this fall.

There can be no doubt that many such stories are pure invention. Others, however, are too detailed – and too widely reported – to be wholly invented. The interesting question is, what genuine powers did men such as Simon Magus possess? The account of him given in the Acts of the Apostles is, understandably, belittling. Describing himself as 'some great one', Simon angered St. Peter by offering him money in exchange for the gift of the Holy Spirit. Christian documents are inclined to regard Simon as a charlatan. He claimed to be able to make himself invisible, change himself into an animal and walk unharmed through fire. The Christians said that all this was achieved by bewitching the senses of the onlookers. Modern writers have taken this to mean that he used some form of hypnosis. For example, legend says that when Simon went to Rome, Nero ordered him to be decapitated by one of his officers. Simon, however, bewitched the officer into decapitating a ram instead. When he reappeared with his head still on his shoulders, Nero was so impressed by his powers that he made Simon his court magician.

But was Simon's means of control over the officer ordinary hypnosis or was it the kind of Psi power exercised by Wolf Messing on the bank clerk? The latter is altogether more likely, because hypnosis takes the co-operation of the person about to be hypnotized. It is unlikely that Simon was able to make himself invisible or turn himself into an animal. But he certainly seemed to have command of the power of thought pressure, just as some people are born with a green thumb.

At this point, it is time to raise the question of how such a power could work. Let us look more closely at some of the recorded examples.

The poet W. B. Yeats was a member of the Order of the Golden Dawn, one of the first and best known occult societies of late nineteenth-century England. In his autobiography, Yeats describes an incident that occurred on a walk taken by one of the other Golden Dawn members and MacGregor Mathers, one of the order's founders. 'Look at those sheep', said Mathers. 'I am going to imagine myself a ram.' The sheep immediately began to run after him.

Mathers could also use his strange powers on people, just as the Swedish playwright August Strindberg, believed he himself could. Once, when Strindberg was eating alone in a restaurant, he recognized two friends among some drunk people at another table. To his dismay, one of them began to approach him. Strindberg fixed his eyes on the man. At this, the friend looked bewildered and returned to his table apparently convinced that Strindberg was a stranger.

Strindberg once attempted to practice black magic and he believed that his later suffering and bad luck was a result of this dabbling with evil forces. It was when he was separated from his second wife. He wanted desperately to bring about a reconciliation and had to think of a way of seeing her. He decided to use his telepathic powers to make his daughter just sick enough to require a visit from him. Using a photograph of the girl, he tried to bring about her illness. When the two children of his first marriage got sick a short time later, he felt that he was responsible and that his use of the evil eye had misfired. Strindberg dates his misfortunes from then on.

One of the most celebrated German criminal cases of 1936, concerned a hypnotist named Franz Walter, who liked to pose as a doctor. One day, boarding a train to Heidelberg, he entered a carriage occupied by a young woman. Walter talked to her and discovered she was on her way to see a doctor about stomach pains. Walter sympathized, told her he was a doctor, and invited her to have coffee with him. She felt frightened and wanted to refuse but when Walter took her hand, she found she could not. She later recalled that 'it seemed to me as if I no longer had a will of my own.' Walter had somehow hypnotized her without her consent. Later, when he wrote to her ordering her to come to him in another town, she felt strangely giddy and immediately went to him.

Under hypnosis, she was raped by Walter, who then ordered her to become a prostitute and to give him her earnings. When she later married, he hypnotized her into making several attempts on her husband's life. The husband eventually reported her behaviour to the police and a police doctor, Ludwig Mayer, recognized some of the symptoms of hypnotism. He managed to de-hypnotize her and unlock the memories of her ordeals, which Walter had ordered her to forget. Walter was tried, found guilty and sentenced to 10 years in prison.

There is a link between these examples. Mathers' ability to attract the sheep is an example of the kind of telepathy that can exist between humans and animals. But Mathers was deceiving the sheep in the same sort of way that Wolf Messing deceived the bank clerk. Telepathy can be used for a kind of hypnosis or suggestion. In the case of Strindberg and his drunk friend, the playwright projected the suggestion, 'I am not Strindberg' so that the friend turned and walked away. In the Walter case, Dr Mayer established that the hypnotist had hypnotized the young woman against her will. There can be no doubt that Walter immediately recognized her as a good hypnotic subject. It is also clear from Mayer's book on the case that Walter was driven by a 'will to power'. A coarse, rather stupid man, he pretended he was a quali-fied doctor and many incidents in the case reveal the pleasure he took in his power over his victim. The interesting point in this case is that Walter did not hypnotize his victim by the usual means – for example, by getting her to focus her eyes on a swinging pendulum – but he did it instantaneously by some kind of suggestion. There was some natural form of sympathy between the two, although it seems akin to the sympathy between a snake and a hypnotized rabbit.

When we look more closely at these cases, we find another interesting link. Mathers was a strange mixture of charlatan and genuine scholar. He liked to pose as a Scottish laird of distinguished ancestry while, in fact, he was the son of a clerk and was born in London. He was a quarrelsome man, intensely jealous of his status as head of the Order of the Golden Dawn. He was also driven by a restless will to power. Strindberg had a paranoid egoism that is evident in much of his work. According to the police doctor, Franz Walter also was an egoist driven by the craving to be admired. Mathers, Strindberg and Walter all lacked a stable background to their lives. It would be scarcely an exaggeration to describe them as homeless wanderers. In all three we see the basic characteristics of the magician – the desire for fame, the will to power, and a natural talent for using thought pressure to dominate others.

After Simon Magus, the most famous magician in European history is Faust, also known as Dr. Faustus. The Faust legend has maintained its potency for almost five centuries and has inspired at least three great works of literature – Christopher Marlowe's *Dr Faustus* (1604), Goethe's *Faust* (1808 and 1832), and Thomas Mann's *Doctor Faustus* (1947) – as well as many musical works. From all these, the picture that emerges of Faust is of a brilliant, proud, restless man who longs to share the secrets of the gods. But these characteristics have evolved over the centuries and as we go backward in time, we come closer to the truth about the person who called himself Faust. Thomas Mann's Faust is a great musician; Goethe's Faust is a restless scholar, chafing against the frustration of being merely human; Marlowe's Faustus is a scholar who has been led into temptation by the lust for power. The book on which all these were based is Johann Spies' *Historia von D. Johann Faustus*, which appeared in Berlin in 1587. Its hero is little more than a magical confidence trickster. Significantly, his chief gift is hypnosis – although, of course, the author does not use that word.

In a typical episode in the Spies book, Faust goes to a Jew and offers to leave behind his arm or leg as security for a loan. The Jew accepts and Faust appears to saw off his leg. Embarrassed and disgusted by this, the Jew later throws the leg into a river – whereupon Faust appears and demands his leg back. The Jew is forced to pay him heavy compensation. In another anecdote, Faust asks a wagoner with a load of hay how much hay he will allow him to eat for a few pence. The wagoner says jokingly, 'As much as you like.' When Faust has eaten half the wagonload, the wagoner repents his generosity and offers Faust a gold piece on condition he leaves the rest undevoured. When he reaches home the wagoner discovers that his load is intact, 'for the delusion which the doctor had raised was vanished.'

Even the Faust of this original book is described as 'a scholar and a gentleman'. He is said to have been the son of honest German peasants, born near Weimar in 1491, but brought up by a well-to-do uncle in Wittenberg. This uncle sent him to university. Faust's 'strong powers of mind' soon distinguish him and his friends urge him to enter the Church. But Faust has greater ambitions. He begins to dabble in sorcery. He studies Chaldean, Greek and Arabic. He takes his degree of Doctor of Divinity and also a medical degree. In due course, he becomes a famous doctor. It is intellectual brilliance that is his downfall, 'the boldness of his profane enquiries' – a quality that later generations would consider a virtue, and for which even Spies has a sneaking admiration. Faust wishes to become a great magician, and this is why he invokes the Devil. Having entered into his pact with the Devil, Faust is corrupted by the Prince of Darkness, who proceeds to fill him with greed and lust for power.

At this point, it is worth quoting the *Historia* on a subject that has some bearing on the lives of magicians. 'It used to be an old saying that the magician, charm he ever so wisely for a year together, was never a sixpence richer for all his efforts.' This belief that unusual powers cannot be used for financial gain is fundamental and persistent. And there seems to be some truth in it. None of the great magicians from Simon Magus to MacGregor Mathers has died rich and most of them have died paupers. The few who have succeeded in living comfortably – Emanuel Swedenborg and Gurdjieff, for example – made their money in other ways than through their dabbling in magic.

When we pass from the Faust legends to the obscure original, as described by some of his contemporaries, we encounter exactly the sort of person that this investigation has led us to expect, a coarse, vulgar, boastful man, with some natural talent and an overmastering desire for fame. We don't know if he was named

Georg Sabellicus or Johannes, but he was often called Faustus
Junior. The first we hear of him is in 1507 when, through the good
offices of a nobleman, he obtained a post as a teacher in a boys'
school in Kreuznach near Frankfurt. Apparently he was a homo-
sexual, for he proceeded to seduce some of his pupils, 'indulging
in the most dastardly kind of lewdness'. When found out, he fled.
In 1509, Johannes Faust was given a degree in theology in
Heidelberg, some 40 miles from Kreuznach. In 1513, the
canon of St. Mary's church in Gotha in eastern Germany,
recorded that he had heard Georg Faust, known as 'the demigod
of Heidelberg', boasting and talking nonsense in an inn in nearby
Erfurt.

The alchemist, Trithemius, recalls a meeting with Faustus
Junior as early as 1507 and dismisses him as a fool, a boaster and
a charlatan. In the few other references we have, he is casting
horoscopes, making prophecies, or being driven from town to
town by his unsavoury reputation as a sodomite and *necromancer*
(one who foretells the future by communicating with the dead).
From Johanne Wier, an acquaintance of Faust who wrote about
him, we learn that Faust was wont to boast about 'his friend the
Devil' – which may have been nothing more than a typical piece
of bombast. A story of Faust's malicious humour recorded by
Wier describes how Faust, when a prisoner in the castle of Baron
Hermann of Batenburg, offered to show the nobleman's chaplain
how to remove his beard without a razor, in exchange for a bottle
of wine. The chaplain was to rub his beard with the 'magic
formula' arsenic. The gullible chaplain did this. His beard fell
out, just as Faust had prophesied – but it took most of the chaplain's skin with it. Wier also tells us that Faust was a drunken
wanderer who spent much of his time in low taverns, impressing
the locals with conjuring tricks. Other contemporary chroniclers
describe him as a liar and 'low juggler'.

We do not know when Faust died – it was probably in the
1540s – but we do know how his legendary fame began. A Swiss
Protestant clergyman, Johanne Gast, once dined with Faust and
was unfavourably impressed by him – perhaps because of Faust's
hints at his pact with the Devil. At all events, Gast later spoke of
Faust in one of his sermons, declaring that he had been strangled
by the Devil and that his corpse had persisted in lying on its face,

although it had been turned on its back five times. This story had the right touch of horror to appeal to the imaginations of his congregation. Soon other stories grew up. One told how the Devil had twisted Faust's head around completely so that it looked down his back. Another recounted how, toward the end of his life, Faust began to hope that he might escape the Devil's clutches – but the trembling of the house at night warned him that the end was near.

The sixteenth century was an age of religious persecution, a time when a man could be executed on the mere suspicion that he did not believe in the Trinity. The very idea of a man selling his soul to the Devil was enough to make Faust's contemporaries turn pale. Little wonder, then, that Spies' *Historia* became one of the most popular works of its time. Phillip Melancthon, a follower of Luther, also preached about Faust. He gilded the lily somewhat with a story that Faust had defeated and eaten a rival magician in Vienna. Luther also has two slighting references to Faust in his *Table Talk*, from which it is clear that he regarded Faust as a common charlatan, rather than a demonic wonder worker. The only powers that some of Faust's educated contemporaries were willing to grant him, were the gifts of casting accurate horoscopes and of foretelling the future. In 1535, for instance, Faust correctly predicted that the Bishop of Munster would recapture the city and in 1540, he foretold the defeat of the European armies In Venezuela.

Legend has made Faust the most famous figure in the history of necromancy. But when we peer through the legendary mist, what do we find? Most of the more sensational stories about the man as told by people who knew him, tell of feats that have been more or less duplicated by other men of strange powers down the ages. It is difficult to decide whether this helps to support or to discredit Faust's credentials as a magician. When we try to sift fact from legend, it becomes clear that Faust knew something about hypnosis. It may be that he also knew how to conjure poltergeists. The priest, Gast, claimed that when Faust was angered by the poor hospitality offered to him by some monks, he sent a poltergeist to trouble them. Apparently the rattling spirit created such a furore that the monks had to abandon their monastery. Accounts made it plain that Faust was stupid, boastful and malicious. The same is true of many men of strange powers. As we shall see, Faust's restless egoism, his desire to impress and his need to bend nature to his will, are characteristic of many of the best-known magicians, from Simon Magus onward. Magicians are not comfortable people to know.

CHAPTER 24

WONDERWORKERS

Are there such things as miracles? Many of the strange phenomena viewed so suspiciously in the West are accepted calmly in the East: yoga is full of wonders and the mystical exercises of Zen Buddhism are designed to integrate mental and physical powers for perfection of action. Also, the stories of Christian saints are full of miraculous happenings, unexplainable by the laws of nature. Swedenborg, scientist and mystic, had amazingly vivid visions of heaven and hell – and then astounded the sceptical with casual feats of clairvoyance in very ordinary matters. Different as they are, the evidence seems to indicate that these wonderworker do have qualities in common.

When Louis Jacolliot, an eminent French lawyer and later a chief justice, went to India in the early 1860s, he was a free-thinker with a profound scepticism about religion. However, when his servant announced one morning that a *fakir* (Hindu holy man) wished to see him, his curiosity got the better of him and he decided to see the man. Jacolliot opened the conversation by saying that he had heard that *fakirs* possess the power to move objects without touching them – a power that is now called psychokinesis. The *fakir* – a thin, bony little man – replied that he himself possessed no such power but that spirits lent him their aid. The Frenchman asked if he might see a demonstration of these powers. The Hindu said that he would demonstrate and requested seven flowerpots filled with earth, seven thin wooden rods each a yard long and seven large leaves from any tree in the garden.

The wooden rods were stuck in the flowerpots so that they were upright. Then a hole was made in the centre of each leaf, and the leaves were impaled on each rod so that they fell down and covered the flowerpots. The fakir stood up, joined his hands above his head and intoned a Hindu prayer. After that he seemed to go into a state of ecstasy, his hands outstretched toward the flowerpots. Suddenly, Jacolliot felt a breeze on his face. During the next 10 minutes, it blew several times. Slowly and gently the leaves began to rise up the wooden rods, then to float downward again. Jacolliot went closer to see if the Hindu could somehow be causing them to move by a trick. But the leaves continued to rise and fall undisturbed as Jacolliot passed between them and the *fakir*. For the remainder of that morning, Jacolliot tried different tests to discover if the *fakir* used trickery. He arranged the flowerpots and rods himself in case of collusion between his servant and the *fakir*. He had the rods fixed into holes bored in a plank. It made no difference; the leaves still rose and fell as before.

Finally, the *fakir* asked Jacolliot if he would like to ask a question of the spirits. In doing so, Jacolliot used an alphabet of brass letters with which he printed his name in his books. Thinking of a dead friend, he began to take letters out of their bag one by one. When he pulled out the letter 'A' the leaves moved. He returned the letter to the bag and repeated the process. This time the leaves moved when he pulled out the letter 'L'. By this process, the leaves slowly spelled out the message, 'Albain Brunier died at Bourg-en-Bresse, 3 January 1856.' This was the friend Jacolliot had been thinking of.

Jacolliot concluded that the Hindu had simply read his mind. He thought of a way to test this suspicion and tried it with the *fakir* next day. As he held the bag containing the letters, he concentrated on changing the name to 'Halbin Pruniet'. The leaves spelled out 'Halbin Pruniet' instead of 'Albain Brunier'; but no amount of concentration could change the date of Brunier's death, or the name of the city in which he died.

Jacolliot had experiences in psychokinesis with other *fakirs*, one of whom was able to hold down a small table so firmly that Jacolliot's attempts to move it only tore off one of its folding leaves. The same *fakir* dropped a papaw seed into a pot filled with damp earth, went into a trance for two hours and caused the seed to sprout into an eight-inch-tall plant. Jacolliot's most startling experience was when a *fakir* named Covindasamy, caused a phosphorescent cloud to form in the air. After a moment, white hands appeared in the cloud. One of them held Jacolliot's hand for a moment. At his request, it plucked a flower from a bowl and dropped it at his feet. Next, the *fakir* conjured up the shade of an old Brahmin priest. When Jacolliot asked it whether it was once alive on earth, the word 'Am' (yes) appeared on its breast in glowing letters as if written with phosphorus. Finally, the *fakir* materialized another shade that moved around the room playing a flute. When the apparition vanished, it left the flute on the ground. It was a flute that Jacolliot had borrowed from a rajah and that he had in his locked house.

What is so impressive about these stories is that Jacolliot does not write as an occultist. The book in which they appear is a sober study of Hinduism and these stories of his experiments are added almost as an afterthought. He is merely interested in recording inexplicable events, to which he attaches no undue importance. Not being concerned with psychical research, which in the 1860s had not yet attracted much attention, he does not attempt to classify the phenomena as the products of extrasensory perception, telepathy or psychokinesis. He puts it that, 'What we call spirit force is called by the Hindus *artahancarasya* or the force of I.' It seems clear that he is referring to what we have called Psi power. The *fakirs* themselves believe that all such phenomena spring from the same source – the spirits. The fact that Jacolliot actually saw entities that appeared to be spirits, suggests that this idea cannot be wholly dismissed.

Most Hindus find nothing strange about such marvels. The ancient Hindu scriptures – the Vedic hymns, the *Upanishads*, the *Bhagavad Gita* – all teach that the human soul, the Atman, is identical with the godhead, Brahman. Thus, if one could penetrate through all a man's outer layers to the very depth of his being, one would find Brahman. Stripped of its religious essence, this echoes the central conviction of occult philosophers – the deeper we penetrate our innermost being, the closer we approach the strange powers that all men possess, but that few can tap or consciously use.

The science of yoga, which is basically a system of meditation, is intended to enable man to gain control over his body and emotions and to move inward toward the 'source of power, meaning and purpose'. A *yogi* assumes one of the traditional yoga postures, withdraws deep into himself, concentrates his gaze and attempts to still his mind. The aim is total inner serenity. In attempting yoga, many westerners make the mistake of simply suspending the mind, as if sitting in church. Consequently, they find it difficult to prevent it from wandering. The more experienced practitioner soon realizes that, although the posture suggests absolute rest, the mind is actually in gear, concentrating with a certain earnestness as if engaged in some difficult and dangerous operation. In the imagery of the Buddhist scriptures, the mind is like a pond and the aim is to still the pond until it becomes a perfect mirror reflecting the moon, man's basic divinity. Great importance is attached to *prana* (breathing) because the breath is identified with life, or the spirit.

Eugen Herrigel, a German professor who taught in Japan for many years, determined to attempt to master the secrets of Zen, the peculiarly Japanese form of Buddhism. A central aim of Zen studies is the total integration of one's mental and physical powers. One of Herrigel's spiritual exercises directed toward this end, was learning how to draw an archer's bow correctly. He watched his Zen master draw the bow without effort and release the arrow casually. It flew to the centre of the target. When Herrigel tried it, he found it almost impossible even to draw the string of the massive bow.

After a long period of frustration, Herrigel was told by the Zen master that he was not breathing correctly. 'Press your breath down gently after breathing in so that the abdominal wall is tightly stretched, and hold it there for a while. Then breathe out as slowly and evenly as possible and, after a short pause, draw a quick breath of air again – out and in continually in a rhythm that will gradually settle itself. If it is done properly, you will feel the shooting becoming easier every day. For through this breathing you will not only discover the source of all spiritual strength, but will also cause this source to flow more abundantly, and to pour more easily through your limbs the more relaxed you are.' It took Herrigel a year to succeed in drawing the bow with this perfect ease. Then came another long struggle, this time to release the arrow without a jerk, 'as if the bow string had cut through the thumb that held it.'

What Herrigel had to learn so painfully was to use his whole being, his subconscious as well as his conscious mind, in drawing and releasing the bow. Once this was learned, he had also learned the basic secret of Zen. This union of every part of one's self also enables men and women to begin to grasp the perfect truth about Being. For Zen Buddhism holds that our central problem is that we have become too self-conscious, or rather, that we have developed what the novelist D. H. Lawrence called 'head consciousness'.

We are all familiar with the sensation of doing some simple physical activity badly because we are thinking about it. For instance, if we are aware of someone staring at the way we walk, we begin to walk awkwardly. If something makes us self-conscious about our accent, we begin to trip over words. According to the mystical tradition, this awkwardness has reached deep into human consciousness so that most of our powers are tied in a knot and unable to find expression. To some extent, relaxation can help to release these powers. For example, the fashionable cult of Transcendental Meditation is basically a kind of self-hypnosis that brings deep relaxation, leading to the release of hidden powers. We are out of tune with ourselves. We oppose ourselves like clumsy adolescents tripping over our own feet. All spiritual disciplines aim at removing this self-division. But, as Zen recognizes, the basic problem is how to arouse our 'true will'.

All the mystical traditions, Western as well as Eastern, recognize that the awakening of the true will can occur in a single flash. That is why the Zen master may sometimes kick his disciple violently. In one of the Zen stories, the disciple is awakened to a state of total enlightenment by such a kick. Similarly, there is a story told of the nineteenth-century Hindu saint, Ramakrishna. When he was a young priest, Ramakrishna became deeply depressed because he seemed unable either to escape from the boredom of everyday existence or to catch a glimpse of Brahman. One day, in despair, he seized a sword and was about to plunge it into himself. Suddenly the Divine Mother revealed herself to him. Ramakrishna was filled with a vision of an endless sea of vitality and self-knowledge and with such deep ecstasy that he became unconscious. Undoubtedly the threat of death aroused his true will – showed him, as it were, the trick of parting the curtain of everyday existence that obstructs our view of reality.

According to Ramakrishna, such powers as Jacolliot's *fakir* exhibited are merely the first consequences of this deeper knowledge of reality and are utterly without value. Again and again, he insists on the triviality of the feats that are traditionally ascribed to *yogis* and *fakirs* – for example, walking on water, moving objects without touching them and climbing a rope that hangs unsupported in the air. The *yogi* who wants to do such things, says Ramakrishna, is at a rudimentary level of spiritual progress. The *yogi* who has tasted *samadhi* – the moment of absolute union with Brahman, the moment in which he realizes that his own soul is Brahman – cares only to strive for continual union. The conjuring tricks he regards with contempt.

Yet these examples of strange powers, called conjuring tricks by Ramakrishna, are a vital part of the Hindu tradition. One of the most extraordinary spiritual autobiographies of this century is Paramhansa Yogananda's *Autobiography of a Yogi*, to which the eminent orientalist, W. Y. Evans-Wentz, wrote an introduction that vouched for its authenticity. The book breathes the essential spirit of the Hindu religion, yet it is so full of tales of miracles that the sceptical westerner's first reaction is to dismiss it as a pack of lies. At the age of eight, Yogananda was dangerously ill with cholera. He was told by his mother to bow mentally, being too weak to move physically, to a picture of a great *yogi* on the wall of his room. As he did so, the room seemed to glow with light and his fever disappeared. Shortly after this, he quarrelled with his sister about some ointment she was using to cure a boil. He told her that the following day her boil would be twice as large and that he would have a boil on his forearm. Both things turned out as he said, and his sister accused him of being a sorcerer.

From this point on the stories become ever more incredible. Yogananda tells of visiting a *yogi* named Pranabananda. The *yogi* told him that a certain friend of his was on his way. At exactly the moment foretold, the friend arrived. Yogananda asked him how he had come to be there. The friend explained that Pranabananda had approached him in the street and told him that Yogananda was waiting in his room. Then the *yogi* had vanished into the crowd. What baffled Yogananda and his friend was that Pranabananda had been with Yogananda throughout the previous hour. It seems, then, that Pranabananda had been able to project his astral body – the spiritual second body.

In another chapter of his autobiography, Yogananda describes visiting the 'perfume saint', a *yogi* able to induce the smell of any perfume. At Yogananda's request, the *yogi* caused a scentless flower to smell of jasmine. When Yogananda arrived home, his sister was also able to smell the scent of jasmine on the flower, thus allaying any suspicion that the *yogi* had managed merely to suggest the perfume to Yogananda.

Some of the most incredible of Yogananda's stories are about Babaji, the nineteenth-century 'Yogi-Christ'. One tells of how he allowed a disciple to hurl himself from a high crag and then resurrected him. Another recounts how he materialized an immense golden palace in the Himalayas. Yogananda tells these stories at second hand and it may be that he intended them to be accepted as myths or parables, rather than as literal truth. But the stories he tells of his own *guru* (religious teacher or spiritual adviser), Sri Yukteswar, are almost as astonishing. Yukteswar also appears simultaneously in two places, Calcutta and Serampore. One day, when his disciples are about to attend a festival in stifling heat, Yukteswar assures them that a cooling umbrella of cloud will be sent to help them. As he said this, the sky clouds over and a gentle rain falls during the festival. However, Yukteswar did not claim to have conjured up the rain himself.

The climax of Yogananda's book is the description of the death and resurrection of Yukteswar. He predicted the time of his death and died exactly when he had foretold. After his death, he appeared to Yogananda in a hotel room in Bombay and Yogananda insists that he was there in the flesh. Before vanishing, Yukteswar explained to his disciple at length that his task was now to serve as a saviour on an astral plane, or another dimension of the world.

It is possible, of course, to dismiss the whole of Yogananda's book as the invention of a religious crank. But before doing so, it is well to bear in mind that most of the strange powers described in it have been observed and vouched for many times in the records of the reputable Society for Psychical Research. Moreover, we know that many *yogis* and *fakirs* have remarkable control over their bodies. Some have survived after being buried alive for some time – a feat that is beyond the understanding of most of us. Until we have a more systematic knowledge of the possibilities of higher states of consciousness, it may be as well to keep an open mind.

How, for example, do we account for the apparently ghastly self-mutilations of the Moslem holy men called the dervishes? Gurdjieff's disciple John G. Bennett, has described a Moslem dervish ceremony that he witnessed twice in Istanbul. The dervishes knelt on the floor, swaying as they chanted the name of Allah. At a certain point of intense emotion, they began to drive spikes and skewers through their cheeks and arms. One old man lay down on the ground and placed a sharp sword, edge downward, across his stomach. Another man stepped onto the sword, balancing himself by holding the hands of two men on either side. When the man stepped down, the old dervish raised the sword from his body and revealed that it had not even made a mark. Bennett examined the sword after the ceremony. It was as sharp as a razor and bore no trace of blood.

The Western temperament is more given to intellectual speculation and is less mystical than the Eastern – which partly explains why the technological advances of the West have been so much greater than those of the East. All the same, the West has produced many great mystics who believe that certain kinds of truth are reached, not through logical reasoning or the experiences of the senses, but through some kind of spiritual intuition. The father of Western mysticism was the Greek philosopher Plato, who lived in the fifth century BC. In his *Symposium*, Plato writes about the teachings of his mentor, Socrates. The older philosopher explains how the lover begins by desiring attractive bodies, then learns to admire beautiful soul and ends by loving the beauty of the universe itself. This, says he, is the true aim of all love.

Socrates' insistence on the love of the impersonal has remained the central theme of Western mysticism ever since. The Greek philosopher Plotinus, who taught in Rome in the third century AD, described the aim of the mystic as 'the flight of the Alone to the Alone'. Later, Christian mystics often used words such as 'darkness' and 'emptiness' to describe the God of the true mystic. In the Middle Ages, when alchemy began to fascinate those of a philosophical turn of mind, mysticism and magic became oddly mixed together. The alchemist sought the Philosopher's Stone, a substance believed capable of turning base metals into gold and the elixir of everlasting life. The mystic sought union with God. For many thinkers, the two kinds of search became identical.

One of the most remarkable of these mystical alchemists was the German shoemaker Jakob Boehme, born in Gorlitz, Silesia in eastern Germany. At the age of 25 (in 1600), Boehme had his first experience of mystical insight. He found himself staring at a pewter dish whose polished surface reflected the sunlight. Gazing into it, Boehme found himself drifting into a kind of ecstasy. He had the sensation of being able to see into the heart of all nature. He walked out to the fields and it seemed to him that the trees and grass were transparent and lit by a kind of flame from within.

How can we explain such mystical ecstasies? They seem to be due to the release of a flood of emotional energy – a flood so powerful that it overwhelms the senses. Many people have experienced something of the kind – perhaps when listening to music or looking at magnificent scenery, so we are inclined to dismiss such experiences as mere emotion. But we fail to understand the possibilities of mere emotion. Boehme's mystical intensities carried him into a realm in which he seemed to see into the heart of the universe. He wrote of a later ecstasy, that 'the Gate was opened to me, so that in a quarter of an hour I knew more than if I had been many years at a university.' He tried to express this insight in a number of strange works. His first book caused him a great deal of trouble – the local clergyman denounced him as a false prophet and the magistrates ordered him to stop writing. Fortunately, he ignored them and produced a number of strange and difficult masterpieces full of the language of the alchemists, attempting to describe the soul's relation to God. Although he died in relative obscurity, his fame afterward spread all over Europe. He influenced another great visionary, the English poet and painter William Blake, whose work vibrates with the same feeling of strange hidden realities lying behind the curtain of the everyday world.

The state of ecstasy can produce remarkable effects. There is reliable evidence that it caused a devoutly religious monk to rise into the air and fly. Giuseppe Desa was born at Apulia, Italy in 1603. He was feeble and sickly as a child. At the age of 22, he joined the Franciscan order and soon became well known for his prayers and fasting. One day after Mass, he suddenly rose into the air, floated above the congregation, and hovered over the altar. The candle flames did not burn him. From this time on, Father Joseph, as he was now known, often levitated and flew considerable distances. Many eminent contemporaries witnessed this strange feat, including the great German philosopher Leibniz. There are so many apparently reliable records of his flights, that it seems probable they were not faked. Significantly, when a hostile and envious superior started to bully and humiliate him, Father Joseph ceased to fly. He recovered his spirits, however, and afterward flew through the air and embraced the statue of the virgin above the altar. A century after his death, he was canonized as St Joseph of Copertino.

Science cannot explain levitation, although there are thousands of well-authenticated cases on record, particularly from India. But then, neither can science explain how John G. Bennett, seriously weakened after a three-day attack of dysentery, could dig furiously for an hour without collapsing. We know little about the powers of the mind because, in most of us, they are undeveloped. If we lived in a world in which there was only the moon and no sun, no one would believe that light could cause sunburn or make forests burst into flames. We know the universe only to the extent of our, as yet, feeble attempts to perceive and measure it and the results are often absurd and contradictory.

One of the most eminent Protestant mystics was also a distinguished scientist and engineer. Emanuel Swedenborg was born in Stockholm in 1688 and began his career as a mathematician. He also studied watchmaking, carpentry and music. Later he became Assessor of the Swedish board of mines and demonstrated his engineering skill when he transported five ships overland for 15 miles, during his country's war with Denmark.

In 1744, when he was 56, Swedenborg had an overpowering dream in which a roaring wind flung him on his face. Then Jesus appeared and spoke the words, 'Well then, do it!' From this time onward, Swedenborg began to go into ecstatic trances and to see visions. His books contain vivid descriptions of journeys he claimed to have made through heaven and hell, under the guidance of angelic spirits.

One's first reaction to this is to conclude that Swedenborg must have gone mad. But people who met him and expected to find a lunatic, were surprised by his sanity and good humour. Moreover, his powers of clairvoyance were witnessed by many. One night, when about to sit down to dinner in Gothenburg, he suddenly turned pale and announced that a great fire had just broken out in Stockholm, 250 miles away. It was threatening his own house, he said. For the next two hours he was in a state of agitation. Then he said with relief, 'Thank heavens, the fire is under control. It had almost reached my doorstep.' The next day he wrote a detailed description of the fire to the governor of Gothenburg and the day after that, a letter arrived confirming to the last detail all that Swedenborg had said.

One day, when Swedenborg was at the royal court, the queen asked him, perhaps mockingly, if he had seen her deceased brother on his visits to heaven. Swedenborg replied gravely that he had not. The queen then remarked that, if Swedenborg met him, perhaps he would give him her greeting. The next time Swedenborg came to court, he told the queen that he had seen her brother and had given him her message. The brother, he said, sent his apologies for not having answered her last letter to him before he died but he would now do so through Swedenborg. The scientist then repeated her brother's reply to various points in her letter. The queen was dumbfounded as she declared, 'No one but God knows this secret.'

About this time, the Dutch ambassador to the Swedish court died. When his widow afterward received an invoice for a silver tea service, she was convinced that her husband had paid for it shortly before his death. But she could not find the receipt. She asked Swedenborg for help. A few days later as she sat with friends, Swedenborg told her, 'Your husband says the receipt is in the bureau upstairs.' 'Impossible', said the widow, 'I have searched it.' Swedenborg said that there was a secret drawer, which he described. The widow went to the bureau, found the secret drawer and opened it. The receipt was inside.

Many of Swedenborg's contemporaries believed that these

remarkable demonstrations proved that his visions of heaven and hell must be true. We should be more cautious. One of his books contains a description of Mars and its inhabitants, that is wholly nonsensical in the light of our present knowledge of the planet. We can only conclude that if Swedenborg had visions – as he almost certainly did – then some of them were false ones.

Of the more modern European wonderworkers, perhaps the most interesting is Jean-Marie-Baptiste Vianney, the curé (parish priest) of Ars. In 1818, at the age of 34, Vianney was appointed to the parish of Ars near Lyon. He was a simple man, not particularly intelligent and generally narrow-minded. Yet his piety and reported understanding of the human soul, soon spread his reputation far afield. He had mystical visions, although he would say little about them – and many seriously ill people who came to see him were cured. His most famous miracle took place during a year of famine when there were only a few cupfuls of wheat left in the village granary. Vianney prayed all night. The next morning when a girl tried to enter the granary, she found the door blocked. Forcing it open, she found the place full of grain – enough to feed most of the parish for months.

This story was not investigated by an independent observer, and one hardly needs to be a sceptic to be suspicious of it. But even allowing for the credulity of the more devoted members of his flock, Vianney seems to have possessed special powers, particularly of telepathy. As his fame spread, people came from far and wide to attend services at his church.

Powerful religious feelings sometimes seem able to release deep and hidden forces in the human soul. But it is important to realize that many of these powers are little more than by-products of our inner evolution. What is impressive about all the mystics, from Boehme to Yogananda, is not the wonders or visions. It is the sense they all share that the everyday world conceals some tremendous reality that all are capable of seeing, if they can discover how to look. We feel something of this kind in the paintings and poetry of William Blake. We feel it in Vincent Van Gogh's evocative painting *Starry Night*, which the artist painted with candles tied around his hat so that he could see the canvas in the dark. Works such as these suggest something of the ecstatic intensity experienced by Boehme, when he found himself looking 'into the heart of nature', or by Ramakrishna when he was over-whelmed by the vision of the Divine Mother. They give us a glimpse of the source of power, meaning and purpose that lies deep inside all human beings.

CHAPTER 25

MAGICIANS AND MYSTICS

Do the rituals of magic really hold the key that unlocks secret powers? What has happened to the men who have claimed success in the strange and mysterious world of spells and symbols? Cornelius Agrippa, living in the sixteenth century, believed he could summon spirits and his enemies feared it was true. Paracelsus, the arrogant physician, was gifted with a magical prowess in healing – and died from a fall while in a drunken stupor. Franz Anton Mesmer healed wealthy invalids in Paris, apparently by summoning powers within the patients that neither he nor they realized they possessed. Is magic a mystery even to the magician?

It was a windy, chilly evening in March 1865, and most of the inhabitants of the French village of Solliés-Farliede were indoors. A limping man approached the cottage of a workman and knocked on the door. The girl who opened it shrank back when she saw the unkempt stranger, whose beard was as tangled as a bird's nest. The man pointed to his mouth, then to his ears and shook his head, indicating that he was deaf-mute. The girl's father came to the door and, after the kindly fashion of country people, invited the tramp in for a meal. The girl, Josephine, kept house for her father. The only other occupant of the small country cottage was Josephine's 15-year-old brother.

From the first moment, Josephine felt terrified of the ugly stranger. His manners were eccentric and uncouth. Instead of filling his glass with wine, he poured in a little at a time, putting the bottle down several times. He made the sign of the cross over his glass before drinking, as if afraid the Devil was in it. After the meal, the girl's father questioned the man by means of pencil and paper. They learned that his name was Timotheus Castellan, that he had been a cork cutter and that he had had to abandon the trade after an injury to his hand. Now, he said, he travelled around the country making a living as a healer and water diviner. Curious neighbours came in to see the magician and all were impressed. That night, the tramp slept in a haystack. Josephine lay on her bed, fully dressed, her mind full of foreboding.

The next day her father and brother went off to work and Castellan went with them. Shortly afterward, however, he returned to the cottage. Josephine let him in and went about her housework. Several neighbours called in at the cottage, having heard about the wonderworker and brought him presents of food. One of them saw Castellan making strange signs in the air behind Josephine's back.

At lunchtime, the two ate together. Suddenly, Castellan stretched out his hand, pointing two fingers at Josephine. She immediately became unconscious. When she woke up, Castellan was sprinkling water on her face. Then he picked her up, carried her into the bedroom, and raped her. Although she was fully conscious, she was unable to move. At one point a neighbour knocked on the door and called her name but she found herself unable to reply.

Later that afternoon Castellan left the cottage, and beckoned to her. In a state of confusion she followed him. Neighbours asked her where she was going but though she answered, her words were unintelligible.

That night the couple stayed at a farmhouse and slept together. The next day they persuaded a farmer at the nearby village of La Cappelude to give them a bed. The farmer and his household were baffled by Josephine's behaviour. Sometimes she seemed like an infatuated newlywed, kissing and caressing the ugly deaf-mute; then suddenly she would turn away, as if nauseated. During the evening, she managed to talk to a girl who lived nearby and asked her if she could stay with her overnight. Castellan overheard their conversation, however, and ordered Josephine to remain with him. He made a sign with his hand. She collapsed in his arms and remained in a trance for an hour.

Two days later, the distraught girl succeeded in giving Castellan the slip. She approached a group of men and asked them to take her home. A search for the tramp began immediately but it turned out later that soon after the girl's escape, he had been arrested for vagrancy. Two doctors examined Josephine and pronounced that the tramp had deprived the girl of her will by 'magnetism' (hypnosis). A court sentenced him to 12 years' hard labour.

What are we to make of this sinister beggar? He was undoubtedly a confidence man and a liar. Josephine declared that she had escaped while he was in conversation with a band of hunters; evidently he could speak and hear normally. It seems clear that Castellan's intention in hypnotizing Josephine was not only to obtain a mistress but also to get a companion whose attractions would persuade country people to provide him with meals and a bed. Yet his powers were certainly genuine. He was a water diviner, healer, and hypnotist of remarkable ability. He was, in short, both a genuine magician and a charlatan – a mixture we have already found in Simon Magus and Faust and will encounter again and again in the history of magic.

The Castellan case, which is well documented, underlines something we should not forget – that magical powers are not confined to a few famous names in history. In every age, there are thousands of such men and women and their powers are of many kinds. Timotheus Castellan evidently recognized Josephine as an easy hypnotic subject as soon as he saw her – just as Franz Walter earmarked his victim on the train. What is more interesting is that Josephine undoubtedly recognized Castellan as a man who might gain power over her. Moreover, if the evidence of the neighbour is to be believed, Castellan did not hypnotize Josephine by the usual methods. He made passes in the air when her back was turned. This suggests that he was exercising some form of thought pressure.

It is a curious fact that the careers of most magicians seem to follow a definite pattern – spectacular rise to power or fame, followed by a long, slow downfall. Timotheus Castellan's downfall obviously began when he mesmerised Josephine. We do not know enough of the historical Faust to know when his career took the downward plunge but the fact that we know nothing about his later years or his death, suggests that his fame evaporated before he was 40-years-old.

Faust and Castellan had another interesting thing in common – both were black magicians. This term may seem quaint in our scientific age but it is less absurd than it sounds. The black magician is, quite simply, a man who wants power for himself, for self-aggrandizement. He wants to be able to vent his spite on enemies and to satisfy all his desires. Black magicians are usually defined as those who have made a pact with the Devil but this is not necessarily the case. A magician may summon the Devil or one of his demons and remain a white magician, so long as his purpose is benevolent. On the other hand, a magician may have no interest in the Devil or may even deny his existence, but if his intentions are malicious and self-centred, he is a black magician.

Faust was not the most celebrated magician of his age. He had two remarkable contemporaries, Cornelius Agrippa and Paracelsus, whose fame greatly and deservedly surpassed his own and who were undoubtedly white magicians. Agrippa and Paracelsus were both students of that strange mystical system of knowledge called the Cabala, whose purpose is to show the fallen man his way back to Paradise and the godhead. The two works that contain the essence of cabalistic teaching – the *Sefer Yetsirah*, Book of Creation and the *Zohar*, Book of Splendour – are of such profound importance in the history of magic that we must say a few words about them here.

The Book of Creation dates from the second century AD. The Book of Splendour appeared in an Aramaic manuscript written by a student named Moses de Léon in the late thirteenth century. It is, however, a tradition that the teachings of both books date from the beginning of human history, when angels taught Adam the secret of how to recover his lost bliss. Cabalists think of man as a being who is tied up and enveloped in a complicated straitjacket – like Houdini before one of his celebrated escapes – and whose problem is to discover how to untie all the knots. Most men do not even realize that they are tied up. The cabalist not only knows it, he knows also that man's highest state is total freedom.

According to the Cabala, when Adam sinned he fell from a state of union with God. He fell down through ten lower states of consciousness into a state of amnesia, in which he totally forgot his divine origin, his true identity. Man's task, therefore, is to clamber back until he once more attains his highest state. The journey is long and hard. It is not simply a matter of climbing, like Jack clambering up the beanstalk, because the 'beanstalk' passes through ten different 'realms'. But even that image is too simple – the beanstalk does not pass straight upward, like a fireman's pole, but wanders from side to side.

The image of the beanstalk is apt because the Cabala is essentially the study of a sacred tree – the Tree of Life. At the top of the tree is God the Creator, who is called Kether (the crown). The nine other branches of the tree are wisdom, beauty, power, understanding, love, endurance, majesty, foundation and kingdom. These are known collectively as the Sefiroth – emanations or potencies and it is they that constitute the realms through which the beanstalk passes. There is a further complication. The traditional picture of the Tree of Life looks rather like a diagram of a chemical molecule, in which the atoms are connected to each other by lines. These lines correspond to the 22 paths of the Cabala that connect the realms.

The Tree of Life no longer grows on earth. How, then, does the aspirant set about climbing it? There are three main ways. First, one may explore the realms on the astral plane. Another way to explore the realms of the Cabala is through inner vision – that is, by achieving a semi-trancelike or visionary state in which the realms appear before the inner eye. A third way is the obvious one – study of the Cabala itself. It is, however, perhaps the most difficult way of all, because its revelations of man's consciousness and destiny are not spoken of directly but lie hidden in an enormously complex system of symbols.

The realms of the Sefiroth, however, are not themselves symbols. According to the Cabala, they are real worlds. For instance, if the wandering astral body finds itself in a realm containing doves and spotted leopards, a land bursting with an almost overwhelming glory of life, it is almost certainly in the realm of Netshah or Venus – symbol of endurance and victory.

The doctrines of the Cabala were probably far above the head of a charlatan such as Faust. But Cornelius Agrippa and Paracelsus were not charlatans. They regarded themselves as scientists and philosophers and they were far more intelligent than Faust. Yet both of them were flawed by the defects we have come to realize are characteristic of so many magicians – a craving to be admired and a crude will to power. When these ambitions are frustrated, even men of genuine powers will often misuse their powers like a charlatan.

Like Faust, Cornelius Agrippa became the subject of many remarkable legends. What was the truth behind such incredible tales? Cornelius Agrippa – whose real name was Heinrich Cornelis – was born in Cologne in 1486. His parents were sufficiently well-off to send him to the recently founded university of Cologne, where he proved to be a brilliant scholar. It was an exciting time for young intellectuals. Gutenberg had invented the printing press some 50 years before Agrippa was born and the printed book had created the same kind of revolution as radio and television were to do five centuries later. Agrippa read everything he could lay his hands on. One day, he discovered the Cabala and it at once appealed to something deep within him. A magician was made.

At the age of 20, Agrippa became a court secretary to the Holy Roman Emperor and a distinguished career seemed assured for him. But Agrippa was a divided man. Part of him, as we have said, craved celebrity and power, but he loathed the world of diplomacy and courtly intrigue by which such success could be achieved. By now he was also obsessed by the ultimate other world of the Cabala.

At about this time, he attended the University of Paris where he studied mysticism and philosophy. There he met a Spaniard named Gerona, who had recently been forced to flee from his estate in Catalonia after a peasants' revolt. Agrippa offered to help him, sensing that if their mission succeeded, Gerona's gratitude might enable Agrippa to settle in Spain and devote his life to study of the Cabala. They went to Catalonia and Agrippa devised a brilliant plan that enabled them to capture a stronghold from the rebels. But they were later besieged, Agrippa was forced to flee and Gerona was captured and probably murdered. The episode was typical of the bad luck that was to pursue Agrippa for the rest of his life.

He returned to his job as court secretary but he felt so frustrated that he left after a few months and began wandering around

Europe. Within a year or two, he had acquired a reputation as a black magician and it was to cause him a great deal of trouble. In 1509, he taught in Dôle, France under the patronage of Queen Margaret of Austria. The local monks became jealous of this patronage, however, and plotted against him. When one of them preached against him in the presence of the queen, Agrippa decided it was time to move on. In 1515, he was knighted on a battlefield in Italy and became Cornelius Agrippa von Nettesheim – a name taken from that of a small village near Cologne.

He was granted a pension by King Francis I of France but this was revoked when Agrippa refused to cast horoscopes for the king's mother. Agrippa was later made official historian by Queen Margaret but was unwise enough to publish a work in which he attempted to demonstrate that all knowledge is useless. This so enraged his academic colleagues that he lost his job. Soon he was imprisoned for debt. Agrippa certainly lacked tact, for after this he again made the mistake of speaking his mind about Queen Margaret, for which he was thrown into prison and tortured. His health broken, he died in 1535 at the age of 49. Legend says that, as he lay on his deathbed, he cursed his wasted life and the black arts that had seduced him. Whereupon his black dog rushed out of the house and threw itself into a river – clearly proving that it was a demon in disguise.

These biographical snippets, however richly spiced with legends, hardly add up to a man of strange powers. The certainty that Agrippa was indeed a magician, however, lies in the three volumes of his treatise *The Occult Philosophy*, which is regarded as one of the great magical texts. The book makes it clear that Agrippa knew all about thought pressure. Magic, he insists, is a faculty that springs from the power of the mind and imagination. There are mysterious relations between the human body and the universe and between the earth on which we live and higher spiritual worlds. Thus, he argued, a stone can teach us about the nature of the stars. Agrippa believed that all nature is bound together by a kind of vast spider's web. Most human beings never learn to use their innate magical powers because they believe that they are cut off from the rest of nature. The magician, on the contrary, knows that his thought, if properly directed, can set the web vibrating and cause effects in far distant places.

Agrippa wrote his extraordinary masterwork when he was only 23-years-old. It shows that, even at this early age, his study of the Cabala had given him some profound insights. Because he was always in danger of being burned as a black magician, he was careful to insist in his book that his knowledge is of a kind that any serious student can acquire from study of the great philosophers and mystics. But he also admits that he has successfully practiced divination and foretelling the future. For example, he describes two methods by which he claims to have detected the identity of thieves. One method is to pivot a sieve on forceps held between the index fingers of two students. The sieve will begin to swing like a pendulum when the name of the guilty person is mentioned. Similarly, if the sieve is pivoted so that it can be made to spin, it will stop spinning when the thief's name is spoken.

Agrippa insists that the success of these and other magical techniques are due to spirits – similar, presumably, to the spirits that help *fakirs* to perform their wonders. The overwhelming impression that emerges from the book is that Agrippa was sensitive – born with the gifts of precognition, telepathy and the ability to influence events by using the power of his mind. His belief that mind is more powerful than matter runs like a thread through the book. *The Occult Philosophy* is the work of a young man – full of vitality and brilliance – and of a dreamer who peered into a world that few of us have the gift to see.

The case of Paracelsus is even more tantalizing than that of Agrippa. His writings prove him to have been a more remarkable man – a great scientist as well as a magician. But, again, seeking the truth about him is like groping about in a fog, so obscured is his life with myth and legend.

He was born as Theophrastus Bombastus von Hohenheim in 1493, the son of an impoverished Swiss nobleman who had become a doctor. He studied medicine in Basel and completed his education at universities in Italy and Germany. His gifts as a physician were immediately apparent and a series of remarkable cures soon earned him a formidable reputation. In 1524, when he was only 29-years-old, he was appointed professor of medicine at Basel University. In nine years, he had become one of the great names in medicine in Europe.

It was at this point that his career, so rich in both achievement and promise, was undermined by the same kind of character defects that brought ruin to Agrippa and that seems to be the hallmark of so many magicians. He was vain-glorious. He chose the pseudonym 'Paracelsus' because it implied that he was greater than Celsus, the famous physician of ancient Rome. He was a heavy drinker and was prey to sudden, violent tempers. One of his first acts as professor at Basel University, was to order his students to hold a public burning of the books of Avicenna, Galen and other famous doctors of the past. This enraged his colleagues, who condemned him as an exhibitionist and a charlatan. When they plotted against him, Paracelsus compounded his unpopularity by calling them names – like many paranoid people he had a powerful gift for invective. For a while his reputation held his enemies at bay and, when he cured the publisher Frobenius of an infected leg that other doctors had decided to amputate, it seemed that he had become invulnerable to attack. Soon after this, however, a patient declined to pay his bill and Paracelsus took him to court. Owing to the plots of his enemies, he lost the case, whereupon he rained such violent abuse on the heads of the judges that a warrant was issued for his arrest. He was forced to flee Basel and his long soul-destroying downfall had begun.

For the remainder of his life, Paracelsus wandered all over Europe as an itinerant doctor, writing book after book (of which few were published in his lifetime) and pouring scorn and invective on his enemies. Fourteen years of wandering and disappointment wore him out. In 1541, when he was 48-years-old, he was invited by the Prince Palatine to settle at his seat in Salzburg. At last he might have found contentment in a quiet life of study. But he continued to drink too much and six months later he rolled down a hill in a drunken stupor and died of his injuries.

Then, ironically, his books began to be published and they spread his fame over Europe once more. They have a range and boldness of imagination that is reminiscent of Leonardo da Vinci's notebooks. Paracelsus, immediately, became a kind of patron saint of occultism – a position he maintains even today, with his writings being studied by a new generation of occultists.

As with Agrippa, it is difficult to discover four centuries later what genuine powers lay behind the many legends of Paracelsus's magical prowess. One thing is clear – most of the stories concern remarkable cures and this suggests that he was primarily gifted with, seemingly, magical powers of healing. For example, we are told that he cured an innkeeper's daughter, who since birth had been paralyzed from the waist down. The medicine he gave her was probably saltpeter in teaspoonfuls of wine. This would obviously have had no effect, but it seems that the hypnotic force of his personality and his natural healing power brought about a cure. We are also again confronted by the paradox of the split personality – a man who was bad-tempered, thin-skinned and boastful, yet who could be taken over by some strange power that rose from his subconscious depths and made him a great healer.

So we reach the odd conclusion that the contemporaries of Agrippa and Parcelsus were probably right when they called them charlatans – but that, at the same time, both men possessed genuine powers. It would be another four centuries before the great Swiss psychologist, Carl Jung attempted to explain these powers scientifically in terms of that vast reservoir of energy known as the subconscious mind.

In the sixteenth century, it was still dangerous for a man of knowledge to gain a reputation as a wizard or sorcerer. The witch hunting craze was spreading across Europe and many people were being burned for being in league with the Devil. This, no doubt, explains why we know so little of the lives of the alchemists who followed in the footsteps of Agrippa and Paracelsus. That remarkable sixteenth-century French physician and prophet, Nostradamus, took care to hide his visions in verse of such obscurity that even nowadays we cannot be certain what most of them mean.

The tide turned in the seventeenth and eighteenth centuries – the age of scientists such as Newton, Huygens and Harvey – and the seeker after forbidden knowledge once again became respectable, at least in Protestant countries. Sir Isaac Newton – one of the greatest names in science and philosophy – spent as much time in his alchemical laboratory as at his telescope.

In 1734 was born one of those remarkable pioneers to whom the modern world owes much but to whom it pays little attention – Franz Anton Mesmer. He was the discoverer of what came to be called mesmerism and later hypnotism. Mesmer, whose parents

Unsolved Mysteries

were Swiss, studied medicine at the University of Vienna and wrote his doctoral thesis on the influence of the planets on human health. He was 40 years of age when he stumbled on the discovery that was to make him famous – and infamous. A wealthy English lady who was passing through Vienna was suffering from stomach cramps and she called on a Jesuit acquaintance of Mesmer's to ask if he could lend her some magnets. She was convinced that magnets relieved her stomach pains. When Mesmer heard of this he was intrigued, for it seemed to complement his own theory that there was some kind of vital fluid in the body that flowed like the tides, producing health or sickness. If these tides existed, might it not be possible to influence their movements by magnets?

Mesmer tried using magnets on his own patients – and they seemed to work. Shortly afterward, while Mesmer was bleeding a patient – the standard cure for most ailments in those days – he observed that the bleeding increased when he came closer and decreased when he moved away. This must mean, he thought, that he himself was a kind of magnet. Mesmer coined the term 'animal magnetism' to describe his strange power and he demonstrated its value when curing a nobleman who was suffering from spasms. For six days, Mesmer had moved his powerful magnets over the patient's body to no effect. Then, on the sixth day, as the patient choked with asthma, Mesmer took hold of his foot. The spasm abated.

It looked as though Mesmer had effected a cure of the patient's vital fluids at last. News of his remedy spread all over Vienna and made him one of the most celebrated doctors in Austria. He began to experiment with 'magnetized water' – vats of water filled with iron filings into which metal rods were fixed. Patients grasped the rods – or one patient held onto a rod while other sufferers held his other hand. Music was played during the treatment and eventually the patients went into a trance or had convulsions. They were cured by the dozen.

Then came a temporary setback. Mesmer failed to cure a blind girl – understandably so, as her blindness was due to a detached retina. A scandal arose, however, and he had to leave Vienna. He moved to Paris and immediately achieved even greater success. His healing sessions began to look like orgies. The patients – men and women together – were lightly clad to help the animal magnetism flow more easily from one patient to the next. As they massaged one another or pressed their thighs together, according to Mesmer's prescribed method, many of them were convinced they could feel the health-giving effect.

The instrument of Mesmer's downfall was the same as that of Paracelsus – envious fellow doctors who denounced him as a charlatan. As with Paracelsus too, Mesmer's arbitrary and auto-cratic behaviour as much as his natural talents, was the cause. When a commission of doctors declared that his cures were due merely to suggestion, rather than to magnetism, Mesmer left France in disgrace. He retired to a villa near Constance in south-western Germany, where he spent his remaining days in peace. The doctors were right that Mesmer cured by suggestion, of course. What they failed to realize was that Mesmer's cures proved that the power of suggestion is a greater force than anyone had suspected. If the subconscious mind can be convinced by suggestion, it can bring about extraordinary cures. This point was underlined a few years later when one of Mesmer's disciples, the Marquis of Puysegur, was trying to 'magnetize' a shepherd boy by stroking his head and, to his astonishment, induced a deep trancelike sleep. He had stumbled on hypnotism. Even today, after almost two centuries, we know little more about the under-lying mechanism of hypnotism than did Puysegur. Once more we confront the strange paradox – that a man can be completely self-deceived about the nature of his powers and nevertheless be a genuine magician.

Nowhere is this more apparent than in the case of the man whose name has become synonymous with seduction – Jacques Casanova, the adventurer and confidence trickster who flourished in the second half of the eighteenth century. Not only was Casanova an accomplished faith healer (he cured an ailing Venetian senator by means of suggestion), but he was also remarkably successful at fortune-telling by means of cards and other oracles. Indeed, the accuracy of his predictions sometimes alarmed Casanova himself. For instance, he told one girl that she would go to Paris and become the king's mistress – and that is exactly what happened. Casanova believed that he somehow conjured up real spirits when he was muttering his bogus incantations. What seems more likely is that he possessed the same occult faculty as Paracelsus or Faust to some degree.

Casanova met and immediately disliked, another charlatan who acquired a reputation as a great magician – the man who called himself the 'Count of Saint-Germain'. When Saint-Germain arrived in Vienna in the mid-1740s, he seemed to be about 30 years old – a man of powerful and dominant personality, with the typical magician's streak of boastfulness and desire to astonish. In Vienna, he was befriended by members of the nobility and was brought to Paris by the Marshal de Belle-Isle. By 1758, he had become a close friend of Louis XV and his mistress, Madame de Pompadour.

Part of Saint-Germain's attraction was his reputation as a man of mystery. No one seemed to have any idea of where or when he was born. But his knowledge of history seemed to be enormous and occasionally he said things that suggested he knew far more about certain events in the remote past than any mere student possibly could know. In short, he implied that he had actually witnessed them in person. He would learnedly discourse on the priesthood of Egypt, in a way that suggested he had studied in ancient Thebes or Heliopolis. Another puzzle was that he was never seen to eat, although it is now known that he had a special diet. He explained that he lived on some elixir of which only he knew the formula. He was a student of alchemy and claimed to have discovered the secret of the Philosopher's Stone. What is certain is that he had learned a great deal about metallurgy and chemistry.

Saint-Germain continued to fascinate students of occultism. Many of them believe he is alive today – possibly in Tibet. The unromantic truth is that he died in his mid-70s in 1784, suffering from rheumatism and morbid depression. Accounts of people who met him indicate that, far from being a man of mystery and an enigma, he struck many intelligent people as a fool, charlatan, boaster and swindler.

If Saint-Germain seems to have been fundamentally a confidence man, the same cannot be said of his famous contemporary, Count Alessandro di Cagliostro. That he was a fraud there can be little doubt, but that he also possessed highly developed occult faculties is fairly certain. His enemies said that Cagliostro's real name was Giuseppe Balsamo and that he had been a confidence trickster in his native Italy. As a schoolboy, he was exuberant and ungovernable and ran away from seminary school several times. In his teens, he became a wanderer like many talented and penniless young men and lived by his wits. But he was also an avid student of alchemy, astrology and ritual magic and he soon had a wide, if not very coherent, knowledge of occultism.

At the age of 26 (in 1769), Cagliostro fell in love with Lorenza, the beautiful 14-year-old daughter of a coppersmith. They married and for many years she was his partner in adventure and fraud, her beauty being one of their greatest assets. When Casanova met them in the south of France the year after their marriage, as they were returning from a pilgrimage to Santiago de Compostella in Spain, they appeared to be people of means, travelling in style and distributing alms to the poor. In Paris, the couple came under the protection of a nobleman, who then seduced Lorenza and tried to make her leave her husband. Cagliostro had her thrown into jail but later reunited with her and took her to England.

In London, he joined the Freemasons. Soon, however, he founded his own masonic order, infusing its ceremonies with occult rituals purportedly based on ancient Egyptian practices that Cagliostro claimed he had discovered in an Egyptian manuscript on a bookstall. Cagliostro was undoubtedly convinced that his Egyptian masonry was the product of divine inspiration. It was certainly the turning point in his fortunes. From London, he journeyed to Venice, Berlin, Nuremberg and Leipzig. In each city, he visited the masonic lodge, made speeches on his Egyptian rite and initiated members. His argument seems to have been that the Egyptian rite was as different from and as superior to established freemasonry, as New Testament Christianity is from Old Testament Judaism. He was feted and admired and became a rich man.

Cagliostro came to Strasbourg in 1780, and soon became the most talked about man in town. Although he was wealthy, he lived modestly in a room above a tobacco shop. His cures became legendary. He was often able to heal the sick simply by the laying on of hands. On one occasion, he successfully delivered a baby after midwives had given up the mother for dead.

It was in Strasbourg that he met the man who was to bring about his downfall – Cardinal de Rohan. He was a churchman who longed for royal favour but who, unfortunately, was disliked by Queen Marie Antoinette. Cagliostro deeply impressed Rohan, who spoke of his luminous and hypnotic eyes with almost religious fervour.

The cardinal's downfall occurred in 1785, in the famous Affair of the Diamond Necklace. A pretty swindler who called herself the Countess de la Motte Valois became Rohan's mistress and persuaded him that the queen wanted him to secretly buy a diamond necklace worth $300,000. In fact, the queen knew nothing of it and the money raised by the cardinal went straight into the countess's pocket. When the jewellers finally approached the queen for a long overdue instalment on the money, the whole affair came to light. The countess was tried and publicly flogged. Rohan and Cagliostro were also tried and, although they were acquitted, the scandal damaged both of them irreparably. In addition, the months that Cagliostro spent in jail before trial broke his nerve – and his luck.

Cagliostro went to London after leaving prison. There, he accurately predicted the nature and date of the French Revolution and of the fall of the Bastille. Then he travelled around Europe, often hounded by the police. Finally, he made the extraordinary error of going to Rome to propagate his Egyptian freemasonry under the nose of the Pope. He was arrested and thrown into the papal prison in the Castel Sant'Angelo and was later transferred to the, even worse, prison of San Leo. Eight years after his arrest in 1787, French soldiers captured San Leo prison and searched for Cagliostro, intending to treat him as a revolutionary hero. In fact, he had been dead for several years – though exactly when and how he died is still unknown.

Of all the great magician-mystics, Cagliostro is the most tragic. One of his enemies said of him that he possessed 'a demonic power that paralyzes the will'. But in retrospect he seems less a demon than a fallen angel. The one magician-mystic who certainly had – and used – a paralytic power of will over others was Rasputin, the sinister, enigmatic Russian monk. His is an extraordinary story.

On 1 January 1917, the temperature in the Russian city of

Petrograd – now Leningrad – was sub-zero. From a bridge over the frozen Neva River, a few spectators watched a group of policemen who stood around a hole in the ice. A diver emerged, grasping the end of a rope that disappeared into the dark water beneath him. When he was out, the policemen heaved on the rope. A body broke the surface and slid onto the ice. The corpse was a bearded man in his late 40s – his face was battered and swollen. He had been bound with ropes but before dying, he had managed to free one hand, which was raised to his chest as if making the sign of the cross. He was wearing only one boot – the other was in the hands of a police inspector who stood nearby. It was this boot, found by a boy, that had led police to the spot.

Grigori Rasputin, who had been murdered three days before, was one of the most notorious figures in Petrograd. Now that he was dead, he would become a legend all over the world – a symbol of evil, cunning and lust. If ever you see a magazine story titled 'Rasputin, the Mad Monk', you can be sure it will be full of lurid details of how Rasputin spent his days in drunken carousing, his nights in sexual debauchery – how he deceived the Tsar and Tsarina into thinking he was a miracle worker, how he was the evil genius who brought about the Russian Revolution and the downfall of the Romanov dynasty. It is all untrue. Yet it makes such a good story that there is little chance that Rasputin will ever receive justice. The truth about him is that he really was a miracle worker and a man of strange powers. He was certainly no saint – very few magicians are – and tales of his heavy drinking and sexual prowess are undoubtedly based on fact. But he was no diabolical schemer.

Rasputin was born in the village of Pokrovskoe in 1870. His father was a fairly well-to-do peasant. As a young man, Rasputin had a reputation for wildness until he visited a monastery and spent four months there in prayer and meditation. For the remainder of his life, he was obsessed by religion. He married at 19 and became a prosperous carter. Then the call came again – he left his family and took to the road as a kind of wandering monk. When eventually he returned, he was a changed man, exuding an extraordinarily powerful magnetism. The young people of his village were fascinated by him. He converted one room in his house into a church and it was always full. The local priest became envious of his following, however, and Rasputin was forced to leave home again.

Rasputin had always possessed the gift of second sight. One day during his childhood, this gift had revealed to him the identity of a peasant who had stolen a horse and hidden it in a barn. Now, on his second round of travels, he also began to develop extraordinary healing powers. He would kneel by the beds of the sick and pray, then he would lay his hands on them and cure many of them. When he came to what is now Leningrad, probably late in 1903, he already had a reputation as a wonderworker. Soon he was accepted in aristocratic society, in spite of his rough, peasant manners.

It was in 1907 that he suddenly became the power behind the throne. Three years before, Tsarina Alexandra had given birth to a longed-for heir to the throne, Prince Alexei. But it was soon apparent that Alexei had inherited haemophilia, a disease that prevents the blood from clotting and from which a victim may bleed to death, even with a small cut. At the age of three, the prince fell and bruised himself so severely that an internal haemorrhage developed. He lay in fever for days and doctors despaired of his life. Then the Tsarina recalled the man of God she had met two years earlier and sent for Rasputin. As soon as he came in, he said calmly, 'Do not worry about the child. He will be all right.' He laid his hand on the boy's forehead, sat down on the edge of the bed and began to talk to him in a quiet voice. Then he knelt and prayed. In a few minutes, the boy was in a deep and peaceful sleep and the crisis was over.

Henceforth, the Tsarina felt a powerful emotional dependence on Rasputin – a dependence nourished by the thinly veiled hostility with which Alexandra, a German, was treated at court. Rasputin's homely strength brought her a feeling of security. The Tsar also began to confide in Rasputin, who became a man of influence at court. Nicholas II was a poor ruler, not so much cruel as weak and too indecisive to stem the rising tide of social discontent. His opponents began to believe that Rasputin was responsible for some of the Tsar's reactionary policies and a host of powerful enemies began to gather. On several occasions, the Tsar had to give way to the pressure and order Rasputin to leave the city. On one such occasion, the young prince fell and hurt himself again. For several days he tossed in agony, until he seemed too weak to survive, The Tsarina dispatched a telegram to Rasputin, and he telegraphed back, 'The illness is not as dangerous as it seems.' From the moment it was received, the prince began to recover.

World War I brought political revolution and military catastrophe to Russia. Its outbreak was marked by a strange coincidence – Rasputin was stabbed by a madwoman at precisely the same moment as the Archduke Franz Ferdinand was shot at Sarajevo. Rasputin hated war and might have been able to dissuade the Tsar from leading Russia into the conflict. But he was in bed recovering from his stab wound, when the moment of decision came.

Rasputin's end was planned by conspirators in the last days of 1916. He was lured to a cellar by Prince Felix Yussupov, a man he trusted. After feeding him poisoned cakes, Yussupov shot him in the back, then he was beaten with an iron bar. Such was his immense vitality that he was still alive when the murderers dropped him through the hole in the ice into the Neva. Among his papers was found a strange testament addressed to the Tsar. It stated that he had a strong feeling he would die by violence before 1 January 1917 and that if he were killed by peasants, the Tsar would reign for many years to come – but if he were killed by aristocrats – as he was – then 'none of your children or relations will remain alive for more than two years'. He was right. The Tsar and his family were all murdered in July 1918 – an amazing example, among many, of Rasputin's gift of precognition.

CHAPTER 26

MAGIC AT WORK

Perhaps it is easy to dismiss the accounts of strange powers among medieval men – it was long ago and the historians were uncritical – but how can we explain the bizarre events in the lives of magicians who lived nearer to our own time? Is it possible that the Roman god Mercury could be summoned up in the twentieth century Paris? And what about the extraordinary Madame Blavatsky, who dealt in wonders, only some of which can be explained away by trickery and fraud? The evidence is mixed but the tales are fascinating . . . and there seems to be no easy answer or a rational, scientific explanation.

It was 11:30 pm at night on 31 December 1913 and the room in Paris was filled with the smell of incense. The room was lit by a flame that burned on an altar. Laid out beside this were a chain, a scourge, a dagger, a jar of oil, a loaf of bread and a flask of wine. The dark, robed man who stood before the altar was Aleister Crowley, an English practitioner of magic who liked to refer to himself as the Beast 666 from Revelations. The naked man beside him was his disciple, Victor Neuberg. Crowley began to intone,

> Hail! Asi! Hail, Hoor-Apep! Let
> The Silence speech beget . . .

As he chanted the words of the ritual, Crowley rang a bell twice, seized the scourge and whipped Neuberg's bare buttocks. Then he took the dagger and scratched a cross on Neuberg's chest above the heart and bound the chain about Neuberg's forehead,·

> The scourge, the dagger, and the chain
> Cleanse body, breast, and brain!

This strange ritual continued until the clock sounded midnight – New Year's Day, 1914. Then the priest and his neophyte began to chant in Latin. Suddenly, the shape of a naked boy seemed to form in the air in front of them. He was surrounded by thousands of golden wands, which glowed with a clear light. Around each wand, two live serpents seemed to be writhing. This was the caduceus, the wand traditionally associated with Mercury, the messenger of the Gods. It indicated that Crowley had succeeded in invoking Mercury – the Roman equivalent of the older Greek god Hermes, traditional founder of magic arts.

To the sceptic, the whole thing sounds absurd and the vision seems to be some kind of hallucination induced with the help of the incense and the orgiastic flogging. We cannot say if this is so with any certainty. What we can say, is that the ceremony Crowley was performing was not some wild invention of his inflamed imagination. It was a traditional magic ceremony of a kind that had been performed thousands of times in the temples of the ancient world. It was no surprise to Crowley that he saw Mercury and his caduceus. He expected to see Mercury, just as a chemist expects to see blue litmus paper turn red when he dips it in acid.

But how is it possible for a modern Westerner to take magic seriously? Is it not a primitive superstition – or, at best, an early form of crude science ? No magician would agree. According to Crowley and most other practicing magicians, magic is quite simply the science of 'causing changes to occur in conformity with will'. This view was put forward by the French magician Eliphas Lévi, of whom Crowley believed himself to be a reincarnation. According to Lévi, magic is based on human will power which is a force 'as real as steam or the galvanic current'. In short, both Lévi and Crowley believed that magic is the directed use of the power that we have labelled thought pressure. Steam is lighter than air, yet it can drive an engine. Electricity is invisible, yet it can light a whole city. The will is intangible and invisible, yet magicians believe that, if properly directed, it can change the world.

We might expect ritual magic to be something that changes from age to age, according to the temperament of individual magicians and the cultures to which they belong. To a minor extent this is true. Yet perhaps the most surprising thing about magic, is that the way people have regarded it and the manner in which it has been used have altered little in thousands of years. Anyone who reads about the magic of the ancient Chaldeans or Chinese, or about the modern gypsies or dervishes, soon discovers that certain basic ideas and methods occur again and again. If magic is purely wishful thinking and nonsense, it has managed to be remarkably consistent wishful thinking and nonsense.

The god Hermes Trismegistus whom Crowley invoked, was identical with Thoth, an important god of the ancient Egyptians. Magicians of ancient Alexandria in Egypt declared that Thoth was not a god, but a king who had reigned for more than 3000 years and had written various books on religion and magic. This king was known in Greek as Hermes Trismegistus, Thrice-Greatest Hermes. According to legend, he was buried in the great pyramid of Giza and when his body was uncovered he was found to be holding an emerald tablet that contained an inscription beginning, 'As above, so below'. This has two meanings, one religious and one magical. Its religious meaning is that God is identical with the soul – a belief that is one of the central tenets of Hinduism. The magical meaning is that a man is a small model of the universe. Man is the *microcosm* (from Greek words meaning little world) and the universe is the *macrocosm* (great world). Man and the universe are connected by thousands of fine threads – a doctrine later elaborated by Paracelsus. You might say that man is an organ of the universe, just as the heart is an organ of the body. That is why students of magic believe that astrology, which claims that celestial bodies influence human affairs, can predict future events.

Like the Cabala, the many works attributed to Hermes Trismegistus – which in fact were probably written in Alexandria between 300 BC and AD 300 – were a source of inspiration to many great thinkers of the Middle Ages and after. They were studied not only by mystics such as Albertus Magnus, the thirteenth century Christian bishop who taught St. Thomas Aquinas, but also by Agrippa and Paracelsus. We have already argued that the success of most magicians is due to their possession of strange powers. The question we must now ask is this – can certain rituals, such as those enacted by Crowley, confer magical powers? For evidence, let us look at the careers of three of the most celebrated occultists of the last four centuries.

Dr. John Dee, the most highly regarded magician of Shakespeare's time, is almost unique among magicians in that he possessed practically no occult powers. Perhaps this is why he managed to avoid the usual magician's destiny of spectacular success and tragic downfall.

He was born in 1527, the son of a minor official in the court of King Henry VIII. From childhood on, he was an avid reader and when he went to Cambridge University at the age of 15, he allowed himself only four hours sleep a night. After Cambridge, he went to the University of Louvain in Belgium, where Agrippa had also studied. When Dee read Agrippa's *Occult Philosophy*, he knew that he had stumbled on his life's work – the pursuit of magical knowledge. At the age of 23, he gave a series of free lectures on geometry in Rheims, France, and was so popular that he was offered a professorship. But he preferred to return to England to pursue his occult studies.

When Elizabeth I came to the throne in 1558, she asked Dee to cast a suitable date for her coronation. Dee did so and from this time on he enjoyed royal protection. Even so, as one suspected of magical practices, he still had to behave with extreme caution. Moreover, Queen Elizabeth was notoriously stingy – her patronage did nothing to improve Dee's finances and he remained poor all his life. Dee married a lady-in-waiting who bore him eight children. He lived quietly and studied astrology, crystal gazing and alchemy.

The aim of crystal gazing is to induce a semi-trancelike state in which the subconscious mind projects future events as images in the crystal. Dee was too much of an intellectual to be good at this. He realized that what he needed was a working partner with natural occult faculties, especially in scrying. In 1582 he met Edward Kelley, a young Irishman who claimed to have second sight. Kelley was undoubtedly a crook – he had had both his ears cut off for forgery – but it seems equally certain that he did possess second sight and that he was also a medium. Dee's wife took an immediate dislike to the Irishman, but when Kelley went into a trance and began to get in touch with spirits, Dee was so delighted that he overruled his wife s objections.

How did Dee and Kelley go about summoning the spirits? One famous print shows them in a graveyard practicing necromancy. From what we know of the pious Dee, however, it seems unlikely that he went in for this sort of thing. We can learn more from his *Spiritual Diaries*. It is clear that he went into training before endeavouring to summon the spirits. He abstained for three days from sexual intercourse, overeating and the consumption of alcohol and he took care to shave his beard and cut his nails. Then began a two-week period of magical invocations in Latin and Hebrew, beginning at dawn and continuing until noon, then beginning again at sunset and continuing until midnight. Kelley, meanwhile, gazed intently into the crystal ball. At the end of 14 days, Kelley would begin to see angels and demons in the crystal. Later, these spirits would walk about the room. Dee, however, does not seem to have seen the spirits but he recorded lengthy dialogues he had with them.

One's instant response to this, is the conviction that Kelley made Dee believe that nonexistent spirits had manifested themselves. The trouble with this view is that the conversations, which came via the mouth of Kelley, were often so crammed with abstruse magical lore that it is almost inconceivable that the illiterate Irishman could have made them up as he went along. Dee, of course, was familiar with the lore and certain of the demons quoted chunks of Agrippa's *Occult Philosophy*. This makes it possible that Dee transmitted them telepathically to Kelley. The likeliest explanation, however, is that Kelley was a natural medium.

Count Adalbert Laski, a servant of Henry III of France, was so impressed by these seances of Dee and Kelley, that he invited them to visit the king of Germany. Dee and his family and Kelley and his wife, spent four years travelling around Europe as guests of various kings and noblemen, and their performances were sensationally successful.

Kelley was a difficult man, given to sudden tantrums and to fits of boredom and depression – but in spite of their ups and downs, he and Dee continued to work together for many years. They finally separated while they were still on their travels in Europe. Kelley achieved some success on his own as an alchemist and scryer but eventually died in prison. Dee returned to England in 1589 and lived for another 19 years, hoping in vain that the spirits would lead him to a crock of gold. Today his reputation among occultists is secure, for he was the first magician on record to make use of spirit communication. He was 200 years before his time – but in spite of his lack of worldly success, he remains one of the great names in the history of magic.

In 1801, there appeared in London a work called *The Magus or Celestial Intelligencer* by Francis Barrett. It was supposed to be 'a complete system of occult philosophy'. Nowadays, it is not highly regarded by students and adepts of the magic arts, because many of the rituals it details are garbled and inaccurate. Nevertheless, it was an important work for it was almost the first attempt at a serious description of magical practices since Agrippa's *Occult Philosophy*, nearly three centuries earlier. After Agrippa's time, fear of persecution had driven the magicians underground for 200 years.

The Age of Reason, as thinkers and writers of mid-eighteenth century Europe called their period, had made magic superfluous – or at least unfashionable. But the tide soon turned again. All over western Europe, novels such as Horace Walpole's *The Castle of Otranto* began to appear, in which high adventure and crimes of passion were mixed with supernatural events. Of course, most readers did not really believe in the supernatural trappings of such stories – but their enormous popularity shows that ghosts, magic and the paranormal continued to fascinate. At the end of *The Magus*, Barrett printed an advertisement asking for students to help him found a 'magic circle', and an active group was established at Cambridge.

Nine years after publication of *The Magus*, there was born in Paris a remarkable man who, more than any other, was responsible for the great magical revival that swept across Europe in the nineteenth-century – Alphonse-Louis Constant, better known as Eliphas Lévi. The son of a poor shoemaker, Lévi was a dreamy, sickly, highly intelligent and imaginative child with powerful religious inclinations. At the age of 12 (in 1822), he decided he was destined for the Church. He had a craving to belong to some spiritual order, some great organization, that would enable him to devote his life to the truths of the spirit. His teacher at the seminary of Saint Nicholas du Chardonnet was Abbot Frere-Colonna, a remarkable idealist who believed that man was slowly ascending toward God and that a great age of the Holy Spirit was at hand. The abbot had studied Mesmer's doctrines and believed that they were inspired by the Devil. He devoted some time to denouncing them in class, but succeeded only in awakening young Lévi's interest in such forbidden matters. When the abbot was dismissed through the intrigues of jealous colleagues, Lévi's disillusion with the Church began.

Lévi still hungered for a faith, however. He became a subdeacon and one of his chief tasks was teaching the catechism to young girls. One day, a poor woman begged him to prepare her daughter for first communion and Lévi's initial feelings of protectiveness developed into a wild infatuation for the girl. Nothing came of it but the experience convinced him that he was not intended for the priesthood. When he turned away from his vocation, his mother committed suicide.

After 14 years in a seminary, Lévi found the world a hard place to adjust to. He still wanted to be a believer and dreamed of Frere-Colonna's spiritual rebirth of mankind. So, although he began to write for radical newspapers – and spent time in prison on sedition charges as a result – his search for a faith continued. He discovered the writings of Swedenborg and then the Cabala, with its doctrine that man can overcome original sin and rise toward the godhead. Honoré de Balzac's mystical novel *Louis Lambert*, was also a vital influence. Lévi studied that strange fortune-telling deck of cards known as the Tarot and linked its 22 cards of the Major Arcana with the 22 paths of the Cabala. Lévi came to certain important conclusions about magic. The first was that the will is a far greater power than we realize and that magic is learning how to use this power. The second was that all space is permeated with a medium that Lévi called astral light, which can take the impression of thoughts and feelings and is the medium through which thoughts are conveyed in telepathy. Third, he believed deeply in the microcosm-macrocosm doctrine enshrined in Hermes Trismegistus's inscription, 'As above, so below'.

Lévi was in his 40s when his *Dogma and Ritual of High Magic* was published in 1856 and it established a reputation that was consolidated four years later by his History of Magic. In the first book, he describes one of the most curious incidents of his life. On a visit to London, he records, he was asked to try to raise the spirit of the ancient Greek magician, Apollonius of Tyana. After a month of preparation and fasting, Lévi spent 12 hours in ritual incantations. At last, the shade of Apollonius appeared in a grey shroud and telepathically answered questions Lévi put to it about the future of two of his acquaintances. It prophesied the death of both, Lévi's description of the invocation has considerable dramatic quality,

'I kindled two fires with the requisite prepared substances, and began reading the invocations of the "Ritual" in a voice at first low, but rising by degrees. The smoke spread, the flame caused the objects on which it fell to waver, then it went out, the smoke still floating white and slow about the marble altar. I seemed to feel a quaking of the earth, my ears tingled, my heart beat quickly. I heaped more twigs and perfumes on the chafing dishes, and as the flames again burst up, I beheld distinctly, before the altar, the figure of a man of more than normal size, which dissolved and vanished away. I re-commenced the evocations, and placed myself within a circle which I had drawn previously between the tripod and the altar. Thereupon, the mirror which was behind the altar seemed to brighten in its depth, and a wan form was outlined therein, which increased and seemed to approach by degrees. Three times, and with closed eyes, I invoked Apollonius. When I again looked forth there was a man in front of me, wrapped from head to foot in a species of shroud, which seemed more grey than white. He was lean, melancholy, and beardless, and did not altogether correspond to my preconceived notion of Apollonius. I experienced an abnormally cold sensation, and when I endeavoured to question the phantom, I could not articulate a syllable. I therefore placed my hand upon the sign of the pentagram, and pointed the sword at the figure, commanding it mentally to obey and not alarm me, in virtue of the said sign. The form thereupon became vague, and suddenly disappeared. I directed it to return, and presently felt, as it were, a breath close by me; something touched my hand which was holding the sword, and the arm became immediately benumbed as far as the elbow. I divined that the sword displeased the spirit, and I therefore placed it point downward, close by me, within the circle. The human figure reappeared immediately, but I experienced such an intense weakness in all my limbs, and a swooning sensation came so quickly over me, that I made two steps to sit down, whereupon I fell into profound lethargy, accompanied by dreams, of which I had only a confused recollection when I came to myself. For several subsequent days, the arm remained benumbed and painful.'

In spite of these setbacks, Lévi persisted and, according to his own account, was able to consult the spirit on two more occasions on some fine points of cabalism.

Lévi was a widely respected magician for the remainder of his life, and attracted many disciples. That he had occult powers – or that his disciples were convinced he had – is certain. A disciple to whom Lévi had given a prayer to recite before he fell asleep, found that the words of the prayer were glowing in the dark, and that Lévi's spirit was standing by his bed. It seems likely that Lévi possessed the power of projecting his astral body.

His books strike the modern reader as wildly imaginative and confused, but they exerted an immense influence on a whole generation of students of the occult. His death, in 1875, was mourned by hundreds of occultists in France, Germany and England, who regarded him as the great master.

In 1831, when Lévi was still studying for the priesthood, there was born in Russia a woman who was to exert an even greater influence than he on nineteenth-century occultism – Elena Hahn, later Petrovna but known as Madame Blavatsky. Born into an aristocratic family, she married at 16, left her husband soon after and began to travel around the world. She was an explosive, charming, delightful personality. For a while, she worked as a bareback rider in a circus and dabbled in many odd interests. She had undoubted mediumistic powers and throughout her life, odd manifestations were apt to occur in her presence – inexplicable rappings, ringing of bells and movements of objects. In fact, it seems that she had the power of raising poltergeists. After living carelessly, until she was just past 40 and then wondering how to make a living, she decided to turn her occult abilities to account and become a medium.

On going to the United States she met Colonel Olcott, a lawyer and journalist who became her lifelong admirer and tireless publicist. She told Olcott that she was in touch with a certain spiritual Brotherhood of Luxor (presumably priests of ancient Egypt) and he believed her – as he believed everything else she told him. Together they formed the Theosophical Society, a movement for the study of ancient wisdom. For three years it flourished in America. In 1879, as interest seemed to wane, they decided to move to India, which Madame Blavatsky regarded as the fountainhead of spiritual wisdom.

In Bombay, Theosophy was an immediate success. The charismatic personality of Madame Blavatsky fascinated the Hindus even more than it had fascinated the Americans. She claimed that the Secret Masters in Tibet, a group of spiritual initiates, had imparted their wisdom to her. When disciples asked her questions about these matters, paper notes fell from the air. The notes contained detailed replies to the questions and were signed 'Koot Hoom'. These notes later became famous as the Mahatma Letters. Koot Hoomi, a semi-divine Master, was even seen by some devotees one moonlight night.

In 1884 the bombshell came. A housekeeper with whom Madame Blavatsky had quarrelled told a Western journalist that most of the magical effects were merely tricks. The Mahatma Letters were simply dropped through a crack in the ceiling of the room in which the disciples had gathered and the seven-foot-tall Koot Hoomi was actually a model carried around on someone's shoulders. Examination of a cabinet in which many manifestations had occurred revealed a secret panel. The Society for Psychical Research, which had been investigating her powers, issued a sceptical report.

It might seem that the Blavatsky reputation was irretrievable. Not a bit of it. Madame Blavatsky set sail for London – and soon the Theosophical Society was flourishing again, although it never achieved anything like its earlier success. Once again, accounts of Madame Blavatsky's magical powers began to circulate among occultists. The poet W. B. Yeats, a serious and long-term student of the occult, reported that when he visited Madame Blavatsky, her cuckoo clock made hooting noises at him. A. P. Sinnett, who later became her faithful disciple, complained when he visited her that he had attempted to raise spirits at seances but could not even get rapping sounds. 'Oh, raps are the easiest thing to get', she replied – and raps immediately sounded from all parts of the room.

When Madame Blavatsky died in 1891, six years after the fiasco that drove her out of India, she left behind a host of disciples who firmly believed in the existence of Koot Hoomi and the Tibetan Masters. She also left behind two huge books, *Isis Unveiled* and *The Secret Doctrine*, in which she explains that the earth is destined to evolve through seven 'root races', of which we are the fifth. Much of these enormous, bewildering books is taken up with descriptions of the root races.

In retrospect, it seems fairly certain that Madame Blavatsky was a genuine medium of unusual powers. It is more certain that, when her somewhat erratic powers were feeble, she helped them out with trickery – a temptation to which dozens of bona-fide mediums and magicians have succumbed. She was, in short, both a charlatan and a genuine magician and her hypnotically powerful personality made her one of the most remarkable women of the nineteenth century.

CHAPTER 27

THE GREAT MAGICAL REVIVAL

What went on in the secret chambers of the Golden Dawn? The meeting place of the magical society was in an ordinary London street and the members led ordinary lives in the city – but once behind the forbidden door, dressed in vivid magical robes, they were wholly caught up in a deliberate attempt to make contact with the mysterious forces of the universe and to explore the possibilities of the deepest subconscious levels of the human will. Armed with secret regalia and following ancient ritual, they set out to contact demons and angels on the astral pathways of the spirit world.

One day, in 1885, a middle-aged clergyman named Woodford was passing an idle hour at a secondhand bookstall on Farringdon Street in London. Among the dusty volumes he came upon a bound, handwritten manuscript that was obviously in cipher. Woodford was a student of the occult and he recognized certain symbols of the Cabala in the text. He bought the manuscript but, after several unsuccessful attempts to decode it, put it aside. Two years later, in the summer of 1887, he sent the manuscript to a friend Dr. William Wynn Westcott, a coroner who was interested in occultism and freemasonry. Westcott was familiar with the first major work on ciphers, the *Steganographia* by the fifteenth-century alchemist, Abbot Johann Trithemius, and it did not take him long to conclude that the mysterious pages were actually written in Trithemius's code. When deciphered, they proved to be five magical rituals for introducing newcomers into a secret society, together with notes on various cabalistic matters.

Concealed among the pages, Wescott found a letter in German, which stated that anyone interested in these rituals should contact a certain Fräulein Sprengel at an address in Stuttgart. Westcott lost no time in writing to her. Fräulein Sprengel replied, divulging that she was a member of a German magical order. A correspondence about magic ensued and eventually Fräulein Sprengel gave Westcott permission to found an English branch of the order and to use the rituals to initiate members. Accordingly, in 1888, Westcott founded a society called The Isis-Urania Temple of the Golden Dawn. (Its pretentious title perhaps reflects the influence of Madame Blavatsky, who had arrived in London from India a few months previously.) Two other students of the occult were cofounders – William Woodman, a retired doctor who had studied the Cabala in Hebrew and Samuel Liddell Mathers, an eccentric scholar of aristocratic leanings. Before long, the Golden Dawn had branches in Edinburgh, Weston-super-Mare and Bradford, and an enthusiastic following of displaced intellectuals and cranks. Its members included the beautiful actress Florence Farr, the poet W. B. Yeats and the young, and as yet unknown, Aleister Crowley.

This, at any rate, is the story of the founding of the Golden Dawn as put about by Westcott and Mathers. In recent years Ellic Howe, the historian of magic, has looked into the matter closely and has concluded that Fräulein Sprengel never existed. The cipher manuscript was probably genuine but it came from a collection of occultist Fred Hockley, who died in 1885 and not from a bookstall in Farringdon Street. Westcott, probably with the connivance of Mathers, forged various letters in German purporting to come from Fräulein Sprengel. His aim evidently was to give the society a certain authority rooted in ancient practices. Mathers was later to denounce the Sprengel letters as forgeries, although he must have known about them from the beginning. Westcott seems to have been a Jekyll and Hyde character. Indeed, his split personality was so marked, that he wrote in two completely different styles of handwriting. As for Mathers, who was to change his name to MacGregor Mathers and pose as a Scottish aristocrat, he was one of these curious figures who seem to occur so often in the history of magic – a kind of confidence trickster whose aim was not so much to swindle as to gain respect, admiration and power.

Does all this mean, then, that the Order of the Golden Dawn was nothing more than a combination of chicanery and wishful thinking? By no means. Its members did, beyond question, pursue serious and genuine studies of the magical arts. At this point, then, we must have a closer look at the whole subject of magic and those who practice it.

First of all, we have to admit that common sense insists that magic is bound to be nonsense. How could some semi-religious ceremony have the slightest influence on the real world? Clergymen in church may pray for rain, or prosperity, or victory in battle but they do not expect their prayers to produce a definite effect – they merely hope that God will pay attention. So why should some magic ceremony, not even addressed to God, have the power to influence actual events?

This is, I repeat, the commonsense view, the so-called scientific approach. But every day, thousands of events occur that science refuses to recognize because they appear to flout scientific laws. Dowsing, telepathy, precognition of future events and spectres of the living are only a few examples. And what of those strange, heightened states of consciousness such as the one that John G. Bennett experienced while at Gurdjieff's Institute? Perhaps we cannot really blame scientists for declining to pay too much attention to these things. The aim of science is to describe the universe in terms of natural laws, especially laws that forge unbreakable links between cause and effect – between an occurrence and the forces that make it happen. It is the apparent absence of such a link in magical events that makes scientists sceptical of them. The occultist responds to such scepticism by claiming that scientists refuse, or are unable, to spread their net of inquiry wide enough to encompass strange events. What is beyond dispute is that such events do occur.

When we try to take account of occult events and to devise some kind of theory that helps to account for them, we discover an interesting thing. Such a theory has already existed for thousands of years. It does not matter whether we call it magic, occultism, shamanism, or the Hermetic tradition as based on the works of Hermes Trismegistus. It all amounts to the same thing. Its basic assertion is that there is a far more intimate connection between man and nature than we are inclined to believe. The world is full of unseen forces and laws of whose nature we have no inkling. Perhaps there is some strange medium that stretches throughout space – such as Eliphas Lévi's astral light – that transmits these forces as the air transmits sound waves.

How do we make contact with such forces? The answer seems to be that you have to want to with an intense inner compulsion. In his autobiography, the painter Oscar Kokoschka tells of how his mother, who was having tea with his aunt one day in Prague, Czechoslovakia, suddenly leaped to her feet and announced that she must rush home because her youngest son was bleeding. The aunt tried to persuade her that her idea was nonsense but his mother hurried home – and found that her son had cut his leg with a hatchet while trying to chop down a tree. He would certainly have bled to death if she had arrived any later. This story – and hundreds of others like it equally well attested – indicates that strange powers come into operation where our deepest desires or needs are involved. As we go through our everyday lives, we do not need to exercise much will power – but occasionally, something stirs us to some really deep effort. It is this kind of effort that is likely to produce magical effects. The twentieth-century poet Robert Graves, remarked that many young men use a form of unconscious 'sorcery' to seduce young women. This is another word for thought pressure.

We could say, then, that organizations such as the Hermetic Order of the Golden Dawn, set out to experiment with will power, and to explore the possibilities of reaching deep subconscious levels of the will. Perhaps their magic was a hit-and-miss affair that worked only occasionally, but at least they were trying to learn about the possibilities of the true will.

The magic practiced by the members of the Golden Dawn was based on a number of simple principles. To begin with, they believed that certain basic symbols or ideas have a deep meaning for all human beings. On one occasion, Mathers handed Florence Farr a piece of cardboard with a geometrical symbol on it and told her to close her eyes and place it against her forehead. She immediately saw in her mind's eye a cliff top above the sea, with gulls shrieking. Mathers had shown her the water symbol from the Cabala. There is a close connection between such symbols and the theory of archetypes of the psychologist Carl Jung, who believed that certain symbols are able to strike a chord in the unconscious mind of every human being.

The Golden Dawn taught its students to try to train their imagination, which is the trigger of the will, and gain control over it. One of their exercises was to control likes and dislikes until they could like something they normally hated and hate something they usually liked. Another exercise was to attempt to see the world through other people's eyes, rather than their own – in other words, to completely change their normal point of view. Many modern psychologists would agree that such exercises are valuable and healthy. They are, in fact, similar to exercises practiced in yoga and other meditation disciplines.

The Golden Dawn also made a genuine attempt to draw together all that was best in the ancient magical traditions – Hermeticism, Cabalism, Enochian magic (based on the Apocryphal *Book of Enoch*, which tells of the fall of the Angels and their magic practices) and such magic textbooks as *The Key of Solomon*, *The Magic of Abrahemelin the Mage*, and the *Grimoire of Pope Honorius*.

On the face of it, the Golden Dawn should have been a wholly beneficial and healthy influence. Unfortunately, too many of its leading figures were driven by the craving that has been the downfall of so many magicians – the will to power, not only over themselves but also over everyone else. Gerald Yorke, a friend of Aleister Crowley, concluded that the story of the Golden Dawn showed that 'the majority of those who attempt to tread the occult path of power become the victims of their creative imagination, inflate their egos, and fall.' There was a great deal of infighting for the leadership of the Golden Dawn. Dr Westcott saw himself as the leader, but MacGregor Mathers felt the position should rightly be his. Mathers claimed to be in direct touch with Secret Chiefs, semi-divine spirits, who dictated new rituals to him through his wife as a medium. Then there was A. E. Waite, a learned American historian of magic. His interests, however, were more mystical than magical and he was not a very inspiring person. Finally, there was Aleister Crowley, a remarkable and demonic magician whose career brought ruin to many others as well as himself.

Crowley was the son of a wealthy and puritanical brewer. He

was born in Leamington near Stratford-upon-Avon in 1875. His birthplace gave him opportunity to remark with typical bombast and arrogance, 'It is a strange coincidence that one small county [Leamington and Stratford are in Warwickshire] should have given England her two greatest poets – for one must not forget Shakespeare.' It sounds like a joke but in fact Crowley was convinced that he was a great poet. However, though his verse shows considerable talent, he lacked the discipline and sense of language to be even a good poet.

Crowley was a spoiled child who developed an intense dislike of the Plymouth Brethren, the strict religious sect to which his father belonged. He was also obsessed by sex. His first of numerous seductions occurred, with a young servant, when he was 14-years-old. At university, he wrote a great deal of poetry which he published at his own expense. He also developed an incurable desire that lasted all his life to shock respectable people. In his late teens he discovered Mathers' translation of a book called *The Kabbalah Unveiled,* as well as a work by A. E. Waite on ceremonial magic. He quickly established contact with the Golden Dawn.

By the time Crowley entered the Golden Dawn in 1898, the struggle for its control had already been going on for some time. In 1891, Mathers had returned from France to announce that he had met three of the Secret Chiefs in Paris and had various magical secrets imparted to him. Dr Woodman died that year and for the next six years there was a certain amount of tension within the movement. Dr Westcott resigned from the Order – apparently having been told by his superiors on the London Council that magic was not a suitable occupation for a respectable public official. Mathers spent a great deal of time in Paris working on magical manuscripts at the Bibliothèque Nationale, so the struggle for leadership of the movement continued.

In August 1899, Crowley rented a house in Boleskine, Scotland on the shores of Loch Ness, conferred on himself the title 'Laird of Boleskine', donned a kilt and proceeded to practice the magic of Abrahamelin the Mage – a system which, he claimed, he had learned about in the writings of John Dee.

In December 1899, convinced that it was time he moved up to a higher grade in the Golden Dawn, Crowley went to London to demand initiation. This was refused through the efforts of Yeats and various other senior members, who regarded him as an overgrown juvenile delinquent. Crowley therefore went to Paris and persuaded Mathers to perform the necessary rituals. He also took the opportunity to stir up trouble, convincing Mathers that he had a revolt on his hands. Mathers sent him back to London with instructions to break into the Golden Dawn headquarters and to put new locks on all the doors. Yeats, Florence Farr and the other London initiates were enraged.

The legal wrangle that ensued in 1901 broke up the original Golden Dawn, 13 years after it had been founded. One group of members, under the leadership of A. E. Waite, managed to continue for another four years, still calling themselves the Golden Dawn. Another group, including Yeats, Florence Farr and the novelist Arthur Machen, was led until 1905 by Dr. R. W. Felkin, who then founded a magical society called the Stella Matutina or Morning Star. Finally, in the 1920s, a talented young medium and occultist who called herself Dion Fortune, founded the Society of the Inner Light, based on Golden Dawn rituals obtained from Mrs. Mathers – Mathers himself having died in the influenza epidemic of 1918.

The same year of the legal problems, the Golden Dawn had received another blow in the form of a sudden spate of unwelcome publicity. It happened when a couple of confidence tricksters, who called themselves Mr and Mrs Horos, were accused of raping a 16-year-old girl. Mrs Horos had learned that it was supposed to have been Fräulein Sprengel who had given the Golden Dawn its charter. She went to Paris and introduced herself to Mathers as Fräulein Sprengel. Oddly enough, Mathers was taken in – which could argue that he was not at that time aware that Fräulein Sprengel had been invented by Westcott. Mathers soon became suspicious of the couple, whereupon Mrs. Moros and her husband stole some of the rituals of the Golden Dawn and fled to London. There they launched into a career of confidence trickery based on a mixture of spurious occultism, extortion and sex. When charged with their crimes, they claimed to be leaders of the Golden Dawn. As a consequence, many of the most intimate secrets of the order were made public and sensationalized by the press. The publicity, combined with the power struggles within it, sealed the fate of the Golden Dawn.

Crowley had decided to get away before the Horos scandal broke. Late in 1900 he had gone to Mexico, where he studied the Cabala, practiced yoga and – according to his own account – finally became a true magician. When he returned to Paris in 1902, he tried to persuade Mathers to take up yoga. Mathers declined and their relation became several degrees colder. Eventually it turned into hatred, with Mathers and Crowley pronouncing magical curses on one another. Crowley claimed that his curses were actually responsible for the death of Mathers.

Back in England, Crowley married Rose Kelly and they travelled to Ceylon and Egypt. They called themselves the Prince and Princess Chioa Khan. In Cairo, Crowley performed various rituals with the intention of invoking the Egyptian god, Horus. On 8 April 1904, he received instructions from his wife, who had taken to uttering strange messages while in a trancelike state, to go into a room he had furnished as a temple. Suddenly, he heard a disembodied voice ordering him to write. What Crowley wrote was an odd document called *The Book of the Law*, which became the cornerstone of his later teaching. He claimed that it was dictated by Aiwass, one of the Secret Chiefs. Its basic teaching was expressed in the phrase, 'Do what you will'.

In 1905, Crowley went to the Himalayas to attempt the climb of Kanchenjunga, third highest mountain in the world. During the climb he quarrelled with the rest of the team and, when they were buried in an avalanche, made no attempt to help them. Several were killed. He deserted his wife and baby in India, where the baby died of typhoid. Rose later became an alcoholic and died insane. In a magazine called *The Equinox*, Crowley began to publish the secret rituals of the Golden Dawn. Mathers took him to court for this but lost his case.

In 1912, Crowley received a communication from another magical organization, the Order of the Temple of the Orient, reproaching him for publishing its secrets. Puzzled by the accusation, Crowley went to see Theodor Reuss, one of the OTO's leaders. It appeared that the secret in question was something called sex magic. It arose from the system of yoga known as Tantra, which attempts to use the power of sexual energy to fuel the drive toward higher consciousness. The OTO had, it seems, developed its own form of Tantric techniques. Crowley was fascinated and promptly availed himself of Reuss's permission to set up an English branch of the OTO. Magical ritual performed by Crowley often involved sex magic – with his disciple Victor Neuberg, it was an act of sodomy. Sex magic remained one of Crowley's central enthusiasms for the rest of his life – though addiction to heroin and cocaine lessened his sex drive in later years.

In the United States during World War I, Crowley had an endless series of mistresses, each of whom he liked to call the 'Scarlet Woman'. He undoubtedly had an exceptional sexual appetite but it must also be said, that he genuinely believed that sex magic heightened his self-awareness and enabled him to tap increasingly profound levels of consciousness. At all events, during this period Crowley steadily developed a kind of hypnotic power that it is as difficult to account for as it is to describe. William Seabrook, an American writer on the occult, witnessed the use of this power one day when he and Crowley were walking on Fifth Avenue in New York City. Crowley began to follow a complete stranger who was walking along the sidewalk. Crowley followed a few yards behind, keeping in perfect step with him. Suddenly, Crowley allowed his knees to buckle and dropped momentarily to the ground. At exactly the same moment, the man he was following collapsed in precisely the same manner.

By the early 1920s Crowley, who was suffering from asthma, was almost permanently in debt. A legacy of $12,000 enabled him to move to a small farmhouse in Cefalu, Italy. He called it the Abbey of Thelema, which means 'Do what you will', began to practice magic and invited disciples to join him. He provided apparently limitless quantities of drugs for anyone who wished to use them and attractive women devotees were expected to help Crowley practice his sex magic. Even with the legacy, however, the money problem remained pressing. Crowley wrote a novel called *Diary of a Drug Fiend* and started his *Confessions*, which he called his hagiography (the biography of a saint). He announced that the earth had now passed beyond Christianity and had entered the new epoch of Crowleyanity. But when one of his disciples died after sacrificing a cat and drinking its blood, the resulting newspaper scandal drove Crowley out of Sicily.

The British press denounced him as 'the wickedest man in the world' and, although he loved the publicity, he soon discovered that his notoriety made publishers shy away from his books. He deserted his disciples, one of whom committed suicide, and married again. His second wife, like the first, became insane. Hoping to make money, he sued the English sculptress Nina Hamnett for calling him a black magician. But when witnesses described Crowley's magic, the judge stopped the case, declaring he had never heard such 'dreadful, horrible, blasphemous, and abominable stuff'.

By the outbreak of World War II, Crowley had added alcoholism to his drug addiction, even though his daily intake of heroin at that time would have killed a dozen ordinary men. Every now and again he found rich disciples to support him until, inevitably, they lost patience with him. He retired to a rooming house near Hastings in southern England and died there in December 1947, at the age of 72. John Symonds, a writer who had met him in his last years, later wrote his biography – a hilarious but often disturbing book. Other friends, notably Richard Cammell and Israel Regardie, wrote more sober and admiring accounts of his career. But it was not until the magical revival, which began in the mid-1960s, that Crowley's reputation began to rise again. Nowadays, more than a dozen of his books are in print and a new generation ardently practices the magic rituals described in them. The Beast has finally achieved the fame he craved. Nonetheless (and fortunately), the great age of Crowley-anity seems as far away as ever.

CHAPTER 28

THEY LIVE AMONG US

Is it possible to trap the mysterious powers of the mind in the laboratory, and to examine and investigate them by means of scientific tests? With the present revival in occult phenomena, more and more scientists are trying to find a method by which many strangely gifted individuals can be accurately and reliably tested. As scientists work to define their powers, some gifted clairvoyants work with police, and many of their successes have been electrifying. Whether these talents lie within the human subconscious, or in contact with spirits or intelligences from some other world, there is clearly much more to discover.

In Paris, in the year 1960, there appeared on the bookstalls a volume with the euphonious title *Le Matin de Magiciens* (The Morning of Magicians), by Louis Pauwels and Jacques Bergier. It is a curious hodgepodge of a book, as the authors themselves recognized, for they wrote in the first chapter, 'Skip chapters if you want to; begin where you like, and read in any direction; this book is a multiple-use tool, like the knives campers use . . .' To everyone's astonishment the book became a best seller, running through edition after edition in France. Serious critics were irritated and baffled by its success – they pointed out that the book was merely a series of wild speculations on magic, alchemy, telepathy, prophecy, strange cults, the Great Pyramid, Hitler's astrologers, the Cabala, flying saucers and a thousand other topics. This mass of eccentricity was held together by one simple theme – the world is a stranger and richer place than science is willing to recognize.

It was a message that apparently had wide appeal in France, especially to the young. They were less interested in the book's argument about the narrowness of science, than in the imaginative appeal of its magical wonders. Other writers saw that there was money to be made out of the occult. Books on astrology, reincarnation and visitors from outer space rolled off the presses and there was no sign of any loss of interest. The craze spread to other countries, notably Germany, the United Kingdom and the United States. In 1968, a German book called *Remembrance of the Future* made a fortune and a name for its author, Erich von Daniken. Translated into English as *Chariots of the Gods?*, it sold more copies than any other book except the Bible. Daniken's thesis was that the earth was visited thousands of years ago by spacemen who left signs of their presence in many ancient cultures. Stanley Kubrick's film *2001, A Space Odyssey*, was based on the same idea. It became a kind of cult classic and its admirers went to see it again and again, just as they might attend a religious ceremony. The great occult boom had arrived.

Curiously enough, a powerful resurgence of interest in the occult has occurred toward the end of every century for the past 400 years. Is this pure chance – or is there, as some people believe, a hidden law that governs such apparently cyclic occult revivals? The question is impossible to answer but it is clear that we are now in the middle of the most widespread occult revival in history. One of its most significant and encouraging features is that it has captured the interest of a large number of scientists. All over the world, universities and other institutions have established laboratories of parapsychology – the scientific investigation of extrasensory perception, clairvoyance, psychokinesis and other psychic phenomena.

In the Netherlands, a famous Institute of Parapsychology was set up at the University of Utrecht, with Professor Willem H. C. Tenhaeff in charge. Tenhaeff has devoted much time to testing the powers of the psychic, Gerard Croiset.

Croiset was born in 1909. He was unfortunate in being an unhealthy child and in having to spend much of his childhood in foster homes. But from an early age he somehow knew about things that were happening in other places. Once, when a teacher returned to school after a day's absence, Croiset was able to tell him that he had spent the day in a distant place with a girl who wore a red rose in her dress and whom he would shortly marry. The teacher was amazed. He had, in fact, taken the day off to see his fiancee, who had worn a red rose.

When he was 25-years-old, Croiset visited the house of an acquaintance and picked up a stick lying on a table. Immediately his mind became crowded with images of an automobile accident and of a body lying on the roadside in a grassy place. The owner of the stick was astonished – it was an accurate description of an incident that frequently occupied his own mind. He told Croiset that he must be clairvoyant. Croiset now began to develop his faculty and had clear visions of the future – of the Nazi invasion of the Netherlands and of the loss of the Dutch East Indies to the Japanese, for example.

In the 1970s, Croiset became internationally known as a psychometrist – a person with the gift of reading the past associations of objects by holding them in his hand. The authenticity of this faculty in Croiset cannot be doubted, for he has been employed on numerous occasions by the Dutch police – and often with remarkable success. In 1949, for instance, Croiset was asked to help in a case of a sex crime. The police had suspects but were by no means certain which, if any, was guilty. Croiset was handed two wrapped objects. Without opening the first, he declared correctly that it was a tobacco box. He described the house from which it came and the two middle-aged brothers who lived in the house. He went on to give detailed descriptions of the characters of each of the brothers and he identified them as the rapists. The second package contained a sack. Croiset immediately saw a cow in connection with it and, in fact, it was used as a cow blanket. He described how the two brothers had taken the girl, a mentally retarded child, to a cowshed with hay on the floor and raped her. After that, the girl had been put into the sack and the brothers had discussed what to do with her. One wanted to bury her alive, the other to drown her. The brothers quarrelled over this and the girl was allowed to live.

The two men, who had been among the suspects, were tried separately and convicted. Croiset again correctly foretold that one of them would commit suicide within a week or two of conviction. He was also able to tell the police that the brother had committed other crimes – among them the rape of a Jewish girl in hiding from the Nazis during the war. He was even able to show them the house where this crime had taken place.

Another Dutchman has become even more famous than Gerard Croiset as a psychometrist who occasionally aids the police. He is Pieter van der Hurk, better known as Peter Hurkos. He also has scored some remarkable hits. In 1958, he was asked by the police of Miami, Florida to sit in the cab of a murdered cab driver and give them his impressions of the killer. As he sat there, Hurkos described the murder of the driver in detail. Then he described the killer as tall and thin, with a tattoo on his right arm and a rolling walk like a sailor. His name, Hurkos said, was Smitty and he had also been responsible for another murder in Miami – that of a man shot to death in his apartment. The police were stunned. There had been such a murder recently but, as far as they knew, it had no connection with the killing of the cab driver. They searched their files and came up with a photograph of an ex-sailor named Charles Smith. Shortly afterward, a waitress interviewed by the police recognized the man in the photograph as a drunk sailor who had boasted to her of killing two men. A wanted alert went out for Smith, who was arrested in New Orleans and sent back to Miami. He confessed to the murder of the cab driver and was sentenced to life imprisonment.

Unlike Croiset, Hurkos was not born clairvoyant. He acquired his extraordinary gift in the Netherlands during World War II, as the result of an accident. Knocked unconscious after a fall from a ladder, he woke up in the hospital with a fractured skull. As he recovered, he found to his amazement that he could read people's thoughts and seemed to know the future. Once when a nurse took his pulse, he told her to be careful or she might lose a suitcase belonging to a friend. The nurse had, in fact, just arrived at the hospital by train and had left a friend's suitcase behind in the dining car. Hurkos told another patient that he ought to be ashamed of himself for selling the gold watch his father had left him when he died. This, too, was true.

His new faculty almost cost Hurkos his life. A patient who had been discharged from the hospital came to shake his hand – and, in that moment of contact, Hurkos knew that the man would shortly be murdered in the street. The victim was involved in resistance against the Nazis. When gossip about Hurkos' prediction reached the Dutch underground movement, it was assumed that Hurkos was a German counter-espionage agent and a member was sent to kill him. It took Hurkos some fast talking to convince his would-be assassin that he was not in the pay of the Nazis.

When Hurkos came out of the hospital, he found that he was unable to do normal work. He no longer possessed the power of concentration required for everyday tasks. This is significant. It may well be that psychic powers are inherent in all of us, but that we unconsciously suppress them – not because they are of little help to us in everyday circumstances, but because they would actually impede our survival in the modern world. Croiset had become bankrupt as a grocer, before he began to use his clair-voyant powers. Likewise, it was only after someone suggested that Hurkos exploit his extraordinary gift on the stage, that he made enough money to support himself.

It is also interesting that Croiset was frequently sick as a child and that Hurkos' gifts emerged only after an accident. This is not to suggest that strange powers are necessarily accompanied by sickness, but only that sickness may be one of the factors which releases psychic sensitivity. On the other hand, many healthy people have deliberately cultivated their psychic powers because they needed them. The tiger hunter Jim Corbett, whose *Man Eaters of Kumaon* has become a modern classic, recounts how his life was saved again and again by his 'jungle sensitiveness' – his sudden intuitive knowledge that a man-eater was lying in wait for him.

Dowsing – the ability to detect underground water, among other things – has long bemused scientists and sceptics alike. As with many other forms of ESP, it seems essentially against the perceived laws of nature, yet for centuries dowsers around the world have been making a comfortable living successfully finding underground streams and sites for wells. Colin Wilson here describes working with one of Britain's best known dowsers:

'A psychic whom I myself have met is the British dowser, Robert Leftwich. Leftwich was described in a magazine article as a man of tremendous energy. The article had discussed his dowsing abilities, which he had successfully demonstrated on television, and also his power to project his astral body. Leftwich had also explained how he had used his psychic powers as a child at school. When the class was instructed to learn a long poem by heart, Leftwich would memorize only a few lines. The teacher customarily looked around the class and chose someone to recite each successive passage of the poem. When the passage that he had learned was coming up, Leftwich would will the teacher to ask him to recite. He claimed that the trick had always worked.

'I was anxious to meet a man who seemed to combine psychic abilities with enormous zest and vitality. I visited him at his home in Sussex, and later he came to my home in Cornwall. His dowsing abilities are undoubtedly remarkable. He demonstrated the dowsing in the house. I hid a coin under a carpet while he was out of the room. He came in with his divining rod and walked around. The rod bent downward violently as he stood over the coin. He explained that for him dowsing is a matter of tuning in the mind to the specific object. If he had been looking for some other object – a playing card or a matchbox – the rod would have ignored the coin, and dipped over the card or matches. He further explained that the rod could also be made to react over everything except what he was looking for. To demonstrate he walked around the room again, and this time the rod twisted violently in his hands until he stood above the coin; then it became still.

'We also did thought transference tests with playing cards. I chose a card from the deck while Leftwich stood on the other side of the room, and tried to transmit its identity to him. His score was exceptionally high. But he is convinced that his powers do not depend just on telepathy, so we tried another test. I shuffled a deck of cards and threw the cards face down on the table. At a certain point he said, "Stop. That's the ace of clubs." He was right. He scored four out of seven on this test.

'Leftwich also demonstrated a form of telepathic dowsing. He stood with his back to my wife, and asked her to walk away from him across the garden. We knew where underground waterpipes were located, but he did not. At a certain point, however, he called "Stop!" She had just crossed an underground waterpipe, and he had located it by using her mind as a transmitter.'

The usual explanation of dowsing is that the mind tunes in to some form of electric field. This was the explanation put forward by the philosopher, Professor C. E. M. Joad in one of the British

Broadcasting Corporation's *Brains Trust* broadcasts of 1946. But after suggesting that water emits some form of electrical radiation that can be detected by the dowser, Joad went on to admit that he had no idea of the explanation of map dowsing. The map dowser holds a pendulum over a map and the pendulum begins to swing or vibrate when it is held over the substance he is looking for – water, oil, minerals or even gold. Joad described how he had witnessed map dowsing in action. A large-scale map, from which all rivers and streams had been carefully removed, was laid out on a table. The map dowser went over it with a pendulum, on the end of which was a small bobbin that could spin. The bobbin spun every time the pendulum was suspended over a place where the dowser detected water. At the end of the session, the dowser had located every river, stream and pond in the area.

Obviously, Joad's theory about radiation cannot explain this. Then how can it be explained? Once again, we are driven to return to the hypothesis that the secret lies in our own minds, but not necessarily in the subconscious mind – the Freudian 'basement' that is supposed to contain all our most primitive animal impulses. Leftwich, like many other occultists, believes that the answer may lie in a part of the mind which could be called the 'superconscious'. If the mind can have a subconscious basement, might it not also possess a superconscious 'attic'?

It was nearly a century ago, that respectable scientists such as Sir William Crookes and Sir Oliver Lodge began to take an interest in the paranormal. At that time, it looked as if the answers to the questions raised might rest reassuringly within the concepts of life after death and of a universe of benevolent spirits doing their best to give help and guidance to the living on earth. But since that time, every decade has revealed new mysteries, and the problem of finding a single explanation becomes increasingly difficult.

Let us take a look at some of the experiences of Dr Andrija Puharich, a researcher whom Aldous Huxley described as 'one of the most brilliant minds on parapsychology'. In 1952, Dr Puharich investigated the case of Harry Stone, a young Dutch sculptor. In deep trance states, Stone spoke ancient Egyptian and wrote hieroglyphics – neither of which he had the slightest knowledge of in his normal state. The messages purported to come from the Ra Ho Tep, an Egyptian of the Fourth Dynasty about 2700 BC.

In 1963, Puharich heard about José Arigó, a Brazilian healer called the 'surgeon of the rusty knife'. In April of that year, he went to Arigó's town to watch the wonderworker in action. The surgeon proved to be a barrel-chested peasant who thought himself possessed by the spirit of a dead German doctor. Puharich watched Arigó deal with 200 patients in four hours, performing many operations without anaesthetic and at great speed. Arigó removed a tumour from Puharich's own arm in a few seconds. Puharich felt nothing and the flesh healed in four days, without disinfectant or antibiotics. In 1971, Arigó was killed in a car accident. Puharich received the news by telephone but was unable to confirm it from any of the news agencies. Later that day, he discovered that Arigó had been killed that morning as his caller had said. But when Puharich looked for the phone number of the caller, which he had written on a notepad, it had vanished. Moreover, his secretary who had been with him throughout the day could not recollect him taking the phone call.

This anecdote is recounted in Puharich's most baffling book, *Uri, a Journal of the Mystery of Uri Geller*. Puharich was drawn to Geller by accounts of his feats of mind reading, spoon bending and his curious power over watches. At his first meeting with Geller, Puharich witnessed some remarkable feats. Geller told a woman to hold a ring in her hand and placed his left hand over her clenched fist for 30 seconds. At the end of that time the ring was found to be broken into two pieces. Geller also demonstrated his powers of telepathy by performing a reading of the future. He wrote three numbers on a pad and placed it face down on the table. Then he asked Puharich to think of three numbers. Puharich selected the numbers 4, 3 and 2. Uri then turned over the pad – on which was written the figures 4, 3, 2. Geller explained that his experiment did not involve precognition, because he had transmitted the numbers to Puharich. In still other demonstrations of his strange powers, Geller changed the time on Puharich's watch as Puharich held it in his own hand, and raised the temperature of a metal thermometer by eight degrees without touching it.

If this were all it would be remarkable enough. But Puharich goes on to make such a startling claim that one's first response is to doubt his sincerity. Briefly, he says that Geller is a kind of saviour or messiah, controlled by beings from outer space that are hovering a few million miles away in a spaceship called *Spectra*. These beings had apparently visited earth on a number of previous occasions and had also selected the patriarch Abraham and the Pharoah Imhotep as avatars, or incarnations of a divine being.

Given the present worldwide interest in the occult, one might expect Puharich's book to have created a sensation and become a best seller. Instead, it was received with a mixture of indifference and hostility. This is not to say that most critics thought Puharich was a liar. Many of them obviously felt that Puharich was sincere but mistaken. Geller told Colin Wilson that everything in Puharich's book is factually accurate but that he himself does not necessarily accept the notion that he is a messiah. This raises some fascinating questions, not merely about Geller and Puharich but also about the whole subject of the occult. The fact that a person possesses certain powers, proves nothing about the source of those powers. Impressive documentary evidence seems to prove, beyond all doubt, that the Victorian medium Daniel Dunglass Home was able to wash his face in red hot coals without getting singed, and could cause heavy tables to float through the air. But this does not prove, as he claimed, that his powers came from spirits rather than from his own subconscious mind. Joan of Arc declared that she had been ordered to save France by St. Michael and St. Catherine, and the Church that had sanctified her, apparently accepts her claim. But did her voices have any greater reality than those of the beings that visited Geller? In the long history of messianic religious movements, dozens of messiahs have astounded their followers by apparently genuine miracles, such as levitating, healing the sick and conferring immunity against weapons. But as their promises about the end of the world have proven untrue, we must conclude that most of them were self-deceivers, however authentic their strange powers. Similarly, Puharich's claims regarding Geller's gifts may be true – but this does not prove that Geller is a messiah or that the spaceship *Spectra* exists.

This still leaves us with the basic question – what is the source of energy or power behind these events, and behind so many psychic phenomena? There seem to be two possibilities – what we have called the superconscious, or spirits of celestial intelligences. The problem with the idea of a superconscious is that, while it is easy enough to understand its role in map dowsing or precognition, it is altogether more difficult to understand why it should conceive flying saucers and beings from outer space. Is it possible that the superconscious possesses a sense of humour? Many students of the paranormal would say that this is, indeed, a possibility, to the extent that the activities of the superconscious may be completely freakish and unexplainable.

Consider the curious case of the Abbot Vachère of Mirebeau in France. In 1913, the abbot was regarded as a kindly and conscientious member of the church, well liked by the Pope himself but without any remarkable talent. He was in his 60th year when the first of a series of strange and rather embarrassing events began, and drops of reddish moisture began to ooze from the hands and feet of the figure of Jesus in a painting that hung in Vachère's private chapel. Vachère reported the matter to his Bishop who asked to see the picture. It was dispatched to the Bishop, but failed to bleed. When it was returned to its chapel, however, the bleeding started again.

Later, a gang of workmen were building Stations of the Cross near the abbot's home and Vachère pinned up an ordinary colour print of Jesus in their hut. This also began to bleed. The bishop investigated, decided that Vachère was a fraud and excommunicated the abbot. The bewildered and unhappy Vachère visited his friends at Aix-la-Chapelle; with him in the house, a statue and a picture belonging to his hostess began to bleed.

Many people felt that the bleeding indicated that Abbot Vachère was a saint or, at least, that he had been selected by God for some special destiny. The Church had no reason to think so and refused to investigate the phenomena which, however, continued to occur until the abbot died in 1921.

The evidence leaves little doubt that the phenomena were genuine. On the other hand, the Church probably showed common sense in refusing to accept them as evidence of sanctity. Possibly the bleeding statues and pictures were a trick perpetrated by the abbot's superconscious. In any event, like the *fakirs'* wonders, the phenomena were spiritually worthless.

This story illustrates the fact that most human beings, churchmen as well as scientists, find supernatural phenomena embarrassing and prefer to ignore them. Such phenomena fail to conform to the laws of nature as we know them. Consequently, they tend to be regarded as irrelevant freaks rather than as interesting pieces of some, as yet, unsolved universal jigsaw puzzle.

A similar attitude was shown toward a series of experiments made by Dr Jule Eisenbud, a psychiatrist and member of the faculty of the University of Colorado Medical School. In 1963, Eisenbud published an article arguing that it is impossible to devise a truly repeatable experiment in the field of paranormal phenomena. A correspondent disagreed and sent him a magazine clipping about a man called Ted Serios. According to the article, Serios could take photographs by means of the mind alone. He would take a polaroid camera in his hands, stare hard into the lens and somehow produce photographs of recognizable places, of faces or people, or of objects such as cars and buses.

Eisenbud's interest was aroused and he arranged a demonstration. Serios proved to be a bellhop of alcoholic tendencies, who also claimed to have the power of projecting his astral body. But the second claim was unconnected with the ability he demonstrated to Eisenbud. He stared down a small paper tube, which he called his 'gismo', toward the camera lens. After a number of failures, he succeeded in producing two blurry pictures of a water tower and a hotel. In considerable excitement, Eisenbud immediately got in touch with various scientists and told them what had happened. To his astonishment, they showed only polite interest and had no wish to see a demonstration. Eisenbud was encountering the reaction we have mentioned above – the embarrassment effect produced by freakish, and apparently inexplicable, events.

Eisenbud refused to be deterred, however. He continued to test Serios and some of the resulting 'thought photographs' were spectacular. Naturally Eisenbud's first suspicion – like that of everybody else who tested Serios – had been that the trick lay in the gismo. Serios insisted that the tube of paper merely helped him to concentrate and close examination of the gismo revealed nothing suspicious. Eisenbud concluded that Serios's powers were genuine, even if they made no sense in terms of any scientific law.

Charles Reynolds and David Eisendrath, two reporters who had watched Serios at work, were convinced he was a fake. They constructed a small device that could be hidden inside the gismo, with a lens at one end and a piece of unexposed film at the other. When this was pointed at the camera, the result was a picture not unlike those that Serios had produced. The account of their invention was printed in *Popular Photography* in 1967 and it gave all the sceptics fresh ammunition. Since then, their article has been cited by people who believe that Serios is a fake, as evidence that he performed his thought photography by sleight of hand. In March 1974, *Time* magazine ran an article on the occult revival and included a brief account of Serios and the *Popular Photography* article. *Time* concluded, 'Many of Serios's followers were shattered. Again, the millennium was deferred.'

Now it is certainly possible that Serios is a fraud. But Reynolds and Eisendrath have done nothing to prove the contention. They merely demonstrated that they themselves could construct a gismo fitted with a lens and film. Dr Eisenbud vainly pointed out that he and other experimenters had examined Serios's gismo for such fraud and had found none.

My aim here is not to defend Serios – although thought photography is no less extraordinary than paintings that bleed or spoons that bend – but to point out that orthodox science is still a long way from taking a balanced and truly scientific attitude toward paranormal phenomena. There exists a deeply ingrained emotional prejudice that is just as likely to obscure the truth, as are the wishful thinking of gullible parapsychologists and the dishonesty of fraudulent psychics.

Finally, if we discard the idea of the superconscious, is it remotely possible that some of these strange forces come from outside man? Might there be other intelligences – either spirits of the dead or creatures from other worlds – that are controlling or influencing the destiny of this planet?

The idea of life outside earth has received support from a number of scientists, but it must be admitted, that the evidence is far from convincing. Some scientists have suggested that certain radio signals received from outer space may have been sent by intelligent beings. We also have the curious accounts of people who claim to have been in communication with creatures from flying saucers.

William Paley, a late eighteenth-century British theologian, used his watch as an argument for the existence of God. He argued that when we open the back and see the works, it is impossible not to recognize that it has been created by an intelligent mind. Therefore when we contemplate the universe, which is far more complex than a watch, how is it possible not to believe that it was created by an intelligent being? The followers of the scientist Charles Darwin were contemptuous of this argument. They insisted that the complexity of the universe – like the complexity of a snow crystal – is due to the operation of natural laws. This argument is not very convincing either, for the complexity of the universe is infinitely greater than that of a snow crystal. Next time you take a walk in the countryside, look at every living thing – trees, flowers, insects, birds, rivers, clouds. Then ask yourself whether you can imagine that they could have been produced by purely mechanical laws.

Intelligences from outer space or the human superconscious mind? Either explanation is possible and it may be that there is truth in both. But for the human race at this point in history, the most fruitful line of inquiry undoubtedly lies within ourselves. The secret of the powers of shamans, of magicians, of psychics and clairvoyants probably lies in some unexplored part of our inner space. When man invents a spacecraft that will carry him to his own inner moons and planets, he will have discovered the secret that every magician has sought – a secret more fascinating than the Philosopher's Stone or the Elixir of Life.

CHAPTER 29

IN SEARCH OF THE UNKNOWN

Are we able to obtain information about the world only through our senses? Or is it possible for mind to transcend the everyday rules and make direct contact with another mind, or even with matter? Scientists trying to come to grips with the increasing evidence that such contact is possible, have classified and defined various types of psychic experience – experience which appears to happen to people of all ages and places and stations in life. It is not only the magician who is gifted with mysterious powers: the evidence shows that all humans may have some degree of psychic ability.

It was the custom of Madame D, a Frenchwoman, to take a bath every evening about six o'clock. One evening, shortly after getting into the tub, she began to feel ill. She didn't know that a leak in a gas pipe, or an inadequately closed valve, had let gas escape into the bathroom. Mme. D managed to press a call bell located near the tub just before she was overcome by the fumes and slid down into the water. An instant later, her husband rushed into the bathroom, pulled her out of the water and restored her to consciousness.

After she was able to talk again, her husband asked her if she had experienced a fleeting vision of her past life in minute detail – as drowning people are said to. Mme. D replied that she had seen a vision, but not the kind one would expect. Instead of seeing her husband and children and events from her past, she had seen the face of a casual acquaintance, Mme. J. 'She was near me', said Mme. D, 'looking at me sadly. It was impossible in those few moments to remove her from my eyes and thoughts.'

The next morning, completely recovered, Mme. D received word of the death of Mme. J. The woman had been drinking rather heavily on the previous evening, had gone into the bathroom to take a bath and had drowned in the tub before she could call for help. The time – about six o'clock.

Was it sheer coincidence that at the moment of her near tragedy, Mme. D should think of a woman she knew only slightly, who at the same time was undergoing a similar experience? A strictly rational view of this incident (adapted from René Warcollier's *Experiments in Telepathy*) would indicate a 'yes' answer. Mme. D had no way of knowing by normal means that the other woman's life was in danger at that moment. The persistent image of Mme. J was simply – according to his viewpoint – a peculiar mental association, a trick of the mind with no causal relationship to Mme. J's crisis. In other words, a coincidence.

All of us experience odd coincidences at one time or another, even if they're not as dramatic as the vision of Mme. D. We may suddenly, for no apparent reason, think of a song that was popular perhaps 15 or 20 years ago, switch on the radio and hear that particular song being played. Or we think of a friend, and a moment later that friend telephones.

Although we are sometimes tempted to think there may be a connection between the two events, most of us don't really believe in such a connection. Our everyday experience tells us that the only way we can get information is through our senses. We cannot know that the radio station is playing the song we thought of, until we switch it on and hear it. We cannot know that the friend is dialling our number because we cannot hear or see the friend at that moment. On answering the phone we may say, 'I must be psychic, I was just thinking of you!' But we don't seriously believe that our mind can, so to speak, bypass the senses and get information the senses cannot supply.

Increasingly, however, evidence is suggesting that it *is* possible for the mind to transcend the senses. Some of the evidence is startling, such as the experience of Mme. D. Some of it is somewhat unexciting, such as the ability to guess correctly, more often than chance would allow, which card will turn up next as one goes through the pack. Not all of the evidence is conclusive. But there is enough strong evidence to suggest that occasionally – perhaps frequently – direct mind-to-mind contact does take place. Today, there are many scientists who would agree that some kind of mental link existed between Mme. D and Mme. J at the moment both were in danger. How such a link is established no one cay say – but that it can be established, is one of the more exciting discoveries of modern science.

Not only is mind-to-mind contact possible, but it also seems possible that some minds can get information from inanimate objects without using the senses. This apparently is something that the wife of the American novelist, Upton Sinclair was able to do. Back in the 1920s, Mrs Sinclair discovered that she could reproduce drawings in sealed envelopes, and in his book *Mental Radio,* Sinclair tells the story of the discovery. Mrs Sinclair had experienced a certain amount of pain from illnesses and had learned to exert mental control over this pain. She developed the ability to relax completely, to clear her mind of random thoughts and to concentrate on a single idea. Her awakening interest in psychic powers developed further, when the Sinclairs became acquainted with a young man named Jan, who performed an amazing variety of mental and physical feats including levitation. Mrs Sinclair established a strong rapport with Jan and was often able to describe in detail what he was doing at a given moment when he was far away from her. One day, she jotted down a dream she had about him, in which he brought her a little basket of flowers – pink roses and violets. She sketched the outline of the basket and flowers. The next day she received a letter from him. In it, through slits cut in the paper, he had inserted some violets and pink cosmos. The shape that the flowers made on the paper roughly followed the outline of the squat basket she had drawn.

Over the next year or two, Mrs Sinclair did 290 drawings attempting to copy drawings made by her husband, his secretary and her own brother-in-law. She occasionally wrote comments on her drawings to compensate for her limitations as an artist and to express more precisely the image in her mind's eye. Sometimes she simply wrote what she saw. In an early experiment, her brother-in-law, who was in Pasadena some 40 miles away, drew a picture of a fork. At the same agreed-upon-time,

Mrs Sinclair directed her powers of concentration toward his mind and finally wrote, 'See a table fork. Nothing else.' In some cases, only part of the original drawing seemed to come through – for Sinclair's drawing of a steamboat, she did only the smoke-stack with smoke coming out of it. Partial successes often resembled the shape of the original drawing – a pocket watch, for example, was seen as a wheel.

Out of the 290 drawings, the Sinclairs counted 65 as successes, 155 as partial successes and the remaining 70 as failures. Acutely aware that most thoughtful people of his day regarded anything suggesting the occult with a certain amount of contempt, Sinclair went to great pains to stress his and his wife's commitment to a rational view of the world. His socialist friends were critical of this aberration on the part of one of their spokesmen, and one of them wrote a newspaper article entitled 'Sinclair Goes Spooky'. Sinclair answered their objections with all the eloquence he could command, stating, 'I don't like to believe in telepathy, because I don't know what to make of it, and I don't know to what view of the universe it will lead me, and I would a whole lot rather give all my time to my muck-raking job . . . In short, there isn't a thing in the world that leads me to this act, except the conviction which has been forced upon me that telepathy is real, and that loyalty to the nature of the universe makes it necessary for me to say so.' If he were writing today, he would not need to be so defensive. Parapsychology – the branch of psychology dealing with telepathy and other psychic abilities – has established itself as a scientific discipline. In 1969, the Parapsychological Association (an international organization of parapsychologists) finally won membership in the American Association for the Advancement of Science. The parapsychologists' bid for membership was championed by the world-renowned anthropologist, Margaret Mead. Her plea for their admission to the prestigious scientific body included these words, 'The whole history of scientific advance is full of scientists investigating phenomena that the Establishment did not believe were there. I submit that we vote in favour of this association's work.' The final vote was six to one in favour of admission.

The British magazine, *New Scientist*, found in a poll of its readers a few years ago that 70 per cent of the respondents, mainly scientists and technicians, believed in the possibility of extrasensory perception. Of course, to believe in the possibility of something is not the same as believing in the thing itself. Even so, the high percentage suggests that the suspicious, if not hostile, attitude of scientists toward parapsychology is not as prevalent as it was in the past.

Mainstream science has impressive achievements to its credit – technological innovations that were inconceivable a century ago that have given us undreamed-of control over our environment and the forces of nature. But in spite of all the great changes it has effected in our environment, there are certain aspects of ourselves that mainstream science has not been able to make any sense of, aspects that not only fail to fit into its picture of reality but also actually challenge that picture. As the awareness grows that the human is a threatened species, and that our swift technological advance has disrupted delicate balances in nature that are essential to our survival, more and more people are opening their minds to alternatives to the scientific-rationalist view of the world. Cultures, philosophies and religions that were formerly regarded as primitive and barbarous, are being looked at with new interest. People are asking whether, in travelling so far so fast, we might not have left something behind. Might there not be something useful for us to learn both from neglected areas of the human psyche and from backward or primitive areas of the world?

In 1973, the Parapsychology Foundation of New York sponsored a conference in London on the theme 'Parapsychology and Anthropology'. The highlight of the conference was a paper entitled 'African Apprenticeship' read by an Englishman named Adrian Boshier, who is also a witch doctor.

After years of living among the tribesmen of South Africa, Boshier had become accepted by them as a brother. Finally they invited him to undergo the 12 degrees of initiation that would qualify him as a witch doctor. Boshier's experiences have convinced him that the secrets and magical rites of the *sangomas*, as they call themselves, are not merely superstition. They are, in more colourful guise, the same kinds of phenomena studied in western parapsychology laboratories. The difference is that, whereas in the West these phenomena are viewed with suspicion, the tribesmen Boshier knew accepted them as true.

In his paper for the London conference, Boshier gave several examples of the psychic powers of the *sangomas*. On one occasion he had narrowly escaped being attacked by a leopard while he was exploring an ancient copper mine. Later, on his way back to Johannesburg, he passed through a village in which lived an old, woman *sangoma*, whom he knew. He found her sitting in her 'hut of the spirits', throwing the bones that she used as aids to divination. She became agitated, for she said she could make no sense of what the bones were telling her. 'All I can see is the underworld, the underground', she said. Boshier told her about his exploration of the ancient mines, which put her mind at rest. But she warned him, 'You must be very careful when you go down there, as the gods of the underworld can be very dangerous. Also, I see you here in my bones next to the leopard. The leopard, too, was in that place, and he does not like people in his home. You must be very careful of this animal – I see you were right next to him.'

Tales of the psychic powers of witch doctors have been told by European travellers ever since Africa was opened up to trade and exploration in the nineteenth century. A typically strange story was told by a hunter and merchant named D. Leslie, in a book privately published in Edinburgh in 1875.

Leslie had sent out his local elephant hunters with instructions to meet him on a certain date at a selected spot. They failed to turn up, so he consulted a local witch doctor who demanded to know the number of missing hunters and their names. He then made eight fires, one for each hunter, threw in some roots that produced a sickly smelling smoke, took some medicine and fell into trance.

After about 10 minutes, he came out of the trance. He raked through the ashes of each of the fires in turn, and told Leslie what had happened to each of his hunters. One had died of fever and his gun was lost; another had been killed by an elephant but his gun had been recovered by another member of the party; a third had killed four elephants and was bringing back their tusks. The survivors, he said, would not be home for three months and would travel by a different route than that previously chosen. Three months later, Leslie was able to confirm every detail of the witch doctor's account.

Of course, such stories do not prove anything. They are the testimonies of individuals, not supported or confirmed by independent investigation and we know very well that we cannot always trust the evidence of our senses, or the reliability of our memory. We see and remember what we want to, often for reasons of which we are not aware. It may be argued that man's mind is avid for wonders, mysteries and sensations and is uncritical and easily deceived when it comes across them. Marvellous tales told by travellers have enthralled listeners in taverns, at firesides and around campfires, throughout human history. Today, tales that are equally marvellous, sensational and inexplicable, enthrall readers of scientific books as well.

In a New York parapsychology laboratory in 1973, the artist and well-known psychic, Ingo Swann, underwent a number of tests, carefully observed by scientists and recorded by a television camera. In one test he sat in a chair in the middle of the room and tried to 'see' the contents of a cardboard box suspended from the ceiling. No one present knew what was in the box and the only way to see into it would have been to climb on a ladder. After concentrating for several minutes with his eyes closed, Swann sketched the shapes and identified the colours of the hidden objects. The test was repeated eight times, and each time he scored a hit. Explaining how he did it, Swann said that he went into trance, then felt his spirit float to the ceiling, look into the box and return to his body. This claim the scientists could neither prove nor disprove, but their electronic equipment did record a noticeable change in his brainwave output before he drew each picture.

Other people have reported the experience of travelling out of the body, but their accounts – usually involving an illness or other crisis – have little value as evidence. The experiments with Ingo Swann illustrate how, in the last few decades, the study of the strange and unexplained faculties of the human mind has progressed from the anecdotal stage to the experimental. There are still, however, some critics of parapsychology who reject the experimental evidence and say that delusion, wishful thinking and outright lying are as rife in the laboratory as in the tavern. Although scientific opinion is more favourable to parapsychology than it was 40 or 50 years ago, the psychic area is still clouded with emotion, distrust and vagueness and it is difficult for the layman to make sense of it all.

Parapsychology – or as it is sometimes called, psychical research – includes the study of several phenomena which are often referred to by the umbrella-term 'psi' (pronounced 'sigh'). These phenomena fall into two groups, mental and physical. The mental phenomena are covered by the term ESP (extrasensory perception) and include telepathy, clairvoyance, psychometry, precognition and retrocognition. The physical phenomena include psychokinesis or PK (also called telekinesis), in its various forms including teleportation, levitation, and psychic healing; materialization and dematerialization; and out of body projection.

Telepathy is a word coined by the early psychical researcher, F. W. H. Myers to denote the 'transmission of thought independently of the recognized channels of sense'. In an autobiographical book, *The Infinite Hive*, the English psychical researcher, Rosalind Heywood gives a fascinating account of numerous telepathic experiences that occurred in her own life. She recalls an occasion in 1944, during World War II, when her husband was due home on his first leave since the Normandy landings. His train from the Channel port of Folkestone was expected at 8 pm. At 6:30 pm, Mrs. Heywood lay down for a short rest after a hard day's work. She had been resting for 10 minutes when she got a compulsive urge to phone the station and check the time of the train. She learned that it would arrive an hour earlier than expected. She then got a strong impression that her husband wanted her to meet him at the station and to have a porter ready. She just managed to reach the station and get a porter in time to meet her husband's train. He was delighted at his welcome and he confirmed that during the journey from Folkestone, he had deliberately tried to send her a mental message that the train would be early and he would need help. The telephone booths at Folkestone had had mile-long lines of people waiting for them, he explained, so he had decided to try telepathic communication instead.

Clairvoyance is the ability of a person to receive extrasensory knowledge of a thing or an event that is not known to any other human being at the time. If an experimenter in a parapsychology laboratory shuffles a deck of cards and gives the deck to the subject and the subject succeeds in guessing the correct order of the cards in the shuffled deck, the feat may be called clairvoyant. Examples of pure clairvoyance are fairly rare, for usually some person – however distant – knows the information; and in such cases telepathy, not clairvoyance, is the likelier explanation. For example, the witch doctor who divined the fate of Leslie's hunters may have received the knowledge telepathically from one of the survivors. Similarly, Ingo Swann's discovery of the contents of the box may have been due neither to out-of-the-body projection nor to clairvoyance, but to telepathy with the absent person who placed the items in the box.

Psychometry, or object-reading, is a special kind of clairvoyance in which the subject receives information about a person extrasensorily, by handling an object associated with that person. In his book *Supernormal Faculties in Man*, the French parapsychologist, Eugène Osty described how the psychic Mme. Morel, once traced a missing person. She was given a scarf from his wardrobe but not told his name. After describing a forest and giving its approximate location, she focused on the body that she saw flying on the ground there, and said, 'He is bald, has a long nose . . . a little white hair above his ears and at the back of his head . . . wearing a long coat . . . soft shirt . . . hands closed . . . I see one finger which has been hurt . . . very old and wrinkled . . . pendant lips . . . Forehead much furrowed, very high and open . . . He is lying on his right side, one leg bent under him . . .' The search team found the man's body lying where she had said it was, in exactly that position.

Precognition and **retrocognition** are the terms for paranormal knowledge of future and past events, respectively. There are many puzzling accounts of precognition on record. In 1956, the American psychic Jeane Dixon wrote in a magazine article, 'the 1960 election will be won by a Democrat, but he will be assassinated or die in office.' A few weeks before President Kennedy's assassination in Dallas she told a friend who was close to the Kennedys, 'The President has just made a decision to go someplace in the South that will be fatal for him. You must get word to him not to make the trip.'

Retrocognition is less frequently reported, for it is obviously more difficult to distinguish paranormal knowledge of the past from normal knowledge. The classic case is that of two English women, Miss Moberly and Miss Jourdain. On a visit to the Palace of Versailles on a summer afternoon in 1901, they found (or imagined) themselves thrown back in time to the eighteenth century and saw the costumed courtiers and all the paths and buildings as they had been in the days of Marie Antoinette. Fifty years later, in 1951, two other Englishwomen visiting Dieppe on the coast of Normandy woke in the middle of the night to sounds of battle. Nothing was visible from their hotel window, but they distinctly heard the sound of gunfire coming from the direction of the beach, tanks rumbling along the roads and aircraft zooming overhead. Later, it was discovered that the occasion was precisely the ninth anniversary of the 1942 Dieppe Raid by Allied Forces and that the women's account of their experience corresponded exactly with the time schedule of the actual invasion.

Psychokinesis is the movement of objects by mental energy, or the power of 'mind over matter'. A California man recounts how, two nights after his wife's death, he had a strong sensation that she was present in the room, so he said, 'If you are here and can hear me, give me a sign.' He had no sooner spoken the words, than a heavy model chariot with two horses crashed to the floor from a mantelpiece where it had stood for 12 years. Whether the power that moved it came from his wife's spirit, from the man himself, or from a natural cause is arguable but the accumulated evidence on such phenomena – including clocks stopping or starting for no apparent reason, pictures falling from walls and vases being hurled across rooms – testifies to the reality of psychokinesis.

Teleportation – less well authenticated than the kinds of phenomena mentioned above – is the ability to move an object from one place to another by psychic means. Andrija Puharich, the scientist who conducted a long series of experiments with Israeli psychic Uri Geller, claims that on one occasion Geller teleported, to Israel, a camera case that Puharich had left in his home near New York and that he had said he needed.

Levitation is the ability to rise from the ground or to raise material objects by paranormal means. Tales of levitations by saints or mystics are found in the literature of religions the world over. They are also common in the records of seances with nineteenth-century mediums. The most famous, controversial and spectacular case was that performed by the British medium Daniel Dunglas Home, usually referred to as DD. In front of several distinguished witnesses, Home levitated, floated out of a third-story window and re-entered the building through the window of another room.

Psychic healing has a long history and includes some of the miracle cures performed by Christ and many of the Christian saints. Today, psychic healing or faith healing, is practiced not only by members of the clergy in the form of laying-on-of-hands, but also by people who, without representing any religious viewpoint, seem to be able to will a person to health. A different aspect of the same apparent power has been demonstrated in controlled experiments with plants, in which those plants that had prayers said over them developed into noticeably healthier specimens than the control group over which no prayers were said.

A bizarre variant of psychic healing is psychic surgery. In recent years, many Europeans and Americans in terminal stages of illness have been going to the Philippines and Brazil and returning home to tell incredulous friends and doctors how local healers have apparently removed tumours from their bodies, simply by massaging and kneading the flesh with their bare hands. Although some observers have been convinced that removal of tissue actually takes place in these treatments, others maintain that the operation is simply a conjuring trick.

Materialization, like psychic surgery, is a highly controversial phenomenon and most psychical researchers would deny that it actually occurs. As the name implies, it involves the creation of material objects – sometimes living organisms – apparently out of nothing, or out of a substance called ectoplasm that exudes from a medium's body. Dematerialization is the reverse process, the causing of the materialized objects to disappear. One extraordinary story of materialization involved a seal. A zoologist named Mr Bolton had cared for and prolonged the life of a large seal that had been harpooned, but in spite of his efforts, it had finally died. Ten days after the seal's death, Bolton was at a

Spiritualist seance when the medium cried out from her cabinet, 'Take this great brute away, it is suffocating me.' A seal emerged from the cabinet, waddled and flopped across the room, remained beside Bolton for a few moments, then returned to the cabinet and dematerialized. 'There is no doubt in my mind', Bolton solemnly told a meeting of the London Spiritualist Alliance, 'that it was the identical seal'.

Out-of-the-body projection may be involuntary or deliberate. The files of doctors and psychiatrists the world over contain accounts of people who have had the alarming experience of being literally outside themselves and clearly seeing their own bodies objectively at a distance. Deliberate out-of-the-body projection, or astral travel, is a phenomenon well-documented in the early records of many cultures.

These, then, are the phenomena, the strange powers and experiences that are collectively known as 'psi'. Records attesting to the reality of psychic phenomena come from all ages and places, and from people of acknowledged intelligence and integrity. Yet argument about 'psi' still rages, for the subject arouses people's hopes, fears and prejudices. Perhaps more than any other question it sharply separates two distinct human types – those who believe that the universe is governed by rational and discoverable principles and who abhor the supernatural, and those who believe that anything is possible, that man has great powers as yet undeveloped and that manifestations of the supernatural are glimpses of a superior and more exciting plane of reality than the one on which we normally live. Between the extremes of those who write off 'psi' as rubbish and those who are ready to believe anything provided it confounds reason and science, are the majority of people. This majority takes a cautiously open-minded view. They think there must be something in it, are prepared to believe some things but not others and are intrigued, but rather bewildered, by the whole subject.

There is one thing that can be said without raising anyone's temperature, however. It is that *'psi'* occurs. It's not a very exciting statement, but it gives us something to build on if we want to take a clear look at the subject and make some sense of it. 'Psi' is useful, not only because it is an umbrella term, but also because it is a neutral one. To say that extrasensory perception occurs is more controversial, for it raises the question of how we know that the perceptions are *extra* and not simply a heightened degree of normal sensory perception. Most of the other terms – such as clairvoyance, telepathy, and materialization – have similar pitfalls. To say that 'psi' occurs is simply to say that there are mental and physical events that in the present state of our knowledge, cannot be explained.

'Our knowledge' in this context means the knowledge that modern, mainly Western, culture and science are founded on. 'Psi' phenomena can easily be explained as the work of spirits or occult forces associated with gods, demons, or the planets, but to accept such explanations seems to the modern mind a retreat from reason back into the dark ages of superstition. This is the problem. Not only is 'psi' inexplicable in terms acceptable to the modern mind, but it also appears to undermine certain concepts that are absolutely fundamental in our civilization – notably our ideas of time, causality, energy, mind and matter. This is where attitudes enter the picture. Some people are completely happy with the Western worldview, and with its scientific and technological civilization. Others would like to see it changed for something less materialistic and more spiritual.

In this situation perhaps the first question we should ask is – what is important about 'psi'? If we accept that it occurs, should we go on and ask how, why and when it occurs and risk undermining some of our most cherished and useful ideas and attitudes? Or should we consider it a mildly interesting curiosity and aberration?

The possibility that all humans may have some degree of psychic ability, is one of the most exciting implications of parapsychology. Perhaps the limitations or boundaries of our minds are not real boundaries at all, but artificial ones of our own making. If these boundaries can be transcended, if 'psi' faculties can be developed and trained, the implications for our society are profound. There is a growing feeling in the Western world today that some fundamental changes are essential if civilization is to survive. Many people believe that 'psi' is important because it points the direction those changes might take. In the words of astronaut Edgar Mitchell, 'survival seems to depend more than anything on a transformation of consciousness, an evolution of the mind.'

CHAPTER 30

THE BEGINNINGS OF
PSYCHICAL RESEARCH

*Were the mediums of the nineteenth century able to contact
the spirits of the dead? Following the success of the
American Fox sisters, the fashion of the seance swept across
the United States and Europe, as sceptics joined the uncritical enthusiasts in circles around tables in darkened rooms.
Three scholars set out to discover if there was any genuine
evidence of supernatural phenomena in all the rappings,
table-shifting and materializations. Their methods established a new attitude toward psychic manifestations and
began the modern tradition of scientific analysis. Their
reports pose still unanswered questions about communication from mind to mind.*

The first recorded psychical researcher was King Croesus of
Lydia, who lived in the sixth century BC. In order to test which of
a group of Greek and Egyptian oracles was the most skilled, he
sent emissaries to each of them with instructions to ask them at a
prearranged time, 'What is King Croesus, the son of Alyattes,
doing now?' He contrived something theoretically impossible to
guess. He cut a lamb and a tortoise into pieces and cooked them
together in a brass cauldron. In a brilliant feat of clairvoyance, the
oracle at Delphi got the answer right.

Of course, King Croesus wasn't researching in the interests of
science. He already believed in the supernatural powers of the
oracles and simply wanted to find out which of them was the best,
so that he could engage a reliable adviser. He chose well, for in

time the clairvoyant and precognitive achievements of the Delphic Oracle became legendary. Her fondness for riddles and ambiguities, however, undermined her usefulness as a royal adviser, as King Croesus found to his cost. When she predicted that one of his campaigns would end in the destruction of a great army, he went off to war with buoyant confidence, not dreaming that the doomed army was his own.

So long as people believed in the supernatural as a part of life, there was no chance for scientific psychical research to get off the ground. That such a belief was prevalent in Shakespeare's day is obvious from his plays, in which the supernatural is often the pivot of the drama. In *A Midsummer Night's Dream*, for example, supernatural beings interact with mortals, weaving an intricate web of romantic complications. Shakespeare's audiences accepted the witches in *Macbeth* and the ghost in *Hamlet* at their face value. Modern audiences accept them in the context of the play, but regard them as remnants of an age of superstition. A parapsychologist, engaged in studying unusual kinds of perception, might take a different view and ask questions that the Elizabethans could never have conceived. For example, when the witches greet Macbeth as 'king hereafter', is this precognition on their part, or are they picking up telepathically from Macbeth a wish that he would like to see fulfilled? When the ghost of Hamlet's father relates the circumstances of his death, is the whole incident perhaps an hallucinatory glimpse of the past on Hamlet's part? Such questions indicate some of the areas of concern of modern psychical research. It has not demystified the universe, but has focused attention on a different set of mysteries from those that preoccupied earlier ages – the mysteries of the mind.

Two conditions were necessary for the start of scientific psychical research – a society generally sceptical of all things supernatural and a group of dedicated and intelligent scientists concerned about the limitations of such scepticism. It was not until the mid-nineteenth century that these two conditions were fulfilled. The eighteenth century was sceptical enough but it didn't produce the right people. Perhaps this was because reason had so recently been enthroned as a sovereign principle of knowledge. Few intellectuals of the Age of Reason would have risked ridicule by seriously examining the discredited beliefs of their superstitious forebears. When reason as an ideal gave way to romanticism, with its emphasis on subjective experience, conditions became more favourable for the development of psychical research.

The poet Shelley, one of the major figures of the romantic age, was a morbid dreamer. In one dream, he saw Lord Byron's dead daughter Allegra rise from the Gulf of Spezia, clasp her hands and smile at him. In another, he saw his friends Edward and Jane Williams die horribly in a house flooded by the sea. Not long after these nightmares, Shelley and Edward Williams died together off the coast of Italy, drowned in the Gulf of Spezia.

The great German poet, Goethe reported a less ominous precognitive experience in his autobiography. One day he was riding on horseback along a footpath when he saw his own image riding toward him in the opposite direction, dressed in a suit such as he had never worn. He shook himself out of his reverie and the vision vanished – but eight years later when he was again riding along the same path, he suddenly realized that he was wearing exactly the suit that he had formerly dreamed of.

The novelist, Charles Dickens also experienced a precognitive vision. He fell asleep in his office one evening and dreamed that he saw a lady in a red shawl standing with her back toward him. He didn't recognize her when she turned around, but she introduced herself as Miss Napier. He could make no sense of it, for he had never heard of any Miss Napier. But the following evening some friends visited him. They brought with them a stranger, a lady wearing a red shawl whom they introduced to him as Miss Napier – the lady of the dream.

In spite of his own psychic experiences and his frequent use of clairvoyant dreams and spirit manifestations in his novels, Dickens was strongly antagonistic to the craze for communication with the spirit world that swept through America and England in the middle of the nineteenth century. Perhaps when he heard of the 'spirit rappings' in Hydesville, New York that launched the Spiritualist movement in 1848, he may have remembered how a great English writer of the previous century had been ridiculed for his interest in a similar phenomenon. In 1762, Dr Samuel Johnson visited a house in Cock Lane, London where the ghost of a Mrs Kent was said to be communicating by means of rappings that would occur only in the presence of the 12-year-old daughter of the house, Elizabeth Parsons. The ghost, which soon became famous throughout London, accused Mr Kent of poisoning his wife. After Dr Johnson had written a report on the ghost for a magazine, another investigator discovered that the rappings were produced by the girl Elizabeth, whose father was trying to blackmail Kent. Johnson and the other eminent people who had taken an interest in the affair were left looking rather foolish.

The Cock Lane Ghost affair was an inept attempt at an art that became highly skilled and sophisticated in the second half of the nineteenth century – the fraudulent production of allegedly spiritual phenomena. This was the age of the great physical mediums, nearly all of whom, with the exception of the greatest of them, D. D. Home, were at one time or another exposed in fraud. With fraudulent mediums producing rappings, spirit photographs, materialized spirit forms (always in semidarkness), automatic writing and voices from the beyond that conveyed mundane and sentimental messages for a credulous public, it is not surprising that most serious and intelligent people should find the whole psychic business tasteless, tawdry and repugnant. The characteristic attitude of the intellectuals was well expressed by the philosopher, Thomas Henry Huxley, in a letter declining an invitation to investigate Spiritualistic phenomena, '. . . supposing the phenomena to be genuine – they do not interest me. If anybody would endow me with the faculty of listening to the chatter of old women and curates in the nearest cathedral town, I should decline the privilege having better things to do. And if the folk in the spiritual world do not talk more wisely and sensibly than their friends report them to do, I put them in the same category. The only good that I can see in a demonstration of the truth of ''Spiritualism'' is to furnish an additional argument against suicide. Better live a crossing-sweeper than die and be made to talk twaddle by a ''medium'' hired at a guinea a seance.'

But there were some highly intellectual and talented men who didn't take Huxley's attitude, who thought that among all the dross there might just be the occasional nugget of solid gold, of significant new knowledge. Among them were Henry Sidgwick,

F. W. H. Myers and Edmund Gurney. These three men, all Fellows of Trinity College, Cambridge and all sons of clergymen, were the founding fathers of systematic psychical research. Their individual, distinctive talents and personalities complemented each other and meshed together in a way that made them an ideal team for the investigative and theoretical work to which they devoted the greater part of their lives.

That they were the sons of clergymen is significant because, undoubtedly, a part of their motivation in pursuing psychical research was the hope of finding some grounds for reviving their religious faith, which had been undermined by the prevailing sceptical philosophy of the day. This is made clear by Myers in this famous passage in which he tells how he first broached the subject to Sidgwick, 'In a star-light walk which I shall not forget I asked him, almost with trembling, whether he thought that when Tradition, Intuition, Metaphysic, had failed to solve the riddle of the Universe, there was still a chance that from any actual observable phenomena – ghosts, spirits, whatsoever there might be – some valid knowledge might be drawn as to a World Unseen. Already, it seemed, he had thought that this was possible; steadily, though in no sanguine fashion, he indicated some last grounds for hope; and from that night onwards I resolved to pursue this quest, if it might be, at his side.'

Sidgwick, who in 1883 became professor of Moral Philosophy at Cambridge, possessed as sharp and critical an intellect as any person of his day. Myers' distinction was as a classicist and he was qualified as a musician and a doctor as well. When Myers, Gurney, Sidgwick and some other Cambridge and Oxford scholars, founded the Society for Psychical Research in 1882, Sidgwick became its President and Gurney its Secretary, a job to which he subsequently devoted all his time and in which he did prodigious work. Myers also worked tirelessly as general organizer of the SPR, lecturing, writing, investigating and collecting material for its publications. Another early member of the SPR was Eleanor Sidgwick, wife of Henry Sidgwick and a prominent psychical investigator. Scientifically trained, she conducted some of the most important research done by the Society and, like her husband, served as its President.

The declared aim of the SPR was to 'investigate that large body of debatable phenomena designated by such terms as mesmeric, psychical, and spiritualistic', and to do so 'without prejudice or prepossession of any kind, and in the same spirit of exact and unimpassioned enquiry which has enabled Science to solve so many problems, once not less obscure nor less hotly debated.' Like most intellectuals of their day, the founders of the SPR shared a belief that science was capable of solving virtually any mystery known to man.

Though the marvels performed by professional mediums were on the whole to be distrusted, Myers and Gurney became convinced that they must sometimes be genuine. This belief arose as a result of their investigation of William Stainton Moses, a retired clergyman, an Oxford University degree holder and, in Myers' words, a man of 'manifest sanity and probity' who could not for a moment be suspected of fraud.

The records of the psychic effects produced by Stainton Moses are as sensational and as puzzling as those of the better known D. D. Home. Their authenticity is buttressed by the fact that before Moses discovered his own powers, he distrusted Spiritualism, and is on record as having said of a book about Home that it was the dreariest twaddle he had ever come across. He began to have second thoughts when, through a medium, he received a strikingly accurate description of the spirit presence of a friend of his who had died. A few months after this occurrence, he had his first experience of levitation. From then on, over a period of nine years, Moses experienced and apparently produced phenomena of the most extraordinary and occasionally alarming nature.

Sergeant Cox, a friend of Moses', wrote an account of a curious happening at his own home in June 1873. He and Moses were in the dining room passing half an hour before going out to a dinner party. Cox was opening letters and Moses was reading *The Times* when suddenly, frequent and loud rapping noises came from the dining table. The table was a large mahogany one that could barely be moved by the strenuous efforts of two men. But it began to sway to and fro and then it moved several inches across the floor. Cox, a keen psychical researcher, realized that this was an invaluable opportunity to conduct some experiments. At his suggestion, he and Moses stood two feet away from the table on opposite sides and held their hands about eight inches above it.

After they had been waiting about a minute, the table rocked violently, moved seven inches along the floor and tilted first toward one man and then toward the other. Finally Moses held his hands four inches above the end of the table and asked that it rise and touch his hand three times, which it promptly did.

What is notable in this account is that the noises and movements began unexpectedly and were almost certainly not deliberately produced by Moses. The same is true of all the other strange things that happened to and around him. Once he found himself suddenly levitated, thrown down on his back on the table, then lifted up again and deposited on the sofa, all of which happened without his being in any way hurt. Frequently, small objects from different parts of the house appeared over Moses' head and fell on the table in front of him, having apparently passed through walls or closed doors. When Moses held a seance, his sitters could expect to be caressed by breezes heavy with perfumes, entertained by a variety of musical sounds – although there were no instruments in the room and illuminated by psychic lights emanating from the floor. Materializations of hands and weaving columns of light, that suggested human forms, would appear in the room. An evening with Stainton Moses couldn't have been dull and the wonders must have been enhanced by the thought that such a solemn and august gentleman – free of any financial motive – would be unlikely to stoop to the low dodges of many a professional medium's elaborately rigged seance room.

Moses claimed that the remarkable physical phenomena that occurred in his presence were produced by spirits, to prove the authenticity of messages that they were communicating to the world through him by means of automatic writing. He published these spirit communications in 1883 as *Spirit Teachings*, a book that became the bible of Spiritualism.

Though Myers had no doubts about the integrity of Moses, he was sceptical about the alleged spirit intelligences and thought that there might be some other explanation for both the automatic writing and the physical phenomena. Unfortunately, by the time the Society for Psychical Research was formed, Moses' psychic powers had declined. He could not be studied under the controlled conditions that the Society sought to bring to all its investigations.

Though psychical phenomena were generally accepted at the time – by those who believed them – as proof of the existence of spirits and therefore of the reality of survival after death, the founders of the SPR were well aware that this was really only an hypothesis. However much they may have personally longed to have their religious doubts allayed and to establish some definite proof of personal survival, they tried not to let this longing introduce a bias into their systematic investigative work. This work mainly involved conducting experiments in telepathy and clairvoyance, and collecting anecdotal evidence of these phenomena.

A public appeal for evidence got a substantial response and deluged Gurney and Myers with work. One of the respondents was a Manchester clergyman named Creery, who had for some time been conducting experiments in telepathy with his five daughters. The Creerys became the first subjects of systematic and controlled research into telepathy conducted by the SPR.

The Creery family reproduced their successes before an investigating committee of the SPR under strictly controlled conditions. However, it was later discovered that the girls had cheated in some, less tightly, controlled experiments and Myers and Gurney had to discount the impressive evidence for telepathy gathered in their own work with the Creerys.

In 1883, the year following the Creery experiments, Liverpool businessman, Malcolm Guthrie discovered that some of his employees had been experimenting with thought-transference in their spare time and had obtained remarkable results in transmitting simple drawings. His interest was aroused, so he and a friend, James Birchall, conducted their own experiments with two of the employees, Miss Relph and Miss Edwards, who were said to have shown exceptional ability. These experiments were so successful that they informed the SPR. Edmund Gurney went to Liverpool to supervise some tests himself.

The procedure varied slightly. Normally, the person chosen to do the drawing would do so in another room. The *percipient* – that is, the person who sees in a paranormal way – would be blindfolded and would sit opposite the agent, who would hold the drawing in such a way that the percipient could not have seen it even without the blindfold. The agent would stare intently at the drawing and concentrate on it until the percipient said she was ready to attempt to reproduce it and her blindfold was removed. The period of concentration might last from half a minute, to two or three minutes.

Many of the attempts were failures. In other cases, parts of the diagram would be inverted or transformed in some other way. A vertical line flanked by two circles was interpreted as a pair of scissors. The number of partial or complete successes was strikingly high, many times higher than could be attributed to chance. In one series of trials, all six attempts were either wholly or partially successful.

The Professor of Physics at Liverpool University at this time was young Oliver Lodge, later knighted for his discoveries in the fields of electricity and radio. He heard about the Guthrie experiments and supervised a new series of tests with the young women, introducing some variations of his own and bringing to the work the care and thoroughness that distinguished his work as a research physicist. In one of his variations he had two agents concentrating on different shapes, a square and a cross. The subject, who was used to receiving telepathic transmission from one agent only and didn't know that two were being used in this case, was at first confused but finally drew a cross within a square. The plausible inference seemed to be that the subject had received both messages and assumed, consciously or subconsciously, that they formed a single image.

In addition to their experimental work, the indefatigable Gurney and Myers investigated numerous reported cases of spontaneous telepathic and clairvoyant experiences. Advertisements in *The Times* and other periodicals brought the reports flooding in. In 1883, they wrote 10,000 letters between them and conducted hundreds of interviews. To help with the work, they enlisted an Oxford scholar, Frank Podmore whose scepticism and thoroughness in investigation were an invaluable contribution.

As they sifted and analyzed the many reports, the researchers noticed that the largest single category was of what they called 'crisis apparitions'. In these cases, a person had experienced a vivid, often very realistic, hallucination of another person at a moment later found to coincide with a moment of crisis in that other person's life. The crisis was usually the person's death, or serious injury or illness. In some cases, the hallucination was auditory rather than visual – the person's voice would be heard at the time of his crisis.

After three years of research, Gurney, Myers and Podmore published their evidence for telepathy, both spontaneous and experimental, in the form of a large book entitled *Phantasms of the Living*. This book, the first major work published by the SPR, contained reports of 702 cases of spontaneous psychic experiences, each of them supported by the testimony of more than one person. A summary of a few of these cases will illustrate the kind of material *Phantasms* contains.

A naval commander recalled an occurrence when he was 13-years-old. He had nearly drowned when a boat attempting to land in rough sea on an island near Java, was capsized. On coming to the surface after being repeatedly submerged, he called for his mother, which amused the men who rescued him. When he returned home some months later, he told his family about his narrow escape including how, while he was in the water, he had had a distinct vision of his mother and sisters sitting at home and of his mother sewing something white. They immediately recalled an occasion when they were all sitting just as he said and all had heard a repeated agonized cry of 'Mother!' The experience had deeply troubled his mother, who had noted the date and time of it in a diary the next day. Allowing for the longitudinal difference in time between England and Java, the time they heard the cry was found to correspond exactly with the time of the boy's narrow escape.

Another case, involving an actual drowning, occurred in upstate New York in 1867. A little three-year-old girl was playing dolls one winter afternoon in a room where her father, mother and aunt were also sitting. Suddenly she ran up to her aunt and exclaimed, 'Auntie, Davie is drowned!' Davie was the child's cousin, a boy of nine, of whom she was very fond. He and his older brother lived about 25 miles away and the little girl had not seen them for several months.

The adults had to ask the child to repeat herself twice before they understood what she was saying. Thinking the child didn't know the meaning of what she said, but wishing to avoid a morbid topic of conversation, the mother changed the subject. She did, however, make a note of the time – 4 pm. A few hours later, the family received a telegram from the boys' father saying, 'My little boys, Darius and Davie, were drowned at four o'clock today while skating at Kenks' Lake.'

A local newspaper clipping obtained by the SPR researchers confirmed the date and approximate time of the accident.

A case that has been discussed and argued about ever since it was first published in *Phantasms of the Living*, is the famous 'Verity case'. It is remarkable, partly because it is well documented with supporting letters and also because it contains elements of telepathy, clairvoyance and possibly out-of-the body projection.

S. H. Beard, a young man who was known and trusted by the officers of the SPR, gave Gurney an account of attempts he made to project himself in spirit into the presence of his fiancée, Miss L. S. Verity. 'On a certain Sunday evening', he wrote, 'having been reading of the great power which the human will is capable of exercising, I determined with the whole force of my being that I would be present in spirit in the front bedroom on the second floor of a house situated at 22 Hogarth Road, Kensington, in which slept two ladies of my acquaintance . . . The time at which I determined I would be there was one o'clock in the morning, and I also had a strong intention of making my presence perceptible.'

A few days later, when he visited Miss Verity, she told him that at 1 am on the night in question, she had suddenly awakened and seen him distinctly, standing beside her bed. When he moved toward her she had screamed, awakening her young sister in the next bed, who also saw the apparition. After the figure had vanished, Miss Verity called another sister from an adjoining room and both girls described their vision of Beard, what he was wearing and where he stood, in exactly the same terms. Gurney subsequently met all three girls, obtained signed statements from them and carefully cross-examined them. He had no doubt that their testimony was truthful.

Beard tried the trick again about a year later, when the Veritys were living in a house in Kew, another part of London. On this particular night, his fiancée was sharing a bedroom with a married sister, who had only met Beard once at a ball two years before. It was this sister who saw the apparition of Beard when he projected himself into the bedroom. She wrote in her statement that she had not yet gone to sleep, when she saw the door open and Beard enter the room. She said he came to her bedside and first took her hair in his hand, then took her hand in his and looked intently at the palm. Miss Verity was asleep at the time and the married sister didn't wake her up and tell her about it until the apparition had gone. What the fiancée thought of this apparent fickleness on the part of the spirit of her intended, is not on record.

Beard visited the sisters in Kew the following day. They were astonished when, after they had given him an account of the odd happening of the previous night, he produced from his pocket a paper on which he had written an account of his intentions and his effort to project his image. He had not known that the sister would be visiting them when he conceived the idea.

Gurney again investigated and found the case well corroborated. Intrigued, he asked Beard to send him a note the next time he intended to attempt to project himself. Beard did so. However, he didn't see Miss Verity for two weeks after this attempt. When he did see her, she told him that she had distinctly seen him in her room at midnight on a certain date and that he had stroked her hair. Beard couldn't remember whether the date she gave coincided with his attempt. But Gurney had Beard's letter stating his intention to appear that evening at a certain time and by comparing this with Miss Verity's signed statement, he found that both the date and the time coincided. Coincidence of time is most important in such experiments and in spontaneous apparitions as well. A time gap between the agent's effort to send the image and the seeing of the image by the percipient, will tend to suggest that the apparition is a subjective hallucination by the percipient, weakening the case for its being telepathic.

In his discussion of the Verity case in *Phantasms of the Living*, Gurney noted a significant difference between such evidence for telepathy and the evidence obtained from controlled experiments. In the experimental situation, the agent is thinking about the image or word or idea he is trying to project and if the experiment is successful, the percipient receives an impression that is more or less a copy of the impression in the agent's mind. In the case of a willed apparition, such as the Beard experiments, the minds of agent and percipient are occupied in different ways. The agent is not so much thinking of his own image as mentally reaching out

toward the percipient, trying to imagine where that person is at
the moment, perhaps concentrating on their relationship. 'It is
thus probable', writes Gurney, 'that the percipient's aspect has
formed a larger part of the agent's whole idea than his own; yet it
is *his* aspect, and nothing else, that is telepathically perceived.'
The same is true for crisis apparitions, even though the agent may
not be consciously trying to project his image.

From this observation, Gurney went on to draw a conclusion
about the nature of the telepathic process. 'As long as the impression in the percipient's mind is merely a reproduction of that in
the agent's mind, it is possible to conceive some sort of physical
basis for the fact of the transference.' He cited several examples
from physics, such as the way a permanent magnet brought into a
room will magnetize any iron in that room, or the way an electric
current in one wire will induce a current in a neighbouring wire.
As long as the information transmitted telepathically was essentially the same at either end – sending and receiving – it might be
assumed to travel via some as yet undiscovered physical medium.
But when the percipient saw something *different* from what the
agent was thinking – for example, the image of the agent himself
– a physical basis for telepathy seemed unlikely.

Another argument against a physical basis for telepathy, was
that all known physical forces were known to become weaker as
they travel over great distances. This is not the case with
telepathy. A telepathic message or apparition can be sent as easily
across a continent as across a street. Recently, however, scientists
have discovered that when certain metals are cooled to the
temperature of liquid helium, they will conduct an electric current
with no loss due to resistance or the distance involved. The existence of these so-called 'superconductors' has reintroduced the
possibility that some physical force may be at work in cases of
telepathy. Yet, the nature of this force remains as much a mystery
as when Gurney first discussed the problem nearly a hundred
years ago.

Some of the peculiarities of telepathic transmission emerged in
a series of more than 750 experiments, performed between 1910
and 1924 by Professor Gilbert Murray of Oxford University. A
small group of family and friends took part in the experiments.
While Professor Murray was out of the room, one of them –

usually the person chosen as agent – would choose some image or incident for him to guess. The subject announced would then be written down exactly by the participant taking notes. Murray would re-enter the room, take the hand of the agent and try to determine the subject chosen, while the note-taker recorded his efforts. The subjects were a colourful mixture of incidents from literature and history, sometimes including people known to the participants. Here is a typical example, with Murray's daughter, Mrs Arnold Toynbee, as agent,

Mrs Toynbee: 'I'll think of Rupert [Brooke] meeting Natasha in *War and Peace*. Running in a yellow dress – running through a wood.'

Professor Murray: 'Well, I thought when I came into the room it was about Rupert. Yes, it's fantastic. He's meeting somebody out of a book. He's meeting Natasha in *War and Peace*. I don't know what he is saying – perhaps "Will you run away with me?"'

Mrs T: 'Can you get the scene?'

Professor M: 'No, I can't get it.'

Great care was taken to insure that Professor Murray was out of earshot of the group. However, the possibility that hyperaesthesia (in this case a sharpening of the hearing faculty), could influence the results was considered by the experimenters. Murray himself noticed that while he was concentrating his attention on the experiment, he became acutely sensitive to noises and that perhaps he was subconsciously receiving aural stimuli from this group. On the few occasions when the subject was not spoken aloud within the group, Murray failed to identify it. Most of these failures, however, occurred during a run of failures in which the subject was usually spoken, so it may be that other factors contributed to the lack of success.

Those who reported on the experiments to the SPR, noted that there were many successes that could not be attributed to hyperacute hearing. Sometimes, Murray would guess a scene from a book he had not read and mention details about the scene or characters not spoken aloud when the subject was chosen. The only conceivable way he could have received this information was by telepathy with the agent, or with one of the other participants who knew the book.

A striking example of a miss that indicated a partial hit was an experiment in which a Mr Mellor, acting as agent, said, 'I'm thinking of the operating room in the nursing home in which I was operated [on].' Murray's response was, 'I get an impression of a theatre. No. I can't get it. I'm now guessing – Covent Garden and Oedipus.' Although Mellor had used the phrase 'operating *room*' rather than 'operating theatre', the concept of a theatre of some kind had apparently been transmitted to Murray.

These experiments raisé the possibility of telepathy being increased by the rapport existing between certain members of the same family – an aspect of parapsychology that is attracting some attention today. Murray seemed to be most successful when the agent was his daughter, Mrs Toynbee. Whether this was due partly to a sympathetic relationship between them, or whether it was due to some exceptional ability of hers to concentrate on the subject, remains an open question.

In evaluating the results of the experiments, the participants judged slightly over 33 per cent to be complete successes; about 40 per cent to be failures; and the remainder, partial successes. Of course, given the nature of the material used, judgments of success or failure were to some extent subjective. More accurate means of measuring telepathy were to be developed in the years that followed, as psychical research adopted more of the methods of the laboratory.

CHAPTER 31

HARRY PRICE AND HIS CONTEMPORARIES

Is it possible for a medium to lower the temperature of an entire room during the course of a seance? Is this how she obtains the energy for her eerie manifestations? This was one of the questions tackled by the psychical researcher Harry Price, who spent years in his investigations of the foremost psychics of his day, inventing some fiendishly complicated equipment designed to detect any possible fraud on the part of the medium. Although he unmasked many cheats and charlatans, he undoubtedly had a taste for personal publicity. But some of the enigmas he uncovered remain unexplained to this day.

One winter evening in 1937, a group of six people were gathered together in a large house in a smart London suburb to witness an event which one of them later described as 'the most remarkable case of materialization I have ever witnessed'.

It took a lot to astonish Harry Price, who wrote these words, for he had been in psychical research for many years. He had sat with all the great mediums of Europe and America and knew all the tricks of their trade. He had publicly denounced several of them when he had caught them cheating. But this 'most remarkable' materialization was not produced by a professional medium. The group consisted of some women friends who gathered every Wednesday evening in this suburban house for a seance. Seances were, of course, being held all over London. What made this one remarkable and of interest to Harry Price, was that the group claimed that one of their members' daughter, who had died 16 years before at the age of six, appeared physically in the room.

Price was sceptical but fascinated. He could see no reason why a private circle of respectable people should wish to perpetrate a fraud that would hold them up to ridicule if it were exposed. Nevertheless, he took all the precautions against fraud that he would have taken to an experimental sitting with a professional medium. Before the seance began, he examined the room and its contents thoroughly, had all unnecessary furniture, ornaments and pictures removed to another room, sprinkled starch powder on the floor on both sides of the door and further insured that no one could enter the room by sealing the door and all the windows with masking tape. He initialled the tape so that if someone broke the seal and then re-applied other tape, he would be able to detect the substitution.

When the seance began, the group sat in darkness for some 20 minutes and the bereaved mother, who was sitting next to Price, repeatedly whispered 'Rosalie!' She sobbed quietly. Then she said, 'My darling.' Price became aware of a presence between them and felt something soft and warm touch his hand, which was resting on his knee. Then he was given permission to touch the materialization. To his amazement, he felt the nude figure of a little girl whose height he estimated at about three and a half feet. He felt her all over, put his ear to her chest and heard a heartbeat, and held her wrist, in which he detected a fast-beating pulse. He was next allowed to examine the child by the light emitted from a luminous plaque which had been lying face down on the floor. His eyes confirmed what his hands had felt. Here was a pretty child, aged about six, with long hair falling over her shoulders. He asked her several questions, but the only one that got a reply was, 'Rosalie, do you love your mummy?' Then the child lisped 'Yes.' The mother cried and clasped her to her breast and all the women in the circle dissolved in tears. This highly charged emotional seance ended 15 minutes later and when the lights were put on, there was no sign of Rosalie. A thorough examination of the room, the seals and the starch powder, showed that no one could have entered or left it during the seance.

This is a fairly extreme example of a type of story that continually turns up in the literature of psychical research and that leaves the reader only with a choice of improbabilities. In this case the improbabilities are: a) that Price was lying and made the whole thing up; b) that he was successfully duped; c) that Rosalie was actually a genuine spirit materialization. That he was lying is improbable because he included the story in his book, *Fifty Years of Psychical Research* only reluctantly, at his publisher's request – it is not a story that would help his reputation as a serious psychical researcher. A friend who saw Price on the day after the Rosalie seance described him as 'visibly shaken' by the experience – an unlikely state of mind if he were lying. That Price was duped is improbable because he took elaborate precautions, knew all the methods employed by fraudulent materializing mediums and was convinced that the mother's emotions were genuine. If the materialization was a hoax, she too was a victim of it. The third supposition, that Rosalie was a materialization, is improbable because there is no precedent for such a phenomenon outside legend and folklore. It violates all known laws of nature.

The Rosalie case exemplifies the problem that scientists have when confronted with the evidence of psychical research. To be stuck with a choice between improbabilities is not a situation that holds out much hope for the advancement of knowledge. It is an understandable reaction to shrug off the problem and get on with other work.

But let us stay with the problem for a while. An odd thing about psychical research, is that certain types of phenomena and certain avenues of research seem to prevail at particular times. Levitations and materializations are not much heard of nowadays, but both were frequently observed by the researchers of the period between the two World Wars. The founding members of the SPR (and its sister organization the American SPR), preferred to investigate mental phenomena – telepathy and clairvoyance – partly because experiments were easier to control and their results easier to assess and partly, no doubt, because they were loath to demean themselves in the rough-and-tumble of the seance room. Their colleagues in continental Europe were less cautious, however, and apparently more ready to put their professional reputations in jeopardy by giving credence to the physical manifestations of mediumship.

On the subject of materializations, consider the words of

Professor Charles Richet, a distinguished French researcher and winner of the Nobel Prize for his contribution to physiology, 'I shall not waste time in stating the absurdities, almost the impossibilities, from a psycho-physiological point of view, of this phenomenon. A living being, or living matter, formed under our eyes, which has its proper warmth, apparently a circulation of blood, and a physiological respiration, which has also a kind of psychic personality having a will distinct from the will of the medium is, in a word, a new human being! This is surely the climax of marvels! Nevertheless, it is a fact.'

No doubt Professor Richet was willing to commit himself so unequivocally because he was supported by distinguished contemporaries. His compatriots, Dr. Gustave Geley and Dr. Eugene Osty, the German physician Baron von Schrenck-Notzing, the great English physicists Sir William Crookes and Sir Oliver Lodge, were all convinced that they had witnessed genuine materializations under strictly controlled conditions. They could have been wrong. Nobel Prize winners and eminent physicists are no better qualified than anyone else to see through the wiles and sleight of hand of a clever conjuror. But that they were wrong *all* the time and that *all* the phenomena they saw produced by mediums were fraudulent, is difficult to believe when one reads some of the accounts of their experiences and of the precautions they took against fraud. It is also difficult to imagine how some of the mediums, particularly the young women, could possibly have obtained access to the jealously-guarded secrets of professional conjurors.

One of the most controversial physical mediums of the early twentieth century was Eva Carriere (known in psychical research as Eva C). Her real name was Marthe Beraud. The daughter of a high-ranking French army officer, she was brought up in Algiers. Her psychic powers were discovered by a general, who invited Professor Richet to investigate. Richet was impressed by what he saw – the full-form materialization of an individual who called himself Bien Boa. Although Richet noted a certain artificial quality about Bien Boa's beard, he remained convinced that the figure was produced, paranormally, by the medium. Subsequently, an Arab servant confessed that he was the spirit Bien Boa and this confession was corroborated by Mlle. Beraud. However, her confession described a kind of trickery seemingly impossible to achieve under the conditions imposed by Richet and Richet claimed that her statement simply indicated the mental instability typical of mediums.

A few years later Marthe Beraud appeared in Paris, where she produced impressive psychic phenomena. They were studied by a number of eminent researchers including Schrenck-Notzing – who gave her the pseudonym Eva C – and Gustave Geley. She was also studied by the British SPR with less remarkable results. The most positive results were obtained by the French investigators and in his book *Clairvoyance and Materialization*, Geley published a series of photographs of materializations allegedly produced by Eva while in a trance. Some of the pictures show amorphous doughy masses and others are of fully formed human heads. In a solemn and level-headed accompanying text, Geley relates how on many occasions he saw a material substance (which Richet called 'ectoplasm') emanate from various parts of Eva's body and form itself into organic shapes, which were solid to the touch. Again we are faced with the problem of choosing to believe whether the distinguished professors were liars or the victims of a hoax, or whether, as they claimed, an actual materialization took place. Of course, no scientist is going to accept as evidence a man's sworn testimony on a phenomenon that violates the known laws of nature, even if that man is a Nobel Prize winner. He wants to see a repeatable experiment before he will acknowledge a fact proved, and one trouble with materialization is that the evidence for it cannot be produced on demand. Those who believe in it claim that it is a spontaneous phenomenon, and that one reason why physical mediums have sometimes cheated, is that pressure has been put on them to produce the phenomena to order. Only when the effects do not come spontaneously, they say, does the medium resort to trickery.

Eva C's effects were almost commonplace compared to those produced by Franck Klusky. According to Geley, who devoted a large section of his book to him, Klusky was the supreme physical medium of the age. He was a Polish poet and banker, who only discovered his strange gifts at the age of 46 and was at first reluctant to exploit them. Finally, he was persuaded to participate in serious research. He certainly produced some bizarre effects.

During a seance, a bowl of paraffin wax, kept at melting point by being floated on warm water, was put near him. When a human form materialized, it was asked to plunge a hand, a foot, or part of a face into the wax several times, then to plunge again in a bowl of cold water to set the wax. When the form dematerialized, a wax moulding of it would remain. This could be filled with plaster and in this way several casts of spirit hands and feet were obtained, photographs of which are in Geley's book. In his accounts of the seances, Geley says there was no possibility that Klusky could have produced these effects fraudulently, for he was closely observed and both his hands were held all the time. Moreover, the wrist openings of the wax 'gloves' were too narrow for a living hand to have slipped through without breaking the mould. When the 'spirit' hands were examined by experts, they were found to be smaller than the hands of anyone who had been present at the seance.

Klusky also produced materializations of animals. It was not uncommon for cats, dogs, squirrels and birds to appear in the room. Geley's book contains a picture of Klusky with an immense materialized buzzard on his shoulders. But the most alarming experience for the sitters must have been the appearance of a creature they called *Pithecanthropus*, a large hairy ape man who grunted, ground his teeth, lurched around the room and tried to lick the hands and faces of everybody present.

Klusky produced similar effects independently both for the French investigators and for the Polish SPR, but he would not sit with Harry Price. Price declared that Klusky's mediumship 'is unsatisfactory from the point of view that no scientific body has investigated the alleged miracles.' This must have annoyed Geley and Richet, who considered that their investigations were scientifically unimpeachable. For example, in order to insure that the 'spirit gloves' obtained at Klusky's seances were actually made during the experiment and with their wax, the researchers mixed a small amount of a certain chemical with the wax. This chemical – undetectable at the time of the experiment – would later produce a discolouration in the wax when it was treated in a certain way. Richet was convinced that this and all the other evidence for the reality of materialization added up to a scientifically proved case. He wrote, 'The fact that intelligent forces are projected from an organism that can act mechanically, can move objects and make sounds, is a phenomenon as certainly established as any fact in physics.' He did not consider that this constituted a proof of survival of the spirit after death, however. He inclined rather to the view that materializations were thought-forms projected by the medium or in some cases, perhaps unconsciously, by one of the sitters participating in the seance.

That some kind of energy discharge takes place, both from the medium and from the sitters during a physical seance, was a hypothesis widely discussed during this period. In some sittings he conducted with a young London nurse named Stella Cranshaw, Price obtained objective evidence indicating that energy was absorbed from the environment during a seance. Self-recording thermometers showed a considerable drop in temperature – on one occasion as much as 11°F – and this drop coincided with the occurrence of the more vigorous physical manifestations, such as levitations. At the end of the seance, the room temperature was always marginally higher than at the start, which was to be expected on account of the presence of the sitters. But the dramatic drop coinciding with the climax of the seance, would seem to suggest that energy was somehow borrowed from the environment to produce the effects and then paid back at the end. Here, it seemed, was a genuine hard paranormal fact, a phenomenon objectively recorded, impossible to fake, showing the operation of a physical law quite unknown to contemporary science. It has not been satisfactorily explained to this day.

Harry Price was a prolific inventor of ingenious devices for making his research methods foolproof and scientifically acceptable. To test Stella's powers to move objects by psychic force, he constructed his 'telekinetoscope'. This elaborate invention contained two electrical contacts that normally required a two-ounce pressure to bring them together. They were protected from physical interference by a soap bubble, a glass shade and a cage. When the electrical contact was made a red bulb would light up. At her first attempt, Stella succeeded in completing the circuit and lighting the bulb, and when the telekinetoscope was examined, both the glass shade and the soap bubble were found intact. She had apparently brought the two electrical contacts together by the exertion of psychic force.

Most of Price's complicated inventions were designed to control the medium and prevent fraud. He had an 'electric chair' in which the medium sat with head, arms, feet, hands and seat all in contact with electric light circuits. At any movement, a red signal light was automatically switched off. To insure further that psychokinetic effects were genuinely produced by psychic forces, he developed his 'counterpoise table'. The object to be moved psychokinetically, which could be as light as a handkerchief, was placed on one side of the table. When the object was lifted, the other side of the table would fall, closing an electrical circuit that immediately activated a battery of cameras. Whatever moved the object would, if it were visible, be automatically photographed. Later, Price devised a system of infra-red ray projectors in the ceiling and walls of the seance room, which provided a more sophisticated and satisfactory method of control than the inhibiting electric chair. Each projector was aligned with a photo-electric cell. When mediums took position in a chair, certain rays were obscured by their body and the resulting pattern was recorded in a nearby control room. Even if a medium were left entirely alone in the seance room, every movement could be observed on the control panel, which would also register the movement of any object in the room. In this way, not only was the medium controlled but also any physical phenomena produced were automatically visible to the observer.

Obviously, such sophisticated apparatus required some form of permanent housing and in 1926, Price opened his National Laboratory of Psychical Research in Kensington. One of the first subjects to be studied there was the Romanian peasant girl, Eleonore Zügun.

Eleonore was 12-years-old when the weird effects that made her famous started to happen. In her presence, objects would fly about with no visible agent having thrown them. In other words, she was the focus of poltergeist activity. It seems unlikely that she would have tried to create the phenomena fraudulently, for because of them she was at first persecuted by the superstitious villagers who thought they were the work of the Devil. Eleonore was put in an asylum, where she might have remained had she not come to the attention of an Austrian Countess who was interested in psychic matters. The Countess secured her release, took her to

Vienna and wrote an article about her that was published in the Journal of the American Society for Psychical Research. When Harry Price read the article, he decided to go to Vienna to investigate the phenomena for himself.

His investigation started with a rather alarming incident. He, Eleonore and the Countess were in the latter's study-bedroom in her apartment. He had brought the child a toy which came apart while she was playing with it. She ran over to where he and the Countess were sitting and asked them to fix the toy. They rose to attend to it and while they were doing so, a long steel paper knife shot across the room from behind them, just missing Price's head and hit the door opposite. It clearly couldn't have been thrown by anyone, for there was no one else in the room and the writing desk where it had lain was across the room, in front of a window that was securely fastened.

Several other movements of objects in the room occurred during Price's brief visit and he was so impressed that he persuaded the Countess to bring Eleonore to London. There, in the National Laboratory, under carefully controlled conditions and in front of some distinguished witnesses, numerous PK effects were recorded. One odd feature of these events was that they were accompanied by stigmata on the child's body. Red weals and what looked like teeth marks would appear. Her pulse rate rose in proportion to the violence of the phenomena. Eleonore must have been greatly relieved when, at the onset of puberty, the phenomena abruptly stopped.

Eleonore's case is a classic example of poltergeist activity, in that the events were spontaneous, uncontrolled and unpredictable. A girl who suffered similarly when she was 12 but who retained her psychic powers in adult life, was the Danish medium Anna Rasmussen. She was studied intensively between 1922 and 1928 by Professor Winther of Copenhagen, who in 1927 invited Price to witness a demonstration at his laboratory.

Anna had a 'trance personality' (or 'spirit guide' as Spiritualists would say), named 'Dr Lasaruz', who supposedly brought about the movement of objects. In order to study these psychic powers, Professor Winther used a special device of a sealed glass case in which a number of pendulums of different weights were suspended by silk threads. In a sunlit room, under strict controls and before witnesses, Anna could make any one of the pendulums move in any direction as requested. All the experimenter had to do was ask Dr Lasaruz to move a specific pendulum in a particular direction and it would move accordingly. In his autobiography, Price wrote that he had never seen a more convincing example of psychokinesis than this.

The most famous psychics of the 1920s and 1930s were the Schneider brothers, Willi and Rudi. Like Hitler, they were born in the Austrian village of Braunau. From an early age the brothers showed remarkable psychic powers, and news of the so-called miracles taking place in Braunau reached Baron von Schrenck-Notzing. One of these miracles, witnessed and reported by retired warship commander Fritz Kogelnik, was the full materialization of Willi's spirit control 'Olga', who 'danced the tango very correctly and gracefully'. Willi was the elder brother and the first to show psychic powers. In order to study Willi's powers thoroughly, Schrenck-Notzing arranged for the boy to go to Munich, train for the dental profession at his own expense and be available for psychical research experiments. He invited colleagues and scientists from all over Europe to attend the experiments and in 1922, Harry Price did so.

The control conditions imposed in Schrenck-Notzing's seance room involved the use of a large wooden cage with gauze panels. A heavy table, a hand bell and a heavy music box – all marked with luminous paint so that their movements could be seen in the semi-darkness – were placed inside the cage, which was then locked. Willi was controlled by being dressed in one-piece black tights outlined with luminous bands and buttons. Luminous bracelets were put on his wrists and he was held firmly by two men.

Soon after Willi had gone into trance, the table inside the locked cage gave a resounding bump on the floor and was seen to rise. Then the music box began to play and bump up and down. The music would stop and resume at the command of any of the sitters and when the music box had run down, it was rewound by some unseen agency – an operation that normally required two hands, one to hold the box and the other to work the lever. Then the luminous hand bell rang and jumped about inside the cage. Other phenomena occurred outside the cage. Price dropped a handkerchief on the floor and it rose in the air. A hand-like form appeared, waved to the sitters then slowly dematerialized.

Later Schrenck-Notzing discovered that Rudi Schneider's powers were even greater than Willi's and he arranged similar tests of the younger boy. Price went to Munich again to see Rudi and eventually brought the boy to London to be investigated in Price's own Laboratory.

That the Schneider brothers' effects were genuine, was formally attested by more than 100 distinguished scientists and other scholars who attended Schrenck-Notzing's demonstrations. Nevertheless, they were not above cheating. On one occasion, the cameras linked to Price's counterpoise table caught Rudi in the act of manually removing a handkerchief which, without the resulting photograph, would have been thought to have moved by paranormal means. (There is, however, some doubt about the authenticity of this photo.) In spite of this apparent evidence of cheating, Price was convinced that in most of his seances with Rudi, particularly those at which the electrical-contact method of control was used, as it always was after this incident – the PK affects were genuine. During many of Rudi's seances, the automatic thermograph recorded a significant fall in temperature in the room, as it did at the Stella Cranshaw sittings.

In his autobiography, Harry Price stated several times that he 'would go a long way to see a miracle'. Some of his critics have said that he sometimes went too far, pursuing his investigations in areas that only brought psychical research into disrepute. Any estimate of his contribution to knowledge of the paranormal, must allow for the fact that there was a streak of the publicity seeker in him. He loved to be in the limelight and he had a nose for a good story that would appeal to the press. But personal profit was not among his motives, for he funded most of his research work himself and donated the National Laboratory, which cost him a substantial sum to set up, along with his personal library of 17,000 volumes, to the University of London. He had the courage not to mind making a fool of himself and he justified his more outlandish investigations with the argument that any alleged miracle was worth looking into, if only to prove there was nothing in it. In this way, one could separate the hard core of the genuinely paranormal from the mass of superstition, fraud and delusion that surrounded and obscured it.

In 1931, an old German, magical manuscript entitled *The Blocksberg Tryst* fell into Price's hands. He was immediately interested and, to the dismay of his scientific friends, he announced his intention of going to the Brocken, the highest peak in the Harz Mountains in central Germany, to carry out an experiment in ritual magic. One friend who was not dismayed and fell in with the plan with enthusiasm, was the philosopher Dr C. E. M. Joad and in January 1932, the two improbable 'magicians' set off for Germany. The ritual required the participation of a 'maiden pure in heart' and a white goat, and it involved various incantations, magic formulae, the preparation of a magic circle and a special ointment composed of bats blood, scrapings of church bells, soot and honey. Catching bats proved a hazardous and difficult exercise but finally all the preparations were completed and they had only to wait for a night when there was a full moon, visible from the top of the Brocken. But month after month, the moon was obscured by mist at the crucial time and it was only after several postponements that the ritual was finally staged. If it worked, the 'maiden pure in heart' would be rewarded by having the white goat transformed into a 'youth of surpassing beauty'. Needless to say, the goat remained a goat and the newspapers had a field day. Price and Joad, however, returned to England satisfied that they had struck a blow for sanity and science by discrediting ritual magic and its devotees. The playwright, Bernard Shaw expressed a general opinion of the experiment when he said that he might have been amused to be there but he 'would not dream of making a special journey to see anything so silly!'

That Price was unashamed and unrepentant, was proved by the fact that he undertook another and perhaps even sillier journey a short time after the Brocken adventure. A correspondent in the Isle of Man informed him that a strange talking animal had attached itself to a family living in a farmhouse on the top of a mountain in the centre of the island. Price wrote to the farmer, who confirmed that the animal was an Indian mongoose and that it could not only talk but also converse intelligently, recite nursery rhymes and sing hymns. A friend of Price's, a Captain Macdonald, offered to investigate. When he returned from the island he reported that he had heard the talking mongoose 'indeed had been verbally insulted by it' – but had been unable even to catch a glimpse of it and was unimpressed by the 'phenomena'. Reports of the mongoose's marvellous doings continued to reach Price, however, and some time later he investigated the matter for himself. He was hospitably received by the farmer and regaled with tales of 'Gef's' marvels and mischief, but the 'talking mongoose of Manx' remained as elusive as ever and Price returned to London without any evidence of its existence. Nevertheless, he managed to write a book, *The Haunting of Cashen's Gap*, about his investigations into the strange case.

When Price died in 1948, an era in psychical research came to an end. His flamboyance and his flair for publicity had embarrassed some of his colleagues but he had been a key figure in the field for a quarter of a century. His energy, enthusiasm, curiosity and independence were qualities that enabled him to function as a link-man between American, British and European researchers. And, in the course of his own investigations, he had turned up enough well-attested, inexplicable phenomena to give the most thorough sceptic food for thought.

CHAPTER 32

ESP IN THE LABORATORY

Can a scientist get ESP to work under laboratory conditions? Research in the universities began in the 1930s and continues – each scientist attempting to produce an experiment that will isolate just one aspect of 'psi' phenomena. Instead of the spectacular manifestations of the seance room, modern psychics concentrate on cards, attempting to transmit information about abstract symbols when all normal sensory contact has been rigorously excluded. What do these tests teach us about the possibilities of telepathic or clairvoyant contact? Have the scientists discovered powers we cannot explain? Some of their experiments have produced results which challenge the traditional concept of a logical world.

The scene is a room in the University of London. The year is 1937. A few people are about to engage in an elaborate guessing game, directed by the distinguished mathematician Dr S. G. Soal. The person who is to do the guessing is Frederick Marion, a well-known stage telepathist.

Dr Soal begins the game by handing Marion a small white handkerchief. Marion holds the handkerchief for a few seconds, hands it to one of the experimenters and leaves the room accompanied by Soal and one of the other participants. The door, which has no keyhole, is closed behind them. The next stage of the game is to hide the handkerchief in one of six tin boxes, which are located in various places in the room and numbered one through six. One of the group rolls a die in a box, silently showing the upturned face of the die to the recorder, who makes a note of its number. The handkerchief is then placed in the box whose number corresponds to the number on the die.

One of the participants now pulls over his head a stockinette hood that covers his features, and steps into a curious contraption – a kind of sentry box on wheels, open at the front. Another person slots into the front of the box several pieces of plywood, until the only visible part of the man in the box is his covered head. All of the participants, except the man in the sentry box, now step behind a curtain. The curtain contains eye-holes, which enable them to see what follows.

Dr Soal, Marion and the other experimenter, re-enter the room. While Soal observes the proceedings carefully, Marion begins to walk around the room, trying to guess which of the boxes contains the handkerchief. He is followed by the man in the sentry box, who is wheeled by the other participant. Of the three people Marion can see, the only one who knows where the handkerchief is hidden is the man in the sentry box. As Marion walks around the room, he frequently glances at the hooded head of this man. Eventually he goes to the correct box, lifts its lid and removes the handkerchief.

This bizarre-looking procedure was the final variation in a series of experimental games devised by Soal, to determine whether Marion's ability to find hidden objects was in fact due to telepathy. The experiments had started out rather simply, with the half dozen or so participants remaining in the room, seated around a table and watching Marion as he walked around the room trying to guess the correct box. Under these conditions, he had guessed correctly 38 times out of 91 trials. The odds against scoring this high by chance, are nearly 71 million to one.

It seemed probable, however, that Marion's success might be due not to telepathy but to physical clues from the sitters – clues they gave him unconsciously. In an effort to determine if this was the case and to what extent Marion depended upon such clues, Soal introduced various controls to obstruct clues from being given in the game – a curtain to hide all but one of the sitters, various kinds of hoods to cover the face of the person following Marion, cardboard boxes to cover his body down to his ankles. Even under these conditions, Marion continued to score high. It seemed possible that he was getting clues from another person's footstep – the hesitations, accelerations, starts, stops. Hence the sentry box on wheels, eliminating tell-tale footsteps. Using the wooden panels, Soal varied the amount of coverage of the man's body. In the next-to-last series of experiments, the front of the box was completely covered except for a tiny chink between the panels, through which the man could watch Marion and presumably will him to select the right tin box. Under these conditions, Marion's score dropped to chance level. With no clues, his apparent telepathic powers disappeared. In the final series, in which the man's hooded head was visible, they returned.

Dr Soal's experiments with Marion clearly demonstrated that the man's extraordinary ability was not telepathy but an acute sensitivity to involuntary clues given by his audience – in this case by the hooded man in the sentry box.

'Let's not talk about extrasensory perception', say the critics of the ESP hypothesis, 'until we know all that there is to know about sensory perception.' Perhaps we will find that all the so-called paranormal powers of the human mind are just normal powers, heightened to an extreme degree. Because telepathy, clairvoyance and precognition appear to contradict our basic ideas of physics, time, and space, we certainly ought not to jump to the conclusion that they occur until we have exhausted every other possible explanation of the phenomena, goes the argument.

Laboratory research into ESP in the universities began in the 1930s and it took full account of the sceptics' arguments. It was conducted by men trained in scientific method and they understood clearly that no amount of spontaneous evidence would convince science of the reality of phenomena that conflicted with its basic assumptions. A telepathic apparition of one's cousin at the exact moment his plane is shot down, or a precognitive dream of the San Francisco earthquake, might be dramatic evidence of 'psi' at work but it is not the kind of evidence needed to convince a scientist. What was needed was to bring ESP into the laboratory, where it could be observed and measured and where experiments could be designed, as in the physical sciences, to test hypotheses about it.

The pioneer in this work was Dr J. B. Rhine. In 1927, he and his wife Louisa, who had both taken PhD degrees in botany, went to Duke University in North Carolina to pursue post-doctoral study in psychical research. They chose Duke because its Professor of Psychology, William McDougall (formerly President of both the British and the American SPR) had publicly campaigned for psychical research to become a university study and was able to offer them his personal advice and the facilities of his department.

Six years later, Rhine published his book *Extra-Sensory Perception*, which gave an account of the first years of parapsychological research at Duke. In scientific circles, it was almost as great a bombshell of a book as Darwin's *Origin of Species* had been and it stirred up a scientific controversy that is still raging.

The anecdotal evidence for ESP, such as that published in Gurney's *Phantasms of the Living*, suggests that it is a spontaneous faculty, often connected with crisis situations such as disasters and deaths. If this were true, then getting ESP to work under laboratory conditions would be virtually impossible. However, it is a basic principle of scientific research that small events produced in the laboratory can establish theoretical principles relevant to much larger events. Men never understood thunderstorms until they discovered in the laboratory that sparks are produced between electrically charged objects. Similarly, an apparently trivial example of ESP, such as guessing what is on a card more often than chance would account for, might lead us to the principle underlying more dramatic spontaneous cases of ESP. It was in the hope of finding such a principle that Rhine began his research programme at Duke University. It did not matter if the ESP effects produced in the laboratory were small and relatively undramatic. What did matter, was that they should be measurable and repeatable and that no other hypothesis except the operation of ESP could explain the phenomena.

Previous studies of ESP had used playing cards, numbers or hidden objects as target material. Rhine and his colleagues realized that this was unsatisfactory, for people have favourite cards and numbers, and objects are loaded with associations for them. So new target material was developed, using five relatively neutral symbols – a circle, a cross, three wavy lines, a square and a star. A deck of ESP cards (sometimes called Zener cards, because Dr Zener suggested the symbols), consists of 25 cards, five of each symbol. In making a 'run' through the pack, trying to guess each card or to identify it by extrasensory perception as it is separated from the rest, a subject might be expected to score five hits purely by chance. That is, over a series of runs through the deck, his average score would, according to the laws of chance, be five. If he consistently scores more than five hits through a long series of runs, it is scientifically valid to assume that some factor other than chance is at work. Of course, the extra-chance factor may be some form of cheating or collusion with the experimenter, or it may be due to some fault in the design of the experiment or to the subject's receiving and interpreting clues in a manner that neither he nor the experimenter is consciously aware of. But if these possibilities are adequately guarded against and the subject continues to score significantly above chance expectation, it is scientifically legitimate to claim that ESP has been demonstrated to work.

In his controversial book *Extra-Sensory Perception*, Rhine reported on the work done at Duke with eight subjects who consistently scored significantly above chance in card guessing trials. Of these, the star performer was Hubert Pearce, a young student in the the School of Religion at Duke.

Rhine's way of conducting his experiments – for which he was later severely criticized – was to start off informally with the subject, sometimes over a cup of coffee and gradually to increase the controls. In his work with Pearce, Rhine found that the student usually took a while to adjust to the stricter conditions but after a brief period of low scoring, he would do as well, and sometimes even better, than before. His average score in 600 runs through the 25-card pack was slightly over nine hits per run. These results, said Rhine, 'are positively breath-taking when one calculates their mathematical significance.' The odds against chance accounting for such results, he added, 'are enormous beyond our capacity to appreciate'.

Most of the work with Pearce tested clairvoyance. The experimenter did not look at the cards, so if Pearce was getting the information by extrasensory means, he was getting it from the cards themselves and not telepathically from the mind of the experimenter. There is, however, another interpretation – that Pearce's high scores were due to precognition – that he was fore-seeing the correct answers that would be revealed when the experimenter checked the cards.

In some of the early trials, Pearce and the experimenter – usually Rhine or his main assistant Dr Pratt – would sit facing each other at a table. Pearce would shuffle the pack of cards and the experimenter would cut the pack and place it between them. Pearce would call the top card and remove it from the pack still face down. The experimenter would record the calls and then check them against the pack.

Rhine soon discovered that Pearce could not only deliberately hit the target on an average of nearly 10 tries out of 25, but he could also deliberately miss it. In a series of 225 runs, Pearce averaged less than two hits per run when he was instructed to make wrong calls. He could alternate high-scoring and low-scoring runs apparently by choice. But the most amazing discovery of these early trials with Pearce, was that he could guess down through the pack without a single card being moved. Rhine would place a freshly opened and thoroughly shuffled pack of cards on the table. Pearce would concentrate and write down the order in which he thought the cards were arranged down through the pack. When the results of 65 such runs through the pack were tabulated, Pearce's score was an average of 7.4 hits – significantly above chance level. In one run, urged on by Rhine's offering him $100 for each hit he got in sequence, Pearce got all 25 cards right. He didn't get the $2500, though, for Rhine said the offer was understood to be 'only a figurative one'.

To test Pearce's powers of clairvoyance under stricter condi-tions, Rhine arranged a series of experiments at long distance. After synchronizing their watches, Pearce and the experimenter, Dr Pratt, went into separate buildings on the Duke University campus. (At first they used buildings that were 100 yards apart; later the distance was increased to 250 yards.) At a pre-arranged time, Pratt shuffled and cut a pack of cards, placed them face down on the table in front of him, then removed the top card and put it aside without looking at it. Pearce, in the other building, had a minute in which to write down his guess for that card. Then a second card was removed and so on through the pack. At the end of the run, Pratt made a record of the sequence, then shuffled the pack and ran through the procedure again. When two runs had been completed, Pearce and Pratt sealed up their record sheets and delivered them independently to Dr Rhine. The results of these experiments were even more impressive than many of Pearce's trials at close range. After excluding the first three runs as an 'adjustment phase', Rhine found that over nearly 300 runs at 100 yards, Pearce was averaging 11.4 hits per run.

Pearce was just one of the eight people Rhine discovered among the faculty and students of Duke University who possessed extraordinary ESP ability. When he published *Extra-Sensory Perception* in 1934, he was convinced that he had demonstrated, by unimpeachable scientific method, that ESP occurs and had presented a case that the scientific community as a whole must pay attention to. However, the scientific community remained sceptical for the most part, and in the ensuing controversy, both Rhine's experimental methods and his statistical analysis of the results were criticized. Some of his critics even questioned his integrity.

One of the sceptics was Professor Bernard Riess of Hunter College in New York City. But, unlike most other critics, Professor Riess decided to test the ESP hypothesis by carrying out some experiments of his own. He discovered a promising subject, a young woman who lived near him in White Plains. Following the procedure used in the Pratt-Pearce experiments at Duke, he completed a series of 74 runs over a period of several months. At a pre-arranged time on certain evenings, Professor Riess sitting in his study, would go through a pack of cards while the girl, a quarter of a mile away, would write down the order of the cards. At the conclusion of the series, she was discovered to have averaged the astonishing score of 18 hits per run. 'Heaven knows there is no room for such results in my scientific philosophy!', Riess told a colleague. But with admirable scientific objectivity, he accepted an invitation to publish a report on his experiments in the *Journal of Parapsychology*.

This is the best-ever record of success in ESP trials, but as it was not obtained under laboratory conditions and with qualified witnesses, it remains on the level of anecdotal evidence. Like all other spectacularly high scorers in card-guessing tests, the subject suddenly lost her powers. She underwent an illness and when she recovered and was tested again, her scores were not significantly above chance expectation. The same had happened to Hubert Pearce, who had suddenly lost his ability apparently as a consequence of receiving bad news from home. Parapsychologists are to this day puzzled by this tendency for ESP to manifest itself spectacularly but briefly in some people. However, the very fact that once-successful subjects eventually begin to fail, is one indication that the original positive results were genuine.

One researcher who was highly sceptical when he read Rhine's report of the early work at Duke, was the same Dr Soal who later established – ingeniously if eccentrically – that the stage telepathist Frederick Marion possessed no paranormal powers. Soal's scepticism was not that of the hard-line materialist. Back in the 1920s, he had already shown an interest in psychical phenomena. Soal was sceptical about Rhine's work because he found it difficult to believe that over a short period of time and in one place, Rhine had discovered as many as eight high-scoring subjects. He had conducted similar experiments himself and had failed to discover even one gifted subject. For several years after Rhine's book was published, he worked diligently with numerous subjects but still failed to get any results significantly above chance expectation. When the well-known photographer Basil Shackleton walked into his office one gloomy February afternoon in 1936 and volunteered as a subject, Soal had no reason to suspect that these experiments would yield one of the strangest discoveries of ESP research.

He still had no reason to suspect it after his first experimental session with Shackleton. The photographer had shown remarkable confidence when he volunteered. 'I have come', he had declared, 'not to be tested, but to demonstrate telepathy', and he claimed that with friends at home he could guess through a pack of playing cards from top to bottom and get most of them right. But he was disappointed in the results he produced under Soal's experimental conditions. His scores in six successive runs with the 25-card pack were 10, 7, 7, 6, 6, and 3 hits. He went away somewhat chastened, saying that he needed to have a drink or two before he could get his ESP functioning. But later, when

Soal provided the 'drink or two' and conditions in which Shackleton thought he could function effectively, the subject only averaged 4.1 hits per 25 – well below chance expectation. A series of trials was completed and at the end of it, Soal filed away the unremarkable record of 165 hits out of 800 attempts. He forgot about Shackleton.

Three years later, Soal was persuaded to take another look at his records of the Shackleton experiments. The Cambridge psychical researcher, Whately Carington had conducted some telepathy experiments himself, using pictures. On ten successive evenings, he would draw a picture and hang it in a locked room in his house. His subjects, some of whom were on the other side of the Atlantic, would attempt to identify the picture by ESP and mail in their own drawings. Quite a number of these drawings, Carington noticed, matched well with a picture in his target series but not the one which was the target for the particular evening on which they were drawn. Many of them were uncannily accurate matches with the *next* picture in the series, or with one used as the target drawing on the previous night. The delayed hits were odd enough, but the advance hits indicated that precognition might be at work. At the time the subjects made these drawings, the target drawing had not even been made. In some cases, Carington had not even thought of what he would draw.

Carington termed these advanced and delayed hits a 'displacement effect' and he drew Soal's attention to it. He urged Soal to look through some of the records of his old experiments to see if further evidence of this displacement effect might be found. Soal followed his suggestion though not very optimistically or enthusiastically, for it involved a considerable amount of work. But when he checked Shackleton's scores, his perseverance was at last rewarded. He discovered that this subject, whose attempts at identifying the target card had barely come up to chance expectation, had called either the one before or the one after it in the series with remarkable frequency. When Soal mathematically analyzed the results, he found that the odds against their being obtained by chance were more than 2,500 to one. Shackleton's confidence in his powers of ESP had not been mistaken. He was like a marksman with a quirky bias to hit persistently just to the left or to the right of the bullseye.

Soal got in touch with Shackleton and in 1940 began a new series of experiments with him, using several different agents. He consistently scored one ahead of the target when his guesses were spaced at intervals of about 2.8 seconds, but when Soal speeded up the rate to approximately half the interval, he scored with equal consistency *two* ahead. Shackleton's ability to guess in advance in this way suggested precognition – the ability to foresee the future. Soal noted, however, that the results might also be explained by clairvoyance. Perhaps the subject was not foreseeing what would be in the agent's mind a few moments later but psychically looking into the unturned cards as they lay on the table at that moment. As in Pearce's case, Shackleton's high scores might be attributed either to clairvoyance or to precognition.

Shackleton also improved his ability to identify the immediate target card. Once, Soal asked him to prepare himself for a session the following week when he would be scored only on the target card. Shackleton gave 76 correct calls in 200 trials, a score with odds against chance of more than 10 million to one. He also responded impressively when Soal secretly introduced another variation. Instead of a random arrangement of the five symbols, Soal used a pack consisting of only two symbols – 12 of one symbol followed by 13 of the other. Shackleton's ESP was not thrown by this innovation. In three such non-random sequences introduced without warning in a series of normal random sequences, he scored 7, 12, and 13 direct hits.

When the distinguished Cambridge philosopher, C. D. Broad studied the Soal-Shackleton experiments, he declared, 'There can be no doubt that the events described happened and were correctly reported; that the odds against chance coincidence piled up to billions to one; and that the nature of the events which involved both telepathy and precognition, conflicts with one or more of the basic limiting principles [of science and common sense].'

Another Cambridge philosopher, Professor R. H. Thouless (who coined the umbrella-term, 'psi') wrote in 1942, 'The reality of the phenomena [of ESP] must be regarded as proved as certainly as anything in scientific research can be proved . . . Let us now give up the task of trying to prove again to the satisfaction of the sceptical that the psi effect really exists, and try instead to devote ourselves to the task of finding out all we can about it.'

A great deal had, in fact, already been found out about ESP in the 12 years between the beginning of Rhine's work at Duke University and the time Professor Thouless wrote these words. But it was a puzzling body of knowledge, little more than a series of glimpses of a, still mysterious, paranormal faculty. This faculty could be demonstrated to work and in some cases, to work in obedience to certain laws, but it showed no overall pattern or lawfulness in its occurrence. Professor Thouless was right to emphasize that much remained to be discovered about the nature of ESP and that it was a waste of time to persist with research designed to prove its, already proven, existence.

What precisely had been found out about 'psi' up to this time? First, it had been demonstrated independently by researchers in different countries, that in card guessing tests some people can show a consistent record of success that rules out chance as an explanation – and that can only be explained as the operation of ESP.

This ability seemed to be rare and short-lived. Consistently high scorers were difficult to find and even they often lost their ability suddenly.

ESP, however, was not entirely an involuntary process. Gifted guessers like Pearce or Shackleton seemed able to score high or low, directly on the target card or on one of its neighbours, at will.

ESP was seen to operate most effectively when the subject was relaxed and free from distractions. It could be temporarily destroyed by a depressant drug, such as sodium amytal and restored (but not improved) by a stimulant, such as caffeine. In tests for telepathy, it tended to vary according to the relationship between the subject and the agent.

In the early days of research, it had been assumed that telepathy was the most plausible form of ESP because it was easier to conceive of mind reacting with mind, than of mind reacting with matter or transcending the limitations of time. But the discovery of Pearce's ability to guess down through the pack and of the displacement effect in Carington's and Soal's researches, cast some doubt on this assumption. Some parapsychologists began to wonder if clairvoyance and precognition were perhaps more common than telepathy.

Such ambiguities in experimental results induced researchers to design some very careful and ingenious experiments, in which only one kind of ESP – telepathy, clairvoyance, or precognition – was tested and the others excluded.

ESP appeared to work equally effectively at any distance. This ruled out the possibility of its being explained in terms of any known physical law, for at that time all physical forces were believed to decline, however slightly, with the distance travelled. Although recently, some exceptions to that rule have been discovered, we still don't know how ESP functions. We see only the results of its functioning.

The results themselves are fairly exciting even today – decades after Rhine reported his first experiments with Pearce. And although star subjects like Pearce are rare, some researchers now believe that everyone may possess ESP to some degree. Readers who would like to explore the possibility of ESP in themselves or their friends can easily set up their own simple experiments. This can be undertaken in the spirit of a game, but if it is properly conducted it could produce a valid contribution to current ESP research. The characteristics of the ESP faculty are by no means fully understood today and any parapsychologist would be delighted to hear of the discovery of another consistently high-scoring subject like Hubert Pearce or Basil Shackleton.

Because the ESP faculty functions best when the subject is relaxed and uninhibited, it is a good idea to follow Rhine's approach of starting off informally and not making too much fuss over techniques and precautions. If a subject shows high-scoring ability, the controls and conditions can be tightened up as the experimental series progresses. Initially, it is essential only to insure that the subject cannot obtain normal sensory information about the target cards. If he can see the backs of the cards, make sure there are no distinguishing marks on them. Also, make sure there are no reflecting surfaces in the room that might enable him to glimpse the faces of the cards.

Preliminary experiments might be conducted with the subject

and agent sitting at opposite ends of a five or six-foot long table, fitted with an improvised screen in the middle.

Zener cards are manufactured and sold commercially. The authorized distributor is Haines House of Cards, Norwalk, Ohio. Detailed instructions accompanying the pack explain how to test for clairvoyance and telepathy in several different ways.

Another kind of test can be constructed following a method adapted from one devised by S. G. Soal. Materials needed include five ordinary playing cards – the ace through the five – and five picture cards. Soal used cards with coloured pictures of five animals – an elephant, a giraffe, a lion, a penguin and a zebra. The idea was that animals were more easily visualized than the abstract Zener symbols and so, might be more effective in pure telepathy tests. Cards bearing these symbols can easily be improvised or, alternatively, other picture cards may be used. Ideally, the names of the symbols should begin with different letters so that the subject need write only one letter for each trial.

Three people are required for this telepathy test – the subject, the agent and the experimenter. The subject and the agent sit at opposite ends of the table with the screen between them and the experimenter sits at the side of the table at the agent's end. The experimenter holds the five playing cards. The agent has the five picture cards, which he shuffles and lays face down in a row on the table in front of him. As an extra precaution, they may be laid out in a cardboard box turned on its side, thus screening them from both the subject and the experimenter.

Both the experimenter and the subject have scoring sheets in front of them with lines numbered 1 to 25. To begin, the experimenter shuffles his five playing cards and shows one selected at random to the agent, saying as he does so, 'one'. This signals the subject to be ready to make his first guess. The experimenter then writes the number of the playing card on his scoring sheet and reshuffles the five cards. Meanwhile, the agent notes the number of the playing card shown to him and looks at the face of the appropriate picture card in front of him. If it was a 3, for example, he will look at the third card from the left. The subject writes against the number 1 on his scoring sheet the initial letter (E, G, L, P, or Z, if the animal pictures are used) of his guess at the target picture.

When a run of 25 guesses has been completed, the agent shows the experimenter the order of the target pictures. The experimenter can then assign the letters E, G, L, P, or Z to the corresponding numbers of the playing cards on his scoring sheet. The target cards are then reshuffled and laid out in a different order in preparation for another run. When the desired number of runs have been completed, the letters on the subject's scoring sheet are compared with the actual sequences on the experimenter's sheet.

The experiment can be converted into one testing clairvoyance if the agent does *not* look at the face of each picture card as its number is shown.

If private ESP experimentation is entered into seriously, it must be continued over several sessions and several hundred individual trials, or guesses. Rhine has said that most of his good subjects did not do particularly well in their first hundred trials.

To do well means to score consistently and significantly above the chance expectation of five hits per run of 25 guesses. On a series of 100 or more runs, an average of even six or seven is significant. It would be premature to take it as signifying the operation of ESP, however. The high score might indicate a fault in the procedure. This would be the stage to introduce stricter controls and conditions.

The Soal-Shackleton experiments were conducted with the subject and agent in separate rooms, with the door open so that the subject could hear the experimenter's cue-calls for the synchronization of his guesses. This is one improvement that could be introduced with a successful scorer after the preliminary trials. Another is to ensure randomness in the numbers turned up by the experimenter. It is possible that in shuffling his five cards and picking one out for each guess he might, consciously or unconsciously, choose them in a certain order. This order might be picked up by the subject, or it might correspond to an order that he favours. To eliminate this possibility, the experimenter can prepare in advance lists of 25 random numbers, which he then communicates in sequence to the agent by holding up the corresponding playing cards. Such lists can be compiled from tables of logarithms or from a telephone directory, using the last digits of numbers down a column in the sequence in which they occur and of course, ignoring all digits except those falling into the range 1 to 5.

If, when these extra precautions have been taken, your subject continues to average seven or more hits per run over a long series of trials, you may have reason to suspect a serious case of supernormality – and should lose no time in calling in your nearest parapsychologist.

CHAPTER 33

MIND OVER MATTER

Can objects fly through the air, propelled by the power of thought alone? Unlikely as it may sound, well-documented evidence indicates that intelligent, reliable observers, time and time again, have been presented with situations that appear to offer no other possible explanation. While some scientists investigate poltergeist activity which occurs spontaneously, others attempt to pin down psychokinesis – PK – in the laboratory with long series of tests with dice or blank cubes. The results dictated by chance alone are easy to predict, but what does it mean when the results show that the rolling dice have apparently been influenced by a person thinking about them?

On 14 January 1966, the Miami police were asked to investigate some strange occurrences at a warehouse owned by Tropication Arts, Inc. – a company that dealt in novelty items and souvenirs for the tourist trade. The complaint clerk at the station told Patrolman William Killam, 'This person who called said he had a ghost in his place of business . . . going around breaking ashtrays and he said they were just coming up off the floor and breaking.' Patrolman Killam went off on his assignment muttering something about being sent to deal with 'a lot of nuts'.

When he arrived at the warehouse, the owner told him that the breakages had started about a month earlier. At first he had put it down to carelessness on the part of the staff, but as weeks went by and the rate of breakage increased, he realized that something very peculiar and unnatural was going on. Patrolman Killam listened sceptically, then said he'd better take a look around the warehouse. He walked along the aisles, sometimes stopping to stamp on the floor or shake one of the shelves in order to see if this would dislodge anything. Everything seemed normal and secure. Killam had walked the length of three aisles and was beginning to walk down a fourth, when he saw something that stopped him in his tracks. A highball glass that was standing among others on a shelf suddenly rose into the air, travelled a few feet and smashed onto the floor. Nobody else was near the spot and when Killam shook the shelf roughly, none of the other glasses moved.

Clearly this problem was beyond the capacity of the police. Psychical investigators were called in. They were Dr J. G. Pratt of the Parapsychology Laboratory at Duke University and Dr W. G. Roll of the Psychical Research Foundation. Since their investigation of the 'Seaford Poltergeist' that had tormented a Long Island family in 1958, they had become a kind of flying squad for the investigation of reported poltergeist phenomena. With a team of helpers, they spent some weeks at the Tropication Arts warehouse, recording every incident in great detail, analyzing them and looking for a common factor that would explain them. In all, they recorded 224 incidents, 78 of which they themselves witnessed. The common factor turned out to be a 19-year-old employee, Cuban refugee Julio Vasquez. In most of the records of poltergeist happenings collected over the years, there is commonly mention of the presence of a young person, who is going through some kind of emotional crisis. So the investigators had known what to look for. But their detailed recording of the incidents in this case yielded some interesting new discoveries.

The breakages had all occurred when Julio was in the warehouse, but not always when he was near the objects. Moreover, they nearly all occurred when he had his back toward the object that was moved, and the movements took place on his left side, never on his right. When the movements of the objects were plotted and the distances they travelled were measured, it was found that, as they had moved away from Julio, they had not travelled in a straight line but in a curve. Analysis of the distances the objects travelled in relation to their distance from Julio at the time of the incident, revealed a precise mathematical ratio. This was found to agree with what is known in physics as the 'law of exponential decay'. This is the law that describes the weakening effect in many natural processes – for example, bacterial and radioactive decay and the conversion of light to heat energy as it penetrates water. After studying and interpreting all the data, the investigators reached a conclusion – contrary to the warehouse owners' suspicions, no ghosts were involved. Julio was the poltergeist. The energy that caused the smashing of objects came from him.

The German word *poltergeist* translates as 'boisterous or noisy spirit'. But many modern physichal researchers have come to the conclusion that poltergeist phenomena have nothing to do with spirits. Instead, they are believed to be involuntary PK effects caused by the release of pent-up psychic energy. The question is how this psychic energy gets converted to kinetic energy, capable of moving matter.

For most people, PK is a more difficult concept to come to terms with than ESP. It is difficult enough to accept that mind can interact with mind without any apparent channel of communication, but to propose that mind can interact with matter is even more implausible. Yet today, the idea of psychosomatic illnesses and psychic healing, which most of the medical profession would have scoffed at not so long ago, is widely accepted. It is not so generally realized that these medical phenomena involve a mind-matter interaction that no known laws can explain. Still, the sceptic could point out that psychosomatic illness and psychic healing involve interaction between mind and matter in the same body. What is implausible is that mind can act upon matter outside the body, that a person can influence events in the external material world by pure will.

One day early in 1934, a young man walked into Dr J. B. Rhine's office at Duke University and announced, 'Hey, doc, I've got something to tell you I think you ought to know.' He was, he explained, a professional gambler and it was his experience that when he was in a certain state of mind, which he described as 'hot', he could influence the dice to come up as he wanted them to by exercising his will. He had heard about Dr Rhine's ESP research and thought that Rhine would be the man to take his discovery seriously and investigate it scientifically. He was right.

Within minutes, Dr Rhine and the gambler were crouched on the floor in a corner of the office rolling dice.

Thus began a long experimental programme of PK research at Duke, the results of which were not published until 10 years later. Rhine and his colleagues had had enough trouble getting the scientific community to accept their evidence for ESP and they didn't want to complicate the controversy prematurely by claiming to be able to demonstrate PK in the laboratory as well. So for nine years, the dice-rolling experiments continued quietly at Duke and the results were carefully recorded and analyzed, but not published.

The advantage of using dice in PK experiments, is the same as the advantage of using cards to test ESP – the results can be statistically analyzed and an odds-against-chance calculation can be made. When two dice ('die' in the singular) are thrown together, the sum of the faces can range from 2 to 12. There are 36 combinations of the two dice, 15 of which add up to values of 8 or more and 15 others to values of 6 or less, while 6 combinations produce the sum of 7. The two dice must be distinguishable from each other to produce this variety of results. For example, a three on die 'a' and a four on die 'b' can thus count as a separate score to a four on 'a' and a three on 'b', even though the numbers are the same in both cases.

The target in a PK test can be high scores, low scores, or sevens. Alternatively, a particular number can be made the target. At the end of a run, which at Duke was arbitrarily set as either 24 throws of separate dice, or 12 throws of pairs, or 8 throws of three dice, the deviation from chance expectation can be precisely calculated. The experimenter found that the most convenient procedure was to throw a pair of dice 12 times and to will either high or low combinations to come up. The chance expectation for either result is five hits per run. This figure is arrived at by dividing the number of low or high combinations – which is 15 each – by 3, which is the number of times that 12 (the number of throws) goes into 36 (the number of possible combinations). In other words, the chances of a hit are reduced *in proportion* to the number of attempts. If there were 36 throws in a run, the chance of a hit would rise proportionately to 15. Of course, all such calculations of chance are based on a large number of runs. In the short term, results might deviate sharply from chance expectation without implying that factors other than chance are at work.

The first series of recorded experiments conducted at Duke consisted of 562 runs. There were 3,110 hits, whereas the chance expectation was 2,810 hits (5 times 562). So there were 300 more hits than pure chance would have produced. Calculations based upon probability theory, showed that this result would not come up more than once in a billion times by chance alone.

After this encouraging exploratory stage, the researchers at Duke felt it was time to vary and tighten up the conditions of the experiments, in order to see if the results could be attributed to any cause other than PK. Two possible other causes were the employment of skill by the thrower of the dice and the existence of a physical bias in the dice themselves. Dice on which the marker spots are hollowed out may slightly favour the higher numbers, because their faces have had more material removed and are therefore fractionally lighter than the faces of the lower numbers. To rule out skill as a factor in throwing, the experimenters used various throwing devices, such as a chute with a corrugated surface and an electrically operated release mechanism. To prevent bias in the dice influencing the results, they used special precision-made dice. Also, the targets within series of runs were systematically alternated so that the effect of any bias would be cancelled out. Many more experiments were conducted under such improved conditions at Duke and elsewhere and results, significantly above chance, were continually obtained. Unlike the ESP experiments, however, this research revealed no spectacularly high-scoring subjects. The work suggested that PK was a latent faculty that many, if not most people possessed, but that it rarely manifested itself as more highly developed in one subject than in another.

One of the most positive results in these trials, was obtained in an amusing experiment that took the form of a contest between divinity students and gamblers. A student at the Duke Divinity School conceived the idea that PK might be an operating factor in cases of prayer apparently influencing events in the physical world. He put his idea to Rhine, who suggested that, because the divinity students would be highly motivated to succeed in order to demonstrate the efficacy of prayer, it might be interesting to compare their results with those of another group of strongly motivated individuals. So four young men noted for their success in crap shooting were found and matched against four prospective ministers. After a total of 1,242 runs of a type in which the chance expectancy average was 4.00 hits per run, the gamblers had obtained an average run score of 4.52 and the divinity students an average of 4.51. This was virtually a tie. The interesting result of the experiment, though, was that when the results of both groups were combined and statistically analyzed, they were found to be likely to occur by chance only once in billions of tests. It was clear that motivation was a potent influence in PK trials, whether that motivation was religious or otherwise.

The most conclusive evidence for the operation of PK in the Duke experiments, did not emerge in the course of the experiments themselves but later, when the results were analyzed. In 1943, active research at Duke was at a standstill because of the war, so Rhine and his only remaining research assistant dug out the results of all the dice-rolling experiments of the previous nine years and had another look at them. They found a sharp drop in the above-chance scores from the first run in a test to the later runs. The experimenters had noted such declines at the time of making the tests, but had paid little attention to them. Now, when the separate tests were taken together and the overall pattern discovered to be one of a sharp drop in above-chance scoring, the scores acquired new significance. The same drop occurred in tests using mechanical dice-throwing machines, which, unlike humans, would not suffer the fatigue that often accounts for a scoring decline in many kinds of psychological tests. Reporting on the discovery of these 'position effects' in the book *Mind Over Matter*, Dr Louisa Rhine observed that they showed that PK was not just an ability sometimes to hit a target, 'but a process connected with and expressed according to deep unconscious motivating factors, just as ESP had been found to be'.

This delayed discovery armed the parapsychologists with a strong argument against the charge of fraud, for the evidence of the position effects had lain in the records for years without anyone suspecting it and the patterns could not conceivably have been fraudulently introduced by the original experimenters, for no one had known at the time that such patterns would ever be significant.

When the accounts of the Duke experiments were published, more researchers became interested in PK. W. E. Cox, an amateur, became closely associated with Duke. He was a businessman with a talent for gadgetry. He devised several dice-throwing experiments using a variety of clock mechanisms, mercury switches, electrical relays and complicated structures built in three and five tiers, with different target areas for the dice to be directed to by PK. These experiments introduced a new skill that became known as 'placement PK'. In this case, the object was not to influence a particular face of a die to come up but to influence freely rolling dice to come to rest in a particular place.

The outstanding contribution to research in placement PK was made by Haakon Forwald, a Swedish engineer-physicist. During the early 1950s, he conducted independent experiments, rolling dice down an inclined plane and trying to will them to fall either on the left or the right side of a table. In 1957, he paid a visit to Duke and joined forces with Dr Pratt. The Pratt-Forwald experiment subsequently became widely regarded as the most successful demonstration of PK.

In this experiment, six wooden cubes were released mechanically and rolled down a chute onto a horizontal surface with a dividing line down the middle. The PK task was not to direct the cubes into one of the target areas, but to influence those that fell in one area to roll farther than those that fell in the other. Lines drawn on the table parallel to the centre line, at intervals of one centimetre, enabled the experimenter to measure the degree of displacement of the cubes from the centre. A long series of trials produced a highly significant positive result, with odds against chance of 5000 to one.

By the end of the 1950s, the reality of PK was as firmly established by experimental method and statistical analysis as was that of ESP. But both ESP and PK as studied in the laboratory, seemed to be relatively weak forces. PK research had only established the possibility of mental influence on small objects already in motion. Nobody had managed, under laboratory conditions, to make a stationary object move. Yet this is what happens in poltergeist phenomena and in some of the alleged physical effects produced by mediums in the seance room. All researchers in the field knew Professor Winther's report on the PK feats of the Danish medium, Anna Rasmussen, back in the 1920s, but no such talented subject had appeared on the scene since really scientific methods of control and analysis had been developed. There were, however, other areas of apparent PK activity that might repay scientific study. These included the phenomena of thought-photography, or 'thoughtograph', and psychic healing.

In 1910, the professor of psychology at Tokyo University, Tomokichi Fukurai, tested a woman of reported psychic ability for clairvoyance. He conceived the idea of having her identify clairvoyantly an image imprinted on a film plate which had not been developed. After the test he discovered that another plate had apparently been affected by the clairvoyant's effort at concentration. In later experiments, he asked her to try to transfer specific images, usually geometrical figures or Japanese characters, onto unexposed film plates. No camera was used and the target plate was sandwiched between the others. The woman consistently succeeded in imprinting the middle plate with the designated image, leaving the two outer plates entirely clear. Fukurai published a book on his strange discovery and the ensuing controversy over his work on psychic phenomena forced him to resign his university position.

Another important investigation – this time into psychic healing powers – was carried out in the 1960s. In this case a psychic healer, Oscar Estebany of Montreal, a former Hungarian army colonel, discovered his healing abilities in the 1930s in the course of massaging cavalry horses. He gained a reputation as a healer in Budapest in the 1940s and continued to practice when he moved to Canada in the mid-1950s. Hundreds of cures, mostly of disorders that have defied the efforts of conventional medical practitioners, are attributed to him. In 1961, Estebany agreed to let Dr Bernard Grad of McGill University test his healing power scientifically.

The obvious rational explanation of psychic healing is that it is effected by suggestion. In other words, the patient's faith in the healer effects the cure. Therefore, Dr Grad started his experiments with 300 patients that had no faith in, or knowledge of, Estebany's alleged powers. The patients were mice. Dr Grad inflicted a small identical wound on all 300 mice and divided them into three equal groups. The first group was treated by Estebany, the second by people who claimed no psychic healing powers and the third was left untreated as a control group. The treatment consisted simply of the healer holding each cage of mice for 15 minutes, twice a day. After 16 days, the wounds were measured. It was found that those on the mice that Estebany had treated were only half the size of those on the other two groups of mice.

In another experiment, Dr Grad compared the growth of two groups of potted barley plants. One group was watered with a solution that Estebany had held for 30 minutes and the other was watered with some of the same solution that Estebany had not tried to influence. The psychically treated water consistently promoted stronger and healthier growth in the plants than the untreated water. Dr Grad reported his experiments in the *International Journal of Parapsychology*, but he was unable to offer an explanation of the results.

More searching investigations of Estebany's powers were conducted by Dr M. Justa Smith, research director of the Human Dimensions Institute at Rosary Hill College in Buffalo, New York. Dr Smith, a biochemist who is also a Franciscan nun, reasoned that if psychic healing works, it must work at the enzyme level in the body's cells. Enzymes are the substances that promote chemical changes in the cells, and enzyme failure is the root physical cause of disease. In order to promote health, the chemical reactions of certain enzymes within the body need to be accelerated and others to be slowed down.

Dr Smith had done a great deal of research with the enzyme *trypsin*, which she knew can be severely damaged by exposure to ultraviolet light. She prepared a flask of *trypsin* in solution, damaged its molecular structure with ultraviolet light and had Estebany hold his hands over the sides of the flask. Every 15 minutes, she removed a small quantity of the solution and analyzed it in a highly sensitive machine called a *spectrophotometer*. In earlier experiments with Estebany, Dr Smith had discovered that he could accelerate reactions in healthy enzyme chains, but now she found that he could actually repair damaged molecules. Follow-up experiments with other healers and other enzymes confirmed the discovery. The psychic healers in Dr Smith's experiments had no way of knowing which enzymes were in solution in the flasks they held, or whether an acceleration or deceleration of activity in a particular flask would have a potentially positive effect on the body. Yet, invariably, the healers caused chemical reactions of the kind appropriate in each case. When Dr Smith presented the results of her research to the scientific world she appropriately titled her paper, *Psychic Healing: Myth into Science*.

Whether psychic healing is brought about by energies emanating from the mind of the healer or from his body, is still an open question. Only if it comes from his mind could we accurately term this healing a psychokinetic function. But this is a question of terminology that need not worry us at this point. What such research as Dr Smith's has established, is that some people possess powers that are outside the ken of modern physical science and until these powers are more fully understood, it is convenient to group them under the general idea of PK.

An experiment that demonstrated PK influence at the cellular level, without involving the complicating factors in cases of psychic healing, was made by the English researcher Nigel Richmond. Richmond tried to influence by PK the movement of *paramecia*, which are single-celled organisms about .01 inch long, found in pond water. His method was to place a drop of pond water on a microscope slide, put a paramecium in the centre of the microscopic field, and try to will the organism to swim where he wanted it to. For this purpose, he divided the microscopic field into four quarters using two crossed hairs and assigned each quarter to one of the four suits of playing cards. He determined the target area, each time, by turning up a card from the top of a shuffled deck.

Each attempt to influence the paramecium's direction of exit lasted 15 seconds. If a paramecium swam out of the field of view before the time had elapsed, it was still counted in the scoring by being assigned to the quarter through which it had passed. In all he made 1,495 attempts. Chance expectation for a paramecium hitting the target area was one-fourth of this number, or 373.75. Richmond found that the paramecia hit the target 483 times, a deviation of 109.25 over chance expectation. He also found that the creatures often went into the quarter diagonally opposite the target area. Out of the 1,495 attempts, this area was hit 444 times – 70.25 above chance. Richmond counted these diagonal scores as hits and grouped them with the target-hitting scores because, he wrote, 'I suspect that influence applied in one direction would sometimes have its effects in the diametrically opposed direction. . . .' Whether or not he was justified in giving equal value to these opposite scores, the fact remains that he got considerably above-chance results for his target quarters. His experiment seemed to indicate that his mind influenced the movements of other living organisms, by the power of PK.

Some parapsychologists, however, have raised the question whether the results might not show telepathy at work between the experimenter and the paramecia. This suggestion sounds preposterous, for telepathy is such an astonishing power that we tend to think of it as restricted to human beings, if we believe in it at all. But many experiments, particularly with dogs, cats and horses, have indicated that the 'psi' faculty – including telepathy and even PK – may not be confined to humans.

In 1970, Dr Helmut Schmidt, now Research Director of the Mind Science Foundation, San Antonio, Texas, reported some experiments testing the PK ability of a cat. The point of the experiment was to see if the cat could manage to exert PK to turn on a lamp, by which it could warm itself, more often than the lamp would turn on by chance.

The governing mechanism for the lamp was a device called a random number generator. One of the chief problems in 'psi' research is insuring randomness in the target materials. If one is testing for clairvoyance or for PK, it is important to eliminate the possibility of the experimenter knowing – even unconsciously – which card will turn up, for example, or which times the light will go on. If the experimenter or anyone else knows the answer, one would have to include the possibility of telepathy in any positive results. The most random known process in nature, is the rate of decay of radioactive particles. In a pile of strontium atoms, for instance, half of the atoms will disintegrate over a period of 20 years. There is no way, however, of knowing which ones will disintegrate during this period, or at what time they will do so. When the disintegration takes place, energy is emitted, and the random number generator uses this energy to turn on nine lights arranged in a circle, one at a time. The lights go on in a clockwise or counterclockwise direction depending on the decay rate of the strontium nuclei. The experimental subject's task is to make the lights go on in a given direction. This in turn governs the turning on and off of the generator. Success means that the subject has influenced, presumably by PK, the behaviour of subatomic particles.

The cat used in Schmidt's experiments obviously couldn't know about the subatomic particles, but it clearly had an interest in turning on the lamp that was attached to the generator. For half an hour every afternoon, the cat was put into a shack inside which the temperature was 0°C – not cold enough to cause the cat serious discomfort, but not the kind of temperature a cat likes. In one part of the shack was the 200-Watt lamp, going on and off at intervals of a few seconds or less. Every second a number was being generated that would determine whether the lamp was on or off.

For the first five experiments in the series, the cat went straight to the lamp on entering the shack and at the end of the 30 minutes was found curled up next to it. The experimenters found that the light had been on slightly more than 50 per cent of the time. More specifically, out of the 9,000 numbers generated one per second during the five sessions, 4,615 had turned on the lamp – 115 more than the 4,500 expected according to chance. These results were interesting, but not startling.

Schmidt continued the experiment for another five afternoons. It was found that the cat's behaviour changed. When the door was opened at the end of the sixth session, it dashed out of the shack. In none of the remaining sessions was it found sitting by the lamp as it had at first. 'It seemed to have developed a dislike for the flashing lamp', reported Schmidt. Moreover, the generator turned on by chance fewer times than expected, during the second series of five sessions. Was the animal capable of exerting PK but resentful at being bullied into performing? This is a tempting conclusion for anyone who knows cats. Unfortunately, the experiment was too short to prove anything. The onset of warm weather, affecting the temperature inside the shack, forced Schmidt to discontinue the tests. Over a period of

10 days, the variation from chance in both directions was too slight to indicate with any certainty the existence of feline PK.

A significant discovery about PK that has emerged from research done so far, is that it is goal-oriented. That is, when it functions, it seems to accomplish an aimed-for result directly, without the person, animal, or lower organism that exercises it having any conscious conception, so far as we can tell, of the processes that lead to this result. This is the stumbling block for the rational mind. We can possibly conceive of will as a consciously controlled operative force influencing events in the material world. But the idea of will divorced from consciousness, working on the world without any guiding idea of *how* it works, without any programme, is hard to swallow. It conflicts with our understanding of natural processes as being governed by laws of cause and effect. Yet there seems no way out of this puzzle. We just have to admit that Nature is under no obligation to conform to the laws that we have evolved, to further our understanding of how it functions.

The most gifted psychics who produce PK effects, never have any idea how they do it. Anna Rasmussen believed that her spirit guide, Dr Lasaruz, was responsible for hers. In more recent years, Uri Geller has attributed his powers to extraterrestrial beings. But such hypotheses are at present unprovable. Since the 1970s, research into PK has entered a new phase with the discovery of extraordinarily gifted subjects comparable to Anna Rasmussen and the Schneider brothers. Early research at Duke University and elsewhere, suggested that PK is a faculty that many people possess in a weak form, but that cannot be developed to a spectacular degree. The comparatively recent appearances of Uri Geller and Ingo Swann have challenged this idea.

The investigations of Geller and the resulting controversies have been widely reported, but the New York artist Ingo Swann is less well known. Like Geller, he has been studied by scientists at the Stanford Research Institute in Menlo Park, California.

At the Stanford Institute, physicists Harold Puthoff and Russell Targ, supervised an experiment in which Swann was required to psychokinetically disturb the inner workings of a *magnetometer*. This is a device that produces electric current from a radioactive core sunk deep in a well. The current decreases at a uniform rate in relation to the decay rate of the magnetic field within the instrument. The output of current is recorded in the form of a continuous wave on a moving chart. The magnetometer is shielded by special metals so that no other magnetic influences can reach it. The physicists described to Swann how the magnetometer functioned, and told him that if he could affect the magnetic field within it, the change would show on the output recording. Swann then focused his attention on the interior of the magnetometer, whereupon the frequency of the output immediately doubled. In the course of the experiment, he was able to cause other changes, which show up clearly on the chart. Puthoff and Targ emphasize in their report that this was not a fully controlled scientific experiment, for it left open the question whether Swann had in fact disturbed the process of subatomic emission in the radioactive core, or whether he had affected the recording device. Either way, of course, the effect he produced in the laboratory equipment could only have been produced by the operation of PK.

Dr Gertrude Schmeidler, a professor of psychology at the City University, New York, had also conducted experiments with Swann. Starting from the question of whether PK energy generates heat, as all other forms of energy do, she designed an experiment using *thermistors* – extremely sensitive temperature detectors – connected to the palms of Swann's hands and also lodged in thermos bottles on the other side of a large room. The thermistors in the bottles were the targets and Swann was instructed to employ his PK faculty to heat or cool them as directed by the experimenter. He succeeded in doing this with an effort of concentration and Dr Schmeidler noted that his skin temperature correspondingly decreased and increased. She also noted that a *thermistor* in a bottle several feet from the target cooled down when the target bottle heated up. This fact raises an interesting speculation about psychic energy. As Dr Schmeidler put it, 'Rather than Ingo transferring all of his energy to the thermistor target, it appears that he drew on energy from the environment, and when he cooled the target he transferred the energy back.'

This is exactly what earlier researcher Harry Price inferred from the thermograph records obtained during sittings with the mediums Stella Cranshaw and Rudi Schneider. Such startling physical phenomena have only rarely occurred in the parapsychological laboratory, but the combination of sophisticated modern research methods and the appearance of gifted psychics like Geller, Swann and a few others, has enabled contemporary parapsychologists to make rapid progress toward solving the puzzle of PK.

CHAPTER 34

PARAPSYCHOLOGY AND HUMAN EVOLUTION

What is the future for parapsychology? Will it be possible for scientists to study 'psi' phenomena more as they naturally occur, rather than in artificial situations using test cards and dice? The trend now appears to be a concern with discovering under what conditions 'psi' abilities function and what they may indicate about the potential of the human mind. Is everybody capable of some degree of ESP? To what extent does personality influence the workings of 'psi'? Parapsychologists today do not seem to need to prove that 'psi' faculties exist – rather they seek to explore and develop them.

A young woman reclines at ease in a chair in a soundproof room. She can see nothing because her eyes are covered by what looks like coloured ping-pong balls cut in half. She can hear nothing, for she has on a headset through which comes only the uniform low hiss of 'white noise'. She is in a state of 'sensory deprivation'. She will remain in this state for a period of 30 minutes and at some point during this time, a friend in another room will view a series of stereoscopic slides, concentrate hard on the pictures and try to communicate them telepathically to the young woman who has no idea when, during the 30 minutes, the attempt will take place. Throughout the entire period, she gives a running commentary on what she thinks and visualizes, which is tape recorded.

This experiment was designed by Charles Honorton, director

of research in the Division of Parapsychology and Psychophysics at the Maimonides Medical Centre, Brooklyn, New York. It tests his theory that 'conscious sensory isolation increases access to internal mentation processes.' In other words, when nothing is coming in from outside by way of the senses, a person will be more aware of what is going on inside on a purely mental level. The theory also proposed that in a state of sensory deprivation, a person will be more susceptible than he normally is to non-sensory influences from outside, such as telepathic communication.

In this particular experiment, the theme of the target series of slides is Las Vegas. The agent views the slides, concentrating on each picture in turn and gradually the subject's commentary begins to home in on the target. She reports that she sees bright neon lights, street scenes with a lot of activity, theatre marquees. . . . The brightly illuminated buildings could be nightclubs. . . . It could be some place such as Las Vegas. The sending period comes to an end, but the subject's continuous report on her thoughts and mental imagery continues until the prescribed time has elapsed. She is then shown four different sets of slides and asked to select one which has some correspondences with her recent stream of thought. She has no hesitation in selecting the target set, the scenes of Las Vegas. This experiment will be recorded as an unqualified hit.

Out of 27 series of such experiments, each series including 50 sessions with different subjects, Honorton reports that 20 produced a statistically significant proportion of hits. In one successful experiment, the target theme of the slides viewed by the agent was 'rare coins'. Part of the subject's commentary during the sending period ran, '. . . now I see circles, an enormous amount of them. Their sizes are not the same . . . some are really large, and others are very tiny – no larger than a penny. They just keep flashing in front of me, all these different size circles . . . Now I see colours . . . two in particular, gold and silver, seem to stand out more than all the others. I sense something important. I can't tell what but but I get a feeling of importance, respect, value.' On another occasion the target theme was 'the US Air Force Academy', and part of the subject's commentary went, 'An airplane floating over the clouds . . . planes passing overhead . . . thunder and angry clouds . . .

airplanes . . . ultrasound . . . a blaze of fire, red flames . . . a giant bird flying . . . six stripes on an army uniform, V-shaped . . . the sensation of going forward very fast. . . .'

Not all the recorded hits are as unambiguous and direct as these. In assessing results, experimenters have to take into account the fact that there is not always a direct and literal correspondence between an external event and our mental reconstruction of it. For instance, on one occasion when the target pictures were taken from a news magazine story about the secret bombing of Cambodia, the subject reported images of former President Nixon cleaning his nose! Honorton doesn't say whether he counted that a hit.

This type of experiment exemplifies several characteristics of most of the current work in parapsychology. First, it is less concerned with proving that 'psi' phenomena occur than with discovering under what conditions they occur and what they tell us about the properties and potentials of the human mind. Second, it doesn't necessarily revolve around work with exceptionally gifted individuals. There is a growing belief that most, if not all, people possess 'psi' to some degree. Third, it depends less on the closed-option type of test, such as card-guessing and gives the subject's mind freer range and more interesting challenges. Fourth, it seeks to create conditions favourable to the functioning of the 'psi' faculty by putting the subject into an altered state of consciousness. Finally, it employs electronic and other technological aids to induce, observe and measure 'psi' functions.

These characteristics, taken together, constitute a revolution in parapsychology. The subject has broadened out and converged with other areas of scientific investigation and with aspects of modern social and cultural life. Perhaps, in fact, this trend in parapsychology is less a revolution than a return to origins. One of the older generation of British psychical researchers, G. N. M. Tyrrell, said in his Presidential Address to the SPR in 1945, 'Let us now, before the restricted view of the laboratory worker gains too firm a hold, try to realize how wide our subject is. We should try once more to see it through the eyes of Frederic Myers as a subject which lies at the meeting place of religion, philosophy and science, whose business is to grasp all that can be grasped of the nature of human personality.'

Parapsychologists today are tending to return to this broader view of their subject and to transcend, 'the restricted view of the laboratory worker'. Many of them believe that the traditional methods of science as adapted to parapsychological research by Rhine and his colleagues in the 1930s, are self-defeating in the study of 'psi' functions, for they inhibit their operation. They believe that the little that can be learned about 'psi' from card guessing, dice throwing and odds-against-chance computations have already been learned and it is time for new and more imaginative approaches. Especially talented subjects are always interesting to parapsychologists, but the best and most interesting research being done today does not involve a quest for freak superminds. It combines the broadly humanistic outlook of the founders of psychical research, with the technological sophistication of the modern physicist.

Modern studies in telepathy illustrate this. The eminent Cambridge philosopher, C. D. Broad pointed out that to think of telepathy as transfer of information or imagery from one mind to another is too restrictive. He preferred to speak of 'telepathic interaction'. This phrase suggests the idea that one mind might act upon another without their thoughts or experiences necessarily corresponding and he suggested that telepathic interaction takes place in life more commonly than we might suppose and quite often without our noticing it. An experiment conducted by Douglas Dean of the Newark College of Engineering demonstrated Broad's concept.

Dean used a device called a *plethysmograph*, which measures fluctuations in blood volume in any part of the body. The index finger of the subject was connected to this device. In another room, the agent was given a list of names and instructed to concentrate on the names one at a time in random order, making a note of the time at which he concentrated on each name. At the same time he was to visualize the subject and his location. Some of the names were of people listed in a telephone directory, but others were of people emotionally connected to the subject, such as his wife, his mother, or his child. Now when a person receives information that has emotional significance for him, his body may react in certain ways including change in blood pressure. In this experiment, the plethysmograph frequently registered significant changes in the subject's blood volume when the agent concentrated on names of people the subject was close to. But when the agent was thinking about an unfamiliar name, there were no such changes. The significant point of this experiment is that the subject was never *consciously* aware of what the agent was thinking. He never said, for instance, 'Now he's thinking of Mary, my wife.' Without the plethysmograph, nobody would have known that a telepathic interaction was taking place. In Dean's experiments, about one person out of four showed a measurable response to telepathic messages of emotional content. The implication would seem to be, that many of us may be physiologically reacting to other people's thoughts, even though we may not be able consciously to formulate the impressions they are making on us.

The dream telepathy experiments of Dr Montague Ullman and Dr Stanley Krippner at the Maimonides Hospital, are perhaps the best-known modern investigations of telepathy. They have established clearly that telepathic communication is neither a rare occurrence confined mainly to times of crisis, nor a special aptitude possessed by a few rare individuals.

The subject of Ullman and Krippner's experiments were ordinary people who volunteered to spend a night at the dream laboratory wired to an EEG (electroencephalograph) and to report on their dreams when they were awakened. It had been found that when a person is dreaming his eyes make rapid movements beneath the closed lids. The EEG monitored these movements and enabled the experimenter, in another room, to see when the subject was dreaming and to awaken him to obtain a report on his dream while it was still vivid to him. In yet another room in the laboratory, sat the agent. At the beginning of the session, he selected an envelope from a group of 12, using a special method to ensure a random choice. Each of the envelopes contained a postcard reproduction of a painting. The agent had to concentrate on this picture throughout the night and attempt to transmit his impressions of it to the sleeping subject. In the morning, the tapes of the subject's dream reports and the target picture were given to independent judges who assessed the dreams for their correspondence, if any, to the target picture.

What emerged strongly from hundreds of such experiments –

and from the many spontaneous cases of dream telepathy collected by Ullman and Krippner – is that telepathic communication to a sleeping subject is a fairly frequent occurrence. However, the process is more of an infiltration of the dreamer's consciousness than a complete invasion of it. The target picture was never transmitted whole, as an image, but was broken up and elements from it were interwoven with the sleeper's ongoing dream. Sometimes these elements were translated by the dreamer into an analogous form, just as in dreams we normally express material from real life in symbolic forms. For instance, one target picture was of two dogs standing with bared teeth over a piece of meat. The subject dreamed that she was at a dinner party with several other people, among them two friends who were noted for their greed and concern that others shouldn't get more than they did, especially of meat – 'because in Israel', she explained, 'they don't have so much meat.' She was eating 'something like rib steak' and was very aware of her friends eyeing her plate. There were no dogs in her dream, but it clearly incorporated the themes of greed and the eating of meat that were in the target picture.

A more literal correspondence was obtained with a picture showing a group of Mexican revolutionaries riding against a background of mountains and dark clouds. Part of the sleeper's account of his first dream of the night went, 'A storm. Rainstorm. It reminds me of travelling . . . approaching a rainstorm, thunder cloud, rainy . . . a very distant scene . . . For some reason, I got a feeling, now, of New Mexico when I lived there. There are a lot of mountains around New Mexico. Indians, Pueblos. Now my thoughts go to almost as though I were thinking of another civilization.'

This is pretty well a direct hit and there are many others given in Ullman, Krippner and Vaughan's book, *Dream Telepathy*, which gives a detailed account of the work of the Maimonides Dream Laboratory team. Research such as this, along with Dean's work with the plethysmograph, has corroborated Professor Broad's idea that telepathy may not be a paranormal phenomenen at all, but rather a feature of everyday life which generally goes unrecognized.

So perhaps all of us are psychic. This is one of the conclusions that contemporary parapsychologists are reaching. Clearly, however, some are more psychic than others and another major area of present day research is into the conditions and personality factors that favour 'psi' functions.

The pioneer of this type of research is Dr Gertrude Schmeidler of the City University of New York. In the late 1940s and early 1950s, Dr Schmeidler conducted thousands of clairvoyance experiments with standard Zener cards, asking each subject before the test began whether he or she believed that ESP was possible under the conditions of the experiment. The purpose of the question was to 'separate the sheep from the goats'. Believers in the possibility of ESP were called sheep and disbelievers goats. Analysis of thousands of runs showed that sheep consistently scored slightly above chance, while goats scored slightly below it. Belief in success appeared to have a positive influence on scoring and disbelief, a negative influence. Dr Schmeidler also discovered that the difference between the two groups was sharpened by making the experimental conditions pleasanter for the sheep than for the goats.

Another early researcher into the effect of personality factors was Dr Betty Humphrey of the Duke Parapsychology Laboratory. Before administering an ESP test, she asked the subject to draw anything he wished on a blank sheet of paper. This is a standard psychological test. People who produce bold, uninhibited drawings using all available space are categorized as 'expansive' types and those who produce drawings that are small, timid or conventional are categorized as 'compressive'. The terms correspond more or less to the more common ones of 'extrovert' and 'introvert'. Dr. Humphrey found that her expansive subjects consistently scored positively in standard ESP tests, whereas the compressives tended to score below chance.

Dr Margaret Anderson and Rhea White carried research into the classroom in order to study the effect of interpersonal relations on 'psi' functioning. They found that the highest scores were turned in by pupils who liked and were liked by the teacher who administered the test. Approximately, chance results were obtained when the teacher-pupil relationship involved no particular feeling on either side, and significantly below chance results were obtained when the pupil and teacher positively disliked each other.

These relatively simple pioneer experiments of the 1940s and 1950s, established that personality factors and interpersonal relationships affect 'psi' functioning. A great deal more research has been and is still being done in this area and it has become increasingly sophisticated.

All the experiments described so far were with subjects in normal states of consciousness. The next logical step, after examining the factors that encourage 'psi' in normal states, was to find out whether deliberately induced alterations in states of consciousness would amplify the 'psi' faculty. Rhine, in his early work at Duke, had discovered that the depressant drug sodium amytal adversely affects the 'psi' faculty and that the stimulant caffeine restores it to a normal level. Dr Schmeidler went into hospitals and discovered that in the passive states of mind following concussion or childbirth, 'psi' functioning was significantly enhanced. Evidence from the fields of religion and anthropology, as well as early psychical research with mediums, testified to the fact that the trance state is conducive to 'psi'. Now, with the development of the EEG and other electronic aids, it has become possible for a person after a little training to induce, at will, a state of mind favourable to 'psi'.

The 'psi' faculty has always been thought to be elusive and uncontrollable, but a new medical technique called 'biofeedback' may succeed in bringing it under control. The principle of biofeedback is that a person who is provided with immediate knowledge of his internal body processes, can learn to control some that normally operate involuntarily. In a typical biofeedback session, a subject sits comfortably in a chair with electrodes attached to the back of the head, right forearm and two fingers of the right hand. He wears a special jacket equipped with a respiration gauge. He aims to self-regulate muscle tension, body temperature, and brain wave rhythm. The electrodes detect changes in these internal states and relay the information back to the subject, by means of three bars of light on a screen in front of him. The bars, like that of a mercury thermometer, become taller or shorter in response to changes in the physiological state that each is monitoring.

The subject first aims to achieve complete relaxation and can watch the progress of this effort on the feedback meter wired to the muscle in his forearm. Having achieved this, he concentrates on raising temperature, while the electrodes attached to his fingers measure his success and relay the information to the second bar on the screen. He then tries to induce an extremely calm, yet alert, state of consciousness that is characterized by distinctive patterns of brain activity, called alpha rhythms. When the subject manages to produce alpha rhythms for a period of 10 seconds, the third bar on the screen rises to its maximum height.

An alpha state has been found to be the state of consciousness most favourable to 'psi' functioning. In 1971, Charles Honorton ran a significant experiment with subjects who had been trained to put themselves into an alpha state. It was a straightforward clairvoyance card test, but each subject was required to go through two series of guesses. For the first series, the subject lay in a semi-dark room with his eyes closed and made his guesses when the EEG indicated that he was in an alpha state. For the second series, he sat with open eyes under bright light – conditions which inhibit the production of alpha rhythms. The results showed a consistent and highly significant difference between the scores attained under the different conditions and demonstrated that the alpha state of profound calm, combined with alertness, is especially favourable for the occurrence of 'psi'.

Dr Elmer Green of the Menninger Foundation in Topeka, Kansas, is an expert on biofeedback and voluntary control of internal states. He has conducted experiments with two masters of mind-body control, the Indian yogi Swami Rama and the American mystic, Jack Schwarz. Swami Rama demonstrated control of the arteries in his wrist by simultaneously warming up one spot on the palm of his hand and cooling another spot only two inches away, until there was a difference of 9°F between them. He slowed down his heartbeats from 70 a minute to 52, taking less than a minute to effect the change. Then, for the sake of the experiment and to demonstrate what yogic training could achieve, he offered to stop his heartbeat completely for three or four minutes. Dr Green said that an arrest of 10 seconds would be enough to prove his point and the Swami promptly obliged but extended the period to 17 seconds. This made some of the observers start to panic. He also demonstrated what he called 'yogic sleep'. He went into a deep sleep, snoring gently and the

EEG showed heavy delta waves that are characteristic of a mental state of total oblivion to the world. Every five minutes, a laboratory assistant made a statement in a very low voice. When the prearranged period of 25 minutes had elapsed, Swami Rama promptly sat up and repeated word for word every statement that the assistant had made. It was as if he had been deeply asleep and wide awake at the same time.

Jack Schwarz, says Green, is 'one of the greatest talents in the country and probably the world in the realm of voluntary bodily controls.' In his early teens, he was drawn to Eastern philosophy and began to practice meditation regularly. He taught himself to perform many of the feats attributed to Hindu and Muslim *fakirs*. At the age of 16, he was able to lie on a bed of sharp nails and to allow a man to stand on his stomach while he was doing so. At Green's laboratory, he demonstrated his powers of pain control by allowing burning cigarettes to be held against his forearm, and by driving a knitting needle through his biceps. When the needle was removed a little blood appeared, but Schwarz said, 'Now it stops', and the bleeding immediately stopped. While he was performing these and similar feats, the EEG recorded a steady production of alpha rhythms.

According to Green, both Swami Rama and Jack Schwarz are able to report correctly on the past, present and future conditions, both physical and mental, of people they do not know and have never seen. Schwarz claims also to be able to read people's auras. He amazed a visiting psychiatrist at the Menninger Foundation by giving a detailed account of the doctor's own medical history and condition.

Anyone, says Schwarz, can do what he does. It is a matter of training and practice. Today, with the EEG and biofeedback techniques, the training can be greatly speeded up. Some years ago, the so-called autonomic physiological systems, which include blood flow, temperature and brain waves, were thought to be inaccessible to control by the will but today students can learn to regulate them after just a few training sessions. There are indications that 'psi' faculties may also be brought under control by similar methods.

A man who has developed psychic faculties in himself and others, without using the biofeedback method, is the New York psychologist, Lawrence LeShan. In an important book *The Medium, the Mystic and the Physicist*, LeShan describes how he made himself a psychic healer. His training as an experimental psychologist predisposed him to believe that the alleged evidence for the paranormal 'must be due to bad, experimental design, false memories, hysteria, and chicanery'. On the other hand, he thought that if the evidence were valid it could be of tremendous importance for science and life and he decided to try to discover the truth for himself. He remembered that the great French chemist, Lavoisier had stated authoritatively that meteorites were an impossible fable because it was obvious that there were no stones in the sky and LeShan didn't want to risk committing a similar error by dismissing 'psi' as impossible, just because it didn't fit in with prevailing scientific ideas of reality.

LeShan started his independent inquiry by investigating the evidence provided by sensitives. (The term 'sensitive' is generally used instead of 'medium' today, because it doesn't suggest an intermediary between the world of the living and the spirits of the dead.) He was fortunate in that one of the most gifted, serious, and respected sensitives of modern times, the late Eileen Garrett, was then living in New York and willing to co-operate with him. He spent more than 500 hours questioning Eileen Garrett and designed several experiments in which she willingly participated. On one occasion, when Mrs Garrett was in Florida and LeShan was going to join her the following day, he prepared an experiment in psychometry in advance. While in his office in New York, he collected several different objects, including an old Greek coin, a woman's comb, a fossil fish, a bit of stone from Mt Vesuvius, a scrap of bandage and an ancient Babylonian clay tablet. He wrapped each object in tissue, sealed it in a small box and put the box into a manila envelope. Another person put the envelopes, which were numbered, into larger envelopes marked with different numbers. This person had the list of both code numbers but did not know which objects were in which envelopes. Thus, no one, including LeShan, could convey any information about the content of any envelope to Eileen Garrett. Mrs Garrett was to be given the envelopes in turn and would attempt to describe details of the history of the object it contained.

While assembling the materials, LeShan found that he needed

another box, so he went to a neighbouring office and asked a secretary, whom he only knew by sight, if she could provide one. The secretary went into his office to find out what size of box would be needed and in the course of their conversation she picked up and examined the clay tablet. A suitable box was found in LeShan's own office and he forgot the whole small incident. Two weeks later and 1,500 miles away, LeShan and Eileen Garrett tried the psychometry experiment. She picked up an envelope – later found to contain the clay tablet – and immediately said there was 'a woman associated with this'. She described the secretary in such detail. LeShan says, that it would have been possible to pick her out of a line-up of 10,000 women. She even mentioned two scars that proved to be there.

Such evidence as this convinced LeShan of the reality of paranormal faculties. After examining the testimony of Eileen Garrett and other sensitives, as well as the writings of the great mystics and some modern physicists, he formulated a theory that two distinct orders of reality exist. One he called 'Sensory Reality' and the other 'Clairvoyant Reality'. Paranormal faculties develop, he says, when a person moves out of the Sensory and into the Clairvoyant Reality. The difference between the two is largely a difference of thought and attitude, of ways of looking at the world. Most of us live, most of the time, on the level of 'Sensory Reality' basing our thoughts on the information conveyed through our senses. We see people and things as separate entities and we consider the most important things about them to be the properties that make them individual. From the other point of view, that of 'Clairvoyant Reality', the important thing about an individual is her relationship to the rest of the universe. All beings – and even inanimate substances like rock, water and earth – are seen as parts of a whole. Time, also, is perceived differently – it does not necessarily flow in one direction at an even pace. Our everyday concepts of past, present and future are seen as illusions.

In distinguishing and describing these two kinds of reality, LeShan quotes several modern physicists. The atomic physicist, J. Robert Oppenheimer, for example, acknowledged the existence of two realities in these words, 'These two ways of thinking, the way of time and history and the way of eternity and timelessness, are both parts of man's efforts to comprehend the world in which he lives. Neither is comprehended in the other nor reducible to it. They are, as we have learned to say in physics, complementary views, each supplementing the other, neither telling the whole story.'

Having provisionally accepted the existence of a separate plane of reality in which 'psi' is possible, LeShan wanted to test this theory with reference to a particular aspect of 'psi'. He chose psychic healing as his area of study. After reading the available literature on the subject and observing and talking with a number of healers, he came to the conclusion that there are two basic types of psychic healing. In Type 1, the healer goes into an altered state of consciousness in which he views himself and the patient as one. He doesn't touch the patient, or attempt to do anything – he just concentrates on a sense of being at one with the patient and with the universe and on deep intense caring. In Type 2, the healer tries to heal, to turn on a flow of energy. He lays his hands on the patient's body on either side of the affected area and often the patient remarks that he feels heat in that part of his body.

LeShan then began to train himself to achieve the state of consciousness required for Type 1 healing. His goal was to attain awareness of 'Clairvoyant Reality' and in that state to become one with the patient for a few moments. His training consisted of learning to meditate. After a period of a year and a half, he learned to achieve a state of mind in which he could heal.

His attempts were not always successful. He also points out that when healing did take place, it might in some cases be due to other causes. Yet in many cases, the positive biological changes that occurred seemed almost certainly due to the healing encounter. Sometimes he supplemented the Type 1 approach with a Type 2 laying on of hands, frequently with successful results.

As a scientist, LeShan couldn't accept a successful experiment as valid unless it was repeatable. It was possible, he suggested, that he had been a natural psychic healer all along without realizing it. If the technique he had developed was the cause of his success, then it should work for others, he reasoned.

It does. Since 1970, LeShan has been holding training seminars for groups of psychologists and students and many acts of healing have been carried out by these people, in the course of the work.

Various side-effects have been noticed, particularly intense tele-pathic communication between members of the groups and between healer and patient.

Le Shan's work is characteristic of some of the best being done in the area of parapsychology today, for it does not aim primarily to prove the existence of the 'psi' faculties but rather to explore and develop them and to bring them into operation in daily life. It demands a degree of personal commitment and a shift of theoret-ical viewpoint that perhaps few orthodox scientists would be capable of. In the last analysis, however, such work is a genuine contribution to science, for it is bringing what was thought to be unknowable and unpredictable into the realm of the known and the controllable. It suggests that, what today we call paranormal, we may in the not too distant future regard as entirely normal.

The early psychical researchers asked, 'Is there life after death?' Today's parapsychologists are asking, 'Are there latent faculties in man that can be developed to enhance life *before* death?' And that is a revolution.